AF556000

ECONOMIC THEORY

ECONOMIC THEORY

Dr. Chandra Kant Singh

RANDOM PUBLICATIONS

NEW DELHI - 110 002 (INDIA)

Economic Theory

ISBN 978-93-51114-56-7

Published in 2014 in India by
RANDOM PUBLICATIONS
4376-A/4B, Gali Murari Lal, Ansari Road
New Delhi-110 002
Phone: +9111-43580356, 23289044
E-mail: randomexports@gmail.com; sales@randompublications.com; info@randompublications.com

Reprinted 2021

Type Setting by: Friends Media, Delhi-110089
Digitally Printed at: Replika Press Pvt. Ltd.

Preface

Economics is the social science that studies the behaviour of individuals, households, and organizations, when they manage or use scarce resources, which have alternative uses, to achieve desired ends. Agents are assumed to act rationally, have multiple desirable ends in sight, limited resources to obtain these ends, a set of stable preferences, a definite overall guiding objective, and the capability of making a choice. There exists an economic problem, subject to study by economic science, when a decision has to be made by one or more resource-controlling players to attain the best possible outcome under bounded rational conditions. Economic theory is a broad concept for the explanation and understanding of the movement of goods in a market. Theoretical economic concepts typically have scientific backing or studies to prove or disprove a stated hypothesis. National governments also have an interest in theories of economics. Politicians rely on studies of government spending, tax collections, money supply, and consumer spending data to make laws or set policy. Different economic theories exist that focus on different aspects of government policy regarding economics. Classical economic theory tends to favour a free market system. Under this theory, little government intervention is necessary to help support a society. Classical economists believe that individuals allowed to act in their own self-interests will present a strong group of consumers. Terms like capitalism and supply side economics also describe this theory. The protection of personal property through courts of law is often a major component of free market economics. Another classic economic theory is command economies driven by national governments. Terms associated with these economies include socialism and communism. The main ideas behind these theories are that governments control the majority of economic resources. Governments allocate resources, give jobs to certain classes or people, and regulate the economy through heavy taxation. The redistribution of wealth attempts to ensure an equal status for all individuals living under the government's umbrella.

A more modern economic concept is Keynesian economics. This theory is a slight combination between the two previous theories. Keynesian theory dictates that targeted government spending and intervention into a national economy helps keep goods moving when free markets become inefficient. Government spending controls do not often exist under Keynesian economics as governments may not have spending limits. Another inherent issue is the inability to control employment, as government spending does not always result in job creation. While other economic theories exist, these are often the main ones a government uses to guide its fiscal and monetary policy. Economists often spend copious time collecting data and reviewing financial information to help provide information for making decisions. These studies and information-gathering sessions represent the science that backs up economic theory. Economic methodology is also important; methodology dictates the best way to collect data and make it useful for economic decision making. Typically, economic theory uses a model individual to describe actions taken by people in economic environments. The theory — known as homo economicus — describes humans as rational and self-interested people who make judgments about their lives. Through this theory, economists attempt to determine how individuals will react to certain economic situations. Free market economies most often ascribe to this theory.

This book is for students with little or no previous knowledge of economic theory who intend to study the subject systematically and provides a general introduction to the theory while not including the special problems of international trade, public finance and welfare economics.

I thank all members of my team who have helped in the preparation of the book. My special thanks go to "Random Publications" who have published the book.

— *Dr. Chandra Kant Singh*

Contents

1

Introduction

Economics is the social science that studies the behaviour of individuals, groups, and organisations (called economic actors, players, or agents), when they manage or use scarce resources, which have alternative uses, to achieve desired ends. Agents are assumed to act rational, have multiple ends in sights (all desirable), limited resources to obtain them, a set of stable preferences, a definite overall guiding objective, and the capability of making a choice. There exist an economic problem, subject of study of the economic science, when a decision (choice) has to be made by one or more resources controlling players, to attain the best possible outcome under bounded rational conditions, in other words, to maximize value subject to the constrains imposed by the information the agents have, the cognitive limitations of their minds, and the finite amount of time they have to take a decision. So, the science centres on the activities of the economic agents that comprise society. They are the focus of economic analysis.

Economics traditional concern is to gain an understanding of the processes that govern the production, distribution and consumption of goods and services in an exchange economy. But there are purposes, (ends) such as reducing crime or protecting from it, for example, that an agent may want to spend resources on. Economics may study how the agent determines the amount of resources to allocate for this purpose, aside from the traditional concern of economics.

An approach to understanding the processes of production, distribution, and consumption, through the study of agent behaviour under scarcity, may go as follows: The continuous interplay (exchange or trade) done by economic actors in all markets sets the prices for all goods and services which, in turn, make the rational managing of scarce resources possible. At the same time, the decisions (choices) made by the same actors, while they are pursuing their own interest (their overall guiding objective), determine the level of output (production), consumption, savings, and investment, in an economy, as well as the remuneration (distribution) paid to the owners of labour (in the form of wages), capital (in the form of profits) and land (in the form of rent). Each period, as if they were in a giant feedback system, economic players influence the pricing processes and the economy, and are in turn influenced by them until a steady state (equilibrium) of all variables involved is reached or until an external shock throw the whole system toward a new equilibrium point. Because of the autonomous actions of rational interacting agents, the economy is a complex adaptive system.

The term *economics* comes from the Ancient Greek ïÒêïíïìßá (*oikonomia*, "management of a household, administration") from ïÒêïò (*oikos*, "house") and íüìïò (*nomos*, "custom" or "law"), hence "rules of the house(hold for good management)". Political economy was the earlier name for the subject, but economists in the late 19th century suggested "economics" as a shorter term for "economic science" to stablish itself as a separate discipine aside of political and other social sciences.

A focus of the subject is how economic agents behave and interact and how economies work. Consistent with this, a primary textbook distinction is between microeconomics and macroeconomics. Microeconomics examines the behaviour of basic elements in the economy, including individual agents (such as households and firms or as buyers and sellers) and markets, their interactions and the consecuented outcomes. Macroeconomics analyzes the entire economy (meaning aggregated production, consumption, savings, and investment) and issues affecting it, including unemployment of resources (labour, capital, and land), inflation, economic growth, and the public policies that address them (monetary and fiscal policies, and other policies).

Other broad distinctions include those between positive economics (describing "what is") and normative economics (advocating "what ought to be"); between economic theory and applied economics; between rational and behavioural economics; and between mainstream economics (more "orthodox" and dealing with the "rationality-individualism-equilibrium nexus") and heterodox economics (more "radical" and dealing with the "institutions-history-social structure nexus"). Besides the traditional concern in production, distribution, and consumption in an economy, economic analysis may be applied throughout society, as *in* business, finance, health care, and government, but also *to* such diverse subjects as crime, education, the family, law, politics, religion, social institutions, war, and science; because, all of these subjects have an important economic aspect to consider. Take education, for example, the time, effort and expenses incurred for procuring it, plus the foregone income and experience, can be weighted against future benefits it may bring to the agent or the economy. At the turn of the 21st century, the expanding domain of economics in the social sciences has been described as economic imperialism.

Definitions

There are a variety of modern definitions of economics. Some of the differences may reflect evolving views of the subject or different views among economists. Scottish philosopher Adam Smith (1776) defined what was then called political economy as "an inquiry into the nature and causes of the wealth of nations", in particular as:

a branch of the science of a statesman or legislator [with the twofold objectives of providing] a plentiful revenue or subsistence for the people ... [and] to supply the state or commonwealth with a revenue for the publick services.

J.-B. Say (1803), distinguishing the subject from its public-policy uses, defines it as the science *of* production, distribution, and consumption of wealth. On the satirical side, Thomas Carlyle (1849) coined "the dismal science" as an epithet for classical economics, in this context, commonly linked to the pessimistic analysis of Malthus (1798). John Stuart Mill (1844) defines the subject in a social context as:

The science which traces the laws of such of the phenomena of society as arise from the combined operations of mankind for the production of wealth, in so far as those phenomena are not modified by the pursuit of any other object.

Alfred Marshall provides a still widely cited definition in his textbook *Principles of Economics* (1890) that extends analysis beyond wealth and from the societal to the microeconomic level:

Economics is a study of man in the ordinary business of life. It enquires how he gets his income and how he uses it. Thus, it is on the one side, the study of wealth and on the other and more important side, a part of the study of man.

Lionel Robbins (1932) developed implications of what has been termed "[p]erhaps the most commonly accepted current definition of the subject":

Economics is a science which studies human behaviour as a relationship between ends and scarce means which have alternative uses. Robbins describes the definition as not *classificatory* in "pick[ing] out certain *kinds* of behaviour" but rather *analytical* in "focus[ing] attention on a particular *aspect* of behaviour, the form imposed by the influence of scarcity." He affirmed that previous economist have usually centred their studies on the analysis of wealth: how wealth is created (production), distributed, and consumed; and how wealth can grow . But he said that economics can be used to study other things, such as war, that are outside its usual focus. This is because war has as the goal wining it (as a sought after end), generates both cost and benefits; and, resources (human life and other costs) are used to attain the goal. If the war is not winnable or if the expected costs outweigh the benefits, the deciding actors (assuming they are rational) may never go to war (a decision) but rather explore other alternatives. We cannot define economics as the science that study wealth, war, crime, education, and any other field economic analysis can be applied to.

Some subsequent comments criticized the definition as overly broad in failing to limit its subject matter to analysis of markets. From the 1960s, however, such comments abated as the economic theory of maximizing behaviour and rational-choice modelling expanded the domain of the subject to areas previously treated in other fields. There are other criticisms as well, such as in scarcity not accounting for the macroeconomics of high unemployment. Gary Becker, a contributor to the expansion of economics into new areas, describes the approach he favours as "combining the assumptions of maximizing behaviour, stable preferences, and market equilibrium, used relentlessly and unflinchingly." One commentary characterizes the remark as making economics an approach rather than a subject matter but with great specificity as to the "choice process and the type of social interaction that [such] analysis involves." The same source reviews a range of definitions included in principles of economics textbooks and concludes that the lack of agreement need not affect the subject-matter that the texts treat. Among economists more generally, it argues that a particular definition presented may reflect the direction toward which the author believes economics is evolving, or should evolve.

Microeconomics

Markets

Microeconomics examines how entities, forming a market structure, interact within a market to create a market system. These entities include private and public players with various classifications, typically operating under scarcity of tradeable units and government regulation. The item traded may be a tangible product such as apples or a service such as repair services, legal counsel, or entertainment.

In theory, in a free market the aggregates (sum of) of *quantity demanded* by buyers and *quantity supplied* by sellers will be equal and reach economic equilibrium over time in reaction to price changes; in practice, various issues may prevent equilibrium, and any equilibrium reached may not necessarily morally equitable. For example, if the supply of healthcare services is limited by external factors, the equilibrium price may be unaffordable for many who desire it but cannot pay for it.

Various market structures exist. In perfectly competitive markets, no participants are large enough to have the market power to set the price of a homogeneous product. In other words, every participant is a "price taker" as no participant influences the price of a product. In the real world, markets often experience imperfect competition.

Forms include monopoly (in which there is only one seller of a good), duopoly (in which there are only two sellers of a good), oligopoly (in which there are few sellers of a good), monopolistic competition (in which there are many sellers producing highly differentiated goods), monopsony (in which there is only one buyer of a good), and oligopsony (in which there are few buyers of a good). Unlike perfect competition, imperfect competition invariably means market power is unequally distributed. Firms under imperfect competition have the potential to be "price makers", which means that, by holding a disproportionately high share of market power, they can influence the prices of their products. Microeconomics studies individual markets by simplifying the economic system by assuming that activity in the market being analysed does not affect other markets. This method of analysis is known as partial-equilibrium analysis (supply and demand). This method aggregates (the sum of all activity) in only one market. General-equilibrium theory studies various markets and their behaviour. It aggregates (the sum of all activity) across *all* markets. This method studies both changes in markets and their interactions leading towards equilibrium.

Production, Cost, and Efficiency

In microeconomics, production is the conversion of inputs into outputs. It is an economic process that uses inputs to create a commodity or a service for exchange or direct use. Production is a flow and thus a rate of output per period of time. Distinctions include such production alternatives as for consumption (food, haircuts, etc.) vs. investment goods (new tractors, buildings, roads, etc.), public goods (national defence, small-pox vaccinations, etc.) or private goods (new computers, bananas, etc.), and "guns" vs. "butter".

Opportunity cost refers to the economic cost of production: the value of the next best opportunity foregone. Choices must be made between desirable yet mutually exclusive actions. It has been described as expressing "the basic relationship between scarcity and choice.". The opportunity cost of an activity is an element in ensuring that scarce resources are used efficiently, such that the cost is weighed against the value of that activity in deciding on more or less of it. Opportunity costs are not restricted to monetary or financial costs but could be measured by the real cost of output forgone, leisure, or anything else that provides the alternative benefit (utility).

Inputs used in the production process include such primary factors of production as labour services, capital (durable produced goods used in production, such as an existing factory), and land (including natural resources). Other inputs may include intermediate goods used in production of final goods, such as the steel in a new car.

Economic efficiency describes how well a system generates desired output with a given set of inputs and available technology. Efficiency is improved if more output is generated without changing inputs, or in other words, the amount of "waste" is reduced. A widely accepted general standard is Pareto efficiency, which is reached when no further change can make someone better off without making someone else worse off.

The production–possibility frontier (PPF) is an expository figure for representing scarcity, cost, and efficiency. In the simplest case an economy can produce just two goods (say "guns" and "butter"). The PPF is a table or graph (as at the right) showing the different quantity combinations of the two goods producible with a given technology and total factor inputs, which limit feasible total output. Each point on the curve shows potential total output for the economy, which is the maximum feasible output of one good, given a feasible output quantity of the other good. Scarcity is represented in the figure by people being willing but unable in the aggregate to consume *beyond the PPF* (such as at *X*) and by the negative slope of the curve. If production of one good *increases* along the curve, production of the other good *decreases*, an inverse relationship. This is because increasing output of one good requires transferring inputs to it from production of the other good, decreasing the latter.

The slope of the curve at a point on it gives the trade-off between the two goods. It measures what an additional unit of one good costs in units forgone of the other good, an example of a *real opportunity cost*. Thus, if one more Gun costs 100 units of butter, the opportunity cost of one Gun is 100 Butter. *Along the PPF*, scarcity implies that choosing *more* of one good in the aggregate entails doing with *less* of the other good. Still, in a market economy, movement along the curve may indicate that the choice of the increased output is anticipated to be worth the cost to the agents.

By construction, each point on the curve shows *productive efficiency* in maximizing output for given total inputs. A point *inside* the curve (as at *A*), is feasible but represents *production inefficiency* (wasteful use of inputs), in that output of *one or both goods* could increase by moving in a northeast direction to a point on the curve. Examples cited of such inefficiency include high unemployment during a business-cycle recession or economic organisation of a country that discourages full use of resources. Being on the curve might still not fully satisfy allocative efficiency (also called Pareto efficiency) if it does not produce a mix of goods that consumers prefer over other points. Much applied economics in public policy is concerned with determining how the efficiency of an economy can be improved. Recognising the reality of scarcity and then figuring out how to organise society for the most efficient use of resources has been described as the "essence of economics", where the subject "makes its unique contribution."

Specialisation

Specialisation is considered key to economic efficiency based on theoretical and empirical considerations. Different individuals or nations may have different real opportunity costs of production, say from differences in stocks of human capital per worker or capital/labour ratios. According to theory, this may give a comparative advantage in production of goods that make more intensive use of the relatively more abundant, thus *relatively* cheaper, input.

Even if one region has an absolute advantage as to the ratio of its outputs to inputs in every type of output, it may still specialise in the output in which it has a comparative advantage and thereby gain from trading with a region that lacks any absolute advantage but has a comparative advantage in producing something else.

It has been observed that a high volume of trade occurs among regions even with access to a similar technology and mix of factor inputs, including high-income countries. This has led to investigation of economies of scale and agglomeration to explain specialisation in similar but differentiated product lines, to the overall benefit of respective trading parties or regions. The general theory of specialisation applies to trade among individuals, farms, manufacturers, service providers, and economies. Among each of these production systems, there may be a corresponding *division of labour* with different work groups specialising, or correspondingly different types of capital equipment and differentiated land uses.

An example that combines features above is a country that specialises in the production of high-tech knowledge products, as developed countries do, and trades with developing nations for goods produced in factories where labour is relatively cheap and plentiful, resulting in different in opportunity costs of production. More total output and utility thereby results from specialising in production and trading than if each country produced its own high-tech and low-tech products. Theory and observation set out the conditions such that market prices of outputs and productive inputs select an allocation of factor inputs by comparative advantage, so that (relatively) low-cost inputs go to producing low-cost outputs. In the process, aggregate output may increase as a by-product or by design. Such specialisation of production creates opportunities for *gains from trade* whereby resource owners benefit from trade in the sale of one type of output for other, more highly valued goods. A measure of gains from trade is the *increased income levels* that trade may facilitate.

Supply and Demand

Prices and quantities have been described as the most directly observable attributes of goods produced and exchanged in a market economy. The theory of supply and demand is an organising principle for explaining how prices coordinate the amounts produced and consumed. In microeconomics, it applies to price and output determination for a market with perfect competition, which includes the condition of no buyers or sellers large enough to have price-setting power. For a given market of a commodity, *demand* is the relation of the quantity that all buyers would be prepared to purchase at each unit price of the good. Demand is often represented by a table or a graph showing price and quantity demanded. Demand theory describes individual consumers as rationally choosing the most preferred quantity of each good, given income, prices, tastes, etc. A term for this is "constrained utility maximization" (with income and wealth as the constraints on demand). Here, utility refers to the hypothesized relation of each individual consumer for ranking different commodity bundles as more or less preferred.

The law of demand states that, in general, price and quantity demanded in a given market are inversely related. That is, the higher the price of a product, the less of it people would be prepared to buy of it (other things unchanged). As the price of a commodity falls, consumers move toward it from relatively more expensive goods (the substitution effect). In addition, purchasing power from the price decline increases ability to buy (the income effect). Other factors can change demand; for example an increase in income will shift the demand curve for a normal good outward relative to the origin, as in the figure. All determinants are predominantly taken as constant factors of demand and supply.

Supply is the relation between the price of a good and the quantity available for sale at that price. It may be represented as a table or graph relating price and quantity supplied. Producers, for example business firms, are hypothesized to be *profit-maximizers*, meaning that they attempt to produce and supply the amount of goods that will bring them the highest profit. Supply is typically represented as a directly proportional relation between price and quantity supplied (other things unchanged).

That is, the higher the price at which the good can be sold, the more of it producers will supply. The higher price makes it profitable to increase production. Just as on the demand side, the position of the supply can shift, say from a change in the price of a productive input or a technical improvement. The "Law of Supply" states that, in general, a rise in price leads to an expansion in supply and a fall in price leads to a contraction in supply. Here as well, the determinants of supply, such as price of substitutes, cost of production, technology applied and various factors inputs of production are all taken to be constant for a specific time period of evaluation of supply.

Market equilibrium occurs where quantity supplied equals quantity demanded, the intersection of the supply and demand curves in the figure above. At a price below equilibrium, there is a shortage of quantity supplied compared to quantity demanded. This is posited to bid the price up. At a price above equilibrium, there is a surplus of quantity supplied compared to quantity demanded. This pushes the price down. The model of supply and demand predicts that for given supply and demand curves, price and quantity will stabilize at the price that makes quantity supplied equal to quantity demanded. Similarly, demand-and-supply theory predicts a new price-quantity combination from a shift in demand. For a given quantity of a consumer good, the point on the demand curve indicates the value, or marginal utility, to consumers for that unit. It measures what the consumer would be prepared to pay for that unit. The corresponding point on the supply curve measures marginal cost, the increase in total cost to the supplier for the corresponding unit of the good. The price in equilibrium is determined by supply and demand. In a perfectly competitive market, supply and demand equate marginal cost and marginal utility at equilibrium.

On the supply side of the market, some factors of production are described as (relatively) *variable* in the short run, which affects the cost of changing output levels. Their usage rates can be changed easily, such as electrical power, raw-material inputs, and over-time and temp work. Other inputs are relatively *fixed*, such as plant and equipment and key personnel. In the long run, all inputs may be adjusted by management. These distinctions translate to differences in the elasticity (responsiveness) of the supply curve in the short and long runs and corresponding differences in the price-quantity change from a shift on the supply or demand side of the market.

Marginalist theory, such as above, describes the consumers as attempting to reach most-preferred positions, subject to income and wealth constraints while producers attempt to maximize profits subject to their own constraints, including demand for goods produced, technology, and the price of inputs. For the consumer, that point comes where marginal utility of a good, net of price, reaches zero, leaving no net gain from further consumption increases. Analogously, the producer compares marginal revenue (identical to price for the perfect competitor) against the marginal cost of a good, with *marginal profit* the difference. At the point where marginal profit reaches zero, further increases in production of the good stop. For movement to market equilibrium and for changes in equilibrium, price and quantity also change “at the margin”: more-or-less of something, rather than necessarily all-or-nothing.

Other applications of demand and supply include the distribution of income among the factors of production, including labour and capital, through factor markets. In a competitive labour market for example the quantity of labour employed and the price of labour (the wage rate) depends on the demand for labour (from employers for production) and supply of labour (from potential workers). Labour economics examines the interaction of workers and employers through such markets to explain patterns and changes of wages and other labour income, labour mobility, and (un)employment, productivity through human capital, and related public-policy issues.

Demand-and-supply analysis is used to explain the behaviour of perfectly competitive markets, but as a standard of comparison it can be extended to any type of market. It can also be generalized to explain variables across the economy, for example, total output (estimated as real GDP) and the general price level, as studied in macroeconomics. Tracing the qualitative and quantitative effects of variables that change supply and demand, whether in the short or long run, is a standard exercise in applied economics. Economic theory may also specify conditions such that supply and demand through the market is an efficient mechanism for allocating resources.

Firms

People frequently do not trade directly on markets. Instead, on the supply side, they may work in and produce through *firms*. The most obvious kinds of firms are corporations, partnerships and trusts. According to Ronald Coase people begin to organise their production in firms when the costs of doing business becomes lower than doing it on the market. Firms combine labour and capital, and can achieve far greater economies of scale (when the average cost per unit declines as more units are produced) than individual market trading.

In perfectly competitive markets studied in the theory of supply and demand, there are many producers, none of which significantly influence price. Industrial organisation generalizes from that special case to study the strategic behaviour of firms that do have significant control of price. It considers the structure of such markets and their interactions. Common market structures studied besides perfect competition include monopolistic competition, various forms of oligopoly, and monopoly.

Managerial economics applies microeconomic analysis to specific decisions in business firms or other management units. It draws heavily from quantitative methods such as operations research and programming and from statistical methods such as regression analysis in the absence of certainty and perfect knowledge. A unifying theme is the attempt to optimize business decisions, including unit-cost minimization and profit maximization, given the firm's objectives and constraints imposed by technology and market conditions.

Uncertainty and Game Theory

Uncertainty in economics is an unknown prospect of gain or loss, whether quantifiable as risk or not. Without it, household behaviour would be unaffected by uncertain employment and income prospects, financial and capital markets would reduce to exchange of a single instrument in each market period, and there would be no communications industry. Given its different forms, there are various ways of representing uncertainty and modelling economic agents' responses to it.

Game theory is a branch of applied mathematics that considers strategic interactions between agents, one kind of uncertainty. It provides a mathematical foundation of industrial organisation, discussed above, to model different types of firm behaviour, for example in an oligopolistic industry (few sellers), but equally applicable to wage negotiations, bargaining, contract design, and any situation where individual agents are few enough to have perceptible effects on each other. As a method heavily used in behavioural economics, it postulates that agents choose strategies to maximize their payoffs, given the strategies of other agents with at least partially conflicting interests.

In this, it generalizes maximization approaches developed to analyze market actors such as in the supply and demand model and allows for incomplete information of actors. The field dates from the 1944 classic *Theory of Games and Economic Behaviour* by John von Neumann and Oskar Morgenstern. It has significant applications seemingly outside of economics in such diverse subjects as formulation of nuclear strategies, ethics, political science, and evolutionary biology.

Risk aversion may stimulate activity that in well-functioning markets smooths out risk and communicates information about risk, as in markets for insurance, commodity futures contracts, and financial instruments. Financial economics or simply finance describes the allocation of financial resources. It also analyzes the pricing of financial instruments, the financial structure of companies, the efficiency and fragility of financial markets, financial crises, and related government policy or regulation.

Some market organisations may give rise to inefficiencies associated with uncertainty. Based on George Akerlof's "Market for Lemons" article, the paradigm example is of a dodgy second-hand car market. Customers without knowledge of whether a car is a "lemon" depress its price below what a quality second-hand car would be. Information asymmetry arises here, if the seller has more relevant information than the buyer but no incentive to disclose it. Related problems in insurance are adverse selection, such that those at most risk are most likely to insure (say reckless drivers), and moral hazard, such that insurance results in riskier behaviour (say more reckless driving). Both problems may raise insurance costs and reduce efficiency in driving otherwise willing transactors from the market ("incomplete markets"). Moreover, attempting to reduce one problem, say adverse selection by mandating insurance, may add to another, say moral hazard. Information economics, which studies such problems, has relevance in subjects such as insurance, contract law, mechanism design, monetary economics, and health care. Applied subjects include market and legal remedies to spread or reduce risk, such as warranties, government-mandated partial insurance, restructuring or bankruptcy law, inspection, and regulation for quality and information disclosure.

Market Failure

The term "market failure" encompasses several problems which may undermine standard economic assumptions. Although economists categorise market failures differently, the following categories emerge in the main texts.

Information asymmetries and incomplete markets may result in economic inefficiency but also a possibility of improving efficiency through market, legal, and regulatory remedies, as discussed above.

Natural monopoly, or the overlapping concepts of "practical" and "technical" monopoly, is an extreme case of *failure of competition* as a restraint on producers. Extreme economies of scale are one possible cause.

Public goods are goods which are undersupplied in a typical market. The defining features are that people can consume public goods without having to pay for them and that more than one person can consume the good at the same time.

Externalities occur where there are significant social costs or benefits from production or consumption that are not reflected in market prices. For example, air pollution may generate a negative externality, and education may generate a positive externality (less crime, etc.). Governments often tax and otherwise restrict the sale of goods that have negative externalities and subsidize or otherwise promote the purchase of goods that have positive externalities in an effort to correct the price distortions caused by these externalities. Elementary demand-and-supply theory predicts equilibrium but not the speed of adjustment for changes of equilibrium due to a shift in demand or supply.

In many areas, some form of price stickiness is postulated to account for quantities, rather than prices, adjusting in the short run to changes on the demand side or the supply side. This includes standard analysis of the business cycle in macroeconomics. Analysis often revolves around causes of such price stickiness and their implications for reaching a hypothesized long-run equilibrium. Examples of such price stickiness in particular markets include wage rates in labour markets and posted prices in markets deviating from perfect competition.

Some specialised fields of economics deal in market failure more than others. The economics of the public sector is one example. Much environmental economics concerns externalities or "public bads".

Policy options include regulations that reflect cost-benefit analysis or market solutions that change incentives, such as emission fees or redefinition of property rights.

Public Sector

Public finance is the field of economics that deals with budgeting the revenues and expenditures of a public sector entity, usually government. The subject addresses such matters as tax incidence (who really pays a particular tax), cost-benefit analysis of government programs, effects on economic efficiency and income distribution of different kinds of spending and taxes, and fiscal politics. The latter, an aspect of public choice theory, models public-sector behaviour analogously to microeconomics, involving interactions of self-interested voters, politicians, and bureaucrats.

Much of economics is positive, seeking to describe and predict economic phenomena. Normative economics seeks to identify what economies *ought* to be like.

Welfare economics is a normative branch of economics that uses microeconomic techniques to simultaneously determine the allocative efficiency within an economy and the income distribution associated with it. It attempts to measure social welfare by examining the economic activities of the individuals that comprise society.

Macroeconomics

Macroeconomics examines the economy as a whole to explain broad aggregates and their interactions "top down", that is, using a simplified form of general-equilibrium theory. Such aggregates include national income and output, the unemployment rate, and price inflation and subaggregates like total consumption and investment spending and their components. It also studies effects of monetary policy and fiscal policy. Since at least the 1960s, macroeconomics has been characterized by further integration as to micro-based modelling of sectors, including rationality of players, efficient use of market information, and imperfect competition. This has addressed a long-standing concern about inconsistent developments of the same subject. Macroeconomic analysis also considers factors affecting the long-term level and growth of national income. Such factors include capital accumulation, technological change and labour force growth.

Growth

Growth economics studies factors that explain economic growth – the increase in output per capita of a country over a long period of time. The same factors are used to explain differences in the *level* of output per capita *between* countries, in particular why some countries grow faster than others, and whether countries converge at the same rates of growth. Much-studied factors include the rate of investment, population growth, and technological change. These are represented in theoretical and empirical forms (as in the neoclassical and endogenous growth models) and in growth accounting.

Business Cycle

The economics of a depression were the spur for the creation of "macroeconomics" as a separate discipline field of study. During the Great Depression of the 1930s, John Maynard Keynes authored a book entitled *The General Theory of Employment, Interest and Money* outlining the key theories of Keynesian economics. Keynes contended that aggregate demand for goods might be insufficient during economic downturns, leading to unnecessarily high unemployment and losses of potential output. He therefore advocated active policy responses by the public sector, including monetary policy actions by the central bank and fiscal policy actions by the government to stabilize output over the business cycle. Thus, a central conclusion of Keynesian economics is that, in some situations, no strong automatic mechanism moves output and employment towards full employment levels. John Hicks' IS/LM model has been the most influential interpretation of *The General Theory*.

Over the years, understanding of the business cycle has branched into various research programs, mostly related to or distinct from Keynesianism. The neoclassical synthesis refers to the reconciliation of Keynesian economics with neoclassical economics, stating that Keynesianism is correct in the short run but qualified by neoclassical-like considerations in the intermediate and long run.

New classical macroeconomics, as distinct from the Keynesian view of the business cycle, posits market clearing with imperfect information. It includes Friedman's permanent income hypothesis on consumption and "rational expectations" theory, lead by Robert Lucas, and real business cycle theory. In contrast, the new Keynesian approach retains the rational expectations assumption, however it assumes a variety of market failures. In particular, New Keynesians assume prices and wages are "sticky", which means they do not adjust instantaneously to changes in economic conditions.

Thus, the new classicals assume that prices and wages adjust automatically to attain full employment, whereas the new Keynesians see full employment as being automatically achieved only in the long run, and hence government and central-bank policies are needed because the "long run" may be very long.

Unemployment

The amount of unemployment in an economy is measured by the unemployment rate, the percentage of workers without jobs in the labour force. The labour force only includes workers actively looking for jobs. People who are retired, pursuing education, or discouraged from seeking work by a lack of job prospects are excluded from the labour force. Unemployment can be generally broken down into several types that are related to different causes.

Classical models of unemployment occurs when wages are too high for employers to be willing to hire more workers. Wages may be too high because of minimum wage laws or union activity. Consistent with classical unemployment, frictional unemployment occurs when appropriate job vacancies exist for a worker, but the length of time needed to search for and find the job leads to a period of unemployment.

Structural unemployment covers a variety of possible causes of unemployment including a mismatch between workers' skills and the skills required for open jobs. Large amounts of structural unemployment can occur when an economy is transitioning industries and workers find their previous set of skills are no longer in demand. Structural unemployment is similar to frictional unemployment since both reflect the problem of matching workers with job vacancies, but structural unemployment covers the time needed to acquire new skills not just the short term search process.

While some types of unemployment may occur regardless of the condition of the economy, cyclical unemployment occurs when growth stagnates. Okun's law represents the empirical relationship between unemployment and economic growth. The original version of Okun's law states that a 3% increase in output would lead to a 1% decrease in unemployment.

Inflation and Monetary Policy

Money is a *means of final payment* for goods in most price system economies and the unit of account in which prices are typically stated. A very apt statement by Professor Walker, a well-known economist is that, " Money is what money does." Money has a general acceptability, a relative consistency in value, divisibility, durability, portability, elastic in supply and survives with mass public confidence. It includes currency held by the nonbank public and checkable deposits. It has been described as a social convention, like language, useful to one largely because it is useful to others.

As a medium of exchange, money facilitates trade. It is essentially a measure of value and more importantly, a store of value being a basis for credit creation. Its economic function can be contrasted with barter (non-monetary exchange). Given a diverse array of produced goods and specialised producers, barter may entail a hard-to-locate double coincidence of wants as to what is exchanged, say apples and a book. Money can reduce the transaction cost of exchange because of its ready acceptability. Then it is less costly for the seller to accept money in exchange, rather than what the buyer produces.

At the level of an economy, theory and evidence are consistent with a positive relationship running from the total money supply to the nominal value of total output and to the general price level. For this reason, management of the money supply is a key aspect of monetary policy.

Fiscal Policy

Governments implement fiscal policy by adjusting spending and taxation policies to alter aggregate demand. When aggregate demand falls below the potential output of the economy, there is an output gap where some productive capacity is left unemployed. Governments increase spending and cut taxes to boost aggregate demand. Resources that have been idled can be used by the government.

For example, unemployed home builders can be hired to expand highways. Tax cuts allow consumers to increase their spending, which boosts aggregate demand. Both tax cuts and spending have multiplier effects where the initial increase in demand from the policy percolates through the economy and generates additional economic activity.

The effects of fiscal policy can be limited by crowding out. When there is no output gap, the economy is producing at full capacity and there are no excess productive resources. If the government increases spending in this situation, the government use resources that otherwise would have been used by the private sector, so there is no increase in overall output. Some economists think that crowding out is always an issue while others do not think it is a major issue when output is depressed. Skeptics of fiscal policy also make the argument of Ricardian equivalence. They argue that an increase in debt will have to be paid for with future tax increases, which will cause people to reduce their consumption and save money to pay for the future tax increase. Under Ricardian equivalence, any boost in demand from fiscal policy will be offset by the increased savings rate intended to pay for future higher taxes.

International Economics

International trade studies determinants of goods-and-services flows across international boundaries. It also concerns the size and distribution of gains from trade. Policy applications include estimating the effects of changing tariff rates and trade quotas. International finance is a macroeconomic field which examines the flow of capital across international borders, and the effects of these movements on exchange rates. Increased trade in goods, services and capital between countries is a major effect of contemporary globalization.

The distinct field of *development economics* examines economic aspects of the economic development process in relatively low-income countries focusing on structural change, poverty, and economic growth. Approaches in development economics frequently incorporate social and political factors. Economic systems is the branch of economics that studies the methods and institutions by which societies determine the ownership, direction, and allocation of economic resources. An *economic system* of a society is the unit of analysis.

Among contemporary systems at different ends of the organisational spectrum are socialist systems and capitalist systems, in which most production occurs in respectively state-run and private enterprises. In between are mixed economies. A common element is the interaction of economic and political influences, broadly described as political economy. *Comparative economic systems* studies the relative performance and behaviour of different economies or systems.

Gross Domestic Product (GDP) or Economic Growth

Gross Domestic product means the total value of goods produced and services provided in a country in a year. GDP is customarily reported on annual basis.

$$GDP = C + I + G + (X - M)$$

Practice

Contemporary economics uses mathematics. Economists draw on the tools of calculus, linear algebra, statistics, game theory, and computer science. Professional economists are expected to be familiar with these tools, while a minority specialise in econometrics and mathematical methods.

Theory

Mainstream economic theory relies upon a priori quantitative economic models, which employ a variety of concepts. Theory typically proceeds with an assumption of *ceteris paribus*, which means holding constant explanatory variables other than the one under consideration. When creating theories, the objective is to find ones which are at least as simple in information requirements, more precise in predictions, and more fruitful in generating additional research than prior theories. In microeconomics, principal concepts include supply and demand, marginalism, rational choice theory, opportunity cost, budget constraints, utility, and the theory of the firm. Early macroeconomic models focused on modelling the relationships between aggregate variables, but as the relationships appeared to change over time macroeconomists, including new Keynesians, reformulated their models in microfoundations. The aforementioned microeconomic concepts play a major part in macroeconomic models – for instance, in monetary theory, the quantity theory of money predicts that increases in the money supply increase inflation, and inflation is assumed to be influenced by rational expectations. In development economics, slower growth in developed nations has been sometimes predicted because of the declining marginal returns of investment and capital, and this has been observed in the Four Asian Tigers. Sometimes an economic hypothesis is only *qualitative*, not *quantitative*.

Expositions of economic reasoning often use two-dimensional graphs to illustrate theoretical relationships. At a higher level of generality, Paul Samuelson's treatise *Foundations of Economic Analysis* (1947) used mathematical methods to represent the theory, particularly as to maximizing behavioural relations of agents reaching equilibrium. The book focused on examining the class of statements called *operationally meaningful theorems* in economics, which are theorems that can conceivably be refuted by empirical data.

Empirical Investigation

Economic theories are frequently tested empirically, largely through the use of econometrics using economic data. The controlled experiments common to the physical sciences are difficult and uncommon in economics, and instead broad data is observationally studied; this type of testing is typically regarded as less rigorous than controlled experimentation, and the conclusions typically more tentative. However, the field of experimental economics is growing, and increasing use is being made of natural experiments.

Statistical methods such as regression analysis are common. Practitioners use such methods to estimate the size, economic significance, and statistical significance ("signal strength") of the hypothesized relation(s) and to adjust for noise from other variables. By such means, a hypothesis may gain acceptance, although in a probabilistic, rather than certain, sense. Acceptance is dependent upon the falsifiable hypothesis surviving tcsts. Usc of commonly accepted methods need not produce a final conclusion or even a consensus on a particular question, given different tests, data sets, and prior beliefs.

Criticism based on professional standards and non-replicability of results serve as further checks against bias, errors, and over-generalization, although much economic research has been accused of being non-replicable, and prestigious journals have been accused of not facilitating replication through the provision of the code and data. Like theories, uses of test statistics are themselves open to critical analysis, although critical commentary on papers in economics in prestigious journals such as the *American Economic Review* has declined precipitously in the past 40 years. This has been attributed to journals' incentives to maximize citations in order to rank higher on the Social Science Citation Index (SSCI).

In applied economics, input-output models employing linear programming methods are quite common. Large amounts of data are run through computer programs to analyze the impact of certain policies; IMPLAN is one well-known example.

Experimental economics has promoted the use of scientifically controlled experiments. This has reduced long-noted distinction of economics from natural sciences allowed direct tests of what were previously taken as axioms. In some cases these have found that the axioms are not entirely correct; for example, the ultimatum game has revealed that people reject unequal offers.

In behavioural economics, psychologist Daniel Kahneman won the Nobel Prize in economics in 2002 for his and Amos Tversky's empirical discovery of several cognitive biases and heuristics. Similar empirical testing occurs in neuroeconomics. Another example is the assumption of narrowly selfish preferences versus a model that tests for selfish, altruistic, and cooperative preferences. These techniques have led some to argue that economics is a "genuine science."

Profession

The professionalization of economics, reflected in the growth of graduate programs on the subject, has been described as "the main change in economics since around 1900". Most major universities and many colleges have a major, school, or department in which academic degrees are awarded in the subject, whether in the liberal arts, business, or for professional study. In the private sector, professional economists are employed as consultants and in industry, including banking and finance. Economists also work for various government departments and agencies, for example, the national Treasury, Central Bank or Bureau of Statistics. The Nobel Memorial Prize in Economic Sciences (commonly known as the Nobel Prize in Economics) is a prize awarded to economists each year for outstanding intellectual contributions in the field.

Related Subjects

Economics is one social science among several and has fields bordering on other areas, including economic geography, economic history, public choice, energy economics, cultural economics, family economics and institutional economics. Law and economics, or economic analysis of law, is an approach to legal theory that applies methods of economics to law. It includes the use of economic concepts to explain the effects of legal rules, to assess which legal rules are economically efficient, and to predict what the legal rules will be. A seminal article by Ronald Coase published in 1961 suggested that well-defined property rights could overcome the problems of externalities.

Political economy is the interdisciplinary study that combines economics, law, and political science in explaining how political institutions, the political environment, and the economic system (capitalist, socialist, mixed) influence each other. It studies questions such as how monopoly, rent-seeking behaviour, and externalities should impact government policy. Historians have employed *political economy* to explore the ways in the past that persons and groups with common economic interests have used politics to effect changes beneficial to their interests.

Energy economics is a broad scientific subject area which includes topics related to energy supply and energy demand. Georgescu-Roegen reintroduced the concept of entropy in relation to economics and energy from thermodynamics, as distinguished from what he viewed as the mechanistic foundation of neoclassical economics drawn from Newtonian physics. His work contributed significantly to thermoeconomics and to ecological economics. He also did foundational work which later developed into evolutionary economics.

The sociological subfield of economic sociology arose, primarily through the work of Émile Durkheim, Max Weber and Georg Simmel, as an approach to analysing the effects of economic phenomena in relation to the overarching social paradigm (i.e. modernity). Classic works include Max Weber's *The Protestant Ethic and the Spirit of Capitalism* (1905) and Georg Simmel's *The Philosophy of Money* (1900). More recently, the works of Mark Granovetter, Peter Hedstrom and Richard Swedberg have been influential in this field.

History

Economic writings date from earlier Mesopotamian, Greek, Roman, Indian subcontinent, Chinese, Persian, and Arab civilizations. Notable writers from antiquity through to the 14th century include Aristotle, Xenophon, Chanakya (also known as Kautilya), Qin Shi Huang, Thomas Aquinas, and Ibn Khaldun. The works of Aristotle had a profound influence on Aquinas, who in turn influenced the late scholastics of the 14th to 17th centuries. Joseph Schumpeter described the latter as "coming nearer than any other group to being the 'founders' of scientific economics" as to monetary, interest, and value theory within a natural-law perspective.

Two groups, later called "mercantilists" and "physiocrats", more directly influenced the subsequent development of the subject. Both groups were associated with the rise of economic nationalism and modern capitalism in Europe. Mercantilism was an economic doctrine that flourished from the 16th to 18th century in a prolific pamphlet literature, whether of merchants or statesmen. It held that a nation's wealth depended on its accumulation of gold and silver. Nations without access to mines could obtain gold and silver from trade only by selling goods abroad and restricting imports other than of gold and silver. The doctrine called for importing cheap raw materials to be used in manufacturing goods, which could be exported, and for state regulation to impose protective tariffs on foreign manufactured goods and prohibit manufacturing in the colonies. Physiocrats, a group of 18th century French thinkers and writers, developed the idea of the economy as a circular flow of income and output. Physiocrats believed that only agricultural production generated a clear surplus over cost, so that agriculture was the basis of all wealth. Thus, they opposed the mercantilist policy of promoting manufacturing and trade at the expense of agriculture, including import tariffs. Physiocrats advocated replacing administratively costly tax collections with a single tax on income of land owners. In reaction against copious mercantilist trade regulations, the physiocrats advocated a policy of laissez-faire, which called for minimal government intervention in the economy.

Modern economic analysis is customarily said to have begun with Adam Smith (1723–1790). Smith was harshly critical of the mercantilists but described the physiocratic system "with all its imperfections" as "perhaps the purest approximation to the truth that has yet been published" on the subject.

Classical Political Economy

The publication of Adam Smith's *The Wealth of Nations* in 1776, has been described as "the effective birth of economics as a separate discipline." The book identified land, labour, and capital as the three factors of production and the major contributors to a nation's wealth, as distinct from the Physiocratic idea that only agriculture was productive.

Smith discusses potential benefits of specialisation by division of labour, including increased labour productivity and gains from trade, whether between town and country or across countries. His "theorem" that "the division of labour is limited by the extent of the market" has been described as the "core of a theory of the functions of firm and industry" and a "fundamental principle of economic organisation." To Smith has also been ascribed "the most important substantive proposition in all of economics" and foundation of resource-allocation theory – that, under competition, resource owners (of labour, land, and capital) seek their most profitable uses, resulting in an equal rate of return for all uses in equilibrium (adjusted for apparent differences arising from such factors as training and unemployment).

In an argument that includes "one of the most famous passages in all economics," Smith represents every individual as trying to employ any capital they might command for their own advantage, not that of the society, and for the sake of profit, which is necessary at some level for employing capital in domestic industry, and positively related to the value of produce. In this:

He generally, indeed, neither intends to promote the public interest, nor knows how much he is promoting it. By preferring the support of domestic to that of foreign industry, he intends only his own security; and by directing that industry in such a manner as its produce may be of the greatest value, he intends only his own gain, and he is in this, as in many other cases, led by an invisible hand to promote an end which was no part of his intention. Nor is it always the worse for the society that it was no part of it. By pursuing his own interest he frequently promotes that of the society more effectually than when he really intends to promote it.

Economists have linked Smith's invisible-hand concept to his concern for the common man and woman through economic growth and development, enabling higher levels of consumption, which Smith describes as "the sole end and purpose of all production." He embeds the "invisible hand" in a framework that includes limiting restrictions on competition and foreign trade by government and industry in the same chapter and elsewhere regulation of banking and the interest rate, provision of a "natural system of liberty" — national defence, an egalitarian justice and legal system, and certain institutions and public works with general benefits to the whole society that might otherwise be unprofitable to produce, such as education and roads, canals, and the like. An influential introductory textbook includes parallel discussion and this assessment: "Above all, it is Adam Smith's vision of a self-regulating invisible hand that is his enduring contribution to modern economics."

The Rev. Thomas Robert Malthus (1798) used the idea of diminishing returns to explain low living standards. Human population, he argued, tended to increase geometrically, outstripping the production of food, which increased arithmetically. The force of a rapidly growing population against a limited amount of land meant diminishing returns to labour. The result, he claimed, was chronically low wages, which prevented the standard of living for most of the population from rising above the subsistence level. Economist Julian Lincoln Simon has criticised Malthus's conclusions. While Adam Smith emphasized the production of income, David Ricardo (1817) focused on the distribution of income among landowners, workers, and capitalists. Ricardo saw an inherent conflict between landowners on the one hand and labour and capital on the other. He posited that the growth of population and capital, pressing against a fixed supply of land, pushes up rents and holds down wages and profits. Ricardo was the first to state and prove the principle of comparative advantage, according to which each country should specialise in producing and exporting goods in that it has a lower *relative* cost of production, rather relying only on its own production. It has been termed a "fundamental analytical explanation" for gains from trade. Coming at the end of the Classical tradition, John Stuart Mill (1848) parted company with the earlier classical economists on the inevitability of the distribution of income produced by the market system. Mill pointed to a distinct difference between the market's two roles: allocation of resources and distribution of income. The market might be efficient in allocating resources but not in distributing income, he wrote, making it necessary for society to intervene.

Value theory was important in classical theory. Smith wrote that the "real price of every thing ... is the toil and trouble of acquiring it" as influenced by its scarcity. Smith maintained that, with rent and profit, other costs besides wages also enter the price of a commodity. Other classical economists presented variations on Smith, termed the 'labour theory of value'. Classical economics focused on the tendency of markets to move to long-run equilibrium.

Marxism

Marxist (later, Marxian) economics descends from classical economics. It derives from the work of Karl Marx. The first volume of Marx's major work, *Das Kapital*, was published in German in 1867. In it, Marx focused on the labour theory of value and the theory of surplus value which, he believed, explained the exploitation of labour by capital. The labour theory of value held that the value of an exchanged commodity was determined by the labour that went into its production and the theory of surplus value demonstrated how the workers only got paid a proportion of the value their work had created. The U.S. Export-Import Bank defines a Marxist-Lenninist state as having a centrally planned economy. They are now rare, examples can still be seen in Cuba, North Korea and Laos.

Neoclassical Economics

A body of theory later termed "neoclassical economics" or "marginalism" formed from about 1870 to 1910. The term "economics" was popularized by such neoclassical economists as Alfred Marshall as a concise synonym for 'economic science' and a substitute for the earlier "political economy". This corresponded to the influence on the subject of mathematical methods used in the natural sciences.

Neoclassical economics systematized supply and demand as joint determinants of price and quantity in market equilibrium, affecting both the allocation of output and the distribution of income. It dispensed with the labour theory of value inherited from classical economics in favour of a marginal utility theory of value on the demand side and a more general theory of costs on the supply side. In the 20th century, neoclassical theorists moved away from an earlier notion suggesting that total utility for a society could be measured in favour of ordinal utility, which hypothesizes merely behaviour-based relations across persons.

In microeconomics, neoclassical economics represents incentives and costs as playing a pervasive role in shaping decision making. An immediate example of this is the consumer theory of individual demand, which isolates how prices (as costs) and income affect quantity demanded. In macroeconomics it is reflected in an early and lasting neoclassical synthesis with Keynesian macroeconomics.

Neoclassical economics is occasionally referred as *orthodox economics* whether by its critics or sympathizers. Modern mainstream economics builds on neoclassical economics but with many refinements that either supplement or generalize earlier analysis, such as econometrics, game theory, analysis of market failure and imperfect competition, and the neoclassical model of economic growth for analyzing long-run variables affecting national income.

Keynesian Economics

Keynesian economics derives from John Maynard Keynes, in particular his book *The General Theory of Employment, Interest and Money* (1936), which ushered in contemporary macroeconomics as a distinct field. The book focused on determinants of national income in the short run when prices are relatively inflexible. Keynes attempted to explain in broad theoretical detail why high labour-market unemployment might not be self-correcting due to low "effective demand" and why even price flexibility and monetary policy might be unavailing. The term "revolutionary" has been applied to the book in its impact on economic analysis.

Keynesian economics has two successors. Post-Keynesian economics also concentrates on macroeconomic rigidities and adjustment processes. Research on micro foundations for their models is represented as based on real-life practices rather than simple optimizing models. It is generally associated with the University of Cambridge and the work of Joan Robinson.

New-Keynesian economics is also associated with developments in the Keynesian fashion. Within this group researchers tend to share with other economists the emphasis on models employing micro foundations and optimizing behaviour but with a narrower focus on standard Keynesian themes such as price and wage rigidity. These are usually made to be endogenous features of the models, rather than simply assumed as in older Keynesian-style ones.

Chicago School of Economics

The Chicago School of economics is best known for its free market advocacy and monetarist ideas. According to Milton Friedman and monetarists, market economies are inherently stable if the money supply does not greatly expand or contract. Ben Bernanke, current Chairman of the Federal Reserve, is among the economists today generally accepting Friedman's analysis of the causes of the Great Depression.

Milton Friedman effectively took many of the basic principles set forth by Adam Smith and the classical economists and modernized them. One example of this is his article in the September 1970 issue of The New York Times Magazine, where he claims that the social responsibility of business should be "to use its resources and engage in activities designed to increase its profits ... (through) open and free competition without deception or fraud."

Other Schools and Approaches

Other well-known schools or trends of thought referring to a particular style of economics practiced at and disseminated from well-defined groups of academicians that have become known worldwide, include the Austrian School, the Freiburg School, the School of Lausanne, post-Keynesian economics and the Stockholm school. Contemporary mainstream economics is sometimes separated into the Saltwater approach of those universities along the Eastern and Western coasts of the US, and the Freshwater, or Chicago-school approach.

Within macroeconomics there is, in general order of their appearance in the literature; classical economics, Keynesian economics, the neoclassical synthesis, post-Keynesian economics, monetarism, new classical economics, and supply-side economics. Alternative developments include ecological economics, constitutional economics, institutional economics, evolutionary economics, dependency theory, structuralist economics, world systems theory, econophysics, feminist economics and biophysical economics.

Criticisms

General Criticisms

"The dismal science" is a derogatory alternative name for economics devised by the Victorian historian Thomas Carlyle in the 19th century. It is often stated that Carlyle gave economics the nickname "the dismal science" as a response to the late 18th century writings of The

Reverend Thomas Robert Malthus, who grimly predicted that starvation would result, as projected population growth exceeded the rate of increase in the food supply. However, the actual phrase was coined by Carlyle in the context of a debate with John Stuart Mill on slavery, in which Carlyle argued for slavery, while Mill opposed it.

Some economists, like John Stuart Mill or Léon Walras, have maintained that the production of wealth should not be tied to its distribution.

In *The Wealth of Nations*, Adam Smith addressed many issues that are currently also the subject of debate and dispute. Smith repeatedly attacks groups of politically aligned individuals who attempt to use their collective influence to manipulate a government into doing their bidding. In Smith's day, these were referred to as factions, but are now more commonly called special interests, a term which can comprise international bankers, corporate conglomerations, outright oligopolies, monopolies, trade unions and other groups.

Economics per se, as a social science, is independent of the political acts of any government or other decision-making organisation, however, many policymakers or individuals holding highly ranked positions that can influence other people's lives are known for arbitrarily using a plethora of economic concepts and rhetoric as vehicles to legitimize agendas and value systems, and do not limit their remarks to matters relevant to their responsibilities. The close relation of economic theory and practice with politics is a focus of contention that may shade or distort the most unpretentious original tenets of economics, and is often confused with specific social agendas and value systems.

Notwithstanding, economics legitimately has a role in informing government policy. It is, indeed, in some ways an outgrowth of the older field of political economy. Some academic economic journals are currently focusing increased efforts on gauging the consensus of economists regarding certain policy issues in hopes of effecting a more informed political environment. Currently, there exists a low approval rate from professional economists regarding many public policies. Policy issues featured in a recent survey of AEA economists include trade restrictions, social insurance for those put out of work by international competition, genetically modified foods, curbside recycling, health insurance (several questions), medical malpractice, barriers to entering the medical profession, organ donations, unhealthy foods, mortgage deductions, taxing internet sales, Wal-Mart, casinos, ethanol subsidies, and inflation targeting.

In *Steady State Economics* 1977, Herman Daly argues that there exist logical inconsistencies between the emphasis placed on economic growth and the limited availability of natural resources.

Issues like central bank independence, central bank policies and rhetoric in central bank governors discourse or the premises of macroeconomic policies (monetary and fiscal policy) of the state, are focus of contention and criticism.

Deirdre McCloskey has argued that many empirical economic studies are poorly reported, and she and Stephen Ziliak argue that although her critique has been well-received, practice has not improved. This latter contention is controversial.

A 2002 International Monetary Fund study looked at "consensus forecasts" (the forecasts of large groups of economists) that were made in advance of 60 different national recessions in the 1990s: in 97% of the cases the economists did not predict the contraction a year in advance. On those rare occasions when economists did successfully predict recessions, they significantly underestimated their severity.

Criticisms of Assumptions

Economics has been subject to criticism that it relies on unrealistic, unverifiable, or highly simplified assumptions, in some cases because these assumptions simplify the proofs of desired conclusions. Examples of such assumptions include perfect information, profit maximization and rational choices. The field of information economics includes both mathematical-economical research and also behavioural economics, akin to studies in behavioural psychology.

Nevertheless, prominent mainstream economists such as Keynes and Joskow have observed that much of economics is conceptual rather than quantitative, and difficult to model and formalize quantitatively. In a discussion on oligopoly research, Paul Joskow pointed out in 1975 that in practice, serious students of actual economies tended to use "informal models" based upon qualitative factors specific to particular industries. Joskow had a strong feeling that the important work in oligopoly was done through informal observations while formal models were "trotted out *ex post*". He argued that formal models were largely not important in the empirical work, either, and that the fundamental factor behind the theory of the firm, behaviour, was neglected.

In recent years, feminist critiques of neoclassical economic models gained prominence, leading to the formation of feminist economics. Contrary to common conceptions of economics as a positive and objective science, feminist economists call attention to the social construction of economics and highlight the ways in which its models and methods reflect masculine preferences. Primary criticisms focus on failures to account for: the selfish nature of actors (homo economicus); exogenous tastes; the impossibility of utility comparisons; the exclusion of unpaid work; and the exclusion of class and gender considerations. Feminist economics developed to address these concerns, and the field now includes critical examinations of many areas of economics including paid and unpaid work, economic epistemology and history, globalization, household economics and the care economy. In 1988, Marilyn Waring published the book *If Women Counted*, in which she argues that the discipline of economics ignores women's unpaid work and the value of nature; according to Julie A. Nelson, *If Women Counted* "showed exactly how the unpaid work traditionally done by women has been made invisible within national accounting systems" and "issued a wake-up call to issues of ecological sustainability." Bjørnholt and McKay argue that the financial crisis of 2007–08 and the response to it revealed a crisis of ideas in mainstream economics and within the economics profession, and call for a reshaping of both the economy, economic theory and the economics profession. They argue that such a reshaping should include new advances within feminist economics that take as their starting point the socially responsible, sensible and accountable subject in creating an economy and economic theories that fully acknowledge care for each other as well as the planet.

Philip Mirowski Observes that

The imperatives of the orthodox research programme [of economic science] leave little room for maneuver and less room for originality. ... These mandates ... Appropriate as many mathematical techniques and metaphorical expressions from contemporary respectable science, primarily physics as possible. ... Preserve to the maximum extent possible the attendant nineteenth-century overtones of "natural order" ... Deny strenuously that neoclassical theory slavishly imitates physics. ... Above all, prevent all rival research programmes from encroaching ... by ridiculing all external attempts to appropriate twentieth century physics models. ... All theorizing is [in this way] held hostage to nineteenth-century concepts of energy.

In a series of peer-reviewed journal and conference papers and books published over a period of several decades, John McMurtry has provided extensive criticism of what he terms the "unexamined assumptions and implications [of economics], and their consequent cost to people's lives." Nassim Nicholas Taleb and Michael Perelman are two additional scholars who criticized conventional or mainstream economics. Taleb opposes most economic theorizing, which in his view suffers acutely from the problem of overuse of Plato's Theory of Forms, and calls for cancellation of the Nobel Memorial Prize in Economics, saying that the damage from economic theories can be devastating. Michael Perelman provides extensive criticism of economics and its assumptions in all his books (and especially his books published from 2000 to date), papers and interviews.

Despite these concerns, mainstream graduate programs have become increasingly technical and mathematical.

2

The Scarcity Principle

Scarcity

Scarcity is the fundamental economic problem of having seemingly unlimited human wants and needs in a world of limited resources. It states that society has insufficient productive resources to fulfill all human wants and needs. Additionally, scarcity implies that not all of society's goals can be pursued at the same time; trade-offs are made of one good against others. In an influential 1932 essay, Lionel Robbins defined economics as "the science which studies human behaviour as a relationship between ends and scarce means which have alternative uses." In biology, *scarcity* can refer to the uncommonness or rarity of certain species. Such species are often protected by local, national or international law in order to prevent extinction.

Artificial Scarcity

Artificial scarcity describes the scarcity of items even though the technology and production capacity exists to create an abundance. The term is applied to non-rival resources, i.e. those that do not diminish due to one person's use, although there are other resources which could be categorized as artificially scarce. The inefficiency associated with artificial scarcity is formally known as a deadweight loss.

Examples

The Disney vault is a concept where popular Disney properties are only sold over short time spans, and then locked away for numerous years, in order to give customers added incentive to buy for fear of 'missing out'.

On the audio commentary for season 14 episode Treehouse of Horror XIII, showrunner Al Jean said that The Simpsons destroy many of their animation cells in order to make the remaining ones more valuable.

Economic Shortage

An economic shortage is a disparity between the amount demanded for a product or service and the amount supplied in a market. Specifically, a shortage occurs when there is excess demand; therefore, it is the opposite of a surplus.

Economic shortages are related to price—when the price of an item is set below the equilibrium rate determined by supply and demand, there will be a shortage. In most cases, a shortage will compel firms to increase the price of a product until it reaches market equilibrium. Sometimes, however, external forces cause more permanent shortages—in other words, there is something preventing prices from rising or otherwise keeping supply and demand balanced.

In common use, the term "shortage" may refer to a situation where most people are unable to find a desired good at an affordable price. In the economic use of "shortage", however, the affordability of a good for the majority of people is not an issue: If people wish to have a certain good but cannot afford to pay the market price, their wish is not counted as part of the quantity demanded at that price.

Effects

In the case of government intervention in the market, there is always a trade-off, with positive and negative effects. For example, a price ceiling may cause a shortage, but it will also enable a certain portion of the population to purchase a product that they couldn't afford at market costs. Economic shortages caused by higher transaction costs and opportunity costs (e.g., in the form of lost time) also mean that the distribution process is wasteful. Both of these factors contribute to a decrease in aggregate wealth.

More generally, regardless of their cause, shortages may result in:

- Black markets - illegal markets in which products that are unavailable in conventional markets are sold, or in which products with excess demand are sold at higher prices than in the conventional market.
- Artificial controls on demand, such as rationing.
- Non-monetary bargaining methods, such as time (for example queuing), nepotism, or even violence.

- Price discrimination
- The inability to purchase a product.

Examples

- In the former Soviet Union during the 1980s, prices were artificially low by fiat (i.e., high prices were outlawed). Soviet citizens waited in line (or "queued") for various price-controlled goods and services such as cars, apartments, or some types of clothing. From the point of view of those waiting in line, such goods were in perpetual "short supply"; some of them were willing and able to pay more than the official price ceiling, but were legally prohibited from doing so. This method for determining the allocation of goods in short supply is known as "rationing".

Other examples of economic shortages include:

- 1973 oil crisis, during which long lines and rationing were used to control demand.
- Prohibition, which resulted in the creation of a black market for liquor.

Whether an economic shortage of a certain good or service is beneficial or detrimental to society often depends on one's ethical and political views. For instance, consider the shortage of recreational drugs discussed above, and the controversies around the use of such drugs. Likewise, consider the economic shortage of cars in the Soviet Union during the 1980s:

On the one hand, people had to wait in line to buy a new car; on the other hand, cars were more affordable than they would have been at market prices.

Shortages and "Longages"

Garrett Hardin emphasized that a shortage of supply can just as well be viewed as a "longage" of demand. For instance, a shortage of food can just as well be called a longage of people (overpopulation). By looking at it from this view, he felt the problem could be better dealt with.

Post-Scarcity Economy

Post-scarcity is an alternative form of economics or social engineering in which goods, services and information are universally accessible. This would require a sophisticated system of resource recycling, in conjunction with technologically advanced automated systems capable of converting raw materials into finished goods.

The Scarcity Model

Scarcity is the fundamental economic assumption of having seemingly unlimited human needs and wants in a world of limited resources. It states that society has insufficient productive resources to fulfill all human wants and needs. Alternatively, scarcity implies that not all of society's goals can be pursued at the same time; trade-offs are made of one good against others. As such, the term "post-scarcity economics" may be somewhat paradoxical. To quote a 1932 essay by Lionel Robbins, economics is "the science which studies human behaviour as a relationship between ends and scarce means which have alternative uses."

Economics in any and all forms rests on the assumption of conditions of natural or artificially enforced scarcity, far less than enough to supply everyone. The study of economics and its everyday business control and transactions tells you how each variation of the Price System makes an ideology of how to divide up that scarcity. You will find economics defined in terms of scarcity in every textbook on the subject, usually in the opening chapter. Without scarcity, some of them candidly admit, there would be no need for economics.

—John A. Waring, "Technocracy and Humanism", *Section 3 Newsletter*

However, in Marxist economics, scarcity is said to be peripheral. Human wants in practice are not assumed to be infinite, but variable and ultimately conditioned. Scarcity, instead, is secondary to the issue of differential distribution within a society due to class, primarily between a producing class (e.g. slaves, peasants, the proletariat) and a surplus-taking class (e.g. slave owners, lords, the bourgeoisie).

Leon Trotsky considered development of a post-scarcity economy necessary to "uproot class society and to free women and youth from the stultifying confines of the institution of the family".

Means

Speculative Technology: Most visions of post-scarcity societies assume the existence of new technologies which make it much easier for society to produce nearly all goods in great abundance, given raw materials and energy. More speculative forms of nanotechnology (such as molecular assemblers or nanofactories) raise the possibility of devices that can automatically manufacture any specified goods given the correct instructions and the necessary raw materials and energy. Even before that level of technology can be achieved, fab labs and advanced industrial automation might be able to produce most physical goods that people desire, with a minimal amount of human labour required. As for the raw materials and energy needed as input for such automated production systems, self-replicating automated mining plants set loose in the asteroid belt or other areas of space with huge amounts of untapped raw materials could cause the prices of these materials to plummet. New power sources such as fusion power or solar power satellites could do the same for energy, especially if the power plants/power satellites could themselves be constructed in a highly automated way, so their number would be limited only by raw materials and energy.

Effects

Economic Paradigm: Market economies or planned economies may be unnecessary in a post-scarcity age, though gift or exchange economies may take their place once the scarcity driving earlier types of economy disappears. Post-scarcity societies might also have their market economies limited to the exchange of energy and resources, or of other scarce or even non-material things, such as status or reputation, real estate, or skills and expertise.

Many science-fiction variants also imagine the very concept of ownership to weaken or disappear, as people lose attachment to all but sentimental-value items, knowing that they will always be able to receive or create replacements. Monetary systems in consequence also cease to be a factor. Many stories depict these changes as a positive advancement, freeing humanity from both toil and greed. Others posit that handing production and most other services over to machines and computers will stunt the spirit of humanity, or even lead to a loss of control over humanity's own fate, e.g., Jack Williamson's *With Folded Hands.*

Unavoidable Scarcity

Some things would remain limited in supply even in a post-scarcity society. There is a practical limit to the number of people who can live in any specific, 'in-demand' locale. However, hypothetical machines such as a nanofactory are envisioned as being able to produce any real-world artifact, and some fictions even envision the physical creation of new living space (orbitals or ringworlds) to reduce this scarcity. This would likely further reduce (though not fully eliminate) the value of an 'original' item or a specific locale to live in. Engineers have suggested megascale structures such as an Alderson disk or Dyson sphere to provide abundant living space and energy. Should immersive virtual reality develop to simulate reality so accurately that one could not distinguish it from the physical world, the amount of available virtual space would be vastly increased. Since one need not simulate the world to a quantum level to make it appear completely real, a simulated reality which appears completely real to a user could be simulated on a computer much smaller than the simulated space.

Population growth, if it continued long enough, would also lead to unavoidable scarcity. As pointed out by Thomas Robert Malthus, Paul R. Ehrlich, Albert Allen Bartlett, and others, exponential growth in human population has the capacity to overwhelm any finite supply of resources, even the entire known universe, in a remarkably short time. For example, if the human population continued to grow indefinitely at its 1994 rate, in 1,900 years the mass of the human population would equal the mass of Earth, and in 6,000 years the mass of the human population would equal the estimated mass of the observable universe. Although this would imply the invention of faster than light travel, necessary for humanity to spread throughout the universe as fast as population growth, even at lower growth rates these levels would still be reached in readily imaginable times. So a plausible post-scarcity scenario must imply zero population growth or relatively low population growth, even though possible future technologies such as self-replicating spacecraft could theoretically maintain exponential growth far beyond Earth's carrying capacity.

At present, the total fertility rate is high in poor countries with poor health infrastructure, but it tends to drop to replacement levels or lower once a nation reaches a per capita income of roughly $10,000. In fact, virtually every wealthy OECD nation currently has a total fertility rate that is below replacement levels, implying a coming population decline for the West. Due to the decline in fertility that tends to accompany wealth (of the 233 countries listed by the CIA for fertility, 100 have fertility rates below replacement rates), human population is expected to stabilize at near 9 billion by 2050.This will likely be caused by Demographic Transition.

Fiction

Utopias: Fictional post-scarcity societies include varied settings, such as *The Queendom of Sol* in the series of the same name by Wil McCarthy, "the Festival" and agalmic economics from *Singularity Sky* and *Accelerando* by Charles Stross, and the United Federation of Planets from the Star Trek series. One of the earliest treatments of a transition to a post-scarcity society occurs in *Pandora's Millions* by George O. Smith, in which the development of a "matter duplicator" that can replicate almost any scannable object causes an economic collapse, and a return to a barter economy for the only remaining scarce resource: Skilled human labour. Chaos ensues until the inventors of the matter duplicator discover a substance that explodes when scanned by the duplicator beam. This new substance, "Identium," serves as a new medium of exchange for skilled labour, in a post-scarcity society otherwise primarily devoted to the pursuit of leisure, science, art, the occasional lawsuit, and the sale and exchange of "Certified Uniques" — objects whose chain of provenance can legally establish that they have never been scanned by a duplicator beam.

Kim Stanley Robinson's Mars trilogy describes the beginning development of a highly automated society whose economy was to be based on caloric input/output and had only a few materials valued based on their scarcity. However, the inherent problems of such a system (such as its remaining capitalist elements or the difficulty in fixing the worth of academic work) are not resolved within the timeframe depicted in the trilogy.

An intermediate step to a post-scarcity society is shown in Neal Stephenson's *The Diamond Age*, where fabricator technology allows the growth of any item that one has design plans for - however, the poor receive a lesser amount of energy and resources per day to use, and thus have to wait longer for their items to be fabricated. Also, their items tend to be smaller, as they have no access to large-scale fabricators. This system, fueled by a centrally-distributed matter 'feed' is eventually replaced by the protean 'seed', which is able to take in raw materials from its environment to develop into whatever its program dictates. No longer bound to the aristocratically-controlled feeds, the society moves to a post-scarcity economy.

James P. Hogan has written several works where post-scarcity plays a major role. *Voyage from Yesteryear* details the society of the "Chironians", embryo colonists of Alpha Centauri who have adopted such a lifestyle. *Cradle of Saturn* and its sequel *The Anguished Dawn* is mostly told from the perspective of the "Kronians", a pseudo-religion who colonize Saturn's largest satellite in the process of developing such a society. Both stories are driven by the difficulties of changing an existing economic paradigm, and postulate that a fresh start may be necessary to overcome old thinking about money and possessions.

Rudy Rucker also dealt with this jarring transition in *Realware* in which humans receive an alien device that can instantiate any consumer product they have seen. This leads to a breakdown of the market, with stores blacking out their windows in a vain attempt to prevent people from 'copying' their products. Still, people who do buy the products find them instantly copied once out on the streets.

Iain M. Banks' Culture series centres around an advanced spacefaring civilization that has used artificial intelligences to provide extremely abundant (and in daily practice unlimited) amounts of goods and services using advanced technology, describing a fully post scarcity society, which also attempts to influence other galactic societies towards the advanced cultural stage that freedom from greed and material need has allowed it. As Banks puts it in a 1994 article, "nothing and nobody in the Culture is exploited. It is essentially an automated civilisation in its manufacturing processes, with human labour restricted to something indistinguishable from play, or a hobby."

John C. Wright's novel *The Golden Age* deals with a future voluntary libertarian society spanning the solar system called the Golden Oecumene. Due to technology, nearly everyone is immortal and tremendously wealthy except those living outside society due to exile or by choice. The Sophotechs, a superior line of computer intelligences, do most of the work, research, and simulations required by the society. Throughout the book the main character, Phaethon, has to face off against a technologically superior and unknown enemy while also dealing with a post-scarcity society which is afraid of death and instability more than anything else and does not believe his plight.

Dystopias

There have also been fully dystopian science fiction societies where all people's physical needs are provided for by machines, but this causes humans to become overly docile, uncreative and incurious. Examples include E. M. Forster's 1909 short story "The Machine Stops", Kurt Vonnegut's *Player Piano*, and Arthur C. Clarke's 1956 novel *The City and the Stars. Riders of the Purple Wage*, Philip José Farmer's dystopian 1967 science fiction novella also explores some ramifications of a future wherein technology allows everyone's desires to be met.

Arthur C. Clarke's 1953 novel "Childhood's End" also describes Earth achieving a post-scarcity society when god-like aliens take indirect control of the planet and eradicate war, disease, poverty and other ailments. A lack of competitiveness causes humanity to become disinterested in science and space exploration.

Jack Vance's *The Moon Moth* presents a planet where plenitude has led to a culture of intricacy with an elaborate half-musical language and craftsmanship. The lack of incentive for collaboration is one of the problems faced by the "outlander" main character. In Frederik Pohl's *The Midas Plague,* resources and luxuries are so common, that the *poor* must bear the burden of consuming and disposing of the bounty, as well as working at meaningless jobs to produce more meaningless plenty; the *rich*, conversely, are allowed to live simple but comfortable lifestyles.

In Stanislaw Lem's *Cyberiad*, a central motif is unbounded progress of technology - in the sub-story *The Highest Possible Level of Development civilization*, the inhabitants have become passive, and the visitors have to shoo away machines trying to comfort them. In H.G. Wells' *The Time Machine*, the Time Traveller speculates, based on the Eloi, that mankind had been "armed with a perfected science" which reduced all dangers in nature, epitomized by the quote: "Strength is the outcome of need".

In *A for Anything*, a science fiction novel by Damon Knight, the "Gismo" is a device that can duplicate anything—even humans or another Gismo. Since all material objects have become essentially free, the only commodity of value is human labor, and a feudal society and a slave economy is the result.

The 2008 Pixar film *WALL-E* depicts what appears to be a somewhat humorous post-scarcity dystopia: humans are obese hedonists whose lives are spent entirely on floating recliners.

Indifference Curves

In microeconomic theory, an indifference curve is a graph showing different bundles of goods between which a consumer is *indifferent*. That is, at each point on the curve, the consumer has no preference for one bundle over another. One can equivalently refer to each point on the indifference curve as rendering the same level of utility (satisfaction) for the consumer.

In other words an indifference curve is the locus of various points showing different combinations of two goods providing equal utility to the consumer.

Utility is then a device to represent preferences rather than something from which preferences come. The main use of indifference curves is in the representation of potentially observable demand patterns for individual consumers over commodity bundles.

There are infinitely many indifference curves: one passes through each combination. A collection of (selected) indifference curves, illustrated graphically, is referred to as an indifference map.

History

The theory of indifference curves was developed by Francis Ysidro Edgeworth, who explained in his book "Mathematical Psychics: an Essay on the Application of Mathematics to the Moral Sciences," 1881, the mathematics needed for its drawing; later on, Vilfredo Pareto was the first author to actually draw these curves, in his book "Manual of Political Economy," 1906; and others in the first part of the 20th century. The theory can be derived from William Stanley Jevons's ordinal utility theory, which posits that individuals can always rank any consumption bundles by order of preference.

Map and Properties of Indifference Curves

A graph of indifference curves for an individual consumer associated with different utility levels is called an indifference map. Points yielding different utility levels are each associated with distinct indifference curves and these indifference curves on the indifference map are like contour lines on a topographical map. Each point on the curve represents the same elevation. If you move "off" an indifference curve travelling in a northeast direction (assuming positive marginal utility for the goods) you are essentially climbing a mound of utility. The higher you go the greater the level of utility. The non-satiation requirement means that you will never reach the "top," or a "bliss point," a consumption bundle that is preferred to all others

Indifference curves are typically represented to be:

1. Defined only in the non-negative quadrant of commodity quantities (i.e. the possibility of having negative quantities of any good is ignored).
2. Negatively sloped. That is, as quantity consumed of one good (X) increases, total satisfaction would increase if not offset by a decrease in the quantity consumed of the other good (Y). Equivalently, satiation, such that more of either good (or both) is equally preferred to no increase, is excluded. (If utility $U = f(x, y)$, U, in the third dimension, does not have a local maximum for any x and y values.) The negative slope of the indifference curve reflects the assumption of the monotonicity of consumer's preferences, which generates monotonically increasing utility functions, and the assumption of non-satiation (marginal utility for all goods is always positive); an upward sloping indifference curve would imply that a consumer is indifferent between a bundle A and another bundle B because they lie on the same indifference curve, even in the case in

which the quantity of both goods in bundle B is higher. Because of monotonicity of preferences and non-satiation, a bundle with more of both goods must be preferred to one with less of both, thus the first bundle must yield a higher utility, and lie on a different indifference curve at a higher utility level.

The negative slope of the indifference curve implies that the marginal rate of substitution is always positive;

1. Complete, such that all points on an indifference curve are ranked equally preferred and ranked either more or less preferred than every other point not on the curve. So, with (2), no two curves can intersect (otherwise non-satiation would be violated).
2. Transitive with respect to points on distinct indifference curves. That is, if each point on I_2 is (strictly) preferred to each point on I_1, and each point on I_3 is preferred to each point on I_2, each point on I_3 is preferred to each point on I_1. A negative slope and transitivity exclude indifference curves crossing, since straight lines from the origin on both sides of where they crossed would give opposite and intransitive preference rankings.
3. (Strictly) convex. With (2), convex preferences imply that the indifference curves cannot be concave to the origin, i.e. they will either be straight lines or bulge toward the origin of the indifference curve. If the latter is the case, then as a consumer decreases consumption of one good in successive units, successively larger doses of the other good are required to keep satisfaction unchanged.

Assumptions of Consumer Preference Theory

- Preferences are complete. The consumer has ranked all available alternative combinations of commodities in terms of the satisfaction they provide him.
  - o Assume that there are two consumption bundles A and B each containing two commodities x and y. A consumer can unambiguously determine that one and only one of the following is the case:
    - A is preferred to B $\Rightarrow$ A ^{P} B
    - B is preferred to A $\Rightarrow$ B ^{P} A
    - A is indifferent to B $\Rightarrow$ A ^{I} B
    - Note that this axiom precludes the possibility that the consumer cannot decide, and that a consumer is

able to make this comparison with respect to every conceivable bundle of goods.

- Preferences are reflexive
  - o Means that if A and B are identical in all respects the consumer will recognise this fact and be indifferent in comparing A and B
    - – $A = B \Rightarrow A\ ^{I}\ B$
- Preferences are transitive[nb 1]
  - o If $A\ ^{p}\ B$ and $B\ ^{p}\ C$ then $A\ ^{p}\ C$.
  - o Also $A\ ^{I}\ B$ and $B\ ^{I}\ C$ then $A\ ^{I}\ C$.
    - – This is a consistency assumption.
- Preferences are continuous
  - o If A is preferred to B and C is infinitesimally close to B then A is preferred to C.
  - o $A\ ^{p}\ B\ \&\ C \rightarrow B \Rightarrow A\ ^{p}\ C$.
    - – "Continuous" means infinitely divisible - just like there are infinite numbers between 1 and 2 all bundles are infinitely divisible. This assumption makes indifference curves continuous.
- Preferences exhibit strong monotonicity
  - o if A has more of both x and y than B then A is preferred to B
    - – this assumption is commonly called the "more is better" assumption
    - – an alternative version of this assumption is strong monotonicity which requires that if A and B have the same quantity of one good, but A has more of the other, then A is preferred to B.

It also implies that the commodities are good rather than bad. Examples of bad commodities can be disease, pollution etc. because we always desire less of such things.

- Indifference curves exhibit diminishing marginal rates of substitution
  - o The marginal rate of substitution tells how much 'y' a person is willing to sacrifice to get one more unit of 'x'.
  - o This assumption assures that indifference curves are smooth and convex to the origin.

- This assumption also set the stage for using techniques of constrained optimization because the shape of the curve assures that the first derivative is negative and the second is positive.
- Another name for this assumption is the substitution assumption. It is the most critical assumption of consumer theory: Consumers are willing to give up or trade-off some of one good to get more of another. The fundamental assertion is that there is a maximum amount that "a consumer will give up, of one commodity, to get one unit of another good, in that amount which will leave the consumer indifferent between the new and old situations." The negative slope of the indifference curves represents the willingness of the consumer to make a trade off.

• There are also many sub-assumptions:
  - Irreflexivity - for no x is $x^{p}x$
  - Negative transitivity - if $x^{not\text{-}p}y$ then for any third commodity z, either $x^{not\text{-}p}z$ or $z^{not\text{-}p}y$ or both.

Application

Consumer theory uses indifference curves and budget constraints to generate consumer demand curves. For a single consumer, this is a relatively simple process.

First, let one good be an example market e.g., carrots, and let the other be a composite of all other goods. Budget constraints give a straight line on the indifference map showing all the possible distributions between the two goods; the point of maximum utility is then the point at which an indifference curve is tangent to the budget line (illustrated).

This follows from common sense: if the market values a good more than the household, the household will sell it; if the market values a good less than the household, the household will buy it. The process then continues until the market's and household's marginal rates of substitution are equal.

Now, if the price of carrots were to change, and the price of all other goods were to remain constant, the gradient of the budget line would also change, leading to a different point of tangency and a different quantity demanded. These price / quantity combinations can then be used to deduce a full demand curve. A line connecting all points of tangency between the indifference curve and the budget constraint is called the expansion path.

Examples of Indifference Curves

In Figure depicted earlier, the consumer would rather be on I_3 than I_2, and would rather be on I_2 than I_1, but does not care where he/she is on a given indifference curve. The slope of an indifference curve (in absolute value), known by economists as the marginal rate of substitution, shows the rate at which consumers are willing to give up one good in exchange for more of the other good. For *most* goods the marginal rate of substitution is not constant so their indifference curves are curved. The curves are convex to the origin, describing the negative substitution effect. As price rises for a fixed money income, the consumer seeks less the expensive substitute at a lower indifference curve. The substitution effect is reinforced through the income effect of lower real income (Beattie-LaFrance). An example of a utility function that generates indifference curves of this kind is the Cobb-Douglas function $U(x,y)=x^{\alpha}y^{1-\alpha}, 0 \le \alpha \le 1$.. The negative slope of the indifference curve incorporates the willingness of the consumer to make trade offs.

If two goods are perfect substitutes then the indifference curves will have a constant slope since the consumer would be willing to switch between at a fixed ratio. The marginal rate of substitution between perfect substitutes is likewise constant. An example of a utility function that is associated with indifference curves like these would be.

If two goods are perfect complements then the indifference curves will be L-shaped. Examples of perfect complements include left shoes compared to right shoes: the consumer is no better off having several right shoes if she has only one left shoe - additional right shoes have zero marginal utility without more left shoes, so bundles of goods differing only in the number of right shoes they includes - however many - are equally preferred. The marginal rate of substitution is either zero or infinite. An example of the type of utility function that has an indifference map like that above is the Leontief function: $U(x,y)=\min\{\alpha x, \beta y\}$.

The different shapes of the curves imply different responses to a change in price as shown from demand analysis in consumer theory. The results will only be stated here. A price-budget-line change that kept a consumer in equilibrium on the same indifference curve:

In Figure presented would reduce quantity demanded of a good smoothly as price rose relatively for that good. In Figure presented would have either no effect on quantity demanded of either good (at one end of the budget constraint) or would change quantity demanded from one end of the budget constraint to the other. In Figure depicted would have no effect on equilibrium quantities demanded, since the budget line would rotate around the corner of the indifference curve.

Preference Relations and Utility

Choice theory formally represents consumers by a preference relation, and use this representation to derive indifference curves showing combinations of equal preference to the consumer.

Preference relations:

Let

A be a set of mutually exclusive alternatives among which a consumer can choose.

a and b be generic elements of A.

In the language of the example above, the set A is made of combinations of apples and bananas. The symbol a is one such combination, such as 1 apple and 4 bananas and b is another combination such as 2 apples and 2 bananas.

A preference relation, denoted $\succeq$, is a binary relation define on the set A.

The statement

$$a \succeq b$$

is described as 'a is weakly preferred to b.' That is, is at least as good as b(in preference satisfaction).

The statement

$$a \sim b$$

is described as 'a is weakly preferred to b, and b is weakly preferred to a.' That is, one is *indifferent* to the choice of a or b, meaning not that they are unwanted but that they are equally good in satisfying preferences.

The statement

$$a \succ b$$

is described as 'a is weakly preferred to b, but b is not weakly preferred to a.' One says that 'a is strictly preferred to b.'

The preference relation $\succeq$ is complete if all pairs a,b can be ranked. The relation is a transitive relation if whenever $a \succeq b$ and $b \succeq c$, then $a \succeq c$.

For any element $a \in A$, the corresponding indifference curve, $\mathcal{C}_a$ is made up of all elements of A which are indifferent to a. Formally,

$\mathcal{C}_a = \{b \in A : b \sim a\}$.

Formal Link to Utility Theory

In the example above, an element a of the set A is made of two numbers: The number of apples, call it x, and the number of bananas, call it y

In utility theory, the utility function of an agent is a function that ranks *all* pairs of consumption bundles by order of preference (*completeness*) such that any set of three or more bundles forms a transitive relation. This means that for each bundle (x, y) there is a unique relation, $U(x, y)$, representing the utility (satisfaction) relation associated with (x, y).

The relation $(x, y) \to U(x, y)$ is called the utility function. The range of the function is a set of real numbers. The actual values of the function have no importance. Only the ranking of those values has content for the theory. More precisely, if $U(x, y) \geq U(x', y')$, then the bundle (x, y) is described as at least as good as the bundle (x', y'). If $U(x, y) > U(x', y')$, the bundle (x, y) is described as strictly preferred to the bundle (x', y').

Consider a particular bundle (x_0, y_0) and take the total derivative of $U(x, y)$ about this point:

$dU(x_0, y_0) = U_1(x_0, y_0)dx + U_2(x_0, y_0)dy$ or, without loss of generality,

$$\frac{dU(x_0, y_0)}{dx} = U_1(x_0, y_0).1 + U_2(x_0, y_0)\frac{dy}{dx} \text{ (Eq. 1)}$$

where $U_1(x, y)$ is the partial derivative of $U(x, y)$ with respect to its first argument, evaluated at (x, y). (Likewise for $U_2(x, y)$.)

The indifference curve through (x_0, y_0) must deliver at each bundle on the curve the same utility level as bundle (x_0, y_0). That is, when preferences are represented by a utility function, the indifference curves are the level curves of the utility function. Therefore, if one is to change the quantity of x by dx, without moving off the indifference curve, one must also change the quantity of y by an amount dy such that, in the end, there is no change in U:

$\frac{dU(x_0,y_0)}{dx}=0$, or, substituting *0* into *(Eq. 1)* above to solve for dy/dx:

$$\frac{dU(x_0,y_0)}{dx}=0 \Leftrightarrow \frac{dy}{dx}=-\frac{U_1(x_0,y_0)}{U_2(x_0,y_0)}.$$

Thus, the ratio of marginal utilities gives the absolute value of the slope of the indifference curve at point (x_0,y_0). This ratio is called the marginal rate of substitution between x and y.

Examples

Linear Utility: If the utility function is of the form $U(x,y)=\alpha x+\beta y$ then the marginal utility of x is $U_1(x,y)=\alpha$ and the marginal utility of y is $U_2(x,y)=\beta$ The slope of the indifference curve is, therefore,

$$\frac{dx}{dy}=-\frac{\beta}{\alpha}.$$

Observe that the slope does not depend on x or y: the indifference curves are straight lines.

Cobb-Douglas Utility

If the utility function is of the form $U(x,y)=x^{\alpha}y^{1-\alpha}$ the marginal utility of x is $U_1(x,y)=\alpha(x/y)^{\alpha-1}$ and the marginal utility of y is $U_2(x,y)=(1-\alpha)(x/y)^{\alpha}$ .Where $\alpha<1$. The slope of the indifference curve, and therefore the negative of the marginal rate of substitution, is then

$$\frac{dx}{dy}=-\frac{1-\alpha}{\alpha}\left(\frac{x}{y}\right).$$

CES Utility

A general CES (Constant Elasticity of Substitution) form is

$$U(x,y)=\left(\alpha x^{\rho}+(1-\alpha)y^{\rho}\right)^{1/\rho}$$

where $\alpha\in(0,1)$ and $\rho\leq 1$. (The Cobb-Douglas is a special case of the CES utility, with $\rho=0$.) The marginal utilities are given by

$$U_1(x,y)=\alpha\left(\alpha x^{\rho}+(1-\alpha)y^{\rho}\right)^{(1/\rho)-1}x^{\rho-1}$$

and

$$U_2(x,y)=(1-\alpha)\left(\alpha x^{\rho}+(1-\alpha)y^{\rho}\right)^{(1/\rho)-1}y^{\rho-1}.$$

Therefore, along an indifference curve,

$$\frac{dx}{dy} = -\frac{1-\alpha}{\alpha}\left(\frac{x}{y}\right)^{\rho-1}.$$

These examples might be useful for modelling individual or aggregate demand.

Uncertainty

The economics of uncertainty is a field of economics (primarily microeconomics) that investigates how uncertainty and risk affect the allocation of scarce resources, especially in financial markets and in the provision of insurance. Central to this study is the difference between uncertainty (not knowing which of several possible outcomes might occur) and risk (assigning probabilities to different possible outcomes).

People have different preferences about risk. Some prefer to avoid risk (risk aversion), others are indifferent (risk neutrality), while others enjoy risk (risk loving). Risk aversion in particular is a driving force behind the provision of insurance. Those who dislike risk are willing to pay to avoid it.

Risk and uncertainty are important to financial markets, as well. The exchange of financial instruments, such as stocks and bonds, are based on uncertainty of the future, tempered with attempts to quantify the risk of different possibilities.

Uncertainty and Risk

A cornerstone of the economic analysis of uncertainty is the difference between uncertainty and risk. While closely related concepts that are occasionally (and erroneously) used interchangeably, uncertainty and risk have important differences.

- Uncertainty: Uncertainty is the observation that the future is not known. You don't know what might happen tomorrow. You might step in a puddle of mud on the way to class. Or you might anger an intelligent extraterrestrial life form that retaliates by destroying all life on the planet. You just never know.
- Risk: Risk is assigning quantitative probabilities to alternative future outcomes. While it is possible that you could either step in a mud puddle or your could cause total destruction of the planet, both are not equally likely outcomes. Risk is the process of assigning probabilities to these alternatives (for example,

99.999999999% chance of mud puddle stepping versus 0.000000001% chance of total planet destruction).

While anything is possible (which is the essence of uncertainty) everything is not equally probably (which is the essence of risk). Many who participate in the financial markets and in the insurance industry spend a great deal of time and effort trying to transform uncertainty into risk. This can be accomplished with simple historical extrapolation. If, for example, every winter 5 people out of 100 contract the flu, then the projected risk of this outcome is 5%. In actuality, more sophisticated analysis is frequently used. That is, the risk of flu contraction might be evaluated based on lifestyle, weather conditions, medical treatment, and other factors.

Risk Preferences

Different people have different views, perspectives, and preferences about risk. Some people enjoy a risky situation and others do not. This gives rise to three alternative risk preferences — risk aversion, risk neutrality, and risk loving. As the names suggest, some people prefer to avoid risk (risk aversion), others enjoy engaging in risk (risk loving), and still others are indifferent (risk neutrality).

These three alternatives can be more precisely defined based on the marginal utility of income. Marginal utility is the change in utility resulting from a given change in the consumption of a good. Marginal utility of income is then the change in utility resulting from a given change in income. The standard presumption is that marginal utility declines as more of a good is consumed, that is, decreasing marginal utility. As a general rule the marginal utility of income also declines with an increase in income. However, it can also increase or remain constant. Suppose, for example, that you have $100 of income and are confronted with a $50 wager on the flip of a coin.

If the coin comes up heads, then you win $50 and thus have a total of $150. If the coin comes up tails, then you lose $50 and thus have a total of only $50. Risk preferences determine your willingness to decline the wager and keep the $100 of income that you have (certain income) or agree to the wager not knowing whether you will win or lose (risky income).

It is important to note that the income expected from the wager (so called expected income) is actually equal to certain income ($100). That is, because the coin has an equal chance of coming up heads or tails, if you undertake this wager 100 times, you can expect to win 50 times and lose 50 times. The loses exactly equal the wins and the income you can expect to end up with is $100.

These three alternatives give rise to risk aversion, risk loving, and risk neutrality.

- Risk Aversion: This exists when a person has decreasing marginal utility of income. In this case you prefer the certain income to the risky income. With decreasing marginal utility of income you obtain less utility from the income won than the income lost. Even though the expected income is equal to the certain income, the utility obtained from the certain income exceeds the utility obtained from the expected income. The utility from winning is exceeded by the utility from losing. You are better off not wagering.
- Risk Loving: This exists when a person has increasing marginal utility of income. With increasing marginal utility of income you obtain more utility from the income won than the income lost. Even though the expected income is equal to the certain income, the utility obtained from the expected income exceeds the utility obtained from the certain income. The utility from losing is exceeded by the utility from winning. You are better off wagering.
- Risk Neutrality: This exists when a person has constant marginal utility of income. With constant marginal utility of income you obtain the same utility from the income won as the income lost. Not only is the expected income is equal to the certain income, the utility obtained from the expected income is equal to the utility obtained from the certain income. The utility from losing is matches by the utility from winning. You are equally well off wagering or not wagering.

Most people tend to be risk averse, preferring certain income to an equal amount of risky income. Not only do they prefer certainty over risk, they are willing to pay. This is the essence of insurance. People pay a relatively small insurance premium to avoid the prospect of incurring a much bigger loss. They are thus guaranteed a certain income, net of the insurance premium, and eliminate the risk, albeit a small risk, of a loss of income.

Insurance

Uncertainty of the future and the quantification of this uncertainty as risk is fundamental to the provision of insurance. Insurance is a service that transfers the risk of large losses from an individual to a larger group. The larger group is typically represented by an insurance provider. This transfer of risk is undertaken in exchange for a premium payment. That is, the individual agrees to incur a small guaranteed loss (the premium) but avoids incurring a less likely but much larger loss. For example, a person pays an automobile insurance premium each month (guaranteed), but shifts the (slight) risk of a major expense associated with an accident to the insurance provider.

The insurance provider spreads this slight risk of a large expense for one person over a large group, the vast majority who pay the premium but do not incur the expense. Suppose, for example, that insurance is provided to 100 people and one member of this group is involved in an accident that incurs a cost of $20,000. The insurance provider spreads this $20,000 expense over the 100 people by charging each a premium of $200.

The key is that the insurance provider knows that 1 of the 100 customers will incur the $20,000 expense, it just doesn't know which specific person it will be.

Financial Markets

Risk and uncertainty are also key to financial markets. Financial markets exchange financial instruments or legal claims, such as stocks, bonds, and futures contracts. The most common financial market is the stock market that exchanges corporate stock, which are legal claims representing ownership of corporations.

Those who buy and sell legal claims do so with recognition that the future is uncertain. However, they also attempt to transform this uncertainty into quantifiable risk. For example, you might be willing to buy a few shares of OmniConglomerate, Inc. based on expectations that the company will be more profitable in the near future.

While the future profitability of OmniConglomerate, Inc. is uncertainty, you might be able to assign probabilities to alternative outcomes. Perhaps you know that over the past 20 years, the company has had positive profit three-fourths of the time and a loss only one-fourth of the time. The odds are three to one of a positive profit in the coming year. You might then adjust this probability with other information. Perhaps because you heard that the company is on the verge of obtaining a lucrative government contract. Or perhaps you read that the economy will be prospering and with it the demand for company production will increase.

The accuracy of the information plays a big part in who "wins" and "loses" in the financial markets. If your information is better and the price does increase, then you win. If the seller has better information and the price decreases, then you lose.

The Economics of Information

The economics of information studies the importance of information to the allocation of scarce resources. The standard assumption at the basis of most economic theories is one of perfect information, that buyers and sellers, producers and consumers, have perfect (or at least complete) information.

The economics of information, however, indicates that perfect information is just not possible. While information is beneficial to have, it is also costly to acquire. Like the production of any good, the efficient acquisition of information is a matter of balancing benefits against costs. The primary indication is that perfect, complete, or total information is not economically efficient. That is, most people rationally choose to be ignorant (about some things).

In addition to risk and uncertainty, the economic study of information and the efficient search for information provides useful analysis for a number of important issues, including asymmetric information, adverse selection, moral hazard, and information search.

3

Fundamentals of Supply

Supply and Demand

In microeconomics, supply and demand is an economic model of price determination in a market. It concludes that in a competitive market, the unit price for a particular good will vary until it settles at a point where the quantity demanded by consumers (at current price) will equal the quantity supplied by producers (at current price), resulting in an economic equilibrium for price and quantity.

The four basic laws of supply and demand are:

1. If demand increases and supply remains unchanged, a shortage occurs, leading to a higher equilibrium price.
2. If demand decreases and supply remains unchanged, a surplus occurs, leading to a lower equilibrium price.
3. If demand remains unchanged and supply increases, a surplus occurs, leading to a lower equilibrium price.
4. If demand remains unchanged and supply decreases, a shortage occurs, leading to a higher equilibrium price.

Graphical Representation of Supply and Demand

Although it is normal to regard the quantity demanded and the quantity supplied as functions of the price of the good, the standard graphical representation, usually attributed to Alfred Marshall, has price on the vertical axis and quantity on the horizontal axis, the opposite of the standard convention for the representation of a mathematical function.

Since determinants of supply and demand other than the price of the good in question are not explicitly represented in the supply-demand diagram, changes in the values of these variables are represented by moving the supply and demand curves (often described as "shifts" in the curves). By contrast, responses to changes in the price of the good are represented as movements along unchanged supply and demand curves.

Supply Schedule

A supply schedule is a table that shows the relationship between the price of a good and the quantity supplied.

Under the assumption of perfect competition, supply is determined by marginal cost. Firms will produce additional output while the cost of producing an extra unit of output is less than the price they would receive. By its very nature, conceptualizing a supply curve requires the firm to be a perfect competitor, namely requires the firm to have no influence over the market price. This is true because each point on the supply curve is the answer to the question "If this firm is *faced with* this potential price, how much output will it be able to and willing to sell?" If a firm has market power, its decision of how much output to provide to the market influences the market price, then the firm is not "faced with" any price, and the question is meaningless.

Economists distinguish between the supply curve of an individual firm and between the market supply curve. The market supply curve is obtained by summing the quantities supplied by all suppliers at each potential price. Thus, in the graph of the supply curve, individual firms' supply curves are added horizontally to obtain the market supply curve.

Economists also distinguish the short-run market supply curve from the long-run market supply curve. In this context, two things are assumed constant by definition of the short run: the availability of one or more fixed inputs (typically physical capital), and the number of firms in the industry. In the long run, firms have a chance to adjust their holdings of physical capital, enabling them to better adjust their quantity supplied at any given price. Furthermore, in the long run potential competitors can enter or exit the industry in response to market conditions. For both of these reasons, long-run market supply curves are flatter than their short-run counterparts.

The determinants of supply are:

1. Production costs: how much a good costs to be produced. Production costs are the cost of the inputs, primarily labour, capital, energy and materials. Production costs depend on the technology used in production, and/or technological advances.

2. Firms' expectations about future prices
3. Number of suppliers

Demand Schedule

A demand schedule, depicted graphically as the demand curve, represents the amount of some good that buyers are willing and able to purchase at various prices, assuming all determinants of demand other than the price of the good in question, such as income, tastes and preferences, the price of substitute goods, and the price of complementary goods, remain the same.

Following the law of demand, the demand curve is almost always represented as downward-sloping, meaning that as price decreases, consumers will buy more of the good.

Just like the supply curves reflect marginal cost curves, demand curves are determined by marginal utility curves. Consumers will be willing to buy a given quantity of a good, at a given price, if the marginal utility of additional consumption is equal to the opportunity cost determined by the price, that is, the marginal utility of alternative consumption choices. The demand schedule is defined as the *willingness* and *ability* of a consumer to purchase a given product in a given frame of time.

It is aforementioned, that the demand curve is generally downward-sloping, there may be rare examples of goods that have upward-sloping demand curves. Two different hypothetical types of goods with upward-sloping demand curves are Giffen goods (an inferior but staple good) and Veblen goods (goods made more fashionable by a higher price).

By its very nature, conceptualizing a demand curve requires that the purchaser be a perfect competitor—that is, that the purchaser has no influence over the market price. This is true because each point on the demand curve is the answer to the question "If this buyer is *faced with* this potential price, how much of the product will it purchase?" If a buyer has market power, so its decision of how much to buy influences the market price, then the buyer is not "faced with" any price, and the question is meaningless.

Like with supply curves, economists distinguish between the demand curve of an individual and the market demand curve. The market demand curve is obtained by summing the quantities demanded by all consumers at each potential price. Thus, in the graph of the demand curve, individuals' demand curves are added horizontally to obtain the market demand curve.

The determinants of demand are:

1. Income
2. Tastes and preferences
3. Prices of related goods and services
4. Consumers' expectations about future prices and incomes that can be checked
5. Number of potential consumers

Microeconomics

Figure 5 – "Supply and Demand" Curves

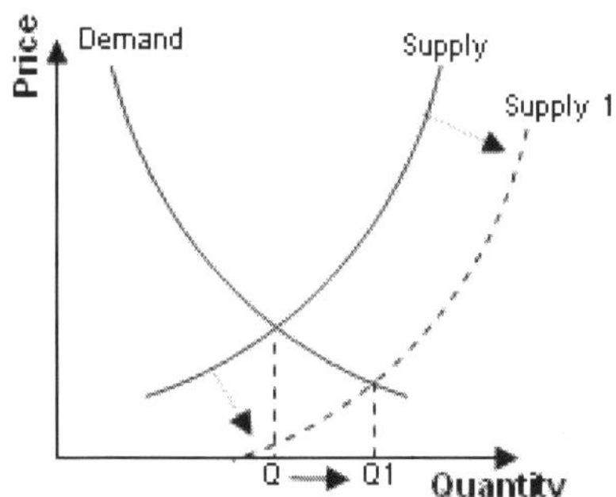

Equilibrium

Equilibrium is defined to be the price-quantity pair where the quantity demanded is equal to the quantity supplied, represented by the intersection of the demand and supply curves.

Market Equilibrium: A situation in a market when the price is such that the quantity that consumers demand is correctly balanced by the quantity that firms wish to supply.

Comparative Static Analysis: Examines the likely effect on the equilibrium of a change in the external conditions affecting the market.

Changes in Market Equilibrium: Practical uses of supply and demand analysis often centre on the different variables that change equilibrium price and quantity, represented as shifts in the respective curves. Comparative statics of such a shift traces the effects from the initial equilibrium to the new equilibrium.

Demand Curve Shifts: When consumers increase the quantity demanded *at a given price*, it is referred to as an *increase in demand.* Increased demand can be represented on the graph as the curve being shifted to the right. At each price point, a greater quantity is demanded, as from the initial curve D1 to the new curve D2. In the diagram, this raises the equilibrium price from P1 to the higher P2. This raises the equilibrium quantity from Q1 to the higher Q2. A movement along the curve is described as a "change in the quantity demanded" to distinguish it from a "change in demand," that is, a shift of the curve. There has been an *increase* in demand which has caused an increase in (equilibrium) quantity. The increase in demand could also come from changing tastes and fashions, incomes, price changes in complementary and substitute goods, market expectations, and number of buyers. This would cause the entire demand curve to shift changing the equilibrium price and quantity. Note in the diagram that the shift of the demand curve, by causing a new equilibrium price to emerge, resulted in *movement along* the supply curve from the point (Q_1, P_1) to the point (Q_2, P_2).

If the Demand Decreases, then the Opposite Happens: a shift of the curve to the left. If the demand starts at D2, and *decreases* to D1, the equilibrium price will decrease, and the equilibrium quantity will also decrease. The quantity supplied at each price is the same as before the demand shift, reflecting the fact that the supply curve has not shifted; but the equilibrium quantity and price are different as a result of the change (shift) in demand.

Supply Curve Shifts: When technological progress occurs, the supply curve shifts. For example, assume that someone invents a better way of growing wheat so that the cost of growing a given quantity of wheat decreases. Otherwise stated, producers will be willing to supply more wheat at every price and this shifts the supply curve S1 outward, to S2—an *increase in supply*. This increase in supply causes the equilibrium price to decrease from P1 to P2. The equilibrium quantity increases from Q1 to Q2 as consumers move along the demand curve to the new lower price. As a result of a supply curve shift, the price and the quantity move in opposite directions. If the quantity supplied *decreases*, the opposite happens. If the supply curve starts at S2, and shifts leftward to S1, the equilibrium price will increase and the equilibrium quantity will decrease as consumers move along the demand curve to the new higher price and associated lower quantity demanded. The quantity demanded at each price is the same as before the supply shift, reflecting the fact that the demand curve has not shifted. But due to the change (shift) in supply, the equilibrium quantity and price have changed.

The movement of the supply curve in response to a change in a non-price determinant of supply is caused by a change in the y-intercept, the constant term of the supply equation. The supply curve shifts up and down the y axis as non-price determinants of demand change.

Partial Equilibrium

Partial equilibrium as the name suggests takes into consideration only a part of the market, ceteris paribus to attain equilibrium.

Jain Proposes (Attributed to George Stigler): "A partial equilibrium is one which is based on only a restricted range of data, a standard example is price of a single product, the prices of all other products being held fixed during the analysis."

The supply-and-demand model is a partial equilibrium model of economic equilibrium, where the clearance on the market of some specific goods is obtained independently from prices and quantities in other markets. In other words, the prices of all substitutes and complements, as well as income levels of consumers are constant. This makes analysis much simpler than in a general equilibrium model which includes an entire economy.

Here the dynamic process is that prices adjust until supply equals demand. It is a powerfully simple technique that allows one to study equilibrium, efficiency and comparative statics. The stringency of the simplifying assumptions inherent in this approach make the model considerably more tractable, but may produce results which, while seemingly precise, do not effectively model real world economic phenomena. Partial equilibrium analysis examines the effects of policy action in creating equilibrium only in that particular sector or market which is directly affected, ignoring its effect in any other market or industry assuming that they being small will have little impact if any.

Hence this analysis is considered to be useful in constricted markets. Léon Walras first formalized the idea of a one-period economic equilibrium of the general economic system, but it was French economist Antoine Augustin Cournot and English political economist Alfred Marshall who developed tractable models to analyze an economic system.

Other Markets

The model of supply and demand also applies to various speciality markets. The model is commonly applied to wages, in the market for labour. The typical roles of supplier and demander are reversed. The suppliers are individuals, who try to sell their labour for the highest price. The demanders of labour are businesses, which try to buy the type of labour they need at the lowest price. The equilibrium price for a certain type of labour is the wage rate. A number of economists (for example Pierangelo Garegnani, Robert L. Vienneau, and Arrigo Opocher & Ian Steedman), building on the work of Piero Sraffa, argue that this model of the labour market, even given all its assumptions, is logically incoherent. Michael Anyadike-Danes and Wyne Godley argue, based on simulation results, that little of the empirical work done with the textbook model constitutes a potentially falsifying test, and, consequently, empirical evidence hardly exists for that model.

This criticism of the application of the model of supply and demand generalizes, particularly to all markets for factors of production.

In both classical and Keynesian economics, the money market is analyzed as a supply-and-demand system with interest rates being the price. The money supply may be a vertical supply curve, if the central bank of a country chooses to use monetary policy to fix its value regardless of the interest rate; in this case the money supply is totally inelastic. On the other hand, the money supply curve is a horizontal line if the central bank is targeting a fixed interest rate and ignoring the value of the money supply; in this case the money supply curve is perfectly elastic. The demand for money intersects with the money supply to determine the interest rate.

Empirical Estimation

Demand and supply relations in a market can be statistically estimated from price, quantity, and other data with sufficient information in the model. This can be done with *simultaneous-equation methods of estimation* in econometrics. Such methods allow solving for the model-relevant "structural coefficients," the estimated algebraic counterparts of the theory. The *Parameter identification problem* is a common issue in "structural estimation." Typically, data on exogenous variables (that is, variables other than price and quantity, both of which are endogenous variables) are needed to perform such an estimation. An alternative to "structural estimation" is reduced-form estimation, which regresses each of the endogenous variables on the respective exogenous variables.

Macroeconomic Uses of Demand and Supply

Demand and supply have also been generalized to explain macroeconomic variables in a market economy, including the quantity of total output and the general price level. The Aggregate Demand-Aggregate Supply model may be the most direct application of supply and demand to macroeconomics, but other macroeconomic models also use supply and demand. Compared to microeconomic uses of demand and supply, different (and more controversial) theoretical considerations apply to such macroeconomic counterparts as aggregate demand and aggregate supply. Demand and supply are also used in macroeconomic theory to relate money supply and money demand to interest rates, and to relate labour supply and labour demand to wage rates.

History

According to Hamid S. Hosseini, the power of supply and demand was understood to some extent by several early Muslim scholars, such as fourteenth-century Mamluk scholar Ibn Taymiyyah, who wrote: "If desire for goods increases while its availability decreases, its price rises. On the other hand, if availability of the good increases and the desire for it decreases, the price comes down."

If desire for goods increases while its availability decreases, its price rises. On the other hand, if availability of the good increases and the desire for it decreases, the price comes down.

—Ibn Taymiyyah,

John Locke's 1691 work *Some Considerations on the Consequences of the Lowering of Interest and the Raising of the Value of Money.* includes an early and clear description of supply and demand and their relationship. In this description demand is rent: "The price of any commodity rises or falls by the proportion of the number of buyer and sellers" and "that which regulates the price... [of goods] is nothing else but their quantity in proportion to their rent."

The phrase "supply and demand" was first used by James Denham-Steuart in his *Inquiry into the Principles of Political Oeconomy*, published in 1767. Adam Smith used the phrase in his 1776 book *The Wealth of Nations*, and David Ricardo titled one chapter of his 1817 work *Principles of Political Economy and Taxation* "On the Influence of Demand and Supply on Price".

In *The Wealth of Nations*, Smith generally assumed that the supply price was fixed but that its "merit" (value) would decrease as its "scarcity" increased, in effect what was later called the law of demand also. Ricardo, in *Principles of Political Economy and Taxation*, more rigorously laid down the idea of the assumptions that were used to build his ideas of supply and demand. Antoine Augustin Cournot first developed a mathematical model of supply and demand in his 1838 *Researches into the Mathematical Principles of Wealth*, including diagrams.

During the late 19th century the marginalist school of thought emerged. This field mainly was started by Stanley Jevons, Carl Menger, and Léon Walras. The key idea was that the price was set by the most expensive price, that is, the price at the margin. This was a substantial change from Adam Smith's thoughts on determining the supply price.

In his 1870 essay "On the Graphical Representation of Supply and Demand", Fleeming Jenkin in the course of "introduc[ing] the diagrammatic method into the English economic literature" published the first drawing of supply and demand curves therein, including comparative statics from a shift of supply or demand and application to the labour market. The model was further developed and popularized by Alfred Marshall in the 1890 textbook *Principles of Economics.*

Criticisms

At least two assumptions are necessary for the validity of the standard model: first, that supply and demand are independent; second, that supply is "constrained by a fixed resource". If these conditions do not hold, then the Marshallian model cannot be sustained. Sraffa's critique focused on the inconsistency (except in implausible circumstances) of partial equilibrium analysis and the rationale for the upward slope of the supply curve in a market for a produced consumption good. The notability of Sraffa's critique is also demonstrated by Paul A. Samuelson's comments and engagements with it over many years, for example:

"What a cleaned-up version of Sraffa (1926) establishes is how *nearly empty* are *all* of Marshall's partial equilibrium boxes. To a logical purist of Wittgenstein and Sraffa class, the *Marshallian partial* equilibrium box of *constant* cost is even more empty than the box of *increasing* cost.". Aggregate excess demand in a market is the difference between the quantity demanded and the quantity supplied as a function of price. In the model with an upward-sloping supply curve and downward-sloping demand curve, the aggregate excess demand function only intersects the axis at one point, namely, at the point where the supply and demand curves intersect. The Sonnenschein–Mantel–Debreu theorem shows that the standard model cannot be rigorously derived in general from general equilibrium theory.

The model of prices being determined by supply and demand assumes perfect competition. But: "economists have no adequate model of how individuals and firms adjust prices in a competitive model. If all participants are price-takers by definition, then the actor who adjusts prices to eliminate excess demand is not specified".

Goodwin, Nelson, Ackerman, and Weisskopf write: "If we mistakenly confuse precision with accuracy, then we might be misled into thinking that an explanation expressed in precise mathematical or graphical terms is somehow more rigorous or useful than one that takes into account particulars of history, institutions or business strategy. This is not the case. Therefore, it is important not to put too much confidence in the apparent precision of supply and demand graphs. Supply and demand analysis is a useful precisely formulated conceptual tool that clever people have devised to help us gain an abstract understanding of a complex world. It does not—nor should it be expected to—give us in addition an accurate and complete description of any particular real world market."

Supply (Economics)

In economics, supply refers to the amount of a product that producers and firms are willing to sell at a given price all other factors being held constant. Usually, supply is plotted as a supply curve showing the relationship of price to the amount of product businesses are willing to sell.

Supply Schedule

A supply schedule is a table which shows how much one or more firms will be willing to supply at particular prices under the existing circumstances. Some of the more important factors affecting supply are the good's own price, the prices of related goods, production costs, technology and expectations of sellers.

Factors Affecting Supply

Innumerable factors and circumstances could affect a seller's willingness or ability to produce and sell a good. Some of the more common factors are:

Good's Own Price: The basic supply relationship is between the price of a good and the quantity supplied. Although there is no "Law of Supply", generally, the relationship is positive, meaning that an increase in price will induce an increase in the quantity supplied.

Prices of Related Goods: For purposes of supply analysis related goods refer to goods from which inputs are derived to be used in the production of the primary good. For example, Spam is made from pork shoulders and ham. Both are derived from pigs. Therefore pigs would be considered a related good to Spam. In this case the relationship would be negative or inverse. If the price of pigs goes up the supply of Spam would decrease (supply curve shifts left) because the cost of production would have increased. A related good may also be a good that can be produced with the firm's existing factors of production. For example, suppose that a firm produces leather belts, and that the firm's managers learn that leather pouches for smartphones are more profitable than belts.

The firm might reduce its production of belts and begin production of cell phone pouches based on this information. Finally, a change in the price of a joint product will affect supply. For example beef products and anani sikim leather are joint products. If a company runs both a beef processing operation and a tannery an increase in the price of steaks would mean that more cattle are processed which would increase the supply of leather.

Conditions of Production: The most significant factor here is the state of technology. If there is a technological advancement in one good's production, the supply increases. Other variables may also affect production conditions. For instance, for agricultural goods, weather is crucial for it may affect the production outputs.

Expectations: Sellers' are concerning future market conditions can directly affect supply. If the seller believes that the demand for his product will sharply increase in the foreseeable future the firm owner may immediately increase production in anticipation of future price increases. The supply curve would shift out.

Price of Inputs: Inputs include land, labour, energy and raw materials. If the price of inputs increases the supply curve will shift left as sellers are less willing or able to sell goods at any given price. For example, if the price of electricity increased a seller may reduce his supply of his product because of the increased costs of production.

Number of Suppliers: The market supply curve is the horizontal summation of the individual supply curves. As more firms enter the industry the market supply curve will shift out driving down prices.

Government Policies and Regulations: Government intervention can have a significant effect on supply. Government intervention can take many forms including environmental and health regulations, hour and wage laws, taxes, electrical and natural gas rates and zoning and land use regulations.

This list is not exhaustive. All facts and circumstances that are relevant to a seller's willingness or ability to produce and sell goods can affect supply. For example, if the forecast is for snow retail sellers will respond by increasing their stocks of snow sleds or skis or winter clothing or bread and milk.

Supply Function and Equation

The supply function is the mathematical expression of the relationship between supply and those factors that affect the willingness and ability of a supplier to offer goods for sale. An example would be the curve implied by $Q_s = f(P; P_{rg})$ where P is the price of the good and P_{rg} is the price of a related good. The semicolon means that the variables to the right are held constant when quantity supplied is plotted against the good's own price. The supply equation is the explicit mathematical expression of the functional relationship. A linear example is $Q_s = 325 + P - 30P_{rg}$. Here 325 is the repository of all non-specified factors that affect supply for the product. The coefficient of P is positive following the general rule that price and quantity supplied are directly related. P_{rg} is the price of a related good. Typically its coefficient is negative because the related good is an input or a source of inputs.

Supply Curve

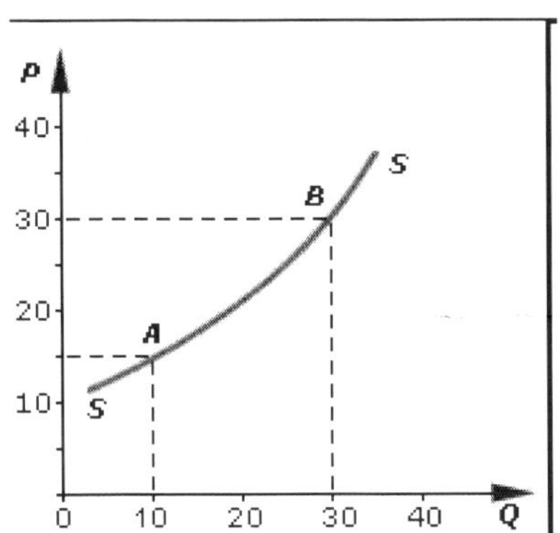

Figure: *An example of a nonlinear supply curve*

The relationship of price and supply curve. The curve is generally positively sloped. The curve depicts the relationship between two variables only; price and quantity supplied. All other factors affecting supply are held constant. However, these factors are part of the supply equation and are implicitly present in the constant term.

Movements versus Shifts

Movements along the curve occur only if there is a change in quantity supplied caused by a change in the good's own price. A shift in the supply curve, referred to as a change in supply, occurs only if a non-price determinant of supply changes. For example, if the price of an ingredient used to produce the good, a related good, were to increase, the supply curve would shift left.

Inverse Supply Equation

By convention in the context of supply and demand graphs, economists graph the dependent variable (quantity) on the horizontal axis and the independent variable (price) on the vertical axis. The *inverse supply equation* is the equation written with the vertical-axis variable isolated on the left side: $P = f(Q)$. As an example, if the supply equation is $Q = 40P - 2P_{rg}$ then the inverse supply equation would be $P = \frac{Q}{40} + \frac{P_{rg}}{20}$.

Marginal Costs and Short-Run Supply Curve

A firm's short-run supply curve is the marginal cost curve above the shutdown point—the short-run marginal cost curve (SRMC) above the minimum average variable cost). The portion of the SRMC below the shutdown point is not part of the supply curve because the firm is not producing any output. The firm's long-run supply curve is that portion of the long-run marginal cost curve above the minimum of the long run average cost curve.

Shape of the Short-Run Supply Curve

The Law of Diminishing Marginal Returns (LDMR) shapes the SRMC curve. The LDMR states that as production increases eventually a point (the point of diminishing marginal returns) will be reached after which additional units of output resulting from fixed increments of the labour input will be successively smaller. That is, beyond the point of diminishing marginal returns the marginal product of labour will continually decrease and hence a continually higher selling price would be necessary to induce the firm to produce more and more output.

From Firm to Market Supply Curve

The market supply curve is the horizontal summation of firm supply curves.

The Shape of the Market Supply Curve

There is no law of supply that "requires" that the market supply curve have a positive slope; the curve may slope down or up or be horizontal or vertical.

Elasticity

The price elasticity of supply (PES) measures the responsiveness of quantity supplied to changes in price, as the percentage change in quantity supplied induced by a one percent change in price. It is calculated for discrete changes as $\left(\frac{\Delta Q}{\Delta P}\right)\times\frac{P}{Q}$ and for smooth changes of differentiable supply functions as $\left(\frac{\partial Q}{\partial P}\right)\times\frac{P}{Q}$. Since supply is usually increasing in price, the price elasticity of supply is usually positive. For example if the PES for a good is 0.67 a 1% rise in price will induce a two-thirds increase in quantity supplied.

Significant Determinants include: Complexity of Production: Much depends on the complexity of the production process. Textile production is relatively simple. The labour is largely unskilled and production facilities are little more than buildings – no special structures are needed. Thus the PES for textiles is elastic. On the other hand, the PES for specific types of motor vehicles is relatively inelastic. Auto manufacture is a multi-stage process that requires specialised equipment, skilled labour, a large suppliers network and large R&D costs.

Time to Respond: The more time a producer has to respond to price changes the more elastic the supply. For example, a cotton farmer cannot immediately respond to an increase in the price of soybeans.

Excess Capacity: A producer who has unused capacity can quickly respond to price changes in his market assuming that variable factors are readily available.

Inventories: A producer who has a supply of goods or available storage capacity can quickly respond to price changes.

Other elasticities can be calculated for non-price determinants of supply. For example, the percentage change the amount of the good supplied caused by a one percent increase in the price of a related good is an input elasticity of supply if the related good is an input in the production process. An example would be the change in the supply of cookies caused by a one percent increase in the price of sugar.

Elasticity along Linear Supply Curves

The slope of a linear supply curve is constant; the elasticity is not. If the linear supply curve intersects the price axis PES will be infinitely elastic at the point of intersection. The coefficient of elasticity decreases as one moves “up” the curve. However, all points on the supply curve will have a coefficient of elasticity greater than one. If the linear supply curve intersects the quantity axis PES will equal zero at the point of intersection and will increase as one moves up the curve; however, all points on the curve will have a coefficient of elasticity less than 1. If the linear supply curve intersects the origin PES equals one at the point of origin and along the curve.

Market Structure and the Supply Curve

There is no such thing as a monopoly supply curve. Perfect competition is the only market structure for which a supply function can be derived. In a perfectly competitive market the price is given by the marketplace from the point of view of the supplier; a manager of a competitive firm can state what quantity of goods will be supplied for any price by simply referring to the firm's marginal cost curve. To generate his supply function the seller could simply initially hypothetically set the price equal to zero and then incrementally increase the price; at each price he could calculate the hypothetical quantity supplied using the marginal cost curve. Following this process the manager could trace out the complete supply function. A monopolist cannot replicate this process, because price is not imposed by the marketplace and hence is not an independent variable from the point of view of the firm; instead, the firm simultaneously chooses both the price and the quantity subject to the stipulation that together they form a point on the customers' demand curve. A change in demand can result in "changes in price with no changes in output, changes in output with no changes in price or both". There is simply not a one to one relationship between price and quantity supplied. There is no single function that relates price to quantity supplied.iyot

Aggregate Supply

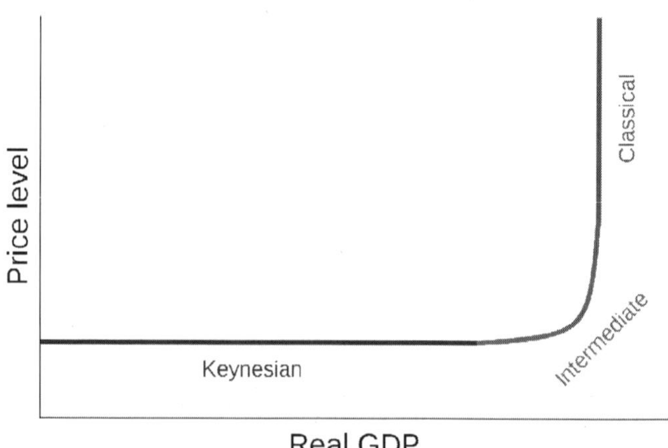

Figure: *Aggregate supply curve showing the three ranges: Keynesian, Intermediate, and Classical.*

In economics, aggregate supply is the total supply of goods and services that firms in a national economy plan on selling during a specific time period. It is the total amount of goods and services that firms are willing to sell at a given price level in an economy.

Analysis

There are two main reasons why Q^s might rise as P rises, i.e., why the AS curve is upward sloping:

- aggregate supply is usually inadequate to supply ample opportunity. Usually this is fixed capital equipment. The AS curve is drawn given some nominal variable, such as the nominal wage rate. In the *short run*, the nominal wage rate is taken as fixed. Thus, rising P implies higher profits that justify expansion of output. In the neoclassical *long run*, on the other hand, the nominal wage rate varies with economic conditions. (High unemployment leads to falling nominal wages — and vice-versa.)
- An alternative model starts with the notion that any economy involves a large number of heterogeneous types of inputs, including both fixed capital equipment and labour. Both main types of inputs can be unemployed. The upward-sloping AS curve arises because (1) some nominal input prices are fixed in the short run (as in the neoclassical theory) and (2) as output rises, more and more production processes encounter bottlenecks. At low levels of demand, there are large numbers of production processes that do not use their fixed capital equipment fully.

  Thus, production can be increased without much in the way of diminishing returns and the average price level need not rise much (if at all) to justify increased production. The AS curve is flat. On the other hand, when demand is high, few production processes have unemployed fixed inputs. Thus, bottlenecks are general. Any increase in demand and production induces increases in prices. Thus, the AS curve is steep or vertical.

AS is targeted by government "supply side policies" which are meant to increase productivity efficiency and national output. Some examples of supply side policies include:

Education and training, research and development, supporting small/medium entrepreneurs, decreasing household and business taxes, making labour market reforms, and investing on infrastructure.

Different Scopes

There are generally three forms of aggregate supply (AS). They are:

1. *Short run aggregate supply* — During the short-run, firms possess one fixed factor of production (usually capital). This does not however prevent outward shifts in the SRAS curve, which will result in increased output/real GDP at a given price. Therefore, a positive correlation between price level and output is shown by the SRAS curve.
2. *Long run aggregate supply* (LRAS) — Over the long run, only capital, labour, and technology affect the LRAS in the macroeconomic model because at this point everything in the economy is assumed to be used optimally. In most situations, the LRAS is viewed as static because it shifts the slowest of the three. The LRAS is shown as perfectly vertical, reflecting economists' belief that changes in aggregate demand (AD) have an only temporary change on the economy's total output.
3. *Medium run aggregate supply* (MRAS) — As an interim between SRAS and LRAS, the MRAS form slopes upward and reflects when capital as well as labour can change. More specifically, the Medium run aggregate supply is like this for three theoretical reasons, namely the Sticky-Wage Theory, the Sticky-Price Theory and the Misperception Theory. When graphing an aggregate supply and demand model, the MRAS is generally graphed after aggregate demand (AD), SRAS, and LRAS have been graphed, and then placed so that the equilibria occur at the same point. The MRAS curve is affected by capital, labour, technology, and wage rate.

In a standard aggregate supply demand model, the output (Y) is the x axis and price (P) is the y axis. An increase in aggregate demand shifts the AD curve rightward, bringing the equilibrium point horizontally along the SRAS until it reaches the new AD. This point is the short run equilibrium.

The AD–AS or aggregate demand–aggregate supply model is a macroeconomic model that explains price level and output through the relationship of aggregate demand and aggregate supply. It is based on the theory of John Maynard Keynes presented in his work *The General Theory of Employment, Interest, and Money*. It is one of the primary simplified representations in the modern field of macroeconomics, and is used by a broad array of economists, from libertarian, Monetarist supporters of laissez-faire, such as Milton

Friedman to Post-Keynesian supporters of economic interventionism, such as Joan Robinson. The conventional "aggregate supply and demand" model is, in actuality, a Keynesian visualization that has come to be a widely accepted image of the theory.

The Classical supply and demand model, which is largely based on Say's law, or that supply creates its own demand, depicts the aggregate supply curve as being vertical at all times (not just in the long-run)

Modelling

The AD/AS model is used to illustrate the Keynesian model of the business cycle. Movements of the two curves can be used to predict the effects that various exogenous events will have on two variables: real GDP and the price level. Furthermore, the model can be incorporated as a component in any of a variety of dynamic models (models of how variables like the price level and others evolve over time). The AD–AS model can be related to the Phillips curve model of wage or price inflation and unemployment.

4

Competition and Monopoly

Competition (Economics)

In economics, competition is the rivalry among sellers trying to achieve such goals as increasing profits, market share, and sales volume by varying the elements of the marketing mix: price, product, distribution, and promotion. Merriam-Webster defines competition in business as "the effort of two or more parties acting independently to secure the business of a third party by offering the most favourable terms." It was described by Adam Smith in *The Wealth of Nations* (1776) and later economists as allocating productive resources to their most highly-valued uses and encouraging efficiency. Smith and other classical economists before Cournot were referring to price and non-price rivalry among producers to sell their goods on best terms by bidding of buyers, not necessarily to a large number of sellers nor to a market in final equilibrium.

Later microeconomic theory distinguished between perfect competition and imperfect competition, concluding that no system of resource allocation is more Pareto efficient than perfect competition. Competition, according to the theory, causes commercial firms to develop new products, services and technologies, which would give consumers greater selection and better products. The greater selection typically causes lower prices for the products, compared to what the price would be if there was no competition (monopoly) or little competition (oligopoly).

It is generally accepted that competition results in lower prices and a greater number of goods delivered to more people. Less competition is perceived to exhibit higher prices with a fewer number of goods delivered to fewer people.

Competition in Practice

Competition is seen as a state which produces gains for the whole economy, through promoting consumer sovereignity. It may also lead to wasted (duplicated) effort and to increased costs (and prices) in some circumstances. In a small number of goods and services, the cost structure means that competition may be inefficient. These situations are known as natural monopoly and are usually publicly provided or tightly regulated. The most common example is water supplies.

Three levels of economic competition have been classified:

1. The most narrow form is direct competition (also called category competition or brand competition), where products that perform the same function compete against each other. For example, a brand of pick-up trucks competes with several different brands of pick-up trucks. Sometimes two companies are rivals and one adds new products to their line so that each company distributes the same thing and they compete.
2. The next form is substitute competition, where products that are close substitutes for one another compete. For example, butter competes with margarine, mayonnaise, and other various sauces and spreads.
3. The broadest form of competition is typically called budget competition. Included in this category is anything that the consumer might want to spend their available money (the so-called discretionary income) on. For example, a family that has $20,000 available may choose to spend it on many different items, which can all be seen as competing with each other for the family's available money.

Competition does not necessarily have to be between companies. For example, business writers sometimes refer to "internal competition". This is competition within companies. The idea was first introduced by Alfred Sloan at General Motors in the 1920s. Sloan deliberately created areas of overlap between divisions of the company so that each division would be competing with the other divisions. For example, the Chevy division would compete with the Pontiac division for some market segments. Also, in 1931, Procter & Gamble initiated a deliberate system of internal brand versus brand rivalry. The company was organised around different brands, with each brand allocated resources, including a dedicated group of employees willing to champion the brand. Each brand manager was given responsibility for the success or failure of the brand and was compensated accordingly. This form of competition thus pitted a brand against another brand. Finally, most businesses also encourage competition between individual employees. An example of this is a contest between sales representatives. The sales representative with the highest sales (or the best improvement in sales) over a period of time would gain benefits from the employer.

It should also be noted that business and economic competition in most countries is often limited or restricted. Competition often is subject to legal restrictions. For example, competition may be legally prohibited as in the case with a government monopoly or a government-granted monopoly. Tariffs or other protectionist measures may also be instituted by government in order to prevent or reduce competition. Depending on the respective economic policy, the pure competition is to a greater or lesser extent regulated by competition policy and competition law. Competition between countries is quite subtle to detect, but is quite evident in the World economy, where countries the US, Japan, the constituents of the European Union, China and the East Asian Tigers each try to outdo the other in the quest for economic supremacy in the global market, harkening to the concept of Kiasuism.Such competition is evident by the policies undertaken by these countries to educate the future workforce. For example, East Asian economies like Singapore, Japan and South Korea tend to emphasize education by allocating a large portion of the budget to this sector, and by implementing programmes such as gifted education, which some detractors criticise as indicative of academic elitism.

Within competitive markets, markets are often defined by their sub-sectors, such as the "short-term" or "long-term" market, the "seasonal" or "summer" market, or the "broad" or "remainder" market. For example, in otherwise competitive market economies, where a large majority of the commercial exchanges are competitively determined by long term contracts and therefore long term market clearing prices, a "remainder market" is one where prices are determined by the small part of the market that deals with the availability of whatever is not cleared via long term transactions. For example, in the sugar industry, about 94% to 95% of the market clearing price is determined by long term supply and purchase contracts. The balance of the market, and world sugar prices, are determined by the ad hoc demand for the 5% to 6% that is not sold via long term contracts; prices in the "remainder market" fluctuate more widely and are determined by short term supply and demand conditions; quoted prices can be significantly higher or lower than the long term market clearing price. Similarly, in the US real estate housing market, appraisal prices can be determined by both short term or long term characteristics depending on short term supply and demand factors; this can result in large price variations for a property at one location.

Bertrand Competition

Bertrand competition is a model of competition used in economics, named after Joseph Louis François Bertrand (1822–1900). It describes interactions among firms (sellers) that set prices and their customers (buyers) that choose quantities at the prices set. The model was formulated in 1883 by Bertrand in a review of Antoine Augustin Cournot's (1838) book in which Cournot had put forward the Cournot model. Cournot argued that when firms choose quantities, the equilibrium outcome involves firms pricing above marginal cost and hence the competitive price. In his review Bertrand argued that if firms chose prices rather than quantities, then the competitive outcome would occur with price equal to marginal cost. The model was not formalized by Bertrand: however, the idea was developed into a mathematical model by Francis Ysidro Edgeworth in 1889.

The model rests on very specific assumptions. There are at least two firms producing a homogeneous (undifferentiated) product and can not cooperate in any way. Firms compete by setting prices simultaneously and consumers want to buy everything from a firm with a lower price (since the product is homogeneous and there are no consumer search costs). If two firms charge the same price, consumers demand is split evenly between them. It is simplest to concentrate on the case of duopoly where there are just two firms, although the results hold for any number of firms greater than 1.

A crucial assumption about the technology is that both firms have the same constant unit cost of production, so that marginal and average costs are the same and equal to the competitive price. This means that as long as the price it sets is above unit cost, the firm is willing to supply any amount that is demanded (it earns profit on each unit sold). If price is equal to unit cost, then it is indifferent to how much it sells, since it earns no profit). Obviously, the firm will never want to set a price below unit cost, but if it did it would not want to sell anything since it would lose money on each unit sold.

The Bertrand Duopoly Equilibrium

Why is the competitive price a Nash equilibrium in the Bertrand model? First, if both firms set the competitive price with price equal to marginal cost (unit cost), neither firm will earn any profits. However, if one firm sets price equal to marginal cost, then if the other firm raises its price above unit cost, then it will earn nothing, since all consumers will buy from the firm still setting the competitive price (recall that it is willing to meet unlimited demand at price equals unit cost even though it earns no profit).

No other price is an equilibrium. If both firms set the same price above unit cost and share the market, then each firm has an incentive to undercut the other by an arbitrarily small amount and capture the whole market and almost double its profits. So there can be no equilibrium with both firms setting the same price above marginal cost. Also, there can be no equilibrium with firms setting different prices.

The firms setting the higher price will earn nothing (the lower priced firm serves all of the customers). Hence the higher priced firm will want to lower its price to undercut the lower-priced firm. Hence the *only* equilibrium in the Bertrand model occurs when both firms set price equal to unit cost (the competitive price).

Note that the Bertrand equilibrium is a *weak* Nash-equilibrium. The firms lose nothing by deviating from the competitive price: it is an equilibrium simply because each firm can earn no more than zero profits given that the other firm sets the competitive price and is willing to meet all demand at that price.

Calculating the Classic Bertrand Model

- MC = constant marginal cost (equals constant unit cost of production).
- p_1 = firm 1's price level
- p_2 = firm 2's price level
- p_M = monopoly price level

Firm 1's optimum price depends on where it believes firm 2 will set its prices. Pricing just below the other firm will obtain full market demand (D), though this is not optimal if the other firm is pricing below marginal cost as that would entail negative profits. In general terms, firm 1's best response function is $p_1''(p_2)$, this gives firm 1 optimal price for each price set by firm 2.

Diagram 1 shows firm 1's reaction function $p_1''(p_2)$, with each firm's strategy on each axis. It shows that when P_2 is less than marginal cost (firm 2 pricing below MC) firm 1 prices at marginal cost, p_1=MC. When firm 2 prices above MC but below monopoly prices, then firm 1 prices just below firm 2. When firm 2 prices above monopoly prices (P) firm 1 prices at monopoly level, $p_1=p^M$.

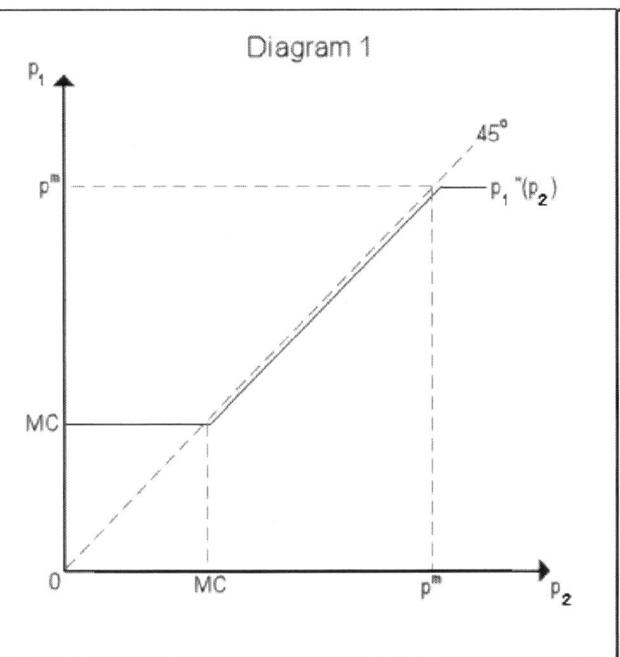

Because firm 2 has the same marginal cost as firm 1, its reaction function is symmetrical with respect to the 45 degree line. Diagram 2 shows both reaction functions.

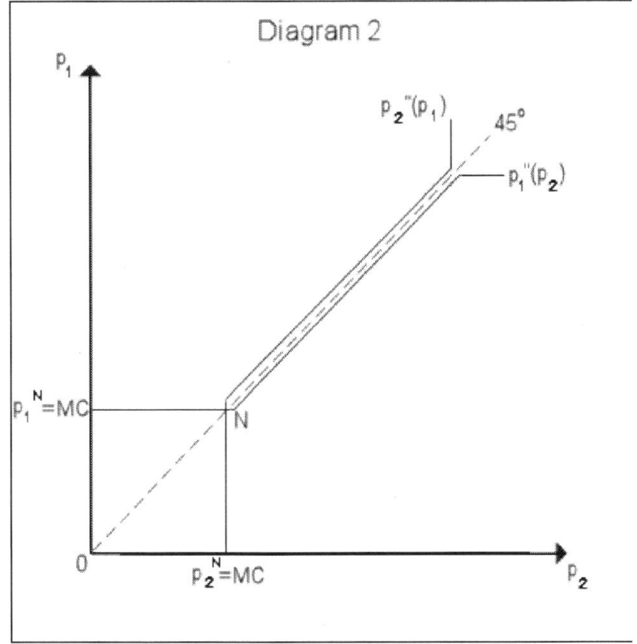

The result of the firms' strategies is a Nash equilibrium, that is, a pair of strategies (prices in this case) where neither firm can increase profits by unilaterally changing price. This is given by the intersection of the reaction curves, Point N on the diagram. At this point $p_1=p_1''(p_2)$, and $p_2=p_2''(p_1)$. As you can see, point N on the diagram is where both firms are pricing at marginal cost.

Another way of thinking about it, a simpler way, is to imagine if both firms set equal prices above marginal cost, firms would get half the market at a higher than MC price. However, by lowering prices just slightly, a firm could gain the whole market, so both firms are tempted to lower prices as much as they can. It would be irrational to price below marginal cost, because the firm would make a loss. Therefore, both firms will lower prices until they reach the MC limit.

If one firm has lower average cost (a superior production technology), it will charge the highest price that is lower than the average cost of the other one (i.e. a price *just* below the lowest price the other firm can manage) and take all the business. This is known as "limit pricing"

Critical Analysis of the Bertrand Model

The Bertrand model rests on some very extreme assumptions. For example, it assumes that consumers want to buy from the lowest priced firm. There are various reasons why this may not hold in many markets: non-price competition and product differentiation, transport and search costs. For example, would someone travel twice as far to save 1% on the price of their vegetables? The Bertrand model can be extended to include product or location differentiation but then the main result – that price is driven down to marginal cost – no longer holds. With search costs, there may be other equilibria apart from the competitive price – the monopoly price or even price dispersion may be equilibria as in the classic "Bargains and Rip-offs" model.

The model also ignores capacity constraints. If a single firm does not have the capacity to supply the whole market then the "price equals marginal cost" result may not hold. The analysis of this case was started by Francis Ysidro Edgeworth and has become known as the Bertrand–Edgeworth model. With capacity constraints, there may not exist any pure strategy Nash equilibrium, the so-called Edgeworth paradox. However, in general there will exist a mixed-strategy Nash equilibrium as shown by HuwDixon.

There is a big incentive to cooperate in the Bertrand model: colluding to charge the monopoly price and sharing the market each is the best that the firms could do in this set up. However not colluding and charging marginal cost, is the non-cooperative outcome and the only Nash equilibrium of this model. If we move from a one-shot game to a repeated game, then perhaps collusion can persist for some time or emerge.

Bertrand Competition versus Cournot Competition

Neither model is necessarily "better." The accuracy of the predictions of each model will vary from industry to industry, depending on the closeness of each model to the industry situation. If capacity and output can be easily changed, Bertrand is generally a better model of duopoly competition. Or, if output and capacity are difficult to adjust, then Cournot is generally a better model. Under some conditions the Cournot model can be recast as a two stage model, where in the first stage firms choose capacities, and in the second they compete in Bertrand fashion. Bertrand predicts a duopoly is enough to push prices down to marginal cost level; a duopoly will result in an outcome exactly equivalent to what prevails under perfect competition.

Bertrand–Edgeworth Model

In microeconomics, the Bertrand–Edgeworth model of price-setting oligopoly looks at what happens when there is a homogenous product (i.e. consumers want to buy from the cheapest seller) where there is a limit to the output of firms which they are willing and able to sell at a particular price. This differs from the Bertrand competition model where it is assumed that firms are willing and able to meet all demand. The limit to output can be considered as a physical capacity constraint which is the same at all prices (as in Edgeworth's work), or to vary with price under other assumptions.

History

Joseph Louis François Bertrand (1822–1900) developed the model of Bertrand competition in oligopoly. This approach was based on the assumption that there are at least two firms producing a homogenous product with constant marginal cost (this could be constant at some positive value, or with zero marginal cost as in Cournot). Consumers buy from the cheapest seller. The Bertrand–Nash equilibrium of this model is to have all (or at least two) firms setting the price equal to marginal cost. The argument is simple: if one firm sets a price above marginal cost then another firm can undercut it by a small amount (often called *epsilon undercutting*, where epsilon represents an arbitrarily small amount) so that the equilibrium is zero (this is sometimes called the Bertrand paradox).

The Bertrand approach assumes that firms are willing and able to supply all demand: there is no limit to the amount that they can produce or sell. Francis Ysidro Edgeworth considered the case where there is a limit to what firms can sell (a capacity constraint): he showed that if there is a fixed limit to what firms can sell, then there may exist no pure-strategy Nash equilibrium (this is sometimes called the Edgeworth paradox).

Martin Shubik developed the Bertrand–Edgeworth model to allow for the firm to be willing to supply only up to its profit maximizing output at the price which it set (under profit maximization this occurs when marginal cost equals price). He considered the case of strictly convex costs, where marginal cost is increasing in output. Shubik showed that if a Nash equilibrium exists, it must be the perfectly competitive price (where demand equals supply, and all firms set price equal to marginal cost). However, this can only happen if market demand is infinitely elastic (horizontal) at the competitive price. In general, as in the Edgeworth paradox, no pure-strategy Nash equilibrium will exist. HuwDixon showed that in general a mixed strategy Nash equilibrium will exist when there are convex costs. Dixon's proof used the Existence Theorem of Partha Dasgupta and Eric Maskin. Under Dixon's assumption of (weakly) convex costs, marginal cost will be non-decreasing. This is consistent with a cost function where marginal cost is flat for a range of outputs, marginal cost is smoothly increasing, or indeed where there is a kink in total cost so that marginal cost makes a discontinuous jump upwards.

Later Developments and Related Models

There have been several responses to the non-existence of pure-strategy equilibrium identified by Francis Ysidro Edgeworth and Martin Shubik. Whilst the existence of mixed-strategy equilibrium was demonstrated by Huw Dixon, it has not proven easy to characterize what the equilibrium actually looks like. However, Allen and Hellwig were able to show that in a large market with many firms, the average price set would tend to the competitive price.

It has been argued that non-pure strategies are not plausible in the context of the Bertrand–Edgworth model. Alternative approaches have included:

- Firms choose the quantity they are willing to sell up to at each price. This is a game in which price and quantity are chosen: as shown by Allen and Hellwig and in a more general case by Huw Dixon that the perfectly competitive price is the unique pure-strategy equilibrium.

- Firms have to meet all demand at the price they set as proposed by Krishnendu Ghosh Dastidar or pay some cost for turning away customers. Whilst this can ensure the existence of a pure-strategy Nash equilibrium, it comes at the cost of generating multiple equilibria. However, as shown by Huw Dixon, if the cost of turning customers away is sufficiently small, then any pure-strategy equilibria that exist will be close to the competitive equilibrium.
- Introducing product differentiation, as proposed by Jean-Pascal Benassy. This is more of a synthesis of monopolistic competition with the Bertrand–Edgeworth model, but Benassy showed that if the elasticity of demand for the firms output is sufficiently high, then any pure strategy equilibrium that existed would be close to the compoetitive outcome.
- "Integer pricing" as explored by Huw Dixon. Rather than treat price as a continuous variable, it is treated as a discrete variable. This means that firms cannot undercut each other by an arbitrarily small amount, one of the necessary ingredients giving rise to the non-existence of a pure strategy equilibrium. This can give rise to multiple pure-strategy equilibria, some of which may be distant from the competitive equilibrium price. More recently, Prabal Roy Chowdhury has combined the notion of discrete pricing with the idea that firms choose prices and the quantities they want to sell at that price as in Allen–Hellwig.
- Epsilon equilibrium in the pure-strategy game. In an epsilon equilibrium, each firm is within epsilon of its optimal price. If the epsilon is small, this might be seen as a plausible equilibrium, due perhaps to menu costs or bounded rationality. For a given epsilon>0, if there are enough firms, then an epsilon-equilibrium exists (this result depends on how one models the residual demand – the demand faced by higher-priced firms given the sales of the lower-priced firms).

Blindspots Analysis

Blindspots analysis (also blind spots analysis) is a method aimed at uncovering obsolete assumptions in a decision maker's mental scheme of the environment.

Michael Porter used the term "blind spots" to refer to conventional wisdom which no longer holds true, but which still guides business strategy. The concept was further popularized by Barbara Tuchman, in her 1984 book, *The March of Folly*, to describe political decisions and strategies which were clearly wrong in their assumptions.

The following method for uncovering blind spots was fully developed by Ben Gilad in his book, *Business Blindspots*. The Gilad method consists of three steps:

Step One: Conducting a Porter's Industry Structure – aka 5 force analysis on a given industry or segment (market), augmented with identification of possible change drivers, which are defined as trends with the potential to have profound (structural) effect on the balance of power among the five forces.

Step Two: Collecting competitive intelligence on the target company's top executives assumptions regarding the same industry structure as in Step One. Sources may include annual reports' letters to shareholders, autobiographies, interviews in the press, public appearances and speeches, industry meetings, congressional testimonies, conference calls with security analysts (transcripts are publicly available), and all other statements regarding vision and beliefs. An alternative technique is known among competitive intelligence professionals as "strategy's reverse engineering" which looks for the underlying assumptions which can rationalize existing strategy.

Step Three: Compare the results of Step Two with the analysis in Step One. Any contradiction with the analysis in Step One is a potential blindspot.

Assumptions Underlying Blindspots Analysis

Underlying Blindspots Analysis is an assumption about the inherent biases of decision making at the top of organisations (business, government or otherwise) exceeding those of their subordinates or outsiders. While top executives in business and government organisations are smart, capable people, they are also vulnerable to several decision biases that come with their powerful positions, from cognitive dissonance, motivated cognitions, to overconfidence and ego-involvement. The impaired ability of leaders to see reality for what it is, and the more objective (less ego-involved) analysis of analysts and mid level planners means that Step 3 of the Blindspots Analysis can be a powerful tool for pointing to potential blinders.

Competitive Advantage

Competitive advantage occurs when an organisation acquires or develops an attribute or combination of attributes that allows it to outperform its competitors. These attributes can include access to natural resources, such as high grade ores or inexpensive power, or access to highly trained and skilled personnel human resources. New technologies such as robotics and information technology can provide competitive advantage, whether as a part of the product itself, as an advantage to the making of the product, or as a competitive aid in the business process (for example, better identification and understanding of customers).

Competitive advantage seeks to address some of the criticisms of comparative advantage. Michael Porter proposed the theory in 1985. Porter emphasizes productivity growth as the focus of national strategies. Competitive advantage rests on the notion that cheap labour is ubiquitous and natural resources are not necessary for a good economy. The other theory, comparative advantage, can lead countries to specialise in exporting primary goods and raw materials that trap countries in low-wage economies due to terms of trade. Competitive advantage attempts to correct for this issue by stressing maximizing scale economies in goods and services that garner premium prices (Stutz and Warf 2009).

The term competitive advantage is the ability gained through attributes and resources to perform at a higher level than others in the same industry or market (Christensen and Fahey 1984, Kay 1994, Porter 1980 cited by Chacarbaghi and Lynch 1999, p. 45). The study of such advantage has attracted profound research interest due to contemporary issues regarding superior performance levels of firms in the present competitive market conditions. "A firm is said to have a competitive advantage when it is implementing a value creating strategy not simultaneously being implemented by any current or potential player" (Barney 1991 cited by Clulow et al.2003, p. 221). Successfully implemented strategies will lift a firm to superior performance by facilitating the firm with competitive advantage to outperform current or potential players (Passemard and Calantone 2000, p. 18). To gain competitive advantage a business strategy of a firm manipulates the various resources over which it has direct control and these resources have the ability to generate competitive advantage (Reed and Fillippi 1990 cited by Rijamampianina 2003, p. 362). Superior performance outcomes and superiority in production resources reflects competitive advantage (Day and Wesley 1988 cited by Lau 2002, p. 125).

Above writings signify competitive advantage as the ability to stay ahead of present or potential competition, thus superior performance reached through competitive advantage will ensure market leadership. Also it provides the understanding that resources held by a firm and the business strategy will have a profound impact on generating competitive advantage. Powell (2001, p. 132) views business strategy as the tool that manipulates the resources and create competitive advantage, hence, viable business strategy may not be adequate unless it possess control over unique resources that has the ability to create such a unique advantage. Summarizing the view points, competitive advantage is a key determinant of superior performance and it will ensure survival and prominent placing in the market. Superior performance being the ultimate desired goal of a firm, competitive advantage becomes the foundation highlighting the significant importance to develop same.

Competitive Strategies/Advantages

Cost Leadership Strategy: The goal of Cost Leadership Strategy is to offer products or services at the lowest cost in the industry. The challenge of this strategy is to earn a suitable profit for the company, rather than operating at a loss and draining profitability from all market players. Companies such as Walmart succeed with this strategy by featuring low prices on key items on which customers are price-aware, while selling other merchandise at less aggressive discounts. Products are to be created at the lowest cost in the industry. An example is to use space in stores for sales and not for storing excess product.

Differentiation Strategy

The goal of Differentiation Strategy is to provide a variety of products, services, or features to consumers that competitors are not yet offering or are unable to offer. This gives a direct advantage to the company which is able to provide a unique product or service that none of its competitors is able to offer. An example is Dell which launched mass-customizations on computers to fit consumers' needs. This allows the company to make its first product to be the star of its sales.

Innovation Strategy

The goal of Innovation Strategy is to leapfrog other market players by the introduction of completely new or notably better products or services. This strategy is typical of technology start-up companies which often intend to "disrupt" the existing marketplace, obsoleting the current market entries with a breakthrough product offering. It is harder for more established companies to pursue this strategy because their product offering has achieved market acceptance. Apple has been a notable example of using this strategy with its introduction of iPod personal music players, and iPad tablets. Many companies invest heavily in their research and development department to achieve such statuses with their innovations.

Operational Effectiveness Strategy

The goal of Operational Effectiveness as a strategy is to perform internal business activities better than competitors, making the company easier or more pleasurable to do business with than other market choices. It improves the characteristics of the company while lowering the time it takes to get the products on the market with a great start. State Farm Insurance pursues this strategy by promoting their agents as "good neighbours" who actively help customers.

Competitiveness

Competitiveness pertains to the ability and performance of a firm, sub-sector or country to sell and supply goods and services in a given market, in relation to the ability and performance of other firms, sub-sectors or countries in the same market. The term may also be applied to markets, where it is used to refer to the extent to which the market structure may be regarded as perfectly competitive. This usage has nothing to do with the extent to which individual firms are "competitive'.

Firm Competitiveness

Empirical observation confirms that resources (capital, labour, technology) and talent tend to concentrate geographically (Easterly and Levine 2002). This result reflects the fact that firms are embedded in inter-firm relationships with networks of suppliers, buyers and even competitors that help them to gain competitive advantages in the sale of its products and services. While arms-length market relationships do provide these benefits, at times there are externalities that arise from linkages among firms in a geographic area or in a specific industry (textiles, leather goods, silicon chips) that cannot be captured or fostered by markets alone. The process of "clusterization," the creation of "value chains," or "industrial districts" are models that highlight the advantages of networks. Within capitalist economic systems, the drive of enterprises is to maintain and improve their own competitiveness, this practically pertains to business sectors.

National Competitiveness

In recent years, the concept of competitiveness has emerged as a new paradigm in economic development. Competitiveness captures the awareness of both the limitations and challenges posed by global competition, at a time when effective government action is constrained by budgetary constraints and the private sector faces significant barriers to competing in domestic and international markets. The Global Competitiveness Report of the World Economic Forum defines competitiveness as "*the set of institutions, policies, and factors that determine the level of productivity of a country*".

The term is also used to refer in a broader sense to the economic competitiveness of countries, regions or cities. Recently, countries are increasingly looking at their competitiveness on global markets. Ireland (1997), Saudi Arabia (2000), Greece (2003), Croatia (2004), Bahrain (2005), the Philippines (2006), Guyana, the Dominican Republic and Spain (2011) are just some examples of countries that have advisory bodies or special government agencies that tackle competitiveness issues. Even regions or cities, such as Dubai or the Basque Country(Spain), are considering the establishment of such a body.

The institutional model applied in the case of National Competitiveness Programs (NCP) varies from country to country, however, there are some common features. The leadership structure of NCPs relies on strong support from the highest level of political authority. High-level support provides credibility with the appropriate actors in the private sector. Usually, the council or governing body will have a designated public sector leader (president, vice-president or minister) and a co-president drawn from the private sector. Notwithstanding the public sector's role in strategy formulation, oversight, and implementation, national competitiveness programs should have strong, dynamic leadership from the private sector at all levels – national, local and firm. From the outset, the program must provide a clear diagnostic of the problems facing the economy and a compelling vision that appeals to a broad set of actors who are willing to seek change and implement an outward-oriented growth strategy. Finally, most programs share a common view on the importance of networks of firms or "clusters" as an organising principal for collective action. Based on a bottom-up approach, programs that support the association among private business leadership, civil society organisations, public institutions and political leadership can better identify barriers to competitiveness; develop joint-decisions on strategic policies and investments; and yield better results in implementation.

National competitiveness is said to be particularly important for small open economies, which rely on trade, and typically foreign direct investment, to provide the scale necessary for productivity increases to drive increases in living standards. The Irish National Competitiveness Council uses a Competitiveness Pyramid structure to simplify the factors that affect national competitiveness. It distinguishes in particular between *policy inputs* in relation to the business environment, the physical infrastructure and the knowledge infrastructure and the *essential conditions* of competitiveness that good policy inputs create, including business performance metrics, productivity, labour supply and prices/costs for business.

Competitiveness is important for any economy that must rely on international trade to balance import of energy and raw materials. The European Union (EU) has enshrined industrial research and technological development (R&D) in her Treaty in order to become more competitive. In 2009, €12 billion of the EU budget (totalling €133.8 billion) will go on projects to boost Europe's competitiveness. The way for the EU to face competitiveness is to invest in education, research, innovation and technological infrastructures.

The International Economic Development Council (IEDC) in Washington, D.C. published the "Innovation Agenda: A Policy Statement on American Competitiveness". This paper summarizes the ideas expressed at the 2007 IEDC Federal Forum and provides policy recommendations for both economic developers and federal policy makers that aim to ensure America remains globally competitive in light of current domestic and international challenges.

International comparisons of national competitiveness are conducted by the World Economic Forum, in its Global Competitiveness Report, and the Institute for Management Development, in its World Competitiveness Yearbook.

Scholarly analyses of national competitiveness have largely been qualitatively descriptive. Systematic efforts by academics to define meaningfully and to quantitatively analyze national competitiveness have been made, with the determinants of national competitiveness econometrically modelled.

A US government sponsored program under the Reagan administration called Project Socrates, was initiated to, 1) determine why US competitiveness was declining, 2) create a solution to restore US competitiveness. The Socrates Team headed by Michael Sekora, a physicist, built an all-source intelligence system to research all competitiveness of mankind from the beginning of time. The research resulted in ten findings which served as the framework for the "Socrates Competitive Strategy System". Among the ten finding on competitiveness was that 'the source of all competitive advantage is the ability to access and utilise technology to satisfy one or more customer needs better than competitors, where technology is defined as any use of science to achieve a function".

Some development economists believe that a sizeable part of Western Europe has now fallen behind the most dynamic amongst Asia's emerging nations, notably because the latter adopted policies more propitious to long-term investments: "Successful countries such as Singapore, Indonesia and South Korea still remember the harsh adjustment mechanisms imposed abruptly upon them by the IMF and World Bank during the 1997–1998 'Asian Crisis' [...] What they have achieved in the past 10 years is all the more remarkable: they have quietly abandoned the "Washington consensus" [the dominant Neoclassical perspective] by investing massively in infrastructure projects [...] this pragmatic approach proved to be very successful."

Criticism

Krugman (1994) argues that, in the context of countries, productivity is what matters and "the world's leading nations are not, to any important degree, in economic competition with each other." Krugman warns that thinking in terms of competitiveness could lead to wasteful spending, protectionism, trade wars, and bad policy.

If the concept of national competitiveness has any substantive meaning it must reside in the factors about a nation that facilitate productivity, and alongside criticism of nebulous and erroneous conceptions of national competitiveness systematic and rigorous attempts like Thompson's need to be elaborated.

Perfect Competition

In economic theory, perfect competition (sometimes called *pure competition*) describes markets such that no participants are large enough to have the market power to set the price of a homogeneous product. Because the conditions for perfect competition are strict, there are few if any perfectly competitive markets. Still, buyers and sellers in some auction-type markets, say for commodities or some financial assets, may approximate the concept. As a Pareto efficient allocation of economic resources, perfect competition serves as a natural benchmark against which to contrast other market structures.

Basic Structural Characteristics

Generally, a perfectly competitive market exists when every participant is a "price taker", and no participant influences the price of the product it buys or sells. Specific characteristics may include:

- Infinite buyers and sellers – An infinite number of consumers with the willingness and ability to buy the product at a certain price, and infinite producers with the willingness and ability to supply the product at a certain price.
- No barriers of entry and exit – No entry and exitbarriers makes it extremely easy to enter or exit a perfectly competitive market.
- Perfect factor mobility – In the long run factors of production are perfectly mobile, allowing free long term adjustments to changing market conditions.
- Perfect information - All consumers and producers are assumed to have perfect knowledge of price, utility, quality and production methods of products.
- Zero transaction costs - Buyers and sellers do not incur costs in making an exchange of goods in a perfectly competitive market.
- Profit maximization - Firms are assumed to sell where marginal costs meet marginal revenue, where the most profit is generated.
- Homogenous products - The qualities and characteristics of a market good or service do not vary between different suppliers.
- Non-increasing returns to scale - The lack of increasing returns to scale (or economies of scale) ensures that there will always be a sufficient number of firms in the industry.
- Property rights - Well defined property rights determine what may be sold, as well as what rights are conferred on the buyer.
- Rational buyers - buyers capable of making rational purchases based on information given
- No externalities - costs or benefits of an activity do not affect third parties

In the short run, perfectly-competitive markets are not productively efficient as output will not occur where marginal cost is equal to average cost (MC=AC). They are allocatively efficient, as output will always occur where marginal cost is equal to marginal revenue (MC=MR). In the long run, perfectly competitive markets are both allocatively and productively efficient.

In perfect competition, any profit-maximizing producer faces a market price equal to its marginal cost (P=MC). This implies that a factor's price equals the factor's marginal revenue product. It allows for derivation of the supply curve on which the neoclassical approach is based. This is also the reason why "a monopoly does not have a supply curve". The abandonment of price taking creates considerable difficulties for the demonstration of a general equilibrium except under other, very specific conditions such as that of monopolistic competition.

Approaches and Conditions

In neoclassical economics there have been two strands of looking at what perfect competition is. The first emphasis is on the inability of any one agent to affect prices. Usually justified by the fact that any one firm or consumer is so small relative to the whole market that their presence or absence leaves the equilibrium price very nearly unaffected. This assumption of negligible impact of each agent on the equilibrium price has been formalized by Aumann (1964) by postulating a continuum of infinitesimal agents. The difference between Aumann's approach and that found in undergraduate textbooks is that in the first, agents have the power to choose their own prices but do not individually affect the market price, while in the second it is simply assumed that agents treat prices as parameters. Both approaches lead to the same result.

The second view of perfect competition conceives of it in terms of agents taking advantage of – and hence, eliminating – profitable exchange opportunities. The faster this arbitrage takes place, the more competitive a market. The implication is that the more competitive a market is under this definition, the faster the average market price will adjust so as to equate supply and demand (and also equate price to marginal costs). In this view, "perfect" competition means that this adjustment takes place instantaneously. This is usually modelled via the use of the Walrasian auctioneer. The widespread recourse to the auctioneer tale appears to have favoured an interpretation of perfect competition as meaning price taking *always*, i.e. also at non-equilibrium prices; but this is rejected e.g. by Arrow (1959) or Mas-Colell et al.

Steve Keen notes, following George Stigler, that if firms do not react strategically to one another, the slope of the demand curve that a firm faces is the same as the slope of the market demand curve. Hence, if firms are to produce at a level that equates marginal cost and marginal revenue, the model of perfect competition must include at least an infinite number of firms, each producing an output quantity of zero. As noted above, an influential model of perfect competition in neoclassical economics assumes that the number of buyers and sellers are both of the power of the continuum, that is, an infinity even larger than the number of natural numbers. K. Vela Velupillai quotes

Maury Osborne as noting the inapplicability of such models to actual economies since money and the commodities sold each have a smallest positive unit. Thus nowadays the dominant intuitive idea of the conditions justifying price taking and thus rendering a market perfectly competitive is an amalgam of several different notions, not all present, nor given equal weight, in all treatments. Besides product homogeneity and absence of collusion, the notion more generally associated with perfect competition is the negligibility of the size of agents, which makes them believe that they can sell as much of the good as they wish at the equilibrium price but nothing at a higher price (in particular, firms are described as each one of them facing a horizontal demand curve). However, also widely accepted as part of the notion of perfectly competitive market are perfect information about price distribution and very quick adjustments (whose joint operation establish the law of one price), to the point sometimes of identifying perfect competition with an essentially instantaneous reaching of equilibrium between supply and demand. Finally, the idea of free entry with free access to technology is also often listed as a characteristic of perfectly competitive markets, probably owing to a difficulty with abandoning completely the older conception of free competition. In recent decades it has been rediscovered that free entry can be a foundation of absence of market power, alternative to negligibility of agents.

Free entry also makes it easier to justify the absence of collusion: any collusion by existing firms can be undermined by entry of new firms. The necessarily long-period nature of the analysis (entry requires time!) also allows a reconciliation of the horizontal demand curve facing each firm according to the theory, with the feeling of businessmen that "contrary to economic theory, sales are by no means unlimited at the current market price" (Arrow 1959 p. 49). Sraffian economists see the assumption of free entry and exit as characteristic of the theory of free competition in Classical economics, an approach that is not expressed in terms of schedules of supply and demand.

Results

In a perfectly competitive market, a firm's demand curve is perfectly elastic. As mentioned above, the perfect competition model, if interpreted as applying also to short-period or very-short-period behaviour, is approximated only by markets of homogeneous products produced and purchased by very many sellers and buyers, usually organised markets for agricultural products or raw materials. In real-world markets, assumptions such as perfect information cannot be verified and are only approximated in organised double-auction markets where most agents wait and observe the behaviour of prices before deciding to exchange (but in the long-period interpretation perfect information is not necessary, the analysis only aims at determining the average around which market prices gravitate, and for gravitation to operate one does not need perfect information).

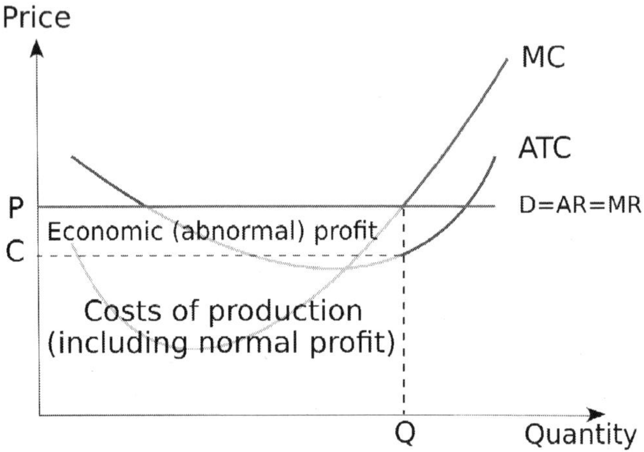

Figure: *In the short run, it is possible for an individual firm to make an economic profit. This situation is shown in this diagram, as the price or average revenue, denoted by P, is above the average cost denoted by C.*

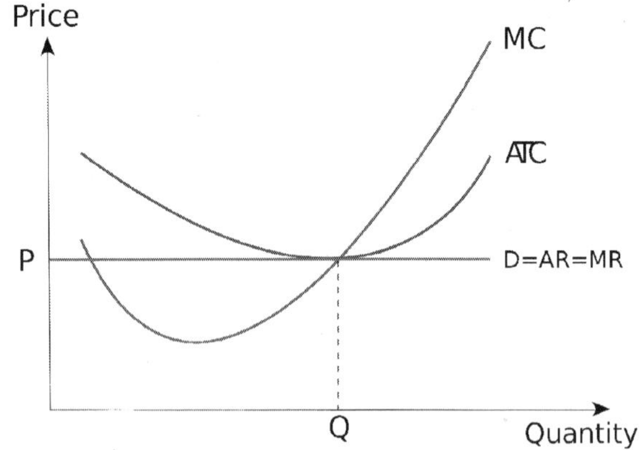

Figure: *However, in the long run, economic profit cannot be sustained. The arrival of new firms or expansion of existing firms (if returns to scale are constant) in the market causes the (horizontal) demand curve of each individual firm to shift downward, bringing down at the same time the price, the average revenue and marginal revenue curve. The final outcome is that, in the long run, the firm will make only normal profit (zero economic profit). Its horizontal demand curve will touch its average total cost curve at its lowest point.*

In the absence of externalities and public goods, perfectly competitive equilibria are Pareto-efficient, i.e. no improvement in the utility of a consumer is possible without a worsening of the utility of some other consumer. This is called the First Theorem of Welfare Economics. The basic reason is that no productive factor with a non-zero marginal product is left unutilised, and the units of each factor are so allocated as to yield the same indirect marginal utility in all uses, a basic efficiency condition (if this indirect marginal utility were higher in one use than in other ones, a Pareto improvement could be achieved by transferring a small amount of the factor to the use where it yields a higher marginal utility).

A simple proof assuming differentiable utility functions and production functions is the following. Let w_j be the 'price' (the rental) of a certain factor j, let MP_{j1} and MP_{j2} be its marginal product in the production of goods 1 and 2, and let p_1 and p_2 be these goods' prices. In equilibrium these prices must equal the respective marginal costs MC_1 and MC_2; remember that marginal cost equals factor 'price' divided by factor marginal productivity (because increasing the production of good by one very small unit through an increase of the employment of factor j requires increasing the factor employment by $1/MP_{ji}$ and thus increasing the cost by w_j/MP_{ji}, and through the condition of cost minimization that marginal products must be proportional to factor 'prices' it can be shown that the cost increase is the same if the output increase is obtained by optimally varying all factors). Optimal factor employment by a price-taking firm requires equality of factor rental and factor marginal revenue product, $w_j=p_iMP_{ji}$, so we obtain $p_1=MC_1=w_j/MP_{j1}$, $p_2=MC_{j2}=w_j/MP_{j2}$.

Now choose any consumer purchasing both goods, and measure his utility in such units that in equilibrium his marginal utility of money (the increase in utility due to the last unit of money spent on each good), $MU_1/p_1=MU_2/p_2$, is 1. Then $p_1=MU_1$, $p_2=MU_2$. The indirect marginal utility of the factor is the increase in the utility of our consumer achieved by an increase in the employment of the factor by one (very small) unit; this increase in utility through allocating the small increase in factor utilisation to good 1 is $MP_{j1}MU_1=MP_{j1}p_1=w_j$, and through allocating it to good 2 it is $MP_{j2}MU_2=MP_{j2}p_2=w_j$ again. With our choice of units the marginal utility of the amount of the factor consumed directly by the optimizing consumer is again w, so the amount supplied of the factor too satisfies the condition of optimal allocation. Monopoly violates this optimal allocation condition, because in a monopolized industry market price is above marginal cost, and this means that factors are underutilised in the monopolized industry, they have a higher indirect marginal utility than in their uses in competitive industries. Of course this theorem is considered irrelevant by economists who do not believe that general equilibrium theory correctly predicts the functioning of market economies; but it is given great importance by neoclassical economists and it is the theoretical reason given by them for combating monopolies and for antitrust legislation.

Profit

In contrast to a monopoly or oligopoly, it is impossible for a firm in perfect competition to earn economic profit in the long run, which is to say that a firm cannot make any more money than is necessary to cover its economic costs. In order not to misinterpret this zero-long-run-profits thesis, it must be remembered that the term 'profit' is also used in other ways. Neoclassical theory defines profit as what is left of revenue after all costs have been subtracted, including normal interest on capital plus the normal excess over it required to cover risk, and normal salary for managerial activity.

Classical economists on the contrary defined profit as what is left after subtracting costs except interest and risk coverage; thus, if one leaves aside risk coverage for simplicity, the neoclassical zero-long-run-profit thesis would be re-expressed in classical parlance as profits coinciding with interest in the long period, i.e. the rate of profit tending to coincide with the rate of interest. Profits in the classical meaning do not tend to disappear in the long period but tend to normal profit.

With this terminology, if a firm is earning abnormal profit in the short term, this will act as a trigger for other firms to enter the market. As other firms enter the market the market supply curve will shift out causing prices to fall. Existing firms will react to this lower price by adjusting their capital stock downward. This adjustment will cause their marginal cost to shift to the left causing the market supply curve to shift inward. However, the net effect of entry by new firms and adjustment by existing firms will be to shift the supply curve outward. The market price will be driven down until all firms are earning normal profit only.

It is important to note that perfect competition is a sufficient condition for allocative and productive efficiency, but it is not a necessary condition. Laboratory experiments in which participants have significant price setting power and little or no information about their counterparts consistently produce efficient results given the proper trading institutions.

The Shutdown Point

In the short run, a firm operating at a loss [R < TC (revenue less than total cost) or P < ATC (price less than unit cost)] must decide whether to continue to operate or temporarily shutdown. The shutdown rule states "in the short run a firm should continue to operate if price exceeds average variable costs." Restated, the rule is that for a firm to continue producing in the short run it must earn sufficient revenue to cover its variable costs. The rationale for the rule is straightforward. By shutting down a firm avoids all variable costs. However, the firm must still pay fixed costs. Because fixed cost must be paid regardless of whether a firm operates they should not be considered in deciding whether to produce or shutdown. Thus in determining whether to shut down a firm should compare total revenue to total variable costs (VC) rather than total costs (FC + VC). If the revenue the firm is receiving is greater than its total variable cost (R > VC) then the firm is covering all variable cost plus there is additional revenue ("contribution"), which can be applied to fixed costs. (The size of the fixed costs is irrelevant as it is a sunk cost. The same consideration is used whether fixed costs are one dollar or one million dollars.) On the other hand if VC > R then the firm is not even covering its production costs and it should immediately shut down. The rule is conventionally stated in terms of price (average revenue) and average variable costs. The rules are equivalent (If you divide both sides of inequality TR > TVC by Q gives P > AVC). If the firm decides to operate, the firm will continue to produce where marginal revenue equals marginal costs because these conditions insure not only profit maximization (loss minimization) but also maximum contribution.

Another way to state the rule is that a firm should compare the profits from operating to those realised if it shutdown and select the option that produces the greater profit. A firm that is shutdown is generating zero revenue and incurring no variable costs. However, the firm still has to pay fixed cost. So the firm's profit equals fixed costs or –FC. An operating firm is generating revenue, incurring variable costs and paying fixed costs. The operating firm's profit is R – VC – FC. The firm should continue to operate if R – VC – FC ≥ –FC, which simplified is R ≥ VC. The difference between revenue, R, and variable costs, VC, is the contribution to fixed costs and any contribution is better than none. Thus, if R ≥ VC then firm should operate. If R < VC the firm should shut down.

A decision to shut down means that the firm is temporarily suspending production. It does not mean that the firm is going out of business (exiting the industry).] If market conditions improve, and prices increase, the firm can resume production. Shutting down is a short-run decision. A firm that has shut down is not producing. The firm still retains its capital assets; however, the firm cannot leave the industry or avoid its fixed costs in the short run. Exit is a long-term decision. A firm that has exited an industry has avoided all commitments and freed all capital for use in more profitable enterprises.

However, a firm cannot continue to incur losses indefinitely. In the long run, the firm will have to earn sufficient revenue to cover all its expenses and must decide whether to continue in business or to leave the industry and pursue profits elsewhere. The long-run decision is based on the relationship of the price and long-run average costs. If $P \geq AC$ then the firm will not exit the industry. If $P < AC$, then the firm will exit the industry. These comparisons will be made after the firm has made the necessary and feasible long-term adjustments. In the long run a firm operates where marginal revenue equals long-run marginal costs.

Short-Run Supply Curve

The short run supply curve for a perfectly competitive firm is the marginal cost (MC) curve at and above the shutdown point. Portions of the marginal cost curve below the shut down point are not part of the SR supply curve because the firm is not producing in that range. Technically the SR supply curve is a discontinuous function composed of the segment of the MC curve at and above minimum of the average variable cost curve and a segment that runs with the vertical axis from the origin to but not including a point "parallel" to minimum average variable costs.

Examples

Though there is no actual perfectly competitive market in the real world, a number of approximations exist:

Perhaps the closest thing to a perfectly competitive market would be a large auction of identical goods with all potential buyers and sellers present. By design, a stock exchange resembles this, not as a complete description (for no markets may satisfy all requirements of the model) but as an approximation. The flaw in considering the stock exchange as an example of Perfect Competition is the fact that large institutional investors (e.g. investment banks) may solely influence the market price. This, of course, violates the condition that "no one seller can influence market price". Horse betting is also quite a close approximation. When placing bets, consumers can just look down the line to see who is offering the best odds, and so no one bookie can offer worse odds than those being offered by the market as a whole, since consumers will just go to another bookie. This makes the bookies price-takers. Furthermore, the product on offer is very homogeneous, with the only differences between individual bets being the pay-off and the horse. Of course, there are not an infinite amount of bookies, and some barriers to entry exist, such as a license and the capital required to set up.

Free software works along lines that approximate perfect competition as well. Anyone is free to enter and leave the market at no cost. All code is freely accessible and modifiable, and individuals are free to behave independently. Free software may be bought or sold at whatever price that the market may allow.

Some believe that one of the prime examples of a perfectly competitive market anywhere in the world is street food in developing countries. This is so since relatively few barriers to entry/exit exist for street vendors. Furthermore, there are often numerous buyers and sellers of a given street food, in addition to consumers/sellers possessing perfect information of the product in question. It is often the case that street vendors may serve a homogenous product, in which little to no variations in the product's nature exist.

Another very near example of perfect competition would be the fish market and the vegetable or fruit vendors who sell at the same place, the bars in "Le Carré" (Liège, Belgium) or the "kebab street" near the Grand Place in Brussels:

1. There are large number of buyers and sellers.
2. There are no entry or exit barriers.
3. There is perfect mobility of the factors, i.e. buyers can easily switch from one seller to the other.
4. The products are homogeneous.

Criticisms

The use of the assumption of perfect competition as the foundation of price theory for product markets is often criticized as representing all agents as passive, thus removing the active attempts to increase one's welfare or profits by price undercutting, product design, advertising, innovation, activities that - the critics argue – characterize most industries and markets. These criticisms point to the frequent lack of realism of the assumptions of product homogeneity and impossibility to differentiate it, but apart from this the accusation of passivity appears correct only for short-period or very-short-period analyses, in long-period analyses the inability of price to diverge from the natural or long-period price is due to active reactions of entry or exit.

Some economists have a different kind of criticism concerning perfect competition model. They are not criticizing the price taker assumption because it makes economic agents too "passive", but because it then raises the question of who sets the prices. Indeed, if everyone is price taker, there is the need for a benevolent planner who gives and sets the prices, in other word, there is a need for a "price maker". Therefore, it makes the perfect competition model appropriate not to describe a decentralize "market" economy but a centralized one. This in turn means that such kind of model has more to do with communism than capitalism.

Another frequent criticism is that it is often not true that in the short run differences between supply and demand cause changes in price; especially in manufacturing, the more common behaviour is alteration of production without nearly any alteration of price.

The critics of the assumption of perfect competition in product markets seldom question the basic neoclassical view of the working of market economies for this reason. The Neo-Austrian school insists strongly on this criticism, and yet the neoclassical view of the working of market economies as fundamentally efficient, reflecting consumer choices and assigning to each agent his contribution to social welfare, is esteemed to be fundamentally correct Some non-neoclassical schools, like Post-Keynesians, reject the neoclassical approach to value and distribution, but not because of their rejection of perfect competition as a reasonable approximation to the working of most product markets; the reasons for rejection of the neoclassical 'vision' are different views of the determinants of income distribution and of aggregated demand.

In particular, the rejection of perfect competition does not generally entail the rejection of free competition as characterizing most product markets; indeed it has been argued that competition is stronger nowadays than in 19th century capitalism, owing to the increasing capacity of big conglomerate firms to enter any industry: therefore the classical idea of a tendency toward a uniform rate of return on investment in all industries owing to free entry is even more valid today; and the reason why General Motors, Texon or Nestle do not enter the computers or pharmaceutical industries is not insurmountable barriers to entry but rather that the rate of return in the latter industries is already sufficiently in line with the average rate of return elsewhere as not to justify entry. On this few economists, it would seem, would disagree, even among the neoclassical ones. Thus when the issue is normal, or long-period, product prices, differences on the validity of the perfect competition assumption do not appear to imply important differences on the existence or not of a tendency of rates of return toward uniformity as long as entry is possible, and what is found fundamentally lacking in the perfect competition model is the absence of marketing expenses and innovation as causes of costs that do enter normal average cost.

The issue is different with respect to factor markets. Here the acceptance or denial of perfect competition in labour markets does make a big difference to the view of the working of market economies. One must distinguish neoclassical from non-neoclassical economists. For the former, absence of perfect competition in labour markets, e.g. due to the existence of trade unions, impedes the smooth working of competition, which if left free to operate would cause a decrease of wages as long as there were unemployment, and would finally ensure the full employment of labour: labour unemployment is due to absence of perfect competition in labour markets. Most non-neoclassical economists deny that a full flexibility of wages would ensure the full employment of labour and find a stickiness of wages an indispensable component of a market economy, without which the economy would lack the regularity and persistence indispensable to its smooth working. This was, for example, John Maynard Keynes's opinion.

Particularly radical is the view of the Sraffian school on this issue: the labour demand curve cannot be determined hence a level of wages ensuring the equality between supply and demand for labour does not exist, and economics should resume the viewpoint of the classical economists, according to whom competition in labour markets does not and cannot mean indefinite price flexibility as long as supply and demand are unequal, it only means a tendency to equality of wages for similar work, but the level of wages is necessarily determined by complex sociopolitical elements; custom, feelings of justice, informal allegiances to classes, as well as overt coalitions such as trade unions, far from being impediments to a smooth working of labour markets that would be able to determine wages even without these elements, are on the contrary indispensable because without them there would be no way to determine wages.

Equilibrium in Perfect Competition

Equilibrium in perfect competition is the point where market demands will be equal to market supply. A firm's price will be determined at this point. In the short run, equilibrium will be affected by demand. In the long run, both demand and supply of a product will affect the equilibrium in perfect competition. A firm will receive only normal profit in the long run at the equilibrium point.

Monopolistic Competition

Monopolistic competition is a type of imperfect competition such that many producers sell products that are differentiated from one another (e.g. by branding or quality) and hence are not perfect substitutes. In monopolistic competition, a firm takes the prices charged by its rivals as given and ignores the impact of its own prices on the prices of other firms. In the presence of coercive government, monopolistic competition will fall into government-granted monopoly. Unlike perfect competition, the firm maintains spare capacity. Models of monopolistic competition are often used to model industries. Textbook examples of industries with market structures similar to monopolistic competition include restaurants, cereal, clothing, shoes, and service industries in large cities. The "founding father" of the theory of monopolistic competition is Edward Hastings Chamberlin, who wrote a pioneering book on the subject, *Theory of Monopolistic Competition* (1933). Joan Robinson published a book *The Economics of Imperfect Competition* with a comparable theme of distinguishing perfect from imperfect competition.

Monopolistically competitive markets have the following characteristics:

- There are many producers and many consumers in the market, and no business has total control over the market price.
- Consumers perceive that there are non-price differences among the competitors' products.
- There are few barriers to entry and exit.
- Producers have a degree of control over price.

The long-run characteristics of a monopolistically competitive market are almost the same as a perfectly competitive market. Two differences between the two are that monopolistic competition produces heterogeneous products and that monopolistic competition involves a great deal of non-price competition, which is based on subtle product differentiation. A firm making profits in the short run will nonetheless only break even in the long run because demand will decrease and average total cost will increase. This means in the long run, a monopolistically competitive firm will make zero economic profit. This illustrates the amount of influence the firm has over the market; because of brand loyalty, it can raise its prices without losing all of its customers. This means that an individual firm's demand curve is downward sloping, in contrast to perfect competition, which has a perfectly elastic demand schedule.

Major Characteristic

- Product differentiation
- Many firms
- No entry and exit cost in the long run
- Open discussion decision making
- No degree of market power
- Buyers and Sellers do not have perfect information (Imperfect Information)

Product Differentiation

MC firms sell products that have real or perceived non-price differences. However, the differences are not so great as to eliminate other goods as substitutes. Technically, the cross price elasticity of demand between goods in such a market is positive. In fact, the XED would be high. MC goods are best described as close but imperfect substitutes. The goods perform the same basic functions but have differences in qualities such as type, style, quality, reputation, appearance, and location that tend to distinguish them from each other. For example, the basic function of motor vehicles is basically the same—to move people and objects from point A to B in reasonable comfort and safety. Yet there are many different types of motor vehicles such as motor scooters, motor cycles, trucks, cars and SUVs and many variations even within these categories.

Many Firms

MC product group and many firms on the side lines prepared to enter the market. A product group is a "collection of similar products". The fact that there are "many firms" gives each MC firm the freedom to set prices without engaging in strategic decision making regarding the prices of other firms and each firm's actions have a negligible impact on the market. For example, a firm could cut prices and increase sales without fear that its actions will prompt retaliatory responses from competitors. How many firms will an MC market structure support at market equilibrium? The answer depends on factors such as fixed costs, economies of scale and the degree of product differentiation. For example, the higher the fixed costs, the fewer firms the market will support. Also the greater the degree of product differentiation—the more the firm can separate itself from the pack—the fewer firms there will be at market equilibrium.

No Entry and Exit Costs

In the long run there are no entry and exit costs. There are numerous firms waiting to enter the market, each with their own "unique" product or in pursuit of positive profits. Any firm unable to cover its costs can leave the market without incurring liquidation costs. This assumption implies that there are low start up costs, no sunk costs and no exit costs.

Independent Decision Making

Each MC firm independently sets the terms of exchange for its product. The firm gives no consideration to what effect its decision may have on competitors. The theory is that any action will have such a negligible effect on the overall market demand that an MC firm can act without fear of prompting heightened competition. In other words each firm feels free to set prices as if it were a monopoly rather than an oligopoly.

Market Power

MC firms have some degree of market power. Market power means that the firm has control over the terms and conditions of exchange. An MC firm can raise its prices without losing all its customers. The firm can also lower prices without triggering a potentially ruinous price war with competitors. The source of an MC firm's market power is not barriers to entry since they are low. Rather, an MC firm has market power because it has relatively few competitors, those competitors do not engage in strategic decision making and the firms sells differentiated product. Market power also means that an MC firm faces a downward sloping demand curve. The demand curve is highly elastic although not "flat".

Imperfect Information

No sellers or buyers have complete market information, like market demand or market supply.

Market Structure comparison

	Number of firms	*Market power*	*Elasticity of demand*	*Product differentiation*	*Excess profits*	*Efficiency*	*Profit maximization condition*	*Pricing power*
Perfect Competition	Infinite	None	Perfectly elastic	None	No	Yes	P=MR=MC	Price taker
Monopolistic competition	Many	Low	Highly elastic (long run)	High	Yes/No (Short/Long)	No	MR=MC	Price setter
Monopoly	One	High	Relatively inelastic	Absolute (across industries)	Yes	No	MR=MC	Price setter

Questions to ask?: - Access to previous historical accounts and up to date accounts to check liabilities and confirm profitability

Inefficiency

There are two sources of inefficiency in the MC market structure. First, at its optimum output the firm charges a price that exceeds marginal costs, The MC firm maximizes profits where marginal revenue = marginal cost. Since the MC firm's demand curve is downward sloping this means that the firm will be charging a price that exceeds marginal costs. The monopoly power possessed by a MC firm means that at its profit maximizing level of production there will be a net loss of consumer (and producer) surplus. The second source of inefficiency is the fact that MC firms operate with excess capacity. That is, the MC firm's profit maximizing output is less than the output associated with minimum average cost. Both a PC and MC firm will operate at a point where demand or price equals average cost. For a PC firm this equilibrium condition occurs where the perfectly elastic demand curve equals minimum average cost. A MC firm's demand curve is not flat but is downward sloping. Thus in the long run the demand curve will be tangential to the long run average cost curve at a point to the left of its minimum. The result is excess capacity.

Problems

While monopolistically competitive firms are inefficient, it is usually the case that the costs of regulating prices for products sold in monopolistic competition exceed the benefits of such regulation. . A monopolistically competitive firm might be said to be marginally inefficient because the firm produces at an output where average total cost is not a minimum. A monopolistically competitive market is productively inefficient market structure because marginal cost is less than price in the long run. Monopolistically competitive markets are also allocatively inefficient, as the price given is higher than Marginal cost. Product differentiation increases total utility by better meeting people's wants than homogenous products in a perfectly competitive market.

Another concern is that monopolistic competition fosters advertising and the creation of brand names. Advertising induces customers into spending more on products because of the name associated with them rather than because of rational factors. Defenders of advertising dispute this, arguing that brand names can represent a guarantee of quality and that advertising helps reduce the cost to consumers of weighing the tradeoffs of numerous competing brands. There are unique information and information processing costs associated with selecting a brand in a monopolistically competitive environment. In a monopoly market, the consumer is faced with a single brand, making information gathering relatively inexpensive. In a perfectly competitive industry, the consumer is faced with many brands, but because the brands are virtually identical information gathering is also relatively inexpensive. In a monopolistically competitive market, the consumer must collect and process information on a large number of different brands to be able to select the best of them. In many cases, the cost of gathering information necessary to selecting the best brand can exceed the benefit of consuming the best brand instead of a randomly selected brand. The result is that the consumer is confused. Some brands gain prestige value and can extract an additional price for that.

Evidence suggests that consumers use information obtained from advertising not only to assess the single brand advertised, but also to infer the possible existence of brands that the consumer has, heretofore, not observed, as well as to infer consumer satisfaction with brands similar to the advertised brand.

Examples

In many U.S. markets, producers practice product differentiation by altering the physical composition of products, using special packaging, or simply claiming to have superior products based on brand images or advertising. Toothpastes, toilet papers, computer software and operating systems are examples of differentiated products.

Oligopoly

An oligopoly is a market form in which a market or industry is dominated by a small number of sellers (oligopolists). Oligopolies can result from various forms of collusion which reduce competition and lead to higher costs for consumers.

With few sellers, each oligopolist is likely to be aware of the actions of the others. The decisions of one firm therefore influence and are influenced by the decisions of other firms. Strategic planning by oligopolists needs to take into account the likely responses of the other market participants.

Description

Oligopoly is a common market form where a small number of firms are in competition. As a quantitative description of oligopoly, the four-firm concentration ratio is often utilised. This measure expresses the market share of the four largest firms in an industry as a percentage. For example, as of fourth quarter 2008, Verizon, AT&T, Sprint, and T-Mobile together control 89% of the US cellular phone market. Oligopolistic competition can give rise to a wide range of different outcomes. In some situations, the firms may employ restrictive trade practices (collusion, market sharing etc.) to raise prices and restrict production in much the same way as a monopoly. Where there is a formal agreement for such collusion, this is known as a cartel. A primary example of such a cartel is OPEC which has a profound influence on the international price of oil.

Firms often collude in an attempt to stabilize unstable markets, so as to reduce the risks inherent in these markets for investment and product development. There are legal restrictions on such collusion in most countries. There does not have to be a formal agreement for collusion to take place (although for the act to be illegal there must be actual communication between companies)–for example, in some industries there may be an acknowledged market leader which informally sets prices to which other producers respond, known as price leadership. In other situations, competition between sellers in an oligopoly can be fierce, with relatively low prices and high production. This could lead to an efficient outcome approaching perfect competition. The competition in an oligopoly can be greater when there are more firms in an industry than if, for example, the firms were only regionally based and did not compete directly with each other.

Thus the welfare analysis of oligopolies is sensitive to the parameter values used to define the market's structure. In particular, the level of dead weight loss is hard to measure. The study of product differentiation indicates that oligopolies might also create excessive levels of differentiation in order to stifle competition.

Oligopoly theory makes heavy use of game theory to model the behaviour of oligopolies:

- Stackelberg'sduopoly. In this model the firms move sequentially.
- Cournot's duopoly. In this model the firms simultaneously choose quantities.
- Bertrand's oligopoly. In this model the firms simultaneously choose prices.

Characteristics

Profit Maximization Conditions: An oligopoly maximizes profits .

Ability to Set Price: Oligopolies are price setters rather than price takers.

Entry and Exit: Barriers to entry are high. The most important barriers are economies of scale, patents, access to expensive and complex technology, and strategic actions by incumbent firms designed to discourage or destroy nascent firms. Additional sources of barriers to entry often result from government regulation favouring existing firms making it difficult for new firms to enter the market.

Number of Firms: "Few" – a "handful" of sellers. There are so few firms that the actions of one firm can influence the actions of the other firms.

Long Run Profits: Oligopolies can retain long run abnormal profits. High barriers of entry prevent sideline firms from entering market to capture excess profits.

Product Differentiation: Product may be homogeneous (steel) or differentiated (automobiles).

Perfect Knowledge: Assumptions about perfect knowledge vary but the knowledge of various economic factors can be generally described as selective. Oligopolies have perfect knowledge of their own cost and demand functions but their inter-firm information may be incomplete. Buyers have only imperfect knowledge as to price, cost and product quality.

Interdependence: The distinctive feature of an oligopoly is interdependence. Oligopolies are typically composed of a few large firms. Each firm is so large that its actions affect market conditions. Therefore the competing firms will be aware of a firm's market actions and will respond appropriately. This means that in contemplating a market action, a firm must take into consideration the possible reactions of all competing firms and the firm's countermoves. It is very much like a game of chess or pool in which a player must anticipate a whole sequence of moves and countermoves in determining how to achieve his or her objectives. For example, an oligopoly considering a price reduction may wish to estimate the likelihood that competing firms would also lower their prices and possibly trigger a ruinous price war. Or if the firm is considering a price increase, it may want to know whether other firms will also increase prices or hold existing prices constant. This high degree of interdependence and need to be aware of what other firms are doing or might do is to be contrasted with lack of interdependence in other market structures. In a perfectly competitive (PC) market there is zero interdependence because no firm is large enough to affect market price. All firms in a *PC* market are price takers, as current market selling price can be followed predictably to maximize short-term profits. In a monopoly, there are no competitors to be concerned about. In a monopolistically-competitive market, each firm's effects on market conditions is so negligible as to be safely ignored by competitors.

Non-Price Competition: Oligopolies tend to compete on terms other than price. Loyalty schemes, advertisement, and product differentiation are all examples of non-price competition.

Modelling

There is no single model describing the operation of an oligopolistic market. The variety and complexity of the models is because you can have two to 10 firms competing on the basis of price, quantity, technological innovations, marketing, advertising and reputation. Fortunately, there are a series of simplified models that attempt to describe market behaviour by considering certain circumstances. Some of the better-known models are the dominant firm model, the Cournot-Nash model, the Bertrand model and the kinked demand model.

Cournot-Nash Model

The Cournot-Nash model is the simplest oligopoly model. The model assumes that there are two "equally positioned firms"; the firms compete on the basis of quantity rather than price and each firm makes an "output decision assuming that the other firm's behaviour is fixed." The market demand curve is assumed to be linear and marginal costs are constant. To find the Cournot-Nash equilibrium one determines how each firm reacts to a change in the output of the other firm. The path to equilibrium is a series of actions and reactions. The pattern continues until a point is reached where neither firm desires "to change what it is doing, given how it believes the other firm will react to any change."

The equilibrium is the intersection of the two firm's reaction functions. The reaction function shows how one firm reacts to the quantity choice of the other firm. For example, assume that the firm 1's demand function is $P = (M - Q_2) - Q_1$ where Q_2 is the quantity produced by the other firm and Q_1 is the amount produced by firm 1, and M=60 is the market. Assume that marginal cost is $C_M=12$. Firm 1 wants to know its maximizing quantity and price. Firm 1 begins the process by following the profit maximization rule of equating marginal revenue to marginal costs. Firm 1's total revenue function is $R_T = Q_1 P = Q_1(M - Q_2 - Q_1) = M Q_1 - Q_1 Q_2 - Q_1^2$. The marginal revenue function is $R_M = \frac{\partial R_T}{\partial Q_1} = M - Q_2 - 2Q_1$.

$$R_M = C_M$$
$$M - Q_2 - 2Q_1 = C_M$$
$$2Q_1 = (M-C_M) - Q_2$$

$Q_1 = (M-C_M)/2 - Q_2/2 = 24 - 0.5\ Q_2$ [1.1]

$Q_2 = 2(M-C_M) - 2Q_2 = 96 - 2\ Q_1$ [1.2]

Equation 1.1 is the reaction function for firm 1. Equation 1.2 is the reaction function for firm 2.

To determine the Cournot-Nash equilibrium you can solve the equations simultaneously. The equilibrium quantities can also be determined graphically. The equilibrium solution would be at the intersection of the two reaction functions. Note that if you graph the functions the axes represent quantities. The reaction functions are not necessarily symmetric. The firms may face differing cost functions in which case the reaction functions would not be identical nor would the equilibrium quantities.

Bertrand Model

The Bertrand model is essentially the Cournot-Nash model except the strategic variable is price rather than quantity.

The model assumptions are:

- There are two firms in the market
- They produce a homogeneous product
- They produce at a constant marginal cost
- Firms choose prices P_A and P_B simultaneously
- Firms outputs are perfect substitutes
- Sales are split evenly if $P_A = P_B$

The only Nash equilibrium is $P_A = P_B = MC$.

Neither firm has any reason to change strategy. If the firm raises prices it will lose all its customers. If the firm lowers price $P < MC$ then it will be losing money on every unit sold.

The Bertrand equilibrium is the same as the competitive result. Each firm will produce where P = marginal costs and there will be zero profits. A generalization of the Bertrand model is the Bertrand-Edgeworth Model that allows for capacity constraints and more general cost functions.

Kinked Demand Curve Model

According to this model, each firm faces a demand curve kinked at the existing price. The conjectural assumptions of the model are; if the firm raises its price above the current existing price, competitors will not follow and the acting firm will lose market share and second if a firm lowers prices below the existing price then their competitors will follow to retain their market share and the firm's output will increase only marginally.

If the assumptions hold then:

- The firm's marginal revenue curve is discontinuous (or rather, not differentiable), and has a gap at the kink
- For prices above the prevailing price the curve is relatively elastic
- For prices below the point the curve is relatively inelastic

The gap in the marginal revenue curve means that marginal costs can fluctuate without changing equilibrium price and quantity. Thus prices tend to be rigid.

Examples

In industrialized economies, barriers to entry have resulted in oligopolies forming in many sectors, with unprecedented levels of competition fueled by increasing globalization. Market shares in an oligopoly are typically determined by product development and advertising. For example, there are now only a small number of manufacturers of civil passenger aircraft, though Brazil (Embraer) and Canada (Bombardier) have participated in the small passenger aircraft market sector. Oligopolies have also arisen in heavily-regulated markets such as wireless communications: in some areas only two or three providers are licensed to operate.

Australia

- Most media outlets are owned either by News Corporation, Time Warner, or by Fairfax Media
- Grocery retailing is dominated by Coles Group and Woolworths.
- Banking is dominated by ANZ, Westpac, NAB, and Commonwealth Bank. To an extent this oligopoly is enshrined in law in what is known as the "Four pillars policy", in order to ensure the stability of Australia's banking system.
- Most of the telecommunications in Australia is delivered by Telstra or Optus. Other brands are virtual network operators (VNO).

Canada

- Six companies (Royal Bank of Canada, Toronto Dominion Bank, Bank of Nova Scotia, Bank of Montreal, Canadian Imperial Bank of Commerce and National Bank of Canada) control the banking industry.

- As of 2008, three companies (Rogers Wireless, Bell Mobility and Telus Mobility) share over 94% of Canada's wireless market.
- 4 companies control the internet service provider market, (Rogers Communications, Bell Canada, Telus, Shaw Communications)
- 8 companies control the oil and gas market, (Husky Energy, Imperial Oil, Nexen, Petro-Canada, Shell Canada, Suncor Energy, Syncrude Canada, Talisman Energy)

India

- The petroleum and gas industry is dominated by Indian Oil, Bharat Petroleum, Hindustan Petroleum and Reliance.
- Most of the telecommunication in India is dominated by Airtel, Vodafone, Idea, Reliance

European Union

- The VHF Data Link market as air-ground part of aeronautical communications is controlled by ARINC and SITA, commonly known as the organisations providing communication services for the exchange of data between air-ground applications in the Commission Regulation (EC) No 29/2009.

United Kingdom

- Five banks (Barclays, Halifax, HSBC, Lloyds TSB and Natwest) dominate the UK banking sector, they were accused of being an oligopoly by the relative newcomer Virgin bank.
- Four companies (Tesco, Sainsbury's, Asda and Morrisons) share 74.4% of the grocery market.
- The detergent market is dominated by two players, Unilever and Procter & Gamble.
- Six utilities (EDF Energy, Centrica, RWE npower, E.on, Scottish Power and Scottish and Southern Energy) share 99% of the retail electricity market.

United States

- Many media industries today are essentially oligopolies.
  - o Six movie studios receive almost 87% of American film revenues.
  - o The television and high speed internet industry is mostly an oligopoly of seven companies: The Walt Disney Company, CBS Corporation, Viacom, Comcast, Hearst Corporation, Time Warner, and News Corporation.

  - o Four wireless providers (AT&T Mobility, Verizon Wireless, T-Mobile, Sprint Nextel) control 89% of the cellular telephone service market. This is not to be confused with cellular telephone manufacturing, an integral portion of the cellular telephone market as a whole.
- Healthcare insurance in the United States consists of very few insurance companies controlling major market share in most states. For example, California's insured population of 20 million is the most competitive in the nation and 44% of that market is dominated by two insurance companies, Anthem and Kaiser Permanente.
- Anheuser-Busch and MillerCoors control about 80% of the beer industry.
- In March 2012, the United States Department of Justice announced that it would sue six major publishers for price fixing in the sale of electronic books. The accused publishers are Apple, Simon & Schuster Inc, Hachette Book Group, Penguin Group, Macmillan, and HarperCollins Publishers.

Worldwide

- The accountancy market is controlled by Price Waterhouse Coopers, KPMG, Deloitte Touche Tohmatsu, and Ernst & Young (commonly known as the Big Four)
- Three leading food processing companies, Kraft Foods, PepsiCo and Nestlé, together achieve a large proportion of global processed food sales. These three companies are often used as an example of "Rule of three", which states that markets often become an oligopoly of three large firms.
- Boeing and Airbus have a duopoly over the airliner market.
- General Electric, Pratt and Whitney and Rolls-Royce plc own more than 50% of the marketshare in the airliner engine market.
- Three credit rating agencies (Standard & Poor's, Moody's, and Fitch Group) dominate their market and extend their crucial importance into the financial sector.
- Nestlé, The Hershey Company and Mars, Incorporated together make most of the candy made worldwide.
- Microsoft, Sony, and Nintendo dominate the video game console market.

Demand Curve

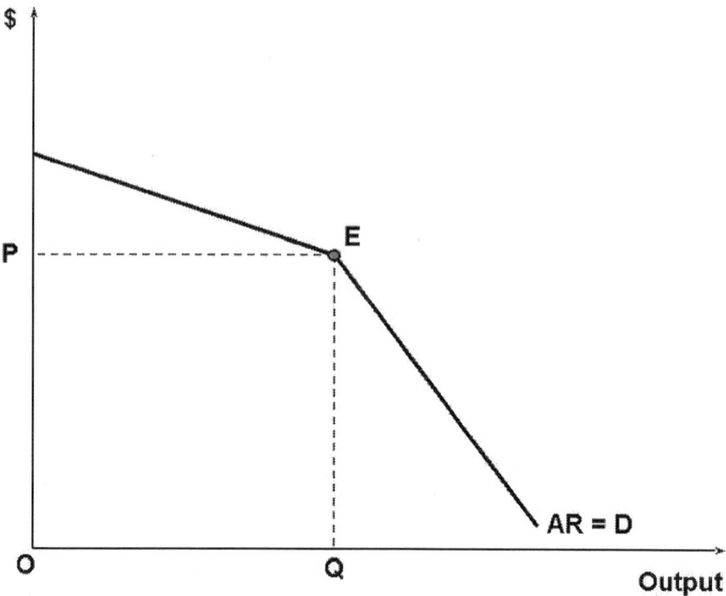

Figure: *Above the kink, demand is relatively elastic because all other firms' prices remain unchanged. Below the kink, demand is relatively inelastic because all other firms will introduce a similar price cut, eventually leading to a price war. Therefore, the best option for the oligopolist is to produce at point E which is the equilibrium point and the kink point. This is a theoretical model proposed in 1947, which has failed to receive conclusive evidence for support.*

In an oligopoly, firms operate under imperfect competition. With the fierce price competitiveness created by this sticky-upwarddemand curve, firms use non-price competition in order to accrue greater revenue and market share.

"Kinked" demand curves are similar to traditional demand curves, as they are downward-sloping. They are distinguished by a hypothesized convex bend with a discontinuity at the bend–"kink". Thus the first derivative at that point is undefined and leads to a jump discontinuity in the marginal revenue curve.

Classical economic theory assumes that a profit-maximizing producer with some market power (either due to oligopoly or monopolistic competition) will set marginal costs equal to marginal revenue. This idea can be envisioned graphically by the intersection of an upward-sloping marginal cost curve and a downward-sloping marginal revenue curve (because the more one sells, the lower the price must be, so the less a producer earns per unit). In classical theory, any change in the marginal cost structure (how much it costs to make each additional unit) or the marginal revenue structure (how much people will pay for each additional unit) will be immediately reflected in a new price and/or quantity sold of the item. This result does not occur if a "kink" exists. Because of this jump discontinuity in the marginal revenue curve, marginal costs could change without necessarily changing the price or quantity.

The motivation behind this kink is the idea that in an oligopolistic or monopolistically competitive market, firms will not raise their prices because even a small price increase will lose many customers. This is because competitors will generally ignore price increases, with the hope of gaining a larger market share as a result of now having comparatively lower prices.

However, even a large price decrease will gain only a few customers because such an action will begin a price war with other firms. The curve is therefore more price-elastic for price increases and less so for price decreases. Firms will often enter the industry in the long run.

Competition Law Theory

Competition law theory covers the strands of thought relating to competition law or antitrust policy.

Classical Perspective

The classical perspective on competition was that certain agreements and business practice could be an unreasonable restraint on the individual liberty of tradespeople to carry on their livelihoods. Restraints were judged as permissible or not by courts as new cases appeared and in the light of changing business circumstances. Hence the courts found specific categories of agreement, specific clauses, to fall foul of their doctrine on economic fairness, and they did not contrive an overarching conception of market power. Earlier theorists like Adam Smith rejected any monopoly power on this basis.

"A monopoly granted either to an individual or to a trading company has the same effect as a secret in trade or manufactures. The monopolists, by keeping the market constantly under-stocked, by never fully supplying the effectual demand, sell their commodities much above the natural price, and raise their emoluments, whether they consist in wages or profit, greatly above their natural rate."

In *The Wealth of Nations* (1776) Adam Smith also pointed out the cartel problem, but did not advocate legal measures to combat them.

"People of the same trade seldom meet together, even for merriment and diversion, but the conversation ends in a conspiracy against the public, or in some contrivance to raise prices. It is impossible indeed to prevent such meetings, by any law which either could be executed, or would be consistent with liberty and justice. But though the law cannot hinder people of the same trade from sometimes assembling together, it ought to do nothing to facilitate such assemblies; much less to render them necessary."

Smith also rejected the very existence of, not just dominant and abusive corporations, but corporations at all.

By the latter half of the nineteenth century it had become clear that large firms had become a fact of the market economy. John Stuart Mill's approach was laid down in his treatise *On Liberty* (1859).

"Again, trade is a social act. Whoever undertakes to sell any description of goods to the public, does what affects the interest of other persons, and of society in general; and thus his conduct, in principle, comes within the jurisdiction of society... both the cheapness and the good quality of commodities are most effectually provided for by leaving the producers and sellers perfectly free, under the sole check of equal freedom to the buyers for supplying themselves elsewhere. This is the so-called doctrine of Free Trade, which rests on grounds different from, though equally solid with, the principle of individual liberty asserted in this Essay. Restrictions on trade, or on production for purposes of trade, are indeed restraints; and all restraint, qua restraint, is an evil..."

Neo-Classical Synthesis

After Mill, there was a shift in economic theory, which emphasised a more precise and theoretical model of competition. A simple neo-classical model of free markets holds that production and distribution of goods and services in competitive free markets maximizes social welfare. This model assumes that new firms can freely enter markets and compete with existing firms, or to use legal language, there are no barriers to entry. By this term economists mean something very specific, that competitive free markets deliver allocative, productive and dynamic efficiency. Allocative efficiency is also known as Pareto efficiency after the Italian economist Vilfredo Pareto and means that resources in an economy over the long run will go precisely to those who are willing and able to pay for them. Because rational producers will keep producing and selling, and buyers will keep buying up to the last marginal unit of possible output - or alternatively rational producers will be reduce their output to the margin at which buyers will buy the same amount as produced - there is no waste, the greatest number wants of the greatest number of people become satisfied and utility is perfected because resources can no longer be reallocated to make anyone better off without making someone else worse off; society has achieved allocative efficiency. Productive efficiency simply means that society is making as much as it can. Free markets are meant to reward those who work hard, and therefore those who will put society's resources towards the frontier of its possible production. Dynamic efficiency refers to the idea that business which constantly competes must research, create and innovate to keep its share of consumers. This traces to Austrian-American political scientist Joseph Schumpeter's notion that a "perennial gale of creative destruction" is ever sweeping through capitalist economies, driving enterprise at the market's mercy. Contrasting with the allocatively, productively and dynamically efficient market model are monopolies, oligopolies, and cartels. When only one or a few firms exist in the market, and there is no credible threat of the entry of competing firms, prices raise above the competitive level, to either a monopolistic or oligopolistic equilibrium price. Production is also decreased, further decreasing social welfare by creating a deadweight loss. Sources of this market power are said to include the existence of externalities, barriers to entry of the market, and the free rider problem. Markets may fail to be efficient for a variety of reasons, so the exception of competition law's intervention to the rule of *laissez faire* is justified. Orthodox economists fully acknowledge that perfect competition is seldom observed in the real world, and so aim for what is called "workable competition". This follows the theory that if one cannot achieve the ideal, then go for the second best option by using the law to tame market operation where it can.

Chicago School

A group of economists and lawyers, who are largely associated with the University of Chicago, advocate an approach to competition law guided by the proposition that some actions that were originally considered to be anticompetitive could actually promote competition. The US Supreme Court has used the Chicago School approach in several recent cases. One view of the Chicago School approach to antitrust is found in United States Circuit Court of Appeals Judge Richard Posner's books *Antitrust law* and *Economic Analysis of Law* Posner once worked in the Department of Justice's antitrust division, has long been a professor at the University of Chicago Law School, and is likely the most widely cited antitrust scholar and jurist in the United States.

Robert Bork was highly critical of court decisions on United States antitrust law in a series of law review articles and his book *The Antitrust Paradox*. Bork argued that both the original intention of antitrust laws and economic efficiency was pursuit *only* of consumer welfare, the protection of competition rather than competitors. Furthermore, only a few acts should be prohibited, namely cartels that fix prices and divide markets, mergers that create monopolies, and dominant firms pricing predatorily, while allowing such practices as vertical agreements and price discrimination on the grounds that it did not harm consumers. Running through the different critiques of US antitrust policy is the common theme that government interference in the operation of free markets does more harm than good. "The only cure for bad theory", writes Bork, "is better theory". The late Harvard Law School Professor Phillip Areeda, who favours more aggressive antitrust policy, in at least one Supreme Court case challenged Robert Bork's preference for non intervention.

Other Critiques

Some economic libertarians have criticised competition law in its entirety, challenging the legitimacy of action against price fixing and cartels.

Policy Developments

Anti-cartel enforcement is a key focus of competition law enforcement policy. In the United States the Antitrust Criminal Penalty Enhancement and Reform Act 2004 raised the maximum imprisonment term for price fixing from three to ten years, and the maximum fine from $10 million to $100 million. In 2007 British Airways and Korean Air pleaded guilty to fixing cargo and passenger flight prices.

These actions complement the private enforcement which has always been an important feature of United States antitrust law. The United States Supreme Court summarised why Congress allows punitive damages in *Hawaii v. Standard Oil.*

"Every violation of the antitrust laws is a blow to the free-enterprise system envisaged by Congress. This system depends on strong competition for its health and vigor, and strong competition depends, in turn, on compliance with antitrust legislation. In enacting these laws, Congress had many means at its disposal to penalize violators. It could have, for example, required violators to compensate federal, state, and local governments for the estimated damage to their respective economies caused by the violations. But, this remedy was not selected. Instead, Congress chose to permit all persons to sue to recover three times their actual damages every time they were injured in their business or property by an antitrust violation." In the EU, the Modernisation Regulation 1/2003 means that the European Commission is no longer the only body capable of public enforcement of European Community competition law. This was done in order to facilitate quicker resolution of competition-related inquiries. In 2005 the Commission issued a Green Paper on *Damages actions for the breach of the EC antitrust rules*, which suggested ways of making private damages claims against cartels easier.

Monopsony

In economics, a monopsony is a market form in which only one buyer interfaces with many sellers.

The microeconomic theory of imperfect competition assumes the monopsonist can dictate terms to its suppliers, as the only purchaser of a good or service, much in the same manner that a monopolist is said to control the market for its buyers in a monopoly, in which only one seller faces many buyers. In addition to its use in microeconomic theory, *monopsony* and *monopsonist* are descriptive terms often used to describe a market where a single buyer substantially controls the market as the major purchaser of goods and services. Examples include the military industry and the space industry.

Etymology

The term was first introduced by Joan Robinson in her influential book, *The Economics of Imperfect Competition*, published in 1933. Robinson credited classics scholar Bertrand Hallward at the University of Cambridge with coining the term.

Examples

A single-payer universal health care system, in which the government is the only "buyer" of health care services, is an example of a monopsony.

During the Cold War, the defence industry in the United States had a monopsonistic element in respect to major defence projects; strategic considerations limited the sole buyer (the United States Department of Defence) to procuring its needs from domestic suppliers, while there were virtually no other parties other than DoD with the interest or resources to purchase many of the suppliers' products. In the post-Cold War world, this has weakened somewhat, as more states have the need and ability to purchase sophisticated military equipment, and DoD is freer to purchase from foreign (particularly European) suppliers. An interesting example of a situation where both a monopoly and a monopsony exist (a bilateral monopoly) involves the market for nuclear-powered aircraft carriers:

the monopsony being with only one purchaser (the United States Navy) and the monopoly being with only one producer (Huntington Ingalls Industries, as their Newport News Shipbuilding division is the only place with the capacity to manufacture, overhaul, and decommission them).

It has also been argued that Walmart, in the United States, functions as a monopsony in certain market segments, as its buying power for a given item may dwarf the remaining market. Another possible monopsony could develop in the exchange between the food industry and farmers.

Prior to 2011, the state of Texas had almost total control over the K-12 textbooks in the whole US due to its market dominance. Although there are over 1,000 independent school districts in the state, the Texas Education Agency formerly set the curriculum for each course that all districts must follow, and therefore also formerly approved which textbooks could be used.

Combined with Texas' large size, in the past Texas' textbook purchases far outweighed those of other buyers. Rule changes in 2011 gave local school boards authority to choose other textbooks, allowing the free market a chance to reassert itself.

Overview

The term "monopsony power", in a manner similar to "monopoly power", is used by economists as a shorthand reference to buyers who face an upwardly sloping supply curve but that are not the only consumer; alternative terms are oligopsony or monopsonistic competition.

Static Monopsony in a Labour Market

The standard, textbook monopsony model refers to static, partial equilibrium in a labour market with just one employer who pays the same wage to all its workers.

This model assumes that the employer is a firm facing an upward-sloping *labour supply curve* (as generally contrasted with an infinitely elastic labour supply curve), represented by the S blue curve in the diagram on the right.

This curve relates the wage paid, w, to the level of employment, L, and is denoted as the increasing function $w(L)$.

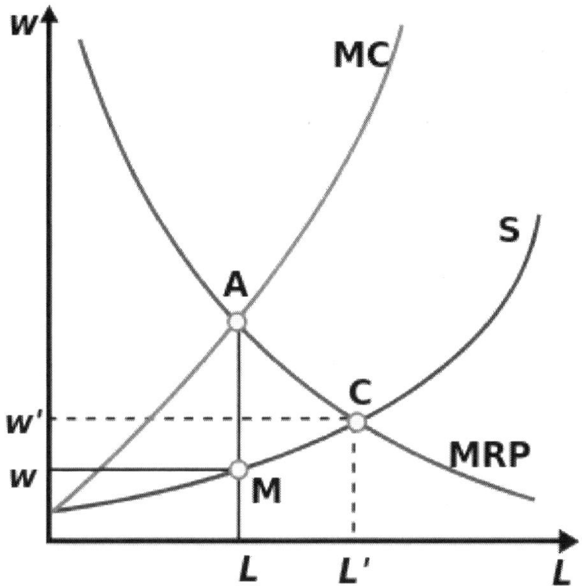

Figure: *A monopsonist employer maximizes profits with employment* L, *that equates demand, given by the marginal revenue product (*MRP*) curve, to marginal cost* MC, *at point* A. *The wage is then determined on the supply curve, at point* M, *and is equal to* w. *By contrast, a competitive labour market would reach equilibrium at point* C, *where supply* S *equals demand. This would lead to employment* L' *and wage* w'.

Total labour costs are then given by $w(L)\cdot L$. Assume now that the firm has a total revenue *R*, which increases with *L* according to the concave function $R(L)$. The firm wants to choose *L* to maximize profits, *P*, which are given by:

$$P(L) = R(L) - w(L)\cdot L \ .$$

This leads to the first-order condition:

$$P'(L) = (R(L) - w(L)\cdot L)'$$

Start solving the derivative of the right hand side with the sum rule:

$$P'(L) = R'(L) - (w(L)\cdot L)'$$

Use the Product rule : $(f\cdot g)' = f'\cdot g + f\cdot g'$ on the right hand side where f=w(L) and g=L:

$$P'(L) = R'(L) - (w(L)'\cdot L + w(L)\cdot L')$$

Since : $L' = (L^1)' = 1L^0 = 1$,

$$P'(L) = R'(L) - (w(L)' \cdot L + w(L) \cdot 1)$$

$$P'(L) = R'(L) - w(L)' \cdot L - w(L)$$

Maximum profits, P_{max}, occurs where $P'(L) = 0$, since that is where a local maximum of the profit curve occurs, so set left hand side equal to 0:

$$0 = R'(L) - w(L)' \cdot L - w(L)$$

Subtracting to put all R terms on one side and all w terms on the other:

$$-R'(L) = -w(L)' \cdot L - w(L)$$

Multiply both sides by -1:

$$R'(L) = w(L)' \cdot L + w(L)$$

The left-hand side of this expression, $R'(L)$, is the *marginal revenue product* of labour (roughly, the extra revenue produced by an extra worker) and is represented by the red *MRP* curve in the diagram. The right-hand side is the *marginal cost* of labour (roughly, the extra cost due to an extra worker) and is represented by the green *MC* curve in the diagram. It should be noticed that this marginal cost is *higher* than the wage $w(L)$ paid to the new worker by the amount

$$w'(L)L \ .$$

This is because the firm has to increase the wage paid to all the workers it already employs whenever it hires an extra worker. In the diagram, this leads to an *MC* curve that is *above* the supply curve *S*.

The first-order condition for maximum profit is then satisfied at point *A* of the diagram, where the *MC* and *MRP* curves intersect. This determines the profit-maximising employment as *L* on the horizontal axis. The corresponding wage *w* is then obtained from the supply curve, through point *M*.

The monopsonistic equilibrium at *M* should now be contrasted with the equilibrium that would obtain under competitive conditions. Suppose a competitor employer entered the market and offered a wage higher than that at *M*. Then every employee of the first employer would choose instead to work for the competitor. Moreover, the competitor would gain all the former profits of the first employer, minus a less-than-offsetting amount from the wage increase of the first employer's employees, plus profits arising from additional employees who decided to work in the market because of the wage increase. But the first employer would respond by offering an even higher wage, poaching the new rival's employees, and so forth. In other words, a group of perfectly competitive firms would be forced, through competition, to intersection *C* rather than *M*. Just as a monopoly is thwarted by the competition to win sales, minimizing prices and maximizing output, competition for employees between the employers in this case would maximize both wages and employment, as shown in the graph.

Welfare Implications

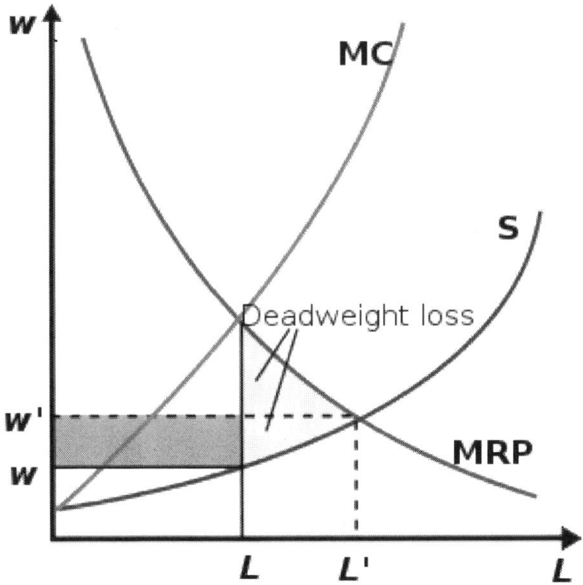

Figure: *The grey rectangle is a measure of the amount of economic welfare transferred from the workers to their employer(s) by monopsony power. The yellow triangle shows the* overall deadweight loss *inflicted on both groups by the monopsonistic restriction of employment. It is thus a measure of the* market failure *caused by monopsony.*

The lower employment and wages caused by monopsony power have two distinct effects on the economic welfare of the people involved. First, it redistributes welfare away from workers and to their employer(s). Secondly, it reduces the aggregate (or social) welfare enjoyed by both groups taken together, as the employers' net gain is smaller than the loss inflicted on workers.

The diagram on the right illustrates both effects, using the standard approach based on the notion of economic surplus. According to this notion, the workers' economic surplus (or net gain from the exchange) is given by the area between the S curve and the horizontal line corresponding to the wage, up to the employment level. Similarly, the employers' surplus is the area between the horizontal line corresponding to the wage and the *MRP* curve, up to the employment level. The *social* surplus is then the sum of these two areas.

Following such definitions, the grey rectangle, in the diagram, is the part of the competitive social surplus that has been redistributed from the workers to their employer(s) under monopsony. By contrast, the yellow triangle is the part of the competitive social surplus that has been lost by *both* parties, as a result of the monopsonistic restriction of employment. This is a net social loss and is called *deadweight loss.* It is a measure of the market failure caused by monopsony power, through a wasteful misallocation of resources.

As the diagram suggests, the size of both effects increases with the difference between the marginal revenue product *MRP* and the market wage determined on the supply curve S. This difference corresponds to the vertical side of the yellow triangle, and can be expressed as a proportion of the market wage, according to the formula:

$$e = \frac{R'(w) - w}{w} \ .$$

The ratio e has been called the rate of exploitation, and it can be easily shown that it equals the reciprocal of the elasticity of the labour supply curve faced by the firm. Thus the rate of exploitation is zero under competitive conditions, when this elasticity tends to infinity. Empirical estimates of e by various means are a common feature of the applied literature devoted to the measurement of observed monopsony power.

Finally, it is important to notice that, while the gray-area redistribution effect could be reversed by fiscal policy (i.e., taxing employers and transferring the tax revenue to the workers), this is not so for the yellow-area deadweight loss.

The market failure can only be addressed in one of two ways: either by breaking up the monopsony through anti-trust intervention, or by regulating the wage policy of firms. The most common kind of regulation is a binding minimum wage higher than the monopsonistic wage.

Minimum Wage

A binding minimum wage can be introduced either by law or through collective bargaining, and its possible effects in a special case are shown in the diagram on the right.

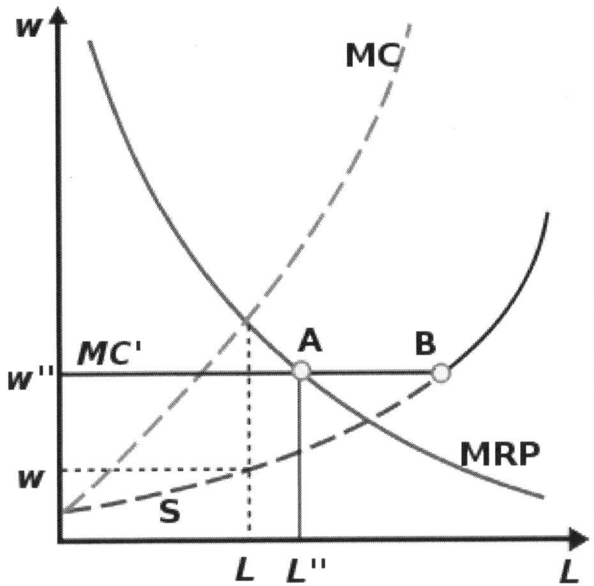

Figure: *With a binding minimum wage of* w" *the marginal cost to the firm becomes the horizontal black* MC' *line, and the firm maximises profits at* A *with a higher employment* L". *However in this example, the minimum wage is higher than the competitive one, leading to* involuntary unemployment *equal to the segment* AB.

Here the minimum wage is *w"*, higher than the monopsonistic *w*. At this given wage the firm can now hire all the workers it wants, up to the supply curve, so that in the relevant employment range its marginal cost of labour becomes effectively constant and equal to *w"*,, as shown by the new black horizontal line *MC'*. Hence the firm maximizes profits at the new intersection point *A*, choosing the employment level *L"*, which is higher than the monopsonistic level *L*. As the reader can check, the rate of exploitation has been reduced to zero.

More generally, a binding minimum wage modifies the form of the supply curve faced by the firm, which becomes:

$$w = \begin{cases} w_{min}, & \text{if } w_{min} \geq w(L) \\ w(L), & \text{if } w_{min} \leq w(L) \end{cases}$$

where $w(L)$ is the original supply curve and w_{min} is the minimum wage. The new curve has thus a horizontal first branch and a kink at the point

$$w(L) = w_{min}$$

as is shown in the diagram by the kinked black curve *MC' S*. The resulting equilibria (the profit-maximizing choices that rational companies will make) can then fall into one of three classes according to the value taken by the minimum wage, as shown by the following table:

Profit Maximizing Choice In A MonopsonisticLabor Market Depends Upon The Minimum Wage Level		
	Minimum Wage	Resulting Equilibrium
First Case	< than monopsony wage	unchanged from monopsony
Second Case	> monopsony wage but <= than competitive wage	at kink of supply curve
Third Case	> competitive wage	at intersection where minimum wage equals *MRP*

As it is now seen, the example illustrated by the diagram belongs to the third regime. As a result, there is an excess supply of labour – i.e. *involuntary unemployment* – equal to the segment *AB*. So, although the exploitation rate has vanished, there is still a deadweight loss to society. This illustrates the problems that may arise when the proper level of the binding minimum wage is not exactly known, or cannot be enforced for political reasons.

Yet, even when it is sub-optimal, a minimum wage higher than the market rate raises the level of employment anyway. This is a highly remarkable result, because it only follows under monopsony. Indeed, under competitive conditions any minimum wage higher than the market rate would actually *reduce* employment, according to classical economic models. Thus, spotting the effects on employment of newly introduced minimum wage regulations is among the indirect ways economists use to pin down monopsony power in selected labour markets.

Wage Discrimination

Just like a monopolist, a monopsonistic employer may find that its profits are maximized if it *discriminates* prices. In this case this means paying different wages to different groups of workers even if their MRP is the same, with lower wages paid to the workers who have a lower elasticity of supply of their labour to the firm. Researchers have used this fact to explain at least part of the observed wage differentials whereby women often earn less than men, even after controlling for observed productivity differentials. Robinson's original application of monopsony (1938) was developed to explain wage differentials between equally productive women and men. Ransom and Oaxaca (2004) found that women's wage elasticity is lower than that of men for employees at a grocery store chain in Missouri, controlling for other factors typically associated with wage determination. Ransom and Lambson (2011) found that female teachers are paid less than male teachers due to differences in labour market mobility constraints facing women and men. Some authors have argued informally that, while this is so for *market* supply, the reverse may somehow be true of the supply to individual firms. In particular, Manning and others have shown that, in the case of the UK Equal Pay Act, implementation has led to higher employment of women. Since the Act was effectively minimum wage legislation for women, this might perhaps be interpreted as a symptom of monopsonistic discrimination.

Dynamic Problems

In many real-world situations a monopsonist firm will have to maximise its profits *through time*, rather than instantaneously as in the previous static model. In all such cases, any short-run outcomes will have to be balanced against longer-run ones, and the resulting equilibrium may differ. The simplest dynamic model to bring out this idea, used in Boal and Ransom (1997), is one where the supply of labour to the firm reacts to wage changes with a lag, due for instance to information costs and search behaviour. Assume hence that the supply function has a distributed-lag specification, leading to:

$$L_t = L(w_t, L_{t-1}) ,$$

where the subscript refers to the time period and L is increasing in both arguments. Inverting this function gives:

$$w_t = w_t(L_t, L_{t-1}) ,$$

with

$$\frac{\partial w_t}{\partial L_t} \geq 0 \quad \text{and} \quad \frac{\partial w_t}{\partial L_{t-1}} \leq 0 .$$

If the firm has a time-discount rate r, the present value of profits is now given by:

$$\sum_{t=1}^{\infty} \left[R_t(L_t) - w_t(L_t, L_{t-1}) L_t \right] \left(\frac{1}{1+r} \right)^{t-1} .$$

The tth first-order condition to maximise this present value is:

$$\frac{dR_t}{dL_t} - w_t - \frac{\partial w_t}{\partial L_t} L_t - \frac{\partial w_{t+1}}{\partial L_t} \frac{L_{t+1}}{1+r} = 0 \ .$$

Define next the short-run simultaneous and lagged inverse supply elasticities respectively as:

$$\epsilon_{SR}^{-1} \overset{\text{def}}{=} \frac{\partial w_t}{\partial L_t} \frac{L_t}{w_t}, \qquad \epsilon_{SRL}^{-1} \overset{\text{def}}{=} \frac{\partial w_{t+1}}{\partial L_t} \frac{L_t}{w_{t+1}} \ .$$

Now, assume these elasticities to be constant over time. Assume further a steady state, with $L_t = L_{t+1}$ and $w_t = w_{t+1}$. Then the first-order condition gives the exploitation rate as:

$$e_t \overset{\text{def}}{=} \frac{MRP_t - w_t}{w_t} = \epsilon_{SR}^{-1} + \frac{\epsilon_{SRL}^{-1}}{1+r} \ .$$

Finally, the steady-state long-run inverse elasticity, ϵ_{LR}^{-1}, is given by the sum of the two short-run inverse elasticities defined above, and so one has:

$$e_t = \epsilon_{SR}^{-1}\left(\frac{r}{1+r}\right) + \epsilon_{LR}^{-1}\left(\frac{1}{1+r}\right) .$$

The exploitation rate is thus a weighted average of the short- and long-run inverse supply elasticities, where the weight of the long-run one is much bigger, because r is much smaller than unity even when the discounting period is one year. It follows that, as the long-run (direct) supply elasticity of labour tends to be much higher than the short-run one, this very simple dynamic model predicts an exploitation rate which is much smaller than the one produced by static analysis. However, less simplified dynamic models tell less simple stories. Even the employment effect of minimum wages is not as clear cut as static models would have.

Empirical Problems

The simplified dynamics sketched above suggests that the frequent observation of short-run relative inelasticity of labour supply to individual firms may not be very relevant to the diagnosis of significant monopsony power. Efforts to measure the size of the exploitation rate in specific labour markets have hence taken various forms:

- direct measurement of wage and MRP
- estimates of the long-run supply elasticity of labour to firms
- cross-sectional comparisons of wages and employer concentration

- correlations between wages and workers' mobility
- structural estimation of equilibrium search models
- employment effects of minimum wages

The results of these empirical works are rarely unambiguous. However, even in cases such as coal miners or nurses, most US studies suggest rates of exploitation probably lower than marginal tax rates on workers' incomes, or union relative wage effects. The better documented instances of significant exploitation are found in the probably rare cases of explicit collusion, such as US baseball before the reserve clause.

Sources of Labour Monopsony Power

The simpler explanation of monopsony power in labour markets is barriers to entry on the *demand* side. In all such cases, oligopsony would result from oligopoly in the product markets of the industries that use that type of labour as input. If the hypothesis was generally true, one would then find a positive statistical correlation between exploitation, on one side, and industry concentration and firm size on the other. However, numerous statistical studies document significant positive correlations between firm or establishment size and *wages*. These results, by themselves inconsistent with the oligopoly-oligopsony hypothesis, may be due to the prevalence of other factors, such as efficiency wages.

However, monopsony power might also be due to circumstances affecting entry of workers on the *supply* side, directly reducing the elasticity of labour supply to firms. Paramount among these are moving costs for workers, which are also a cause of differentiation among potential employees, possibly leading to discrimination. But a similar effect might also be produced by all the institutional factors that limit labour mobility between firms, including job protection legislation. The vetting of employees in the government or the defence sector is another source of monopsonistic competition, as are requirements for professional certification, for example, a medical degree. Finally, as already noticed, a significant reduction in the short-run elasticity of supply may come from information costs and search behaviour.

An alternative that has been suggested as a source of monopsony power is worker preferences over job characteristics (Bhaskar and To, 1999; Bhaskar, Manning and To, 2002). Such job characteristics can include distance from work, type of work, location, the social environment at work, etc. If different workers have different preferences, employers have local monopsony power over workers that strongly prefer working for them.

Finally, monopsony power will occur when the average revenue product of labour increases with the amount of labour employed, due to economies of scale.

In this case, the perfectly competitive solution (workers are paid their marginal revenue product) is not stable.

In the long run, the firm may set wages equal to the average revenue product of labour, or engage in wage discrimination, paying wages closer to marginal product to markets (or workers) with higher elasticity of supply.

Public Administration and Product Markets

The same or similar empirical difficulties dog attempts to identify significant monopsony in non-labour markets, and specifically in markets for intermediate goods bought as inputs by very large firms. Among the most likely US candidates, one finds in the literature:

- *trade in technological knowledge:* Rodriguez (1975)
- *tomatoes for tomato processing:* Just and Chern (1980)
- *beef for the beef packing industry:* Schroeter (1988)
- *western coal for electric utilities:* Atkinson and Kerkvliet (1989)
- *pulpwood and sawlogs:* Murray (1995)
- sophisticated weaponry (i.e. jet fighters, tanks, artillery, etc.)

A related issue is the role of monopsony power from the point of view of anti-trust policy affecting vertical integrations.

It has been argued that vertical integration by a monopsony – whereby the production of the previously bought input becomes an in-house operation – may reduce or eliminate the inefficiencies due to monopsonistic restriction of purchases.

In Australia, the Pharmaceutical Industry can be viewed as a kind of monopsony, as the Commonwealth government is the principal buyer of products through the Pharmaceutical Benefits Scheme (PBS).

In the US, journalists, including *Harper's* and the PBS program *Frontline*, have made the case that Wal-Mart is a monopsonist, dictating terms to suppliers, whilst at the same time a monopolist dictating terms to consumers — at least in certain market segments.

It has been argued that Apple has in some ways become a monopsonist in that it can dictate terms to suppliers of electronic components.

Cournot Competition

Cournot competition is an economic model used to describe an industry structure in which companies compete on the amount of output they will produce, which they decide on independently of each other and at the same time. It is named after Antoine AugustinCournot (1801–1877) who was inspired by observing competition in a spring water duopoly. It has the following features:

- There is more than one firm and all firms produce a homogeneous product, i.e. there is no product differentiation;
- Firms do not cooperate, i.e. there is no collusion;
- Firms have market power, i.e. each firm's output decision affects the good's price;
- The number of firms is fixed;
- Firms compete in quantities, and choose quantities simultaneously;
- The firms are economically rational and act strategically, usually seeking to maximize profit given their competitors' decisions.

An essential assumption of this model is the "not conjecture" that each firm aims to maximize profits, based on the expectation that its own output decision will not have an effect on the decisions of its rivals. Price is a commonly known decreasing function of total output. All firms know N, the total number of firms in the market, and take the output of the others as given. Each firm has a cost function $c_i(q_i)$. Normally the cost functions are treated as common knowledge. The cost functions may be the same or different among firms. The market price is set at a level such that demand equals the total quantity produced by all firms. Each firm takes the quantity set by its competitors as a given, evaluates its residual demand, and then behaves as a monopoly.

History

The state of equilibrium... is therefore *stable*; i.e. if either of the producers, misled as to his true interest, leaves it temporarily, he will be brought back to it.

—Antoine AugustinCournot, *Recherchessur les Principes Mathematiques de la Theorie des Richesses* (1838), translated by Bacon (1897).

Antoine Augustin Cournot (1801-1877) first outlined his theory of competition in his 1838 volume *Recherchessur les Principes-Mathematiques de la Theorie des Richesses* as a way of describing the competition with a market for spring water dominated by two suppliers (a duopoly). The model was one of a number that Cournot set out "explicitly and with mathematical precision" in the volume. Specifically, Cournot constructed profit functions for each firm, and then used partial differentiation to construct a function representing a firm's best response for given (exogenous) output levels of the other firm(s) in the market. He then showed that a stable equilibrium occurs where these functions intersect (i.e. the simultaneous solution of the best response functions of each firm).

The consequence of this is that in equilibrium, each firm's expectations of how other firms will act are shown to be correct; when all is revealed, no firm wants to change its output decision. This idea of stability was later taken up and built upon as a description of Nash equilibria, of which Cournotequilibria are a subset.

Graphically Finding the Cournot Duopoly Equilibrium

This section presents an analysis of the model with 2 firms and constant marginal cost.

p_1 = firm 1 price, p_2 = firm 2 price

q_1 = firm 1 quantity, q_2 = firm 2 quantity

c= marginal cost, identical for both firms

Equilibrium prices will be:

$$p_1 = p_2 = P(q_1 + q_2)$$

This implies that firm 1's profit is given by $\Pi_1 = q_1(P(q_1 + q_2) - c)$

- Calculate firm 1's residual demand: Suppose firm 1 believes firm 2 is producing quantity q_2. What is firm 1's optimal quantity? Consider the diagram 1. If firm 1 decides not to produce anything, then price is given by $P(0 + q_2) = P(q_2)$. If firm 1 produces $q_{1'}$ then price is given by $P(q_{1'} + q_2)$. More generally, for each quantity that firm 1 might decide to set, price is given by the curve $d_1(q_2)$. The curve $d_1(q_2)$ is called firm 1's residual demand; it gives all possible combinations of firm 1's quantity and price for a given value of q_2.
- Determine firm 1's optimum output: To do this we must find where marginal revenue equals marginal cost. Marginal cost (c) is assumed to be constant. Marginal revenue is a curve - $r_1(q_2)$ - with twice the slope of $d_1(q_2)$ and with the same vertical intercept. The point at which the two curves (and $r_1(q_2)$) intersect corresponds to quantity $q_{1''}(q_2)$. Firm 1's

optimum $q_{1''}(q_2)$, depends on what it believes firm 2 is doing. To find an equilibrium, we derive firm 1's optimum for other possible values of q_2. Diagram 2 considers two possible values of q_2. If $q_2 = 0$, then the first firm's residual demand is effectively the market demand, $d_1(0) = D$. The optimal solution is for firm 1 to choose the monopoly quantity; $q_{1''}(0) = q^m$ (q^m is monopoly quantity). If firm 2 were to choose the quantity corresponding to perfect competition, $q_2 = q^c$ such that $P(q^c) = c$, then firm 1's optimum would be to produce nil: $q_{1''}(q^c) = 0$. This is the point at which marginal cost intercepts the marginal revenue corresponding to $d_1(q^c)$.

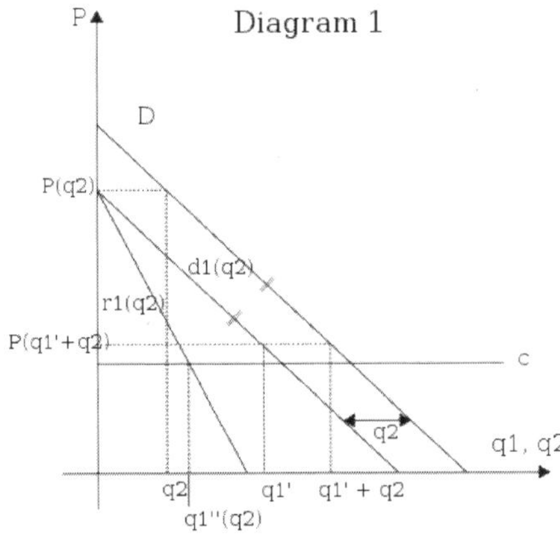

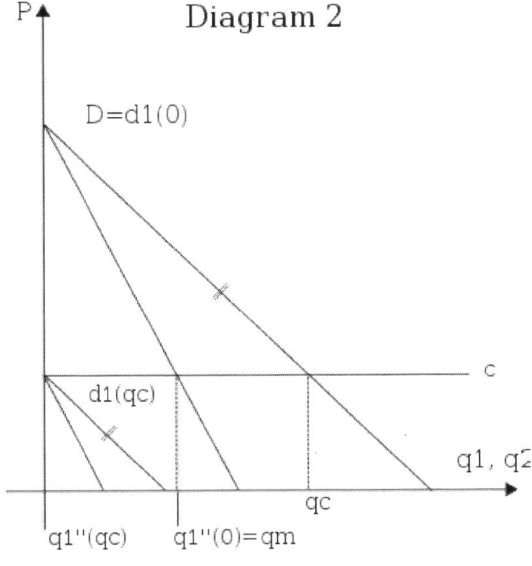

- It can be shown that, given the linear demand and constant marginal cost, the function $q_{1''}(q_2)$ is also linear. Because we have two points, we can draw the entire function $q_{1''}(q_2)$. Note the axis of the graphs has changed, The function $q_{1''}(q_2)$ is firm 1's reaction function, it gives firm 1's optimal choice for each possible choice by firm 2. In other words, it gives firm 1's choice given what it believes firm 2 is doing.

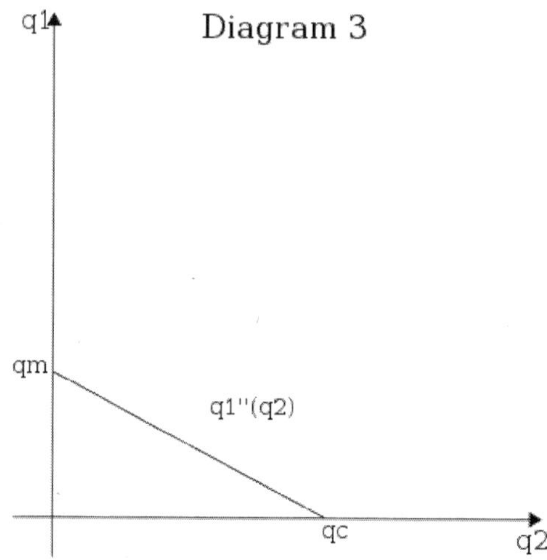

- The last stage in finding the Cournot equilibrium is to find firm 2's reaction function. In this case it is symmetrical to firm 1's as they have the same cost function. The equilibrium is the intersection point of the reaction curves.

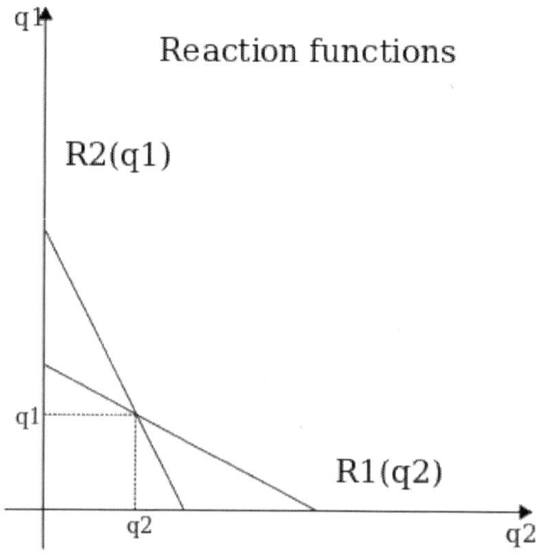

- The prediction of the model is that the firms will choose Nash equilibrium output levels.

Calculating the Equilibrium

In very general terms, let the price function for the (duopoly) industry be $P(q_1+q_2)$ and firm i have the cost structure $C_i(q_i)$. To calculate the Nash equilibrium, the best response functions of the firms must first be calculated.

The profit of firm i is revenue minus cost. Revenue is the product of price and quantity and cost is given by the firm's cost function, so profit is (as described above):

$\Pi_i = P(q_1+q_2)\cdot q_i - C_i(q_i)$.

The best response is to find the value of q_i that maximises Π_i given q_j, with $i \neq j$, i.e. given some output of the opponent firm, the output that maximises profit is found. Hence, the maximum of Π_i with respect to q_i is to be found. First take the derivative of Π_i with respect to q_i:

$$\frac{\partial \Pi_i}{\partial q_i} = \frac{\partial P(q_1+q_2)}{\partial q_i}\cdot q_i + P(q_1+q_2) - \frac{\partial C_i(q_i)}{\partial q_i}$$

Setting this to zero for maximization:

$$\frac{\partial \Pi_i}{\partial q_i} = \frac{\partial P(q_1+q_2)}{\partial q_i}\cdot q_i + P(q_1+q_2) - \frac{\partial C_i(q_i)}{\partial q_i} = 0$$

The values of q_i that satisfy this equation are the best responses. The Nash equilibria are where both q_1 and q_2 are best responses given those values of q_1 and q_2.

An Example

Suppose the industry has the following price structure: $P(q_1+q_2) = a-(q_1+q_2)$ The profit of firm i (with cost structure $C_i(q_i)$ such that $\frac{\partial^2 C_i(q_i)}{\partial q_i^2} = 0$ and $\frac{\partial C_i(q_i)}{\partial q_j} = 0, j \neq i$ for ease of computation) is:

$$\Pi_i = \big(a-(q_1+q_2)\big)\cdot q_i - C_i(q_i)$$

The maximization problem resolves to (from the general case):

$$\frac{\partial\big(a-(q_1+q_2)\big)}{\partial q_i}\cdot q_i + a-(q_1+q_2) - \frac{\partial C_i(q_i)}{\partial q_i} = 0$$

Without loss of generality, consider firm 1's problem:

$$\frac{\partial\left(a-(q_1+q_2)\right)}{\partial q_1}\cdot q_1 + a-(q_1+q_2)-\frac{\partial C_1(q_1)}{\partial q_1}=0$$

$$\Rightarrow -q_1 + a-(q_1+q_2)-\frac{\partial C_1(q_1)}{\partial q_1}=0$$

$$\Rightarrow q_1 = \frac{a-q_2-\frac{\partial C_1(q_1)}{\partial q_1}}{2}$$

By symmetry:

$$\Rightarrow q_2 = \frac{a-q_1-\frac{\partial C_2(q_2)}{\partial q_2}}{2}$$

These are the firms' best response functions. For any value of q_2, firm 1 responds best with any value of q_1 that satisfies the above.

In Nash equilibria, both firms will be playing best responses so solving the above equations simultaneously. Substituting for q_2 in firm 1's best response:

$$q_1 = \frac{a-\left(\frac{a-q_1-\frac{\partial C_2(q_2)}{\partial q_2}}{2}\right)-\frac{\partial C_1(q_1)}{\partial q_1}}{2}$$

$$\Rightarrow q_1^* = \frac{a+\frac{\partial C_2(q_2)}{\partial q_2}-2*\frac{\partial C_1(q_1)}{\partial q_1}}{3}$$

$$\Rightarrow q_2^* = \frac{a+\frac{\partial C_1(q_1)}{\partial q_1}-2^*\frac{\partial C_2(q_2)}{\partial q_2}}{3}$$

The symmetric Nash equilibrium is at (q_1^*, q_2^*). Making suitable assumptions for the partial derivatives (for example, assuming each firm's cost is a linear function of quantity and thus using the slope of that function in the calculation), the equilibrium quantities can be substituted in the assumed industry price structure

$P(q_1+q_2)=a-(q_1+q_2)$

to obtain the equilibrium market price.

Cournot Competition with Many Firms and the Cournot Theorem

For an arbitrary number of firms, $N > 1$, the quantities and price can be derived in a manner analogous to that given above. With linear demand and identical, constant marginal cost the equilibrium values are as follows: edit; we should specify the constants. Given the following results are these;

Market demand; $p(q) = a - bq = a - bQ = p(Q)$

Cost function; $c_i(q_i) = cq_i$, for all i

$$q_i = Q / N = \frac{a-c}{b(N+1)},$$

which is each individual firm's output

$$\sum q_i = Nq = \frac{N(a-c)}{b(N+1)},$$

which is total industry output

$$p = a - b(Nq) = \frac{a+Nc}{N+1},$$

which is the market clearing price, and

$$\Pi_i = \left(\frac{a-c}{N+1}\right)^2 \left(\frac{1}{b}\right),$$ which is each individual firm's profit.

The Cournot Theorem then states that, in absence of fixed costs of production, as the number of firms in the market, N, goes to infinity, market output, Nq, goes to the competitive level and the price converges to marginal cost.

$$\lim_{N \to \infty} p = c$$

Hence with many firms a Cournot market approximates a perfectly competitive market. This result can be generalized to the case of firms with different cost structures (under appropriate restrictions) and non-linear demand. When the market is characterized by fixed costs of production, however, we can endogenize the number of competitors imagining that firms enter in the market until their profits are zero. In our linear example with N firms, when fixed costs for each firm are F, we have the endogenous number of firms:

$$N = \frac{a-c}{\sqrt{Fb}} - 1$$

and a production for each firm equal to:

$$q = \frac{\sqrt{Fb}}{b}$$

This equilibrium is usually known as Cournot equilibrium with endogenous entry, or Marshall equilibrium.

Implications

- Output is greater with Cournot duopoly than monopoly, but lower than perfect competition.
- Price is lower with Cournot duopoly than monopoly, but not as low as with perfect competition.
- According to this model the firms have an incentive to form a cartel, effectively turning the Cournot model into a Monopoly. Cartels are usually illegal, so firms might instead tacitly collude using self-imposing strategies to reduce output which, *ceteris paribus* will raise the price and thus increase profits for all firms involved.

Bertrand versus Cournot

Although both models have similar assumptions, they have very different implications:

- Since the Bertrand model assumes that firms compete on price and not output quantity, it predicts that a duopoly is enough to push prices down to marginal cost level, meaning that a duopoly will result in perfect competition.
- Neither model is necessarily "better." The accuracy of the predictions of each model will vary from industry to industry, depending on the closeness of each model to the industry situation.
- If capacity and output can be easily changed, Bertrand is a better model of duopoly competition. If output and capacity are difficult to adjust, then Cournot is generally a better model.
- Under some conditions the Cournot model can be recast as a two stage model, where in the first stage firms choose capacities, and in the second they compete in Bertrand fashion.

However, as the number of firms increases towards infinity, the Cournot model gives the same result as in Bertrand model: The market price is pushed to marginal cost level.

Monopoly

A monopoly exists when a specific person or enterprise is the only supplier of a particular commodity (this contrasts with a monopsony which relates to a single entity's control of a market to purchase a good or service, and with oligopoly which consists of a few entities dominating an industry). Monopolies are thus characterized by a lack of economic competition to produce the good or service and a lack of viable substitute goods. The verb "monopolize" refers to the *process* by which a company gains the ability to raise prices or exclude competitors. In economics, a monopoly is a single seller. In law, a monopoly is a business entity that has significant market power, that is, the power to charge high prices. Although monopolies may be big businesses, size is not a characteristic of a monopoly. A small business may still have the power to raise prices in a small industry (or market).

A monopoly is distinguished from a monopsony, in which there is only one *buyer* of a product or service; a monopoly may also have monopsony control of a sector of a market. Likewise, a monopoly should be distinguished from a cartel (a form of oligopoly), in which several providers act together to coordinate services, prices or sale of goods. Monopolies, monopsonies and oligopolies are all situations such that one or a few of the entities have market power and therefore interact with their customers (monopoly), suppliers (monopsony) and the other companies (oligopoly) in ways that leave market interactions distorted.

When not legally obliged to do otherwise, monopolies typically maximize their profit by producing fewer goods and selling them at higher prices than would be the case for perfect competition.

Monopolies can be established by a government, form naturally, or form by integration.

In many jurisdictions, competition laws restrict monopolies. Holding a dominant position or a monopoly of a market is often not illegal in itself, however certain categories of behaviour can be considered abusive and therefore incur legal sanctions when a business is dominant. A government-granted monopoly or *legal monopoly*, by contrast, is sanctioned by the state, often to provide an incentive to invest in a risky venture or enrich a domestic interest group. Patents, copyright, and trademarks are sometimes used as examples of government granted monopolies. The government may also reserve the venture for itself, thus forming a government monopoly.

Market Structures

In economics, the idea of monopoly will be important for the study of management structures, which directly concerns normative aspects of economic competition, and provides the basis for topics such as industrial organisation and economics of regulation. There are four basic types of market structures by traditional economic analysis: perfect competition, monopolistic competition, oligopoly and monopoly. A monopoly is a structure in which a single supplier produces and sells a given product. If there is a single seller in a certain industry and there are not any close substitutes for the product, then the market structure is that of a "pure monopoly". Sometimes, there are many sellers in an industry and/or there exist many close substitutes for the goods being produced, but nevertheless companies retain some market power. This is termed monopolistic competition, whereas by oligopoly the companies interact strategically.

In general, the main results from this theory compare price-fixing methods across market structures, analyze the effect of a certain structure on welfare, and vary technological/demand assumptions in order to assess the consequences for an abstract model of society. Most economic textbooks follow the practice of carefully explaining the *perfect competition* model, only because of its usefulness to The boundaries of what constitutes a market and what doesn't are relevant distinctions to make in economic analysis. In a general equilibrium context, a good is a specific concept entangling geographical and time-related characteristics (*grapes sold during October 2009 in Moscow* is a different good from *grapes sold during October 2009 in New York*). Most studies of market structure relax a little their definition of a good, allowing for more flexibility at the identification of substitute-goods. Therefore, one can find an economic analysis of the market of *grapes in Russia*, for example, which is not a market in the strict sense of general equilibrium theory monopoly. understand "departures" from it (the so-called *imperfect competition* models).

The boundaries of what constitutes a market and what doesn't geographical and time-related characteristics (*grapes sold during October 2009 in Moscow* is a different good from *grapes sold during October 2009 in New York*). Most studies of market structure relax a little their definition of a good, allowing for more flexibility at the identification of substitute-goods. Therefore, one can find an economic analysis of the market of *grapes in Russia*, for example, which is not a market in the strict sense of general equilibrium theory monopoly. It are relevant distinctions to make in economic analysis. In a general equilibrium context, a good is a specific concept entangling geographical and time-related characteristics (*grapes sold during October 2009 in Moscow* is a different good from *grapes sold during October 2009 in New York*). Most studies of market structure relax a little their definition of a good, allowing for more flexibility at the identification of substitute-goods. Therefore, one can find an economic analysis of the market of *grapes in Russia*, for example, which is not a market in the strict sense of general equilibrium theory monopoly.

Characteristics

- *Profit Maximizer*: Maximizes profits.
- *Price Maker*: Decides the price of the good or product to be sold, but does so by determining the quantity in order to demand the price desired by the firm.
- *High Barriers to Entry*: Other sellers are unable to enter the market of the monopoly.
- *Single seller*: In a monopoly, there is one seller of the good that produces all the output. Therefore, the whole market is being served by a single company, and for practical purposes, the company is the same as the industry.
- *Price Discrimination*: A monopolist can change the price and quality of the product. He or She sells more quantities charging less price for the product in a very elastic market and sells less quantities charging high price in a less elastic market.

Sources of Monopoly Power

Monopolies derive their market power from barriers to entry – circumstances that prevent or greatly impede a potential competitor's ability to compete in a market. There are three major types of barriers to entry: economic, legal and deliberate.

- *Economic barriers*: Economic barriers include economies of scale, capital requirements, cost advantages and technological superiority.

Economies of scale: Monopolies are characterised by decreasing costs for a relatively large range of production. Decreasing costs coupled with large initial costs give monopolies an advantage over would-be competitors. Monopolies are often in a position to reduce prices below a new entrant's operating costs and thereby prevent them from continuing to compete.

Furthermore, the size of the industry relative to the minimum efficient scale may limit the number of companies that can effectively compete within the industry. If for example the industry is large enough to support one company of minimum efficient scale then other companies entering the industry will operate at a size that is less than MES, meaning that these companies cannot produce at an average cost that is competitive with the dominant company. Finally, if long-term average cost is constantly decreasing, the least cost method to provide a good or service is by a single company.

Capital requirements: Production processes that require large investments of capital, or large research and development costs or substantial sunk costs limit the number of companies in an industry. Large fixed costs also make it difficult for a small company to enter an industry and expand.

Technological superiority: A monopoly may be better able to acquire, integrate and use the best possible technology in producing its goods while entrants do not have the size or finances to use the best available technology. One large company can sometimes produce goods cheaper than several small companies.

***No Substitute Goods*:** A monopoly sells a good for which there is no close substitute. The absence of substitutes makes the demand for the good relatively inelastic enabling monopolies to extract positive profits.

***Control of Natural Resources*:** A prime source of monopoly power is the control of resources that are critical to the production of a final good.

***Network Externalities*:** The use of a product by a person can affect the value of that product to other people. This is the network effect. There is a direct relationship between the proportion of people using a product and the demand for that product. In other words the more people who are using a product the greater the probability of any individual starting to use the product. This effect accounts for fads and fashion trends. It also can play a crucial role in the development or acquisition of market power. The most famous current example is the market dominance of the Microsoft operating system in personal computers.

- *Legal barriers*: Legal rights can provide opportunity to monopolise the market of a good. Intellectual property rights, including patents and copyrights, give a monopolist exclusive control of the production and selling of certain goods. Property rights may give a company exclusive control of the materials necessary to produce a good.
- *Deliberate actions*: A company wanting to monopolise a market may engage in various types of deliberate action to exclude competitors or eliminate competition. Such actions include collusion, lobbying governmental authorities, and force.

In addition to barriers to entry and competition, barriers to exit may be a source of market power. Barriers to exit are market conditions that make it difficult or expensive for a company to end its involvement with a market. Great liquidation costs are a primary barrier for exiting. Market exit and shutdown are separate events. The decision whether to shut down or operate is not affected by exit barriers. A company will shut down if price falls below minimum average variable costs.

Monopoly versus Competitive Markets

While monopoly and perfect competition mark the extremes of market structures there is some similarity. The cost functions are the same. Both monopolies and perfectly competitive companies minimize cost and maximize profit. The shutdown decisions are the same. Both are assumed to have perfectly competitive factors markets. There are distinctions, some of the more important of which are as follows:

- *Marginal revenue and price*: In a perfectly competitive market, price equals marginal cost. In a monopolistic market, however, price is set above marginal cost.
- *Product differentiation*: There is zero product differentiation in a perfectly competitive market. Every product is perfectly homogeneous and a perfect substitute for any other. With a monopoly, there is great to absolute product differentiation in the sense that there is no available substitute for a monopolized good. The monopolist is the sole supplier of the good in question. A customer either buys from the monopolizing entity on its terms or does without.
- *Number of competitors*: PC markets are populated by an infinite number of buyers and sellers. Monopoly involves a single seller.
- *Barriers to Entry*: Barriers to entry are factors and circumstances that prevent entry into market by would-be competitors and limit new companies from operating and expanding within the market. PC markets have free entry and exit. There are no barriers to entry, exit or competition. Monopolies have relatively high barriers to entry. The barriers must be strong enough to prevent or discourage any potential competitor from entering the market.
- *Elasticity of Demand*: The price elasticity of demand is the percentage change of demand caused by a one percent change of relative price. A successful monopoly would have a relatively inelastic demand curve. A low coefficient of elasticity is

indicative of effective barriers to entry. A PC company has a perfectly elastic demand curve. The coefficient of elasticity for a perfectly competitive demand curve is infinite.

- *Excess Profits*: Excess or positive profits are profit more than the normal expected return on investment. A PC company can make excess profits in the short term but excess profits attract competitors, which can enter the market freely and decrease prices, eventually reducing excess profits to zero. A monopoly can preserve excess profits because barriers to entry prevent competitors from entering the market.
- *Profit Maximization*: A PC company maximizes profits by producing such that price equals marginal costs. A monopoly maximises profits by producing where marginal revenue equals marginal costs. The rules are not equivalent. The demand curve for a PC company is perfectly elastic – flat. The demand curve is identical to the average revenue curve and the price line. Since the average revenue curve is constant the marginal revenue curve is also constant and equals the demand curve, Average revenue is the same as price (AR = TR/Q = P x Q/Q = P). Thus the price line is also identical to the demand curve. In sum, D = AR = MR = P.
- *P-Max quantity, price and profit*: If a monopolist obtains control of a formerly perfectly competitive industry, the monopolist would increase prices, reduce production, and realise positive economic profits.
- *Supply Curve*: in a perfectly competitive market there is a well defined supply function with a one to one relationship between price and quantity supplied. In a monopolistic market no such supply relationship exists. A monopolist cannot trace a short term supply curve because for a given price there is not a unique quantity supplied. As Pindyck and Rubenfeld note, a change in demand "can lead to changes in prices with no change in output, changes in output with no change in price or both". Monopolies produce where marginal revenue equals marginal costs. For a specific demand curve the supply "curve" would be the price/quantity combination at the point where marginal revenue equals marginal cost. If the demand curve shifted the marginal revenue curve would shift as well and a new equilibrium and supply "point" would be established. The locus of these points would not be a supply curve in any conventional sense.

The most significant distinction between a PC company and a monopoly is that the monopoly has a downward-sloping demand curve rather than the "perceived" perfectly elastic curve of the PC company. Practically all the variations mentioned above relate to this fact. If there is a downward-sloping demand curve then by necessity there is a distinct marginal revenue curve. The implications of this fact are best made manifest with a linear demand curve. Assume that the inverse demand curve is of the form x = a – by. Then the total revenue curve is TR = ay – by2 and the marginal revenue curve is thus MR = a – 2by. From this several things are evident. First the marginal revenue curve has the same y intercept as the inverse demand curve. Second the slope of the marginal revenue curve is twice that of the inverse demand curve. Third the x intercept of the marginal revenue curve is half that of the inverse demand curve. What is not quite so evident is that the marginal revenue curve is below the inverse demand curve at all points. Since all companies maximise profits by equating MR and MC it must be the case that at the profit-maximizing quantity MR and MC are less than price, which further implies that a monopoly produces less quantity at a higher price than if the market were perfectly competitive.

The fact that a monopoly has a downward-sloping demand curve means that the relationship between total revenue and output for a monopoly is much different than that of competitive companies. Total revenue equals price times quantity. A competitive company has a perfectly elastic demand curve meaning that total revenue is proportional to output. Thus the total revenue curve for a competitive company is a ray with a slope equal to the market price. A competitive company can sell all the output it desires at the market price. For a monopoly to increase sales it must reduce price. Thus the total revenue curve for a monopoly is a parabola that begins at the origin and reaches a maximum value then continuously decreases until total revenue is again zero. Total revenue has its maximum value when the slope of the total revenue function is zero. The slope of the total revenue function is marginal revenue. So the revenue maximizing quantity and price occur when MR = 0. For example assume that the monopoly's demand function is P = 50 – 2Q. The total revenue function would be TR = 50Q – $2Q^2$ and marginal revenue would be 50 – 4Q. Setting marginal revenue equal to zero we have

$$50-4Q=0$$

$$-4Q=-50$$

$$Q=12.5$$

So the revenue maximizing quantity for the monopoly is 12.5 units and the revenue maximizing price is 25.

A company with a monopoly does not experience price pressure from competitors, although it may experience pricing pressure from potential competition. If a company increases prices too much, then others may enter the market if they are able to provide the same good, or a substitute, at a lesser price. The idea that monopolies in markets with easy entry need not be regulated against is known as the "revolution in monopoly theory".

A monopolist can extract only one premium, and getting into complementary markets does not pay. That is, the total profits a monopolist could earn if it sought to leverage its monopoly in one market by monopolizing a complementary market are equal to the extra profits it could earn anyway by charging more for the monopoly product itself. However, the one monopoly profit theorem is not true if customers in the monopoly good are stranded or poorly informed, or if the tied good has high fixed costs. A pure monopoly has the same economic rationality of perfectly competitive companies, i.e. to optimise a profit function given some constraints. By the assumptions of increasing marginal costs, exogenous inputs' prices, and control concentrated on a single agent or entrepreneur, the optimal decision is to equate the marginal cost and marginal revenue of production. Nonetheless, a pure monopoly can – unlike a competitive company – alter the market price for its own convenience: a decrease of production results in a higher price. In the economics' jargon, it is said that pure monopolies have "a downward-sloping demand". An important consequence of such behaviour is worth noticing: typically a monopoly selects a higher price and lesser quantity of output than a price-taking company; again, less is available at a higher price.

The Inverse Elasticity Rule

A monopoly chooses that price that maximizes the difference between total revenue and total cost. The basic markup rule can be expressed as (P – MC)/P = 1/PED. The markup rules indicate that the ratio between profit margin and the price is inversely proportional to the price elasticity of demand. The implication of the rule is that the more elastic the demand for the product the less pricing power the monopoly has.

Market Power

Market power is the ability to increase the product's price above marginal cost without losing all customers. Perfectly competitive (PC) companies have zero market power when it comes to setting prices. All companies of a PC market are price takers. The price is set by the interaction of demand and supply at the market or aggregate level. Individual companies simply take the price determined by the market and produce that quantity of output that maximizes the company's profits. If a PC company attempted to increase prices above the market level all its customers would abandon the company and purchase at the market price from other companies. A monopoly has considerable although not unlimited market power. A monopoly has the power to set prices or quantities although not both. A monopoly is a price maker. The monopoly is the market and prices are set by the monopolist based on his circumstances and not the interaction of demand and supply. The two primary factors determining monopoly market power are the company's demand curve and its cost structure.

Market power is the ability to affect the terms and conditions of exchange so that the price of a product is set by a single company (price is not imposed by the market as in perfect competition). Although a monopoly's market power is great it is still limited by the demand side of the market. A monopoly has a negatively sloped demand curve, not a perfectly inelastic curve. Consequently, any price increase will result in the loss of some customers.

Price Discrimination

Price discrimination allows a monopolist to increase its profit by charging higher prices for identical goods to those who are willing or able to pay more. For example, most economic textbooks cost more in the United States than in developing countries like Ethiopia. In this case, the publisher is using its government-granted copyright monopoly to price discriminate between the generally wealthier American economics students and the generally poorer Ethiopian economics students. Similarly, most patented medications cost more in the U.S. than in other countries with a (presumed) poorer customer base. Typically, a high general price is listed, and various market segments get varying discounts.

This is an example of framing to make the process of charging some people higher prices more socially acceptable. Perfect price discrimination would allow the monopolist to charge each customer the exact maximum amount he would be willing to pay. This would allow the monopolist to extract all the consumer surplus of the market. While such perfect price discrimination is a theoretical construct, advances in information technology and micromarketing may bring it closer to the realm of possibility

It is important to realise that partial price discrimination can cause some customers who are inappropriately pooled with high price customers to be excluded from the market. For example, a poor student in the U.S. might be excluded from purchasing an economics textbook at the U.S. price, which the student may have been able to purchase at the Ethiopian price'. Similarly, a wealthy student in Ethiopia may be able to or willing to buy at the U.S. price, though naturally would hide such a fact from the monopolist so as to pay the reduced third world price. These are deadweight losses and decrease a monopolist's profits. As such, monopolists have substantial economic interest in improving their market information and *market segmenting*.

There is important information for one to remember when considering the monopoly model diagram (and its associated conclusions) displayed here. The result that monopoly prices are higher, and production output lesser, than a competitive company follow from a requirement that the monopoly not charge different prices for different customers. That is, the monopoly is restricted from engaging in price discrimination (this is termed first degree price discrimination, such that all customers are charged the same amount). If the monopoly were permitted to charge individualised prices (this is termed third degree price discrimination), the quantity produced, and the price charged to the *marginal* customer, would be identical to that of a competitive company, thus eliminating the deadweight loss; however, all gains from trade (social welfare) would accrue to the monopolist and none to the consumer. In essence, every consumer would be indifferent between (1) going completely without the product or service and (2) being able to purchase it from the monopolist.

As long as the price elasticity of demand for most customers is less than one in absolute value, it is advantageous for a company to increase its prices: it receives more money for fewer goods. With a price increase, price elasticity tends to increase, and in the optimum case above it will be greater than one for most customers.

A company maximizes profit by selling where marginal revenue equals marginal cost. A company that does not engage in price discrimination will charge the profit maximizing price, P*, to all its customers. In such circumstances there are customers who would be willing to pay a higher price than P* and those who will not pay P* but would buy at a lower price. A price discrimination strategy is to charge less price sensitive buyers a higher price and the more price sensitive buyers a lower price. Thus additional revenue is generated from two sources. The basic problem is to identify customers by their willingness to pay. The purpose of price discrimination is to transfer consumer surplus to the producer. Consumer surplus is the difference between the value of a good to a consumer and the price the consumer must pay in the market to purchase it. Price discrimination is not limited to monopolies.

Market power is a company's ability to increase prices without losing all its customers. Any company that has market power can engage in price discrimination. Perfect competition is the only market form in which price discrimination would be impossible (a perfectly competitive company has a perfectly elastic demand curve and has zero market power).

There are three forms of price discrimination. First degree price discrimination charges each consumer the maximum price the consumer is willing to pay. Second degree price discrimination involves quantity discounts. Third degree price discrimination involves grouping consumers according to willingness to pay as measured by their price elasticities of demand and charging each group a different price. Third degree price discrimination is the most prevalent type.

There are three conditions that must be present for a company to engage in successful price discrimination. First, the company must have market power. Second, the company must be able to sort customers according to their willingness to pay for the good. Third, the firm must be able to prevent resell.

A company must have some degree of market power to practice price discrimination. Without market power a company cannot charge more than the market price. Any market structure characterized by a downward sloping demand curve has market power – monopoly, monopolistic competition and oligopoly. The only market structure that has no market power is perfect competition.

A company wishing to practice price discrimination must be able to prevent middlemen or brokers from acquiring the consumer surplus for themselves. The company accomplishes this by preventing or limiting resale. Many methods are used to prevent resale. For example persons are required to show photographic identification and a boarding pass before boarding an airplane. Most travellers assume that this practice is strictly a matter of security. However, a primary purpose in requesting photographic identification is to confirm that the ticket purchaser is the person about to board the airplane and not someone who has repurchased the ticket from a discount buyer. The inability to prevent resale is the largest obstacle to successful price discrimination. Companies have however developed numerous methods to prevent resale. For example, universities require that students show identification before entering sporting events. Governments may make it illegal to resale tickets or products. In Boston, Red Sox baseball tickets can only be resold legally to the team.

The three basic forms of price discrimination are first, second and third degree price discrimination. In *first degree price discrimination* the company charges the maximum price each customer is willing to pay. The maximum price a consumer is willing to pay for a unit of the good is the reservation price. Thus for each unit the seller tries to set the price equal to the consumer's reservation price. Direct information about a consumer's willingness to pay is rarely available. Sellers tend to rely on secondary information such as where a person lives (postal codes); for example, catalogue retailers can use mail high-priced catalogs to high-income postal codes. First degree price discrimination most frequently occurs in regard to professional services or in transactions involving direct buyer/seller negotiations. For example, an accountant who has prepared a consumer's tax return has information that can be used to charge customers based on an estimate of their ability to pay.

In *second degree price discrimination* or quantity discrimination customers are charged different prices based on how much they buy. There is a single price schedule for all consumers but the prices vary depending on the quantity of the good bought. The theory of second degree price discrimination is a consumer is willing to buy only a certain quantity of a good at a given price. Companies know that consumer's willingness to buy decreases as more units are purchased. The task for the seller is to identify these price points and to reduce the price once one is reached in the hope that a reduced price will trigger additional purchases from the consumer. For example, sell in unit blocks rather than individual units.

In *third degree price discrimination* or multi-market price discrimination the seller divides the consumers into different groups according to their willingness to pay as measured by their price elasticity of demand. Each group of consumers effectively becomes a separate market with its own demand curve and marginal revenue curve. The firm then attempts to maximize profits in each segment by equating MR and MC, Generally the company charges a higher price to the group with a more price inelastic demand and a relatively lesser price to the group with a more elastic demand. Examples of third degree price discrimination abound. Airlines charge higher prices to business travellers than to vacation travellers. The reasoning is that the demand curve for a vacation traveller is relatively elastic while the demand curve for a business traveller is relatively inelastic. Any determinant of price elasticity of demand can be used to segment markets. For example, seniors have a more elastic demand for movies than do young adults because they generally have more free time. Thus theaters will offer discount tickets to seniors.

Example

Assume that by a uniform pricing system the monopolist would sell five units at a price of $10 per unit. Assume that his marginal cost is $5 per unit. Total revenue would be $50, total costs would be $25 and profits would be $25. If the monopolist practiced price discrimination he would sell the first unit for $50 the second unit for $40 and so on. Total revenue would be $150, his total cost would be $25 and his profit would be $125.00. Several things are worth noting. The monopolist acquires all the consumer surplus and eliminates practically all the deadweight loss because he is willing to sell to anyone who is willing to pay at least the marginal cost. Thus the price discrimination promotes efficiency. Secondly, by the pricing scheme price = average revenue and equals marginal revenue. That is the monopolist behaving like a perfectly competitive company. Thirdly, the discriminating monopolist produces a larger quantity than the monopolist operating by a uniform pricing scheme.

Qd	*Price*
1	50
2	40
3	30
4	20
5	10

Classifying Customers

Successful price discrimination requires that companies separate consumers according to their willingness to buy. Determining a customer's willingness to buy a good is difficult. Asking consumers directly is fruitless: consumers don't know, and to the extent they do they are reluctant to share that information with marketers. The two main methods for determining willingness to buy are observation of personal characteristics and consumer actions. As noted information about where a person lives (postal codes), how the person dresses, what kind of car he or she drives, occupation, and income and spending patterns can be helpful in classifying.

Monopoly and Efficiency

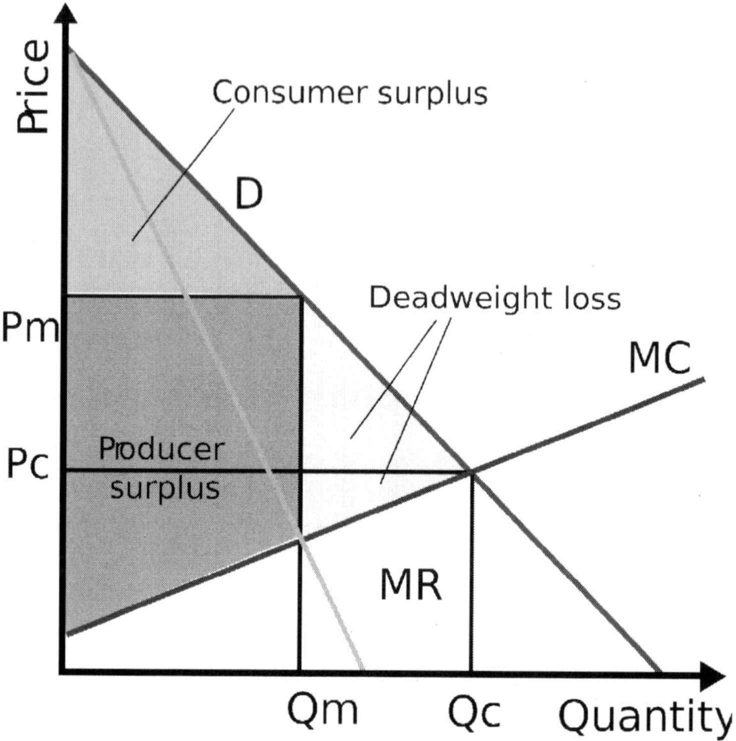

Figure: *Surpluses and deadweight loss created by monopoly price setting*

The price of monopoly is upon every occasion the highest which can be got. The natural price, or the price of free competition, on the contrary, is the lowest which can be taken, not upon every occasion indeed, but for any considerable time together. The one is upon every occasion the highest which can be squeezed out of the buyers, or which it is supposed they will consent to give; the other is the lowest which the sellers can commonly afford to take, and at the same time continue their business.

– Adam Smith (1776), *Wealth of Nations*

Monopoly, besides, is a great enemy to good management.

– Adam Smith (1776), *Wealth of Nations*

According to the standard model, in which a monopolist sets a single price for all consumers, the monopolist will sell a lesser quantity of goods at a higher price than would companies by perfect competition. Because the monopolist ultimately forgoes transactions with consumers who value the product or service more than its cost, monopoly pricing creates a deadweight loss referring to potential gains that went neither to the monopolist nor to consumers. Given the presence of this deadweight loss, the combined surplus (or wealth) for the monopolist and consumers is necessarily less than the total surplus obtained by consumers by perfect competition. Where efficiency is defined by the total gains from trade, the monopoly setting is less efficient than perfect competition.

It is often argued that monopolies tend to become less efficient and less innovative over time, becoming "complacent", because they do not have to be efficient or innovative to compete in the marketplace. Sometimes this very loss of psychological efficiency can increase a potential competitor's value enough to overcome market entry barriers, or provide incentive for research and investment into new alternatives. The theory of contestable markets argues that in some circumstances (private) monopolies are forced to behave *as if* there were competition because of the risk of losing their monopoly to new entrants. This is likely to happen when a market's barriers to entry are low. It might also be because of the availability in the longer term of substitutes in other markets. For example, a canal monopoly, while worth a great deal during the late 18th century United Kingdom, was worth much less during the late 19th century because of the introduction of railways as a substitute.

Natural Monopoly

A natural monopoly is a company that experiences increasing returns to scale over the relevant range of output and relatively high fixed costs. A natural monopoly occurs where the average cost of production "declines throughout the relevant range of product demand". The relevant range of product demand is where the average cost curve is below the demand curve. When this situation occurs, it is always cheaper for one large company to supply the market than multiple smaller companies; in fact, absent government intervention in such markets, will naturally evolve into a monopoly. An early market entrant that takes advantage of the cost structure and can expand rapidly can exclude smaller companies from entering and can drive or buy out other companies. A natural monopoly suffers from the same inefficiencies as any other monopoly. Left to its own devices, a profit-seeking natural monopoly will produce where marginal revenue equals marginal costs. Regulation of natural monopolies is problematic. Fragmenting such monopolies is by definition inefficient. The most frequently used methods dealing with natural monopolies are government regulations and public ownership. Government regulation generally consists of regulatory commissions charged with the principal duty of setting prices. To reduce prices and increase output, regulators often use average cost pricing. By average cost pricing, the price and quantity are determined by the intersection of the average cost curve and the demand curve. This pricing scheme eliminates any positive economic profits since price equals average cost. Average-cost pricing is not perfect. Regulators must estimate average costs. Companies have a reduced incentive to lower costs. Regulation of this type has not been limited to natural monopolies. Average-cost pricing does also have some disadvantages. By setting price equal to the intersection of the demand curve and the average total cost curve, the firm's output is allocatively inefficient as the price exceeds the marginal cost (which is the output quantity for a perfectly competitive and allocatively efficient market).

Government-Granted Monopoly

A government-granted monopoly (also called a "de jure monopoly") is a form of coercive monopoly by which a government grants exclusive privilege to a private individual or company to be the sole provider of a commodity; potential competitors are excluded from the market by law, regulation, or other mechanisms of government enforcement.

Monopolist Shutdown Rule

A monopolist should shut down when price is less than average variable cost for every output level – in other words where the demand curve is entirely below the average variable cost curve. Under these circumstances at the profit maximum level of output (MR = MC) average revenue would be less than average variable costs and the monopolists would be better off shutting down in the short term.

Breaking up Monopolies

When monopolies are not ended by the open market; sometimes a government will either regulate the monopoly, convert it into a publicly owned monopoly environment, or forcibly fragment it. Public utilities, often being naturally efficient with only one operator and therefore less susceptible to efficient breakup, are often strongly regulated or publicly owned.

American Telephone & Telegraph (AT&T) and Standard Oil are debatable examples of the breakup of a private monopoly by government: When AT&T, a monopoly previously protected by force of law, was broken up into various components in 1984, MCI, Sprint, and other companies were able to compete effectively in the long distance phone market.

Law

The existence of a very high market share does not always mean consumers are paying excessive prices since the threat of new entrants to the market can restrain a high-market-share company's price increases. Competition law does not make merely having a monopoly illegal, but rather abusing the power a monopoly may confer, for instance through exclusionary practices (i.e. pricing high just because you are the only one around.) It may also be noted that it is illegal to try to obtain a monopoly, by practices of buying out the competition, or equal practices. If one occurs naturally, such as a competitor going out of business, or lack of competition, is not illegal until such time as the monopoly holder abuses the power.

First it is necessary to determine whether a company is dominant, or whether it behaves "to an appreciable extent independently of its competitors, customers and ultimately of its consumer". As with collusive conduct, market shares are determined with reference to the particular market in which the company and product in question is sold. The Herfindahl-Hirschman Index (HHI) is sometimes used to assess how competitive an industry is. In the US, the merger guidelines state that a post-merger HHI below 1000 is viewed as unconcentrated while HHIs above that will provoke further review.

By European Union law, very large market shares raise a presumption that a company is dominant, which may be rebuttable. If a company has a dominant position, then there is "a special responsibility not to allow its conduct to impair competition on the common market". The lowest yet market share of a company considered "dominant" in the EU was 39.7%.

Certain categories of abusive conduct are usually prohibited by a country's legislation. The main recognised categories are:

- Limiting supply
- Predatory pricing
- Price discrimination
- Refusal to deal and exclusive dealing
- Tying (commerce) and product bundling

Despite wide agreement that the above constitute abusive practices, there is some debate about whether there needs to be a causal connection between the dominant position of a company and its actual abusive conduct. Furthermore, there has been some consideration of what happens when a company merely attempts to abuse its dominant position.

Historical Monopolies

Origin: The term "monopoly" first appears in Aristotle's *Politics*. Aristotle describes Thales of Miletus's cornering of the market in olive presses as a monopoly (*ìïíïðùëβáí*).

The meaning and understanding of the English word 'monopoly' has changed over the years.

Monopolies of Resources

Salt: Vending of common salt (sodium chloride) was historically a natural monopoly. Until recently, a combination of strong sunshine and low humidity or an extension of peat marshes was necessary for producing salt from the sea, the most plentiful source. Changing sea levels periodically caused salt "famines" and communities were forced to depend upon those who controlled the scarce inland mines and salt springs, which were often in hostile areas (e.g. the Sahara desert) requiring well-organised security for transport, storage, and distribution.

The Salt Commission was a legal monopoly in China. Formed in 758, the Commission controlled salt production and sales in order to raise tax revenue for the Tang Dynasty.

The "Gabelle" was a notoriously high tax levied upon salt in the Kingdom of France. The much-hated levy had a role in the beginning of the French Revolution, when strict legal controls specified who was allowed to sell and distribute salt. First instituted in 1286, the Gabelle was not permanently abolished until 1945.

Coal

Robin Gollan argues in *The Coalminers of New South Wales* that anti-competitive practices developed in the coal industry of Australia's Newcastle as a result of the business cycle. The monopoly was generated by formal meetings of the local management of coal companies agreeing to fix a minimum price for sale at dock. This collusion was known as "The Vend". The Vend ended and was reformed repeatedly during the late 19th century, ending by recession in the business cycle. "The Vend" was able to maintain its monopoly due to trade union assistance, and material advantages (primarily coal geography). During the early 20th century, as a result of comparable monopolistic practices in the Australian coastal shipping business, the Vend developed as an informal and illegal collusion between the steamship owners and the coal industry, eventually resulting in the High Court case Adelaide Steamship Co. Ltd v. R. & AG.

Petroleum

Standard Oil was an American oil producing, transporting, refining, and marketing company. Established in 1870, it became the largest oil refiner in the world. John D. Rockefeller was a founder, chairman and major shareholder. The company was an innovator in the development of the business trust. The Standard Oil trust streamlined production and logistics, lowered costs, and undercut competitors. "Trust-busting" critics accused Standard Oil of using aggressive pricing to destroy competitors and form a monopoly that threatened consumers. Its controversial history as one of the world's first and largest multinational corporations ended in 1911, when the United States Supreme Court ruled that Standard was an illegal monopoly. The Standard Oil trust was dissolved into 33 smaller companies; two of its surviving "child" companies are ExxonMobil and the Chevron Corporation.

Steel

U.S. Steel has been accused of being a monopoly. J. P. Morgan and Elbert H. Gary founded U.S. Steel in 1901 by combining Andrew Carnegie's Carnegie Steel Company with Gary's Federal Steel Company and William Henry "Judge" Moore's National Steel Company. At one time, U.S. Steel was the largest steel producer and largest corporation in the world. In its first full year of operation, U.S. Steel made 67 percent of all the steel produced in the United States. However, U.S. Steel's share of the expanding market slipped to 50 percent by 1911, and anti-trust prosecution that year failed.

Diamonds

De Beers settled charges of price fixing in the diamond trade in the 2000s.

Utilities

A public utility (or simply "utility") is an organisation or company that maintains the infrastructure for a public service or provides a set of services for public consumption. Common examples of utilities are electricity, natural gas, water, sewage, cable television, and telephone. In the United States of America, public utilities are often natural monopolies because the infrastructure required to produce and deliver a product such as electricity or water is very expensive to build and maintain.

Western Union was criticized as a "price gouging" monopoly in the late 19th century.

American Telephone & Telegraph was a telecommunications giant. AT&T was broken up in 1984.

In the case of Telecom New Zealand, local loop unbundling was enforced by central government.

Telkom is a semi-privatised, part state-owned South African telecommunications company.

Deutsche Telekom is a former state monopoly, still partially state owned. Deutsche Telekom currently monopolizes high-speed VDSL broadband network. The Long Island Power Authority (LIPA) provided electric service to over 1.1 million customers in Nassau and Suffolk counties of New York, and the Rockaway Peninsula in Queens.

The Comcast Corporation is the largest mass media and communications company in the world by revenue. It is the largest cable company and home Internet service provider in the United States, and the nation's third largest home telephone service provider. Comcast has a monopoly in Boston, Philadelphia, and Chicago.

Transportation

The United Aircraft and Transport Corporation was an aircraft manufacturer holding company that was forced to divest itself of airlines in 1934.

IarnródÉireann, the Irish Railway authority, is a current monopoly as Ireland does not have the size for more companies.

The Long Island Rail Road (LIRR) was founded in 1834, and since the mid-1800s has provided train service between Long Island and New York City. In the 1870s, LIRR became the sole railroad in that area through a series of acquisitions and consolidations. In 2013, the LIRR's commuter rail system is the busiest commuter railroad in North America, serving nearly 335,000 passengers daily.

Foreign Trade

Dutch East India Company was created as a legal trading monopoly in 1602. The *VereenigdeOost-Indische Compagnie* enjoyed huge profits from its spice monopoly through most of the 17th century.

The British Honourable East India Company was created as a legal trading monopoly in 1600. The East India Company was formed for pursuing trade with the East Indies but ended up trading mainly with the Indian subcontinent, North-West Frontier Province, and Balochistan. The Company traded in basic commodities, which included cotton, silk, indigo dye, salt, saltpetre, tea and opium.

Professional Sports

Major League Baseball survived U.S. anti-trust litigation in 1922, though its special status is still in dispute as of 2009.

The National Football League survived anti-trust lawsuit in the 1960s but was convicted of being an illegal monopoly in the 1980s.

Other Examples of Monopolies

- Microsoft has been the defendant in multiple anti-trust suits. They settled anti-trust litigation in the U.S. in 2001. In 2004 Microsoft was fined 493 million euros by the European Commission which was upheld for the most part by the Court of First Instance of the European Communities in 2007. The fine was US$1.35 billion in 2008 for noncompliance with the 2004 rule.
- MPAA (Motion Picture Association of America) has a monopoly over film ratings in the U.S.
- Joint Commission is an organisation that accredits more than 20,000 health care organisations and programs in the United States. The Commission has a monopoly over determining whether a U.S. hospital can participate in the publicly funded Medicare and Medicaid healthcare programs.
- Monsanto has been sued by competitors for anti-trust and monopolistic practices. They have between 70% and 100% of the commercial seed market.
- AAFES has a monopoly on retail sales at overseas U.S. military installations.
- State stores in certain United States, e.g. for liquor.
- The Registered Dietitian union seeks monopoly over nutrition services through state-level licensing schemes.

Countering Monopolies

According to professor Milton Friedman, laws against monopolies cause more harm than good, but unnecessary monopolies should be countered by removing tariffs and other regulation that upholds monopolies.

A monopoly can seldom be established within a country without overt and covert government assistance in the form of a tariff or some other device. It is close to impossible to do so on a world scale. The De Beers diamond monopoly is the only one we know of that appears to have succeeded (and even De Beers are protected by various laws against so called "illicit" diamond trade). – In a world of free trade, international cartels would disappear even more quickly.

However, professor Steve H. Hanke believes that although private monopolies are more efficient than public ones, often by a factor of two, sometimes private natural monopolies, such as local water distribution, should be regulated (not prohibited) by, e.g., price auctions.

Thomas DiLorenzo asserts, however, that during the early days of utility companies where there was little regulation, there were no natural monopolies and there was competition. Only when companies realised that they could gain power through government did monopolies begin to form.

Anti-Competitive Practices

These can include:

- Dumping, where a company sells a product in a competitive market at a loss. Though the company loses money for each sale, the company hopes to force other competitors out of the market, after which the company would be free to raise prices for a greater profit.
- Exclusive dealing, where a retailer or wholesaler is obliged by contract to only purchase from the contracted supplier.
- Price fixing, where companies collude to set prices, effectively dismantling the free market.
- Refusal to deal, e.g., two companies agree not to use a certain vendor
- Dividing territories, an agreement by two companies to stay out of each other's way and reduce competition in the agreed-upon territories.
- Limit Pricing, where the price is set by a monopolist at a level intended to discourage entry into a market.
- Tying, where products that aren't naturally related must be purchased together.
- Resale price maintenance, where resellers are not allowed to set prices independently.
- Religious / minority group doctrine, where businesses must apply tribute to a significant (normally religious) part of the community in order to engage in trade with that community. (A business that does not comply will be 50% worse of than the competitor if they do not comply with the tribute demanded by just 20% of the community)

Also criticized are:

- Absorption of a competitor or competing technology, where the powerful firm effectively co-opts or swallows its competitor rather than see it either compete directly or be absorbed by another firm.
- Subsidies from government which allow a firm to function without being profitable, giving them an advantage over competition or effectively barring competition
- Regulations which place costly restrictions on firms that less wealthy firms cannot afford to implement
- Protectionism, Tariffs and Quotas which give firms insulation from competitive forces
- Patent misuse and copyright misuse, such as fraudulently obtaining a patent, copyright, or other form of intellectual property; or using such legal devices to gain advantage in an unrelated market.
- Digital rights management which prevents owners from selling used media, as would normally be allowed by the first sale doctrine.

Effects

It is usually difficult to practice anti-competitive practices unless the parties involved have significant market power or government backing.

Monopolies and oligopolies are often accused of, and sometimes found guilty of, anti-competitive practices. For this reason, company mergers are often examined closely by government regulators to avoid reducing competition in an industry.

Although anti-competitive practices often enrich those who practice them, they are generally believed to have a negative effect on the economy as a whole, and to disadvantage competing firms and consumers who are not able to avoid their effects, generating a significant social cost. For these reasons, most countries have competition laws to prevent anti-competitive practices, and government regulators to aid the enforcement of these laws.

The argument that anti-competitive practices have a negative effect on the economy arises from the belief that a freely functioning efficient market economy, composed of many market participants each of which has limited market power, will not permit monopoly profits to be earned...and consequently prices to consumers will be lower, and if anything there will be a wider range of products supplied. Some people believe that the realities of the marketplace are sometimes more complex than this or similar theories of competition would suggest. For example, oligopolistic firms may achieve economies of scale that would elude smaller firms. Again, very large firms, whether quasi-monopolies or oligopolies, may achieve levels of sophistication e.g. in business process and/or planning (that benefit end consumers and) that smaller firms would not easily attain.

There are undoubtedly industries (e.g. airlines and pharmaceuticals) in which the levels of investment are so high that only extremely large firms that may be quasi-monopolies in some areas of their businesses can survive.

Many governments regard these market niches as natural monopolies, and believe that the inability to allow full competition is balanced by government regulation. However, the companies in these niches tend to believe that they should avoid regulation, as they are entitled to their monopoly position by fiat.

In some cases, anti-competitive behaviour can be difficult to distinguish from competition. For instance, a distinction must be made between product bundling, which is a legal market strategy, and product tying, which violates anti-trust law. Some advocates of laissez-faire capitalism (such as Monetarists, some Neoclassical economists, and the heterodox economists of the Austrian school) reject the term, seeing all "anti-competitive behaviour" as forms of competition that benefit consumers.

Competition Law

Competition law is law that promotes or seeks to maintain market competition by regulating anti-competitive conduct by companies.

Competition law is known as antitrust law in the United States and anti-monopoly law in China and Russia. In previous years it has been known as trade practices law in the United Kingdom and Australia.

The history of competition law reaches back to the Roman Empire. The business practices of market traders, guilds and governments have always been subject to scrutiny, and sometimes severe sanctions. Since the 20th century, competition law has become global. The two largest and most influential systems of competition regulation are United States antitrust law and European Union competition law. National and regional competition authorities across the world have formed international support and enforcement networks.

Modern competition law has historically evolved on a country level to promote and maintain fair competition in markets principally within the territorial boundaries of nation-states. National competition law usually does not cover activity beyond territorial borders unless it has significant effects at nation-state level. Countries may allow for extraterritorial jurisdiction in competition cases based on so-called effects doctrine. The protection of international competition is governed by international competition agreements. In 1945, during the negotiations preceding the adoption of the General Agreement on Tariffs and Trade (GATT) in 1947, limited international competition obligations were proposed within the *Charter for an International Trade Organisation*. These obligations were not included in GATT, but in 1994, with the conclusion of the Uruguay Round of GATT Multilateral Negotiations, the World Trade Organisation (WTO) was created. The *Agreement Establishing the WTO* included a range of limited provisions on various cross-border competition issues on a sector specific basis.

Principle

Competition law, or antitrust law, has three main elements:

- prohibiting agreements or practices that restrict free trading and competition between business. This includes in particular the repression of free trade caused by cartels.
- banning abusive behaviour by a firm dominating a market, or anti-competitive practices that tend to lead to such a dominant position. Practices controlled in this way may include predatory pricing, tying, price gouging, refusal to deal, and many others.
- supervising the mergers and acquisitions of large corporations, including some joint ventures. Transactions that are considered to threaten the competitive process can be prohibited altogether, or approved subject to "remedies" such as an obligation to divest part of the merged business or to offer licenses or access to facilities to enable other businesses to continue competing.

Substance and practice of competition law varies from jurisdiction to jurisdiction. Protecting the interests of consumers (consumer welfare) and ensuring that entrepreneurs have an opportunity to compete in the market economy are often treated as important objectives. Competition law is closely connected with law on deregulation of access to markets, state aids and subsidies, the privatization of state owned assets and the establishment of independent sector regulators, among other market-oriented supply-side policies. In recent decades, competition law has been viewed as a way to provide better public services. Robert Bork argued that competition laws can produce adverse effects when they reduce competition by protecting inefficient competitors and when costs of legal intervention are greater than benefits for the consumers.

Ideas about competitive law were published during the 18th century with such works as Adam Smith's *The Wealth of Nations*. Different terms were used to describe this area of the law, including "restrictive practices," "the law of monopolies," "combination acts" and the "restraint of trade in india"

History

Roman Legislation: An early example of competition law can be found in Roman law. The *Lex Julia de Annona* was enacted during the Roman Republic around 50 BCE. To protect the grain trade, heavy fines were imposed on anyone directly, deliberately, and insidiously stopping supply ships. Under Diocletian in 301 CE, an edict imposed the death penalty for anyone violating a tariff system, for example by buying up, concealing, or contriving the scarcity of everyday goods. More legislation came under the constitution of Zeno of 483 CE, which can be traced into Florentine Municipal laws of 1322 and 1325. This provided for confiscation of property and banishment for any trade combination or joint action of monopolies private *or* granted by the Emperor. Zeno rescinded all previously granted exclusive rights. Justinian I subsequently introduced legislation to pay officials to manage state monopolies.

Middle Ages

Legislation in England to control monopolies and restrictive practices were in force well before the Norman Conquest. The Domesday Book recorded that "foresteel" (i.e. forestalling, the practice of buying up goods before they reach market and then inflating the prices) was one of three forfeitures that King Edward the Confessor could carry out through England. But concern for fair prices also led to attempts to directly regulate the market. Under Henry III an act was passed in 1266 to fix bread and ale prices in correspondence with grain prices laid down by the assizes. Penalties for breach included amercements, pillory and tumbrel. A 14th century statute labelled forestallers as "oppressors of the poor and the community at large and enemies of the whole country." Under King Edward III the Statute of Labourers of 1349 fixed wages of artificers and workmen and decreed that foodstuffs should be sold at reasonable prices. On top of existing penalties, the statute stated that overcharging merchants must pay the injured party double the sum he received, an idea that has been replicated in punitivetreble damages under US antitrust law. Also under Edward III, the following statutory provision outlawed trade combination.

...we have ordained and established, that no merchant or other shall make Confederacy, Conspiracy, Coin, Imagination, or Murmur, or Evil Device in any point that may turn to the Impeachment, Disturbance, Defeating or Decay of the said Staples, or of anything that to them pertaineth, or may pertain.

In continental Europe competition principles developed in LexMercatoria. Examples of legislation enshrining competition principles include the *constitutionesjurismetallici* by Wenceslaus II of Bohemia between 1283 and 1305, condemning combination of ore traders increasing prices; the Municipal Statutes of Florence in 1322 and 1325 followed Zeno's legislation against state monopolies; and under Emperor Charles V in the Holy Roman Empire a law was passed "to prevent losses resulting from monopolies and improper contracts which many merchants and artisans made in the Netherlands." In 1553 King Henry VIII reintroduced tariffs for foodstuffs, designed to stabilize prices, in the face of fluctuations in supply from overseas. So the legislation read here that whereas,

it is very hard and difficult to put certain prices to any such things... [it is necessary because] prices of such victuals be many times enhanced and raised by the Greedy Covetousness and Appetites of the Owners of such Victuals, by occasion of ingrossing and regrating the same, more than upon any reasonable or just ground or cause, to the great damage and impoverishing of the King's subjects.

Around this time organisations representing various tradesmen and handicrafts people, known as guilds had been developing, and enjoyed many concessions and exemptions from the laws against monopolies. The privileges conferred were not abolished until the Municipal Corporations Act 1835.

Early Competition Law in Europe

The English common law of restraint of trade is the direct predecessor to modern competition law later developed in the US. It is based on the prohibition of agreements that ran counter to public policy, unless the reasonableness of an agreement could be shown. It effectively prohibited agreements designed to restrain another's trade. The 1414 *Dyer's* is the first known restrictive trade agreement to be examined under English common law. A dyer had given a bond not to exercise his trade in the same town as the plaintiff for six months but the plaintiff had promised nothing in return. On hearing the plaintiff's attempt to enforce this restraint, Hull J exclaimed, "per Dieu, if the plaintiff were here, he should go to prison until he had paid a fine to the King." The court denied the collection of a bond for the dyer's breach of agreement because the agreement was held to be a restriction on trade. English courts subsequently decided a range of cases which gradually developed competition related case law, which eventually were transformed into statute law.

Europe around the 16th century was changing quickly. The new world had just been opened up, overseas trade and plunder was pouring wealth through the international economy and attitudes among businessmen were shifting. In 1561 a system of Industrial Monopoly Licenses, similar to modern patents had been introduced into England. But by the reign of Queen Elizabeth I, the system was reputedly much abused and used merely to preserve privileges, encouraging nothing new in the way of innovation or manufacture. In response English courts developed case law on restrictive business practices. The statute followed the unanimous decision in *Darcy v. Allein* 1602, also known as the Case of Monopolies, of the King's bench to declare void the sole right that Queen Elizabeth I had granted to Darcy to import playing cards into England. Darcy, an officer of the Queen's household, claimed damages for the defendant's infringement of this right. The court found the grant void and that three characteristics of monopoly were (1) price increases (2) quality decrease (3) the tendency to reduce artificers to idleness and beggary. This put an end to granted monopolies until King James I began to grant them again. In 1623 Parliament passed the Statute of Monopolies, which for the most part excluded patent rights from its prohibitions, as well as guilds. From King Charles I, through the civil war and to King Charles II, monopolies continued, especially useful for raising revenue. Then in 1684, in *East India Company v. Sandys* it was decided that exclusive rights to trade only outside the realm were legitimate, on the grounds that only large and powerful concerns could trade in the conditions prevailing overseas.

The development of early competition law in England and Europe progressed with the diffusion of Adam Smith's work, who first established the concept of the *market economy*. At the same time industrialisation replaced the individual artisan, or group of artisans, with paid labourers and machine-based production. Commercial success increasingly dependent on maximising production while minimising cost. Therefore the size of a company became increasingly important and a number of European countries responded by enacting laws to regulate large companies which restricted trade. Following the French Revolution in 1789 the law of 14–17 June 1791 declared agreements by members of the same trade that fixed the price of an industry or labour as void, unconstitutional, and hostile to liberty. Similarly the Austrian Penal Code of 1852 established that "agreements... to raise the price of a commodity... to the disadvantage of the public' should be punished as misdemeanours." Austria passed a law in 1870 abolishing the penalties, though such agreements remained void. However, in Germany laws clearly validated agreements between firms to raise prices. Throughout the 18th and 19th century ideas that dominant private companies or legal monopolies could excessively restrict trade were further developed in Europe. However, as in the late 19th century a depression spread through Europe, known as the Panic of 1873, ideas of competition lost favour and it was felt that companies had to co-operate by forming cartels to withstand huge pressures on prices and profits.

Modern Competition Law

While the development of competition law stalled in Europe during the late 19th century, in 1889 Canada enacted what is considered the first competition statute of modern times. The *Act for the Prevention and Suppression of Combinations formed in restraint of Trade* was passed one year before the United States enacted the most famous legal statute on competition law, the Sherman Act of 1890. It was named after Senator John Sherman who argued that the Act "does not announce a new principle of law, but applies old and well recognised principles of common law".

United States Antitrust

The Sherman Act of 1890 attempted to outlaw the restriction of competition by large companies, who co-operated with rivals to fix outputs, prices and market shares, initially through *pools* and later through *trusts.* Trusts first appeared in the US railroads, where the capital requirement of railroad construction precluded competitive services in then scarcely settled territories. This trust allowed railroads to discriminate on rates imposed and services provided to consumers and businesses and to destroy potential competitors. Different trusts could be dominant in different industries. The Standard Oil Company trust in the 1880s controlled a number of markets, including the market in fuel oil, lead and whiskey. Vast numbers of citizens became sufficiently aware and publicly concerned about how the trusts negatively impacted them that the Act became a priority for both major parties. A primary concern of this act is that competitive markets themselves should provide the primary regulation of prices, outputs, interests and profits. Instead, the Act outlawed anticompetitive practices, codifying the common law restraint of trade doctrine. Prof Rudolph Peritz has argued that competition law in the United States has evolved around two sometimes conflicting concepts of competition: first that of individual liberty, free of government intervention, and second a fair competitive environment free of excessive economic power. Since the enactment of the Sherman Act enforcement of competition law has been based on various economic theories adopted by Government.

Section 1 of the Sherman Act declared illegal "every contract, in the form of trust or otherwise, or conspiracy, in restraint of trade or commerce among the several States, or with foreign nations". Section 2 prohibits monopolies, or attempts and conspiracies to monopolize. Following the enactment in 1890 US court applies these principles to business and markets. Courts applied the Act without consistent economic analysis until 1914, when it was complemented by the Clayton Act which specifically prohibited exclusive dealing agreements, particularly tying agreements and interlocking directorates, and mergers achieved by purchasing stock. From 1915 onwards the *rule of reason* analysis was frequently applied by courts to competition cases. However, the period was characterized by the lack of competition law enforcement. From 1936 to 1972 courts' application of anti-trust law was dominated by the *structure-conduct-performance* paradigm of the Harvard School. From 1973 to 1991, the enforcement of anti-trust law was based on efficiency explanations as the Chicago School became dominant, and through legal writings such as Judge Robert Bork's book *The Antitrust Paradox.* Since 1992 game theory has frequently been used in anti-trust cases.

European Union Law

Competition law gained new recognition in Europe in the inter-war years, with Germany enacting its first anti-cartel law in 1923 and Sweden and Norway adopting similar laws in 1925 and 1926 respectively. However, with the Great Depression of 1929 competition law disappeared from Europe and was revived following the Second World War when the United Kingdom and Germany, following pressure from the United States, became the first European countries to adopt fully fledged competition laws. At a regional level EU competition law has its origins in the European Coal and Steel Community (ECSC) agreement between France, Italy, Belgium, the Netherlands,

Luxembourg and Germany in 1951 following the Second World War. The agreement aimed to prevent Germany from re-establishing dominance in the production of coal and steel as it was felt that this dominance had contributed to the outbreak of the war. Article 65 of the agreement banned cartels and article 66 made provisions for concentrations, or mergers, and the abuse of a dominant position by companies. This was the first time that competition law principles were included in a plurilateral regional agreement and established the trans-European model of competition law.

In 1957 competition rules were included in the Treaty of Rome, also known as the EC Treaty, which established the European Economic Community (EEC). The Treaty of Rome established the enactment of competition law as one of the main aims of the EEC through the "institution of a system ensuring that competition in the common market is not distorted". The two central provisions on EU competition law on companies were established in article 85, which prohibited anti-competitive agreements, subject to some exemptions, and article 86 prohibiting the abuse of dominant position. The treaty also established principles on competition law for member states, with article 90 covering public undertakings, and article 92 making provisions on state aid. Regulations on mergers were not included as member states could not establish consensus on the issue at the time.

Today, the Treaty of Lisbon prohibits anti-competitive agreements in Article 101(1), including price fixing. According to Article 101(2) any such agreements are automatically void. Article 101(3) establishes exemptions, if the collusion is for distributional or technological innovation, gives consumers a "fair share" of the benefit and does not include unreasonable restraints that risk eliminating competition anywhere (or compliant with the general principle of European Union law of proportionality).

Article 102 prohibits the abuse of dominant position, such as price discrimination and exclusive dealing. Article 102 allows the European Councilregulations to govern mergers between firms (the current regulation is the Regulation 139/2004/EC). The general test is whether a concentration (i.e. merger or acquisition) with a community dimension (i.e. affects a number of EU member states) might significantly impede effective competition. Articles 106 and 107 provide that member state's right to deliver public services may not be obstructed, but that otherwise public enterprises must adhere to the same competition principles as companies. Article 107 lays down a general rule that the state may not aid or subsidize private parties in distortion of free competition and provides exemptions for charities, regional development objectives and in the event of a natural disaster.

India

India responded positively by opening up its economy by removing controls during the Economic liberalisation. In quest of increasing the efficiency of the nation's economy, the Government of India acknowledged the Liberalization Privatization Globalization era. As a result, Indian market faces competition from within and outside the country. This led to the need of a strong legislation to dispense justice in commercial matters and the Competition Act, 2002 was passed. The history of competition law in India dates back to the 1960s when the first competition law, namely the Monopolies and Restrictive Trade Practices Act (MRTP) was enacted in 1969. But after the economic reforms in 1991, this legislation was found to be obsolete in many aspects and as a result, a new competition law in the form of the Competition Act, 2002 was enacted in 2003. The Competition Commission of India, is the quasi judicial body established for enforcing provisions of the Competition Act.

International Expansion

By 2008 111 countries had enacted competition laws, which is more than 50 percent of countries with a population exceeding 80,000 people. 81 of the 111 countries had adopted their competition laws in the past 20 years, signalling the spread of competition law following the collapse of the Soviet Union and the expansion of the European Union.

Enforcement

At a national level competition law is enforced through competition authorities, as well as private enforcement. The United States Supreme Court explained:

Every violation of the antitrust laws is a blow to the free-enterprise system envisaged by Congress. This system depends on strong competition for its health and vigor, and strong competition depends, in turn, on compliance with antitrust legislation. In enacting these laws, Congress had many means at its disposal to penalize violators. It could have, for example, required violators to compensate federal, state, and local governments for the estimated damage to their respective economies caused by the violations. But, this remedy was not selected. Instead, Congress chose to permit all persons to sue to recover three times their actual damages every time they were injured in their business or property by an antitrust violation.

In the European Union, the Modernisation Regulation 1/2003 means that the European Commission is no longer the only body capable of public enforcement of European Union competition law. This was done to facilitate quicker resolution of competition-related inquiries. In 2005 the Commission issued a Green Paper on *Damages actions for the breach of the EC antitrust rules*, which suggested ways of making private damages claims against cartels easier.

Antitrust administration and legislation can be seen as a balance between:

- guidelines which are clear and specific to the courts, regulators and business but leave little room for discretion that prevents the application of laws from resulting in unintended consequences.
- guidelines which are broad, hence allowing administrators to sway between improving economic outcomes versus succumbing to political policies to redistribute wealth.

Chapter 5 of the post war Havana Charter contained an Antitrust code but this was never incorporated into the WTO's forerunner, the General Agreement on Tariffs and Trade 1947. Office of Fair Trading Director and Professor Richard Whish wrote sceptically that it "seems unlikely at the current stage of its development that the WTO will metamorphose into a global competition authority." Despite that, at the ongoing Doha round of trade talks for the World Trade Organisation, discussion includes the prospect of competition law enforcement moving up to a global level. While it is incapable of enforcement itself, the newly established International Competition Network (ICN) is a way for national authorities to coordinate their own enforcement activities.

Theory

Classical Perspective: Under the doctrine of laissez-faire, antitrust is seen as unnecessary as competition is viewed as a long-term dynamic process where firms compete against each other for market dominance. In some markets a firm may successfully dominate, but it is because of superior skill or innovativeness. However, according to laissez-faire theorists, when it tries to raise prices to take advantage of its monopoly position it creates profitable opportunities for others to compete. A process of creative destruction begins which erodes the monopoly. Therefore, government should not try to break up monopoly but should allow the market to work.

The classical perspective on competition was that certain agreements and business practice could be an unreasonable restraint on the individual liberty of tradespeople to carry on their livelihoods. Restraints were judged as permissible or not by courts as new cases appeared and in the light of changing business circumstances. Hence the courts found specific categories of agreement, specific clauses, to fall foul of their doctrine on economic fairness, and they did not contrive an overarching conception of market power. Earlier theorists like Adam Smith rejected any monopoly power on this basis.

A monopoly granted either to an individual or to a trading company has the same effect as a secret in trade or manufactures. The monopolists, by keeping the market constantly under-stocked, by never fully supplying the effectual demand, sell their commodities much above the natural price, and raise their emoluments, whether they consist in wages or profit, greatly above their natural rate.

In *The Wealth of Nations* (1776) Adam Smith also pointed out the cartel problem, but did not advocate specific legal measures to combat them. People of the same trade seldom meet together, even for merriment and diversion, but the conversation ends in a conspiracy against the public, or in some contrivance to raise prices. It is impossible indeed to prevent such meetings, by any law which either could be executed, or would be consistent with liberty and justice. But though the law cannot hinder people of the same trade from sometimes assembling together, it ought to do nothing to facilitate such assemblies; much less to render them necessary. By the latter half of the 19th century it had become clear that large firms had become a fact of the market economy. John Stuart Mill's approach was laid down in his treatise *On Liberty* (1859).

Again, trade is a social act. Whoever undertakes to sell any description of goods to the public, does what affects the interest of other persons, and of society in general; and thus his conduct, in principle, comes within the jurisdiction of society... both the cheapness and the good quality of commodities are most effectually provided for by leaving the producers and sellers perfectly free, under the sole check of equal freedom to the buyers for supplying themselves elsewhere. This is the so-called doctrine of Free Trade, which rests on grounds different from, though equally solid with, the principle of individual liberty asserted in this Essay. Restrictions on trade, or on production for purposes of trade, are indeed restraints; and all restraint, qua restraint, is an evil...

Neo-Classical Synthesis

After Mill, there was a shift in economic theory, which emphasized a more precise and theoretical model of competition. A simple neoclassical model of free markets holds that production and distribution of goods and services in competitive free markets maximizes social welfare. This model assumes that new firms can freely enter markets and compete with existing firms, or to use legal language, there are no barriers to entry. By this term economists mean something very specific, that competitive free markets deliver allocative, productive and dynamic efficiency. Allocative efficiency is also known as Pareto efficiency after the Italian economist Vilfredo Pareto and means that resources in an economy over the long run will go precisely to those who are willing and able to pay for them.

Because rational producers will keep producing and selling, and buyers will keep buying up to the last marginal unit of possible output – or alternatively rational producers will be reduce their output to the margin at which buyers will buy the same amount as produced – there is no waste, the greatest number wants of the greatest number of people become satisfied and utility is perfected because resources can no longer be reallocated to make anyone better off without making someone else worse off; society has achieved allocative efficiency. Productive efficiency simply means that society is making as much as it can. Free markets are meant to reward those who work hard, and therefore those who will put society's resources towards the frontier of its possible production. Dynamic efficiency refers to the idea that business which constantly competes must research, create and innovate to keep its share of consumers. This traces to Austrian-American political scientist Joseph Schumpeter's notion that a "perennial gale of creative destruction" is ever sweeping through capitalist economies, driving enterprise at the market's mercy. This led Schumpeter to argue that monopolies did not need to be broken up (as with Standard Oil) because the next gale of economic innovation would do the same.

Contrasting with the allocatively, productively and dynamically efficient market model are monopolies, oligopolies, and cartels. When only one or a few firms exist in the market, and there is no credible threat of the entry of competing firms, prices rise above the competitive level, to either a monopolistic or oligopolistic equilibrium price. Production is also decreased, further decreasing social welfare by creating a deadweight loss. Sources of this market power are said to include the existence of externalities, barriers to entry of the market, and the free rider problem. Markets may fail to be efficient for a variety of reasons, so the exception of competition law's intervention to the rule of *laissez faire* is justified if government failure can be avoided. Orthodox economists fully acknowledge that perfect competition is seldom observed in the real world, and so aim for what is called "workable competition". This follows the theory that if one cannot achieve the ideal, then go for the second best option by using the law to tame market operation where it can.

Chicago School

A group of economists and lawyers, who are largely associated with the University of Chicago, advocate an approach to competition law guided by the proposition that some actions that were originally considered to be anticompetitive could actually promote competition. The U.S. Supreme Court has used the Chicago School approach in several recent cases. One view of the Chicago School approach to antitrust is found in United States Circuit Court of Appeals Judge Richard Posner's books *Antitrust Law* and *Economic Analysis of Law*.

Robert Bork was highly critical of court decisions on United States antitrust law in a series of law review articles and his book *The Antitrust Paradox*. Bork argued that both the original intention of antitrust laws and economic efficiency was the pursuit *only* of consumer welfare, the protection of competition rather than competitors. Furthermore, only a few acts should be prohibited, namely cartels that fix prices and divide markets, mergers that create monopolies, and dominant firms pricing predatorily, while allowing such practices as vertical agreements and price discrimination on the grounds that it did not harm consumers.

Running through the different critiques of US antitrust policy is the common theme that government interference in the operation of free markets does more harm than good. "The only cure for bad theory", writes Bork, "is better theory". The late Harvard Law School Professor Philip Areeda, who favours more aggressive antitrust policy, in at least one Supreme Court case challenged Robert Bork's preference for non-intervention.

Practice

Dominance and monopoly: When firms hold large market shares, consumers risk paying higher prices and getting lower quality products than compared to competitive markets. However, the existence of a very high market share does not always mean consumers are paying excessive prices since the threat of new entrants to the market can restrain a high-market-share firm's price increases. Competition law does not make merely having a monopoly illegal, but rather abusing the power that a monopoly may confer, for instance through exclusionary practices.

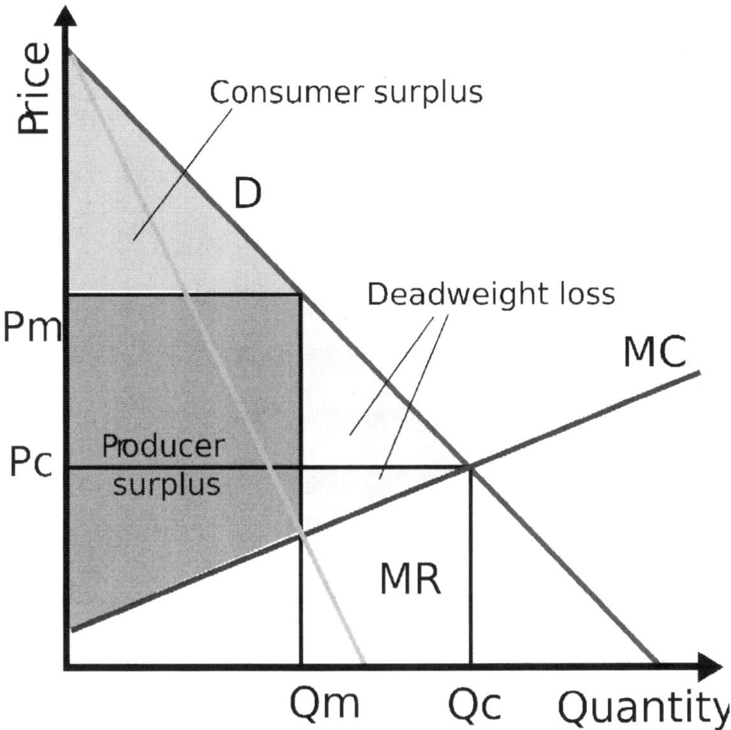

***Figure:** The economist's depiction of deadweight loss to efficiency that monopolies cause*

First it is necessary to determine whether a firm is dominant, or whether it behaves "to an appreciable extent independently of its competitors, customers and ultimately of its consumer." Under EU law, very large market shares raise a presumption that a firm is dominant, which may be rebuttable. If a firm has a dominant position, then there is "a special responsibility not to allow its conduct to impair competition on the common market". Similarly as with collusive conduct, market shares are determined with reference to the particular market in which the firm and product in question is sold.

Then although the lists are seldom closed, certain categories of abusive conduct are usually prohibited under the country's legislation. For instance, limiting production at a shipping port by refusing to raise expenditure and update technology could be abusive. Tying one product into the sale of another can be considered abuse too, being restrictive of consumer choice and depriving competitors of outlets. This was the alleged case in *Microsoft v. Commission* leading to an eventual fine of million for including its Windows Media Player with the Microsoft Windows platform. A refusal to supply a facility which is essential for all businesses attempting to compete to use can constitute an abuse. One example was in a case involving a medical company named *Commercial Solvents*. When it set up its own rival in the tuberculosis drugs market, Commercial Solvents were forced to continue supplying a company named Zoja with the raw materials for the drug. Zoja was the only market competitor, so without the court forcing supply, all competition would have been eliminated.

Forms of abuse relating directly to pricing include price exploitation. It is difficult to prove at what point a dominant firm's prices become "exploitative" and this category of abuse is rarely found. In one case however, a French funeral service was found to have demanded exploitative prices, and this was justified on the basis that prices of funeral services outside the region could be compared. A more tricky issue is predatory pricing. This is the practice of dropping prices of a product so much that one's smaller competitors cannot cover their costs and fall out of business. The Chicago School (economics) considers predatory pricing to be unlikely. However in *France Telecom SA v. Commission* a broadband internet company was forced to pay million for dropping its prices below its own production costs. It had "no interest in applying such prices except that of eliminating competitors" and was being cross-subsidized to capture the lion's share of a booming market. One last category of pricing abuse is price discrimination. An example of this could be offering rebates to industrial customers who export your company's sugar, but not to customers who are selling their goods in the same market as you are in.

Mergers and Acquisitions

A merger or acquisition involves, from a competition law perspective, the concentration of economic power in the hands of fewer than before. This usually means that one firm buys out the shares of another. The reasons for oversight of economic concentrations by the state are the same as the reasons to restrict firms who abuse a position of dominance, only that regulation of mergers and acquisitions attempts to deal with the problem before it arises, *ex ante* prevention of market dominance. In the United States merger regulation began under the Clayton Act, and in the European Union, under the Merger Regulation 139/2004 (known as the "ECMR"). Competition law requires that firms proposing to merge gain authorization from the relevant government authority. The theory behind mergers is that transaction costs can be reduced compared to operating on an open market through bilateral contracts.

Concentrations can increase economies of scale and scope. However often firms take advantage of their increase in market power, their increased market share and decreased number of competitors, which can adversely affect the deal that consumers get. Merger control is about predicting what the market might be like, not knowing and making a judgment. Hence the central provision under EU law asks whether a concentration *would* if it went ahead "significantly impede effective competition... in particular as a result of the creation or strengthening off a dominant position..." and the corresponding provision under US antitrust states similarly,

No person shall acquire, directly or indirectly, the whole or any part of the stock or other share capital... of the assets of one or more persons engaged in commerce or in any activity affecting commerce, where... the effect of such acquisition, of such stocks or assets, or of the use of such stock by the voting or granting of proxies or otherwise, may be substantially to lessen competition, or to tend to create a monopoly.

What amounts to a substantial lessening of, or significant impediment to competition is usually answered through empirical study. The market shares of the merging companies can be assessed and added, although this kind of analysis only gives rise to presumptions, not conclusions. The Herfindahl-Hirschman Index is used to calculate the "density" of the market, or what concentration exists. Aside from the maths, it is important to consider the product in question and the rate of technical innovation in the market.

A further problem of collective dominance, or oligopoly through "economic links" can arise, whereby the new market becomes more conducive to collusion. It is relevant how transparent a market is, because a more concentrated structure could mean firms can coordinate their behaviour more easily, whether firms can deploy deterrents and whether firms are safe from a reaction by their competitors and consumers. The entry of new firms to the market, and any barriers that they might encounter should be considered. If firms are shown to be creating an uncompetitive concentration, in the US they can still argue that they create efficiencies enough to outweigh any detriment, and similar reference to "technical and economic progress" is mentioned in Art. 2 of the ECMR. Another defence might be that a firm which is being taken over is about to fail or go insolvent, and taking it over leaves a no less competitive state than what would happen anyway. Mergers vertically in the market are rarely of concern, although in *AOL/Time Warner* the European Commission required that a joint venture with a competitor Bertelsmann be ceased beforehand. The EU authorities have also focused lately on the effect of conglomerate mergers, where companies acquire a large portfolio of related products, though without necessarily dominant shares in any individual market.

Intellectual Property, Innovation and Competition

Competition law has become increasingly intertwined with intellectual property, such as copyright, trademarks, patents, industrial design rights and in some jurisdictions trade secrets. On the one hand, it is believed that promotion of innovation through enforcement of intellectual property rights promotes competitiveness, while on the other the contrary may be the consequence. The question rests on whether it is legal to acquire monopoly through accumulation of intellectual property rights. In which case, the judgment needs to decide between giving preference to intellectual property rights or towards promoting competitiveness:

- Should antitrust laws accord special treatment to intellectual property.
- Should intellectual rights be revoked or not granted when antitrust laws are violated.

Concerns also arise over anti-competitive effects and consequences due to:

- Intellectual properties that are collaboratively designed with consequence of violating antitrust laws (intentionally or otherwise).
- The further effects on competition when such properties are accepted into industry standards.
- Cross-licensing of intellectual property.
- Bundling of intellectual property rights to long term business transactions or agreements to extend the market exclusiveness of intellectual property rights beyond their statutory duration.
- Trade secrets, if they remain a secret, having an eternal length of life.

Some scholars suggest that a prize instead of patent would solve the problem of deadweight loss, when innovators got their reward from the prize, provided by the government or non-profit organisation, rather than directly selling to the market, see Millennium Prize Problems. However innovators may accept the prize only when it is at least as much as how much they earn from patent, which is a question difficult to determine.

Cartel

A cartel is a formal (explicit) "agreement" among *competing* firms. It is a formal organisation of producers and manufacturers that agree to fix prices, marketing, and production. Cartels usually occur in an oligopolistic industry, where the number of sellers is small (usually because barriers to entry, most notably startup costs, are high) and the products being traded are usually commodities. Cartel members may agree on such matters as price fixing, total industry output, market shares, allocation of customers, allocation of territories, bid rigging, establishment of common sales agencies, and the division of profits or combination of these. The aim of such collusion (also called the cartel agreement) is to increase individual members' profits by reducing competition.

One can distinguish private cartels from public cartels. In the public cartel a government is involved to enforce the cartel agreement, and the government's sovereignty shields such cartels from legal actions. Inversely, private cartels are subject to legal liability under the antitrust laws now found in nearly every nation of the world. Furthermore, the purpose of private cartels is to benefit only those individuals who constitute it, public cartels, in theory, work to pass on benefits to the populace as a whole.

Competition laws often forbid private cartels. Identifying and breaking up cartels is an important part of the competition policy in most countries, although proving the existence of a cartel is rarely easy, as firms are usually not so careless as to put collusion agreements on paper. Several economic studies and legal decisions of antitrust authorities have found that the median price increase achieved by cartels in the last 200 years is around 25%. Private international cartels (those with participants from two or more nations) had an average price increase of 28%, whereas domestic cartels averaged 18%. Fewer than 10% of all cartels in the sample failed to raise market prices.

Origin

The term cartel originated for *alliances of enterprises* roughly around 1880 in Germany. The name was imported into the Anglosphere during the 1930s. Before this, other, less precise terms were common to denominate cartels, for instance: *association, combination, combine* or *pool*. In the 1940s the name *cartel* gained an anti-German bias, being the economic system of the enemy. *Cartels* were the economic structure the American antitrust campaign struggled to ban globally.

Private vs Public Cartel

A distinction is sometimes drawn between *public* and *private* cartels. In the case of public cartels, the government may establish and enforce the rules relating to prices, output and other such matters.

Export cartels and shipping conferences are examples of public cartels. In many countries, depression cartels have been permitted in industries deemed to be requiring price and production stability and/or to permit rationalization of industry structure and excess capacity. In Japan for example, such arrangements have been permitted in the steel, aluminum smelting, ship building and various chemical industries.

Public cartels were also permitted in the United States during the Great Depression in the 1930s and continued to exist for some time after World War II in industries such as coal mining and oil production. Cartels also played an extensive role in the German economy during the inter-war period. International commodity agreements covering products such as coffee, sugar, tin and more recently oil (OPEC) are examples of international cartels with publicly entailed agreements between different national governments. *Crisis cartels* have also been organised by governments for various industries or products in different countries in order to fix prices and ration production and distribution in periods of acute shortages.

Murray Rothbard considered the federal reserve as a public cartel of private banks.

In contrast, private cartels entail an agreement on terms and conditions that provide members mutual advantage, but that are not known or likely to be detected by outside parties. Private cartels in most jurisdictions are viewed as violating antitrust laws.

Long-term Unsustainability

Game theory suggests that cartels are inherently unstable, as the behaviour of members of a cartel is an example of a prisoner's dilemma. Each member of a cartel would be able to make more profit by breaking the agreement (producing a greater quantity or selling at a lower price than that agreed) than it could make by abiding by it. However, if all members break the agreement, all will be worse off.

The incentive to cheat explains why cartels are generally difficult to sustain in the long run. Empirical studies of 20th century cartels have determined that the mean duration of discovered cartels is from 5 to 8 years. However, one private cartel operated peacefully for 134 years before disbanding. There is a danger that once a cartel is broken, the incentives to form the cartel return and the cartel may be re-formed. Whether members of a cartel choose to cheat on the agreement depends on whether the short-term returns to cheating outweigh the long-term losses from the possible breakdown of the cartel. (The equilibrium of a prisoner's dilemma game varies according to whether it is played only once or repeatedly.)

The relative size of these two factors depends in part on how difficult it is for firms to monitor whether the agreement is being adhered to by other firms.

If monitoring is difficult, a member is likely to get away with cheating (and making higher profits) for longer, so members are more likely to cheat and the cartel will be more unstable.

There are several factors that will affect the firms' ability to monitor a cartel:

1. Number of firms in the industry
2. Characteristics of the products sold by the firms
3. Production costs of each member
4. Behaviour of demand
5. Frequency of sales and their characteristics

Number of Firms in Industry

The fewer the number of firms in the industry, the easier for the members of the cartel to monitor the behaviour of other members. Given that detecting a price cut becomes harder as the number of firms increases, the bigger are the gains from price cutting.

The greater the number of firms, the more probable it is that one of those firms is a *maverick* firm; that is, a firm known for pursuing aggressive and independent pricing strategy. Even in the case of a concentrated market, with few firms, the existence of such a firm may undermine the collusive behaviour of the cartel.

Characteristics of Products Sold

Cartels that sell commodities are more stable than those that sell differentiated products. Not only do homogeneous products make agreement on prices and/or quantities easier to negotiate, but also they facilitate monitoring. If goods are homogeneous, firms know that a change in their market share is probably due to a price cut (or quantity increase) by another member. Instead, if products are differentiated, changes in quantity sold by a member may be due to changes in consumer preferences or demand.

Production Costs

Similar cost structures of the firms in a cartel make it easier for them to co-ordinate, as they will have similar maximizing behaviour as regards prices and output. Instead, if firms have different cost structures then each will have different maximizing behaviour, so they will have an incentive to set a different price or quantity. Changes in cost structure (for example when a firm introduces a new technology) also give a cost advantage over rivals, making co-ordination and sustainability more difficult.

Behaviour of Demand

If an industry is characterized by a varying demand (that is, a demand with cyclical fluctuations), it is more difficult for the firms in the cartel to detect whether any change in their sales volume is due to a demand fluctuation or to cheating by another member of the cartel. Therefore, in a market with demand fluctuations, monitoring is more difficult and cartels are less stable.

Characteristics of Sales

If each firm's sales consist of a small number of high-value contracts, then it can make a relatively large short-term gain from cheating on the agreement and thereby winning more of these contracts. If, instead, its sales are high-volume and low-value, then the short-term gain is smaller. Therefore, low frequency of sales coupled with high value in each of these sales make cartels less sustainable. When the demand of the product is fluctuating, parties that are in a cartel are less interested to remain in the cartel, because they are not able to make regular profit.

Antitrust Law

General View: International competition authorities forbid cartels, but the effectiveness of cartel regulation and antitrust law in general is disputed by economic libertarians.

United States

The Sherman Antitrust Act of 1890 outlawed all contracts, combinations and conspiracies that unreasonably restrain interstate and foreign trade. This includes cartel violations, such as price fixing, bid rigging, and customer allocation. Sherman Act violations involving agreements between competitors are usually punishable as federal crimes.

European Union

The EU's competition law explicitly forbids cartels and related practices in its article 81 of the Treaty of Rome. Since the Treaty of Lisbon came into effect, the 81 EC is replaced by 101 TFEU. The article reads:

1. The following shall be prohibited as incompatible with the common market: all agreements between undertakings, decisions by associations of undertakings and concerted practices which may affect trade between Member States and which have as their object or effect the prevention, restriction or distortion of competition within the common market, and in particular those that:
   (a) Directly or indirectly fix purchase or selling prices or any other trading conditions
   (b) Limit or control production, markets, technical development, or investment
   (c) Share markets or sources of supply
   (d) Apply dissimilar conditions to equivalent transactions with other trading parties, thereby placing them at a competitive disadvantage;
   (e) Make the conclusion of contracts subject to acceptance by the other parties of supplementary obligations that, by their nature or according to commercial usage, have no connection with the subject of such contracts
2. Any agreements or decisions prohibited pursuant to this article shall be automatically void.
3. The provisions of paragraph 1 may, however, be declared inapplicable in the case of:
   - Any agreement or category of agreements between undertakings
   - Any decision or category of decisions by associations of undertakings
   - Any concerted practice or category of concerted practices that improve the production or distribution of goods, or promotes technical or economic progress, while allowing consumers a fair share of the resulting benefit, and that does not:

   (a) Impose on the undertakings concerned restrictions which are not indispensable to the attainment of these objectives
   (b) Afford such undertakings the possibility of eliminating competition in respect of a substantial part of the products in question

Article 81 explicitly forbids price fixing and limitation/control of production, the two more frequent cartel-types of collusion. The EU competition law also has regulations on the amount of fines for each type of cartel and a leniency policy by which, if a firm in a cartel, is the first to denounce the collusion agreement it is free of any responsibility. This mechanism has helped a lot in detecting cartel agreements in the EU.

Examples

People of the same trade seldom meet together, even for merriment and diversion, but the conversation ends in a conspiracy against the public, or in some contrivance to raise prices. It is impossible indeed to prevent such meetings, by any law which either could be executed, or would be consistent with liberty and justice.

—Adam Smith, *The Wealth of Nations, 1776*

The most recent example of a cartel was between Unilever and Procter & Gamble who were found guilty of price fixing washing powder in eight European countries. The case that was conducted by the European Commission after a tip off from Germany company, Henkel. The resulting penalty was a 315 million euros fine, split between Unilever (104m Euros) and Procter & Gamble (211m Euros).

De Beers is well known for its monopoloid practices throughout the 20th century, whereby it used its dominant position to manipulate the international diamond market. The company used several methods to exercise this control over the market: Firstly, it convinced independent producers to join its single channel monopoly, it flooded the market with diamonds similar to those of producers who refused to join the cartel, and lastly, it purchased and stockpiled diamonds produced by other manufacturers in order to control prices through supply. As recently as the mid-1980's, De Beers controlled almost 90% of global rough diamond supply, but beginning in the 1990's, the emergence of new competition reduced De Beers market share to less than 40%. While De Beers still sets non-negotiable prices of their own diamonds, they no longer have the market share to fix the global diamond market as a whole.

Another example of an international cartel is the one created by the members of the Asian Racing Federation and documented in the Good Neighbour Policy signed on September 1, 2003. Other well-known examples include:

- Organisation of the Petroleum Exporting Countries (OPEC): As its name suggests, OPEC is organised by sovereign states.

It cannot be held to antitrust enforcement in other jurisdictions by virtue of the doctrine of state immunity under public international law. However, members of the group do frequently break rank to increase production quotas.

- International Match Corporation (IMCO) of IvarKreuger in the 1920s.
- Many trade organisations, especially in industries dominated by only a few major companies, have been accused of being fronts for cartels.
- A well documented, private, international cartel is the lysine cartel of 1992–95.
- Anaconda Copper had a long running cartel.
- Some have argued that even the suppliers of credit can form a cartel to raise the price of credit (the interest rate) or gain political power

Cartel Party theory

In politics a Cartel party or cartel political party is a party which use the resources of the state to maintain its position within the political system. Katz &Mair argue that: "parties in Western Europe have adapted themselves to declining levels of participation and involvement in party activities by not only turning to resources provided by the state but by doing so in a collusive manner".

The concept of the 'cartel party' was first proposed in 1992 as a means of drawing attention to the patterns of inter-party collusion or cooperation rather than competition; and as a way of emphasising the influence of the state on party development. In definitional terms, the cartel party is a type of party that emerges in advanced democratic polities and that is characterised by the interpenetration of party and state and by a pattern of inter-party collusion.

With the development of the cartel party, the goals of politics become self-referential, professional and technocratic, and what little inter-party competition remains becomes focused on the efficient and effective management of the polity. The election campaigns that are conducted by cartel parties are capital-intensive, professionalized and centralized, and are organised on the basis of a strong reliance on the state for financial subventions and for other benefits and privileges. Within the party, the distinction between party members and non-members becomes blurred, in that through primaries, electronic polling, and so on, the parties invite all of their supporters, members or not, to participate in party activities and decision-making. Above all, with the emergence of cartel parties, politics becomes increasingly depoliticised.

Decartelization

Decartelization is the transition of a national economy from monopoly control by groups of large businesses, known as cartels, to a free market economy. This change rarely arises naturally, and is generally the result of regulation by a governing body with monopoly of power to decide what structures it likes. A modern example of decartelization is the economic restructuring of Germany after the fall of the Third Reich in 1945. To truly understand the term "decartelization" requires familiarity with the term "cartel". A cartel is a formal (explicit) agreement among firms. Cartels usually occur in an oligopolistic industry, where there are a small number of sellers and usually involve homogeneous products. Cartel members may agree on such matters as price fixing, total industry output, market shares, allocation of customers, allocation of territories, bid rigging, establishment of common sales agencies, and the division of profits or combination of these. The aim of such collusion is to increase individual member's profits by reducing competition. Competition laws forbid cartels. Identifying and breaking up cartels is an important part of the competition policy in most countries, although proving the existence of a cartel is rarely easy, as firms are usually not so careless as to put agreements to collude on paper.

Historical Background

Examples of alleged and legal monopolies:

- The salt commission, a legal monopoly in China formed in 758.
- British East India Company; created as a legal trading monopoly in 1600.
- Dutch East India Company; created as a legal trading monopoly in 1602.
- U.S. Steel; anti-trust prosecution failed in 1911.
- Standard Oil; broken up in 1911.
- National Football League; survived anti-trust lawsuit in the 1960s, convicted of being an illegal monopoly in the 1980s.
- Major League Baseball; survived U.S. anti-trust litigation in 1922, though its special status is still in dispute as of 2008.
- United Aircraft and Transport Corporation; aircraft manufacturer holding company forced to divest itself of airlines in 1934.

- American Telephone & Telegraph; telecommunications giant broken up in 1982.
- Microsoft; settled anti-trust litigation in the U.S. in 2001; fined by the European Commission in 2004, which was upheld for the most part by the Court of First Instance of the European Communities in 2007. The fine was 1.35 billion USD in 2008 for noncompliance with the 2004 rule.[8][9]
- De Beers; settled charges of price fixing in the diamond trade in the 2000s.
- Apple Inc., Accused of forming a Vertical Monopoly, with iPod, iTunes, iTunes Music Store, and the FairPlay DRM System.
- Joint Commission; has a monopoly over whether or not US hospitals are able to participate in the Medicare and Medicaid programs.
- Telecom New Zealand; local loop unbundling enforced by central government.

Debate

The general debate with decartelization is a national economy controlled by monopolies and cartels, versus a free market economy. With a free market economy, the pros are very clear. It encourages individual initiatives; it determines price of goods through competition, and motivates people to work towards financial freedom. Most individuals would prefer a free market economy, where there are many buyers and sellers in each market, and the prices are determined based on competition alone. The problem is, it is not up to the individuals. In most cases of cartels, these secret arrangements are done "under the radar", and these major companies know how to cover their tracks. It is very difficult to prove that companies have formed a cartel; therefore it is very difficult to dismantle one. In the case with the Third Reich in Germany, the people had no choice. In fact, many people were opposed to the idea of these "cartels" controlling the German economy. During the war, there was a school called Soziate Marktwirtschaft, the "socially conscious free market." Members of this school hated totalitarianism and had propounded their views at some risk during Hitler's regime. Wrote Henry Wallich, "During the Nazi period the school represented a kind of intellectual resistance movement, requiring great personal courage as well as independence of mind." The school's members believed in free markets, along with some slight degree of progression in the income tax system and government action to limit monopoly.

5

Production by the Firm and Industry

Production (Economics)

Production is a process of combining various material inputs and immaterial inputs (plans, know-how) in order to make something for consumption (the output). It is the act of creating output, a good or service which has value and contributes to the utility of individuals. Economic well-being is created in a production process, meaning all economic activities that aim directly or indirectly to satisfy human needs. The degree to which the needs are satisfied is often accepted as a measure of economic well-being. The satisfaction of needs originates from the use of the commodities which are produced. The need satisfaction increases when the quality-price-ratio of the commodities improves and more satisfaction is achieved at less cost. Improving the quality-price-ratio of commodities is to a producer an essential way to enhance the production performance but this kind of gains distributed to customers cannot be measured with production data.

Economic well-being also increases due to the growth of incomes that are gained from the growing and more efficient production. The most important forms of production are

- market production,
- public production and
- production in households.

In order to understand the origin of the economic well-being we must understand these three production processes. All of them have production functions of their own which interact with each other. Market production is the prime source of economic well-being and therefore the "primus motor" of the modern economy. Note that when we later discuss production we refer to market production. When discussing a single unit in the production process, the term "company" is used.

Production as a Source of Economic Well-Being

In principle there are two main activities in an economy, production and consumption. Similarly there are two kinds of actors, producers and consumers. Well-being is made possible by efficient production and by the interaction between producers and consumers. In the interaction, consumers can be identified in two roles both of which generate well-being. Consumers can be both customers of the producers and suppliers to the producers. The customers' well-being arises from the commodities they are buying and the suppliers' well-being is related to the income they receive as compensation for the production inputs they have delivered to the producers.

Stakeholders of Production

Stakeholders of production are persons, groups or organisations with an interest in a producing company. Economic well-being originates in efficient production and it is distributed through the interaction between the company's stakeholders. The stakeholders of companies are economic actors which have an economic interest in a company. Based on the similarities of their interests, stakeholders can be classified into three groups in order to differentiate their interests and mutual relations. The three groups are as follows:

- Customers
- Suppliers
- Producers.

The interests of these stakeholders and their relations to companies are described briefly below. Our purpose is to establish a framework for further analysis.

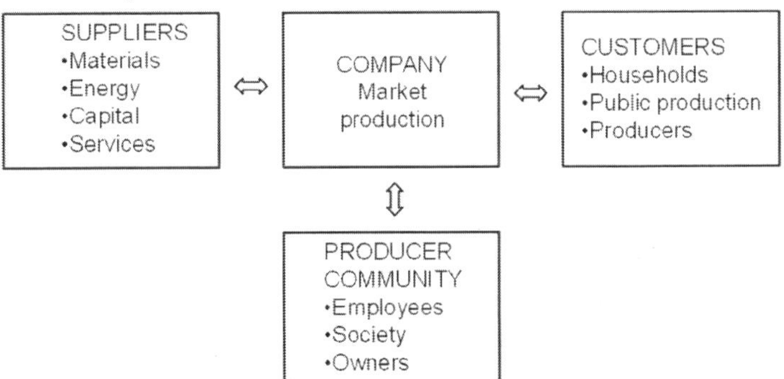

Figure: *Interactive contributions of a company's stakeholders (Saari, 2011,4)*

Customers

The customers of a company are typically consumers, other market producers or producers in the public sector. Each of them has their individual production functions. Due to competition, the price-quality-ratios of commodities tend to improve and this brings the benefits of better productivity to customers. Customers get more for less. In households and the public sector this means that more need satisfaction is achieved at less cost. For this reason the productivity of customers can increase over time even though their incomes remain unchanged.

Suppliers

The suppliers of companies are typically producers of materials, energy, capital, and services. They all have their individual production functions. The changes in prices or qualities of supplied commodities have an effect on both actors' (company and suppliers) production functions. We come to the conclusion that the production functions of the company and its suppliers are in a state of continuous change.

Producer Community

The incomes are generated for those participating in production, i.e., the labour force, society and owners. These stakeholders are referred to here as producer communities or, in shorter form, as producers. The producer communities have a common interest in maximizing their incomes. These parties that contribute to production receive increased incomes from the growing and developing production.

The well-being gained through commodities stems from the price-quality relations of the commodities. Due to competition and development in the market, the price-quality relations of commodities tend to improve over time. Typically the quality of a commodity goes up and the price goes down over time. This development favourably affects the production functions of customers. Customers get more for less. Consumer customers get more satisfaction at less cost. This type of well-being generation can only partially be calculated from the production data. The situation is presented in this study. The producer community (labour force, society, and owners) earns income as compensation for the inputs they have delivered to the production. When the production grows and becomes more efficient, the income tends to increase. In production this brings about an increased ability to pay salaries, taxes and profits. The growth of production and improved productivity generate additional income for the producing community. Similarly the high income level achieved in the community is a result of the high volume of production and its good performance.

This type of well-being generation – as mentioned earlier - can be reliably calculated from the production data.

Main Processes of a Producing Company

A producing company can be divided into sub-processes in different ways; yet, the following five are identified as main processes, each with a logic, objectives, theory and key figures of its own. It is important to examine each of them individually, yet, as a part of the whole, in order to be able to measure and understand them. The main processes of a company are as follows:

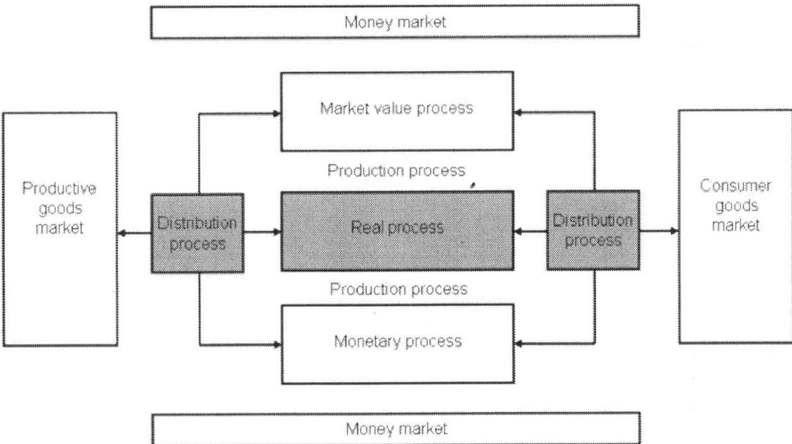

***Figure:** Main processes of a producing company (Saari 2006,3)*

- real process.
- income distribution process
- production process.
- monetary process.
- market value process.

Production output is created in the real process, gains of production are distributed in the income distribution process and these two processes constitute the production process. The production process and its sub-processes, the real process and income distribution process occur simultaneously, and only the production process is identifiable and measurable by the traditional accounting practices. The real process and income distribution process can be identified and measured by extra calculation, and this is why they need to be analysed separately in order to understand the logic of production and its performance. Real process generates the production output from input, and it can be described by means of the production function. It refers to a series of events in production in which production inputs of different quality and quantity are combined into products of different quality and quantity. Products can be physical goods, immaterial services and most often combinations of both. The characteristics created into the product by the producer imply surplus value to the consumer, and on the basis of the market price this value is shared by the consumer and the producer in the marketplace. This is the mechanism through which surplus value originates to the consumer and the producer likewise. It is worth noting that surplus values to customers cannot be measured from any production data. Instead the surplus value to a producer can be measured. It can be expressed both in terms of nominal and real values. The real surplus value to the producer is an outcome of the real process, real income, and measured proportionally it means productivity.

Income distribution process of the production refers to a series of events in which the unit prices of constant-quality products and inputs alter causing a change in income distribution among those participating in the exchange. The magnitude of the change in income distribution is directly proportionate to the change in prices of the output and inputs and to their quantities. Productivity gains are distributed, for example, to customers as lower product sales prices or to staff as higher income pay.

The production process consists of the real process and the income distribution process. A result and a criterion of success of the owner is profitability. The profitability of production is the share of the real process result the owner has been able to keep to himself in the income distribution process. Factors describing the production process are the components of profitability, i.e., returns and costs. They differ from the factors of the real process in that the components of profitability are given at nominal prices whereas in the real process the factors are at periodically fixed prices.

Monetary process refers to events related to financing the business. Market value process refers to a series of events in which investors determine the market value of the company in the investment markets.

Production Growth and Performance

Production growth is often defined as a production increase of an output of a production process. It is usually expressed as a growth percentage depicting growth of the real production output. The real output is the real value of products produced in a production process and when we subtract the real input from the real output we get the real income. The real output and the real income are generated by the real process of production from the real inputs. The real process can be described by means of the production function. The production function is a graphical or mathematical expression showing the relationship between the inputs used in production and the output achieved. Both graphical and mathematical expressions are presented and demonstrated. The production function is a simple description of the mechanism of income generation in production process. It consists of two components. These components are a change in production input and a change in productivity.

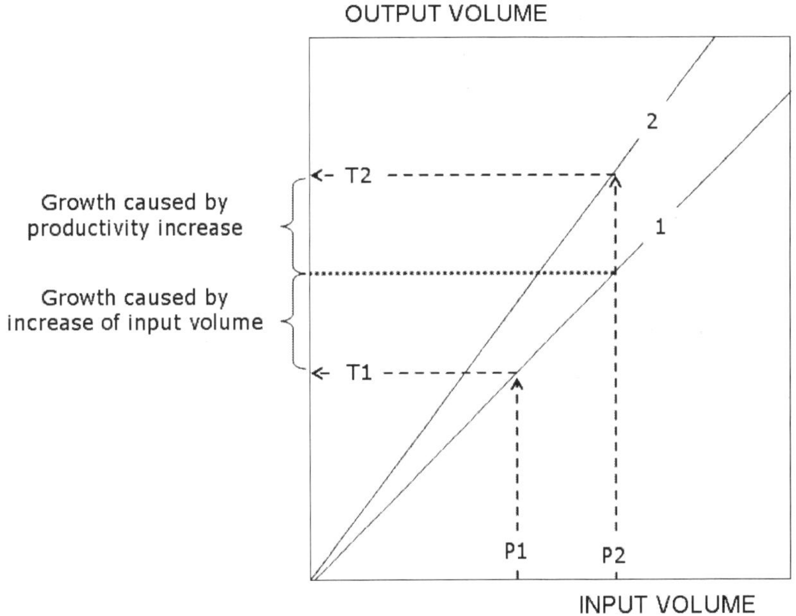

Figure: *Components of economic growth (Saari 2006,2)*

The figure illustrates an income generation process(exaggerated for clarity). The Value T2 (value at time 2) represents the growth in output from Value T1 (value at time 1). Each time of measurement has its own graph of the production function for that time (the straight lines). The output measured at time 2 is greater than the output measured at time one for both of the components of growth: an increase of inputs and an increase of productivity.

The portion of growth caused by the increase in inputs is shown on line 1 and does not change the relation between inputs and outputs. The portion of growth caused by an increase in productivity is shown on line 2 with a steeper slope. So increased productivity represents greater output per unit of input. Production is a process of combining various material inputs and immaterial inputs (plans, know-how) in order to make something for consumption (the output). The methods of combining the inputs of production in the process of making output are often called technology. The production function can be used as a rough measure of relative performance when comparing technologies.

In the case of a single production process (described above) the output is defined as an economic value of products and services produced in the process.

When we want to examine an entity of many production processes we have to sum up the value-added created in the single processes. This is done in order to avoid the double accounting of intermediate inputs. Value-added is obtained by subtracting the intermediate inputs from the outputs. The most well-known and used measure of value-added is the GDP (Gross Domestic Product). It is widely used as a measure of the economic growth of nations and industries.

The growth of production output does not reveal anything about the performance of the production process. The performance of production measures production's ability to generate income. Because the income from production is generated in the real process, we call it the real income. Similarly, as the production function is an expression of the real process, we could also call it "income generated by the production function".

The real income generation follows the logic of the production function. Two components can also be distinguished in the income change: the income growth caused by an increase in production input (production volume) and the income growth caused by an increase in productivity.

The income growth caused by increased production volume is determined by moving along the production function graph. The income growth corresponding to a shift of the production function is generated by the increase in productivity.

The change of real income so signifies a move from the point 1 to the point 2 on the production function (above). When we want to maximize the production performance we have to maximize the income generated by the production function.

The production performance can be measured as an average or an absolute income. Expressing performance both in average (avg.) and absolute (abs.) quantities is helpful for understanding the welfare effects of production. For measurement of the average production performance, we use the known productivity ratio

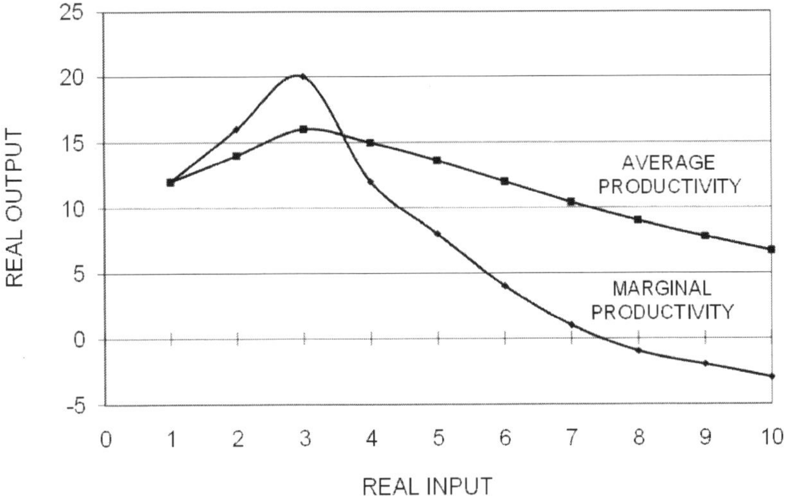

Figure: *Average and marginal productivity (Saari 2011,8)*

- Real output / Real input.

The absolute income of performance is obtained by subtracting the real input from the real output as follows:

- Real income (abs.) = Real output – Real input

The growth of the real income is the increase of the economic value which can be distributed between the production stakeholders. With the aid of the production model we can perform the average and absolute accounting in one calculation. Maximizing production performance requires using the absolute measure, i.e. the real income and its derivatives as a criterion of production performance.

The differences between the absolute and average performance measures can be illustrated by the following graph showing marginal and average productivity. The figure is a traditional expression of average productivity and marginal productivity. The maximum for production performance is achieved at the volume where marginal productivity is zero. The maximum for production performance is the maximum of the real incomes. In this illustrative example the maximum real income is achieved, when the production volume is 7.5 units. The maximum average productivity is reached when the production volume is 3.0 units. It is worth noting that the maximum average productivity is not the same as the maximum of real income.

Figure above is a somewhat exaggerated depiction because the whole production function is shown. In practice, decisions are made in a limited range of the production functions, but the principle is still the same; the maximum real income is aimed for. An important conclusion can be drawn. When we try to maximize the welfare effects of production we have to maximize real income formation. Maximizing productivity leads to a suboptimum, i.e. to losses of incomes.

A practical example illustrates the case. When a jobless person obtains a job in market production we may assume it is a low productivity job. As a result average productivity decreases but the real income per capita increases. Furthermore the well-being of the society also grows. This example reveals the difficulty to interpret the total productivity change correctly. The combination of volume increase and total productivity decrease leads in this case to the improved performance because we are on the "diminishing returns" area of the production function. If we are on the part of "increasing returns" on the production function, the combination of production volume increase and total productivity increase leads to improved production performance. Unfortunately we do not know in practice on which part of the production function we are. Therefore a correct interpretation of a performance change is obtained only by measuring the real income change.

Production Models

A production model is a numerical description of the production process and is based on the prices and the quantities of inputs and outputs. There are two main approaches to operationalize the concept of production function. We can use mathematical formulae, which are typically used in macroeconomics (in growth accounting) or arithmetical models, which are typically used in microeconomics and management accounting. We do not present the former approach here but refer to the survey "Growth accounting" by Hulten 2009.

We use here arithmetical models because they are like the models of management accounting, illustrative and easily understood and applied in practice. Furthermore they are integrated to management accounting, which is a practical advantage. A major advantage of the arithmetical model is its capability to depict production function as a part of production process. Consequently production function can be understood, measured, and examined as a part of production process.

There are different production models according to different interests. Here we use a production income model and a production analysis model in order to demonstrate production function as a phenomenon and a measurable quantity.

Production Income Model

	Period 1			Period 2		
	Quantity	Price	Value	Quantity	Price	Value
Product 1	210.00	7.20	1512	247.25	7.10	1755
Product 2	200.00	7.00	1400	195.03	7.15	1394
Output			2912			3150
Labour	100.00	7.50	750	115.00	7.70	886
Materials	80.00	8.60	688	79.20	8.50	673
Energy	400.00	1.50	600	428.00	1.55	663
Capital	160.00	3.80	608	164.80	3.90	643
Input			2646			2865
Surplus value (abs.)			266.00			285.12
Surplus value (rel.)			*1.101*			*1.100*

Figure: *Profitability of production measured by surplus value (Saari 2006,3)*

The scale of success run by a going concern is manifold, and there are no criteria that might be universally applicable to success. Nevertheless, there is one criterion by which we can generalise the rate of success in production. This criterion is the ability to produce surplus value. As a criterion of profitability, surplus value refers to the difference between returns and costs, taking into consideration the costs of equity in addition to the costs included in the profit and loss statement as usual. Surplus value indicates that the output has more value than the sacrifice made for it, in other words, the output value is higher than the value (production costs) of the used inputs. If the surplus value is positive, the owner's profit expectation has been surpassed. The table presents a surplus value calculation. We call this set of production data a basic example and we use the data through the article in illustrative production models. The basic example is a simplified profitability calculation used for illustration and modelling. Even as reduced, it comprises all phenomena of a real measuring situation and most importantly the change in the output-input mix between two periods. Hence, the basic example works as an illustrative "scale model" of production without any features of a real measuring situation being lost. In practice, there may be hundreds of products and inputs but the logic of measuring does not differ from that presented in the basic example.

In this context we define the quality requirements for the production data used in productivity accounting. The most important criterion of good measurement is the homogenous quality of the measurement object. If the object is not homogenous, then the measurement result may include changes in both quantity and quality but their respective shares will remain unclear. In productivity accounting this criterion requires that every item of output and input must appear in accounting as being homogenous. In other words the inputs and the outputs are not allowed to be aggregated in measuring and accounting. If they are aggregated, they are no longer homogenous and hence the measurement results may be biased.

Both the absolute and relative surplus value have been calculated in the example. Absolute value is the difference of the output and input values and the relative value is their relation, respectively. The surplus value calculation in the example is at a nominal price, calculated at the market price of each period.

Production Analysis Model

A model used here is a typical production analysis model by help of which it is possible to calculate the outcome of the real process, income distribution process and production process. The starting point is a profitability calculation using surplus value as a criterion of profitability. The surplus value calculation is the only valid measure for understanding the connection between profitability and productivity or understanding the connection between real process and production process. A valid measurement of total productivity necessitates considering all production inputs, and the surplus value calculation is the only calculation to conform to the requirement. If we omit an input in productivity or income accounting, this means that the omitted input can be used unlimitedly in production without any impact on accounting results.

Accounting and Interpreting

The process of calculating is best understood by applying the term *ceteris paribus*, i.e. "all other things being the same," stating that at a time only the impact of one changing factor be introduced to the phenomenon being examined. Therefore, the calculation can be presented as a process advancing step by step. First, the impacts of the income distribution process are calculated, and then, the impacts of the real process on the profitability of the production.

The first step of the calculation is to separate the impacts of the real process and the income distribution process, respectively, from the change in profitability (285.12 – 266.00 = 19.12). This takes place by simply creating one auxiliary column (4) in which a surplus value calculation is compiled using the quantities of Period 1 and the prices of Period 2. In the resulting profitability calculation, Columns 3 and 4 depict the impact of a change in income distribution process on the profitability and in Columns 4 and 7 the impact of a change in real process on the profitability.

The accounting results are easily interpreted and understood. We see that the real income has increased by 58.12 units from which 41.12 units come from the increase of productivity growth and the rest 17.00 units come from the production volume growth. The total increase of real income (58.12) is distributed to the stakeholders of production, in this case 39.00 units to the customers and to the suppliers of inputs and the rest 19.12 units to the owners. Here we can make an important conclusion. The income change created in a real process /i.e. by production function) is always distributed to the stakeholders as economic values within the review period. Accordingly the changes in real income and income distribution are always equal in terms of economic value. Based on the accounted changes of productivity and production volume values we can explicitly conclude on which part of the production function the production is. The rules of interpretations are the following:

The production is on the part of "increasing returns" on the production function, when

- productivity and production volume increase or
- productivity and production volume decrease

The production is on the part of "diminishing returns" on the production function, when

- productivity decreases and volume increases or
- productivity increases and volume decreases.

In the basic example the combination of volume growth (+17.00) and productivity growth (+41.12) reports explicitly that the production is on the part of "increasing returns" on the production function (Saari 2006 a, 138–144). Another productivity model (Saari 2011,14) also gives details of the income distribution. Because the accounting techniques of the two models are different, they give differing, although complementary, analytical information. The accounting results are, however, identical. We do not present the model here in detail but we only use its detailed data on income distribution, when the objective functions are formulated in the next section.

Objective Functions

An efficient way to improve the understanding of production performance is to formulate different objective functions according to the objectives of the different interest groups. Formulating the objective function necessitates defining the variable to be maximized (or minimized). After that other variables are considered as constraints. The most familiar objective function is profit maximization which is also included in this case. Profit maximization is an objective function that stems from the owner's interest and all other variables are constraints in relation to maximizing of profits.

The Procedure for Formulating Objective Functions

The procedure for formulating different objective functions, in terms of the production model, is introduced next. In the income formation from production the following objective functions can be identified:

- Maximizing the real income
- Maximizing the producer income
- Maximizing the owner income.

These cases are illustrated using the numbers from the basic example. The following symbols are used in the presentation: The equal sign (=) signifies the starting point of the computation or the result of computing and the plus or minus sign (+ / -) signifies a variable that is to be added or subtracted from the function. A producer means here the producer community, i.e. labour force, society and owners.

Objective function formulations can be expressed in a single calculation which concisely illustrates the logic of the income generation, the income distribution and the variables to be maximized.

The calculation resembles an income statement starting with the income generation and ending with the income distribution. The income generation and the distribution are always in balance so that their amounts are equal. In this case it is 58.12 units. The income which has been generated in the real process is distributed to the stakeholders during the same period. There are three variables which can be maximized. They are the real income, the producer income and the owner income. Producer income and owner income are practical quantities because they are addable quantities and they can be computed quite easily. Real income is normally not an addable quantity and in many cases it is difficult to calculate.

The Dual Approach for the Formulation

Here we have to add that the change of real income can also be computed from the changes in income distribution. We have to identify the unit price changes of outputs and inputs and calculate their profit impacts (i.e. unit price change x quantity). The change of real income is the sum of these profit impacts and the change of owner income. This approach is called the dual approach because the framework is seen in terms of prices instead of quantities (ONS 3, 23).

The dual approach has been recognised in growth accounting for long but its interpretation has remained unclear. The following question has remained unanswered:

"Quantity based estimates of the residual are interpreted as a shift in the production function, but what is the interpretation of the price-based growth estimates?" (Hulten 2009, 18). We have demonstrated above that the real income change is achieved by quantitative changes in production and the income distribution change to the stakeholders is its dual. In this case the duality means that the same accounting result is obtained by accounting the change of the total income generation (real income) and by accounting the change of the total income distribution.

List of Production Functions

The production functions listed below, and their properties are shown for the case of two factors of production, capital (K), and labour (L), mostly for heuristic purposes. These functions and their properties are easily generalizable to include additional factors of production (like land, natural resources, entrepreneurship, etc.)

A production function can also be seen as the dynamics of national output/national income. This list is to collect production functions & the dynamics of national output/income that have been used in literature & textbooks.

Technology

There are three common ways to incorporate technology (or the efficiency with which factors of production are used) into a production function:

- Hicks-neutral technology, or "factor augmenting": $Y = AF(K,L)$
- Harrod-neutral technology, or "labour augmenting": $Y = F(K, AL)$
- Solow-neutral technology, or "capital augmenting": $Y = F(AK, L)$

Elasticity of Substitution

The elasticity of substitution between factors of production is a measure of how easily one factor can be substituted for another.

With two factors of production, say, K and L, it is a measure of the curvature of a production isoquant. The mathematical definition is:

$$\mathrm{E} = [\frac{\partial(slope)}{\partial(L/K)}\frac{L/K}{slope}]^{-1}$$

where "slope" denotes the slope of the isoquant, given by:

$$slope = -\frac{\partial F(K,L)/\partial K}{\partial F(K,L)/\partial L}$$

Returns to Scale

Returns to scale can be

- Increasing returns to scale: doubling all input usages more than doubles output.
- Decreasing returns to scale: doubling all input usages less than doubles output.
- Constant returns to scale: doubling all input usages exactly doubles output.

Some Famous Forms

- Constant elasticity of substitution (CES) function:

$Y = A[\alpha K^{\gamma} + (1-\alpha)L^{\gamma}]^{\frac{1}{\gamma}}$, with $\gamma \in [-\infty, 1]$ which includes the special cases of:

- Linear production (or perfect substitutes)

  $Y = A[\alpha K + (1-\alpha)L]$ when $\gamma = 1$
- Cobb-Douglas (or imperfect complements)

  $Y = AK^{\alpha}L^{1-\alpha}$ when $\gamma \to 0$
- Leontief production function (or perfect complements)

  $Y = Min[K, L]$ when $\gamma \to -\infty$
- Translog (generalization of the above)

  $$ln(Y) = ln(A) + aL * ln(L) + aK * ln(K) + bLL * ln(L) * ln(L) +$$
  $$+ bKK * ln(K) * ln(K) + bLK * ln(L) * ln(K)$$
- The PAR production technology

The PAR production functions have such flexible limiting properties which are lacking in the CES technology. The Cobb-Douglas production function (a=0) as well as the Leontief production function ($a \to \infty$) are special cases of the PAR technology. The general form of the PAR production function is as follows:

Y = A*[c*(D^\-a -L^\-a)/((D/L)^\-a*c-1)]^\-(1/a) (a^1 0)(c^1 0)(D^1 L)

= A**[c*(D^\-a -L^\-a)/(-a*ln(D/L))]^\-(1/a)

(a^1 0)(c = 0)(D^1 L)

= A* D^\((1-c)/2)* L^\((1+c)/2) (a = 0)(-1≤-c≤1)(D^1 L)

= A*D (D = L)

If a=-1, then

Y = A*c*(D-L)/[(D/L)^\c-1] (a = -1)(c^1 0)(D^1 L)

= A*(D-L)/[ln(D/L)] (a = -1)(c = 0)(D^1 L)

In the above equation, Y is the physical output of production, D is input 1, L is input 2, "c" is the distribution limit parameter and "a" is the substitution parameter. Features of PAR technology are thoroughly examined by Tenhunen (1990).

Production Theory

Production theory is the study of production, or the economic process of converting inputs into outputs. Production uses resources to create a good or service that is suitable for use, gift-giving in a gift economy, or exchange in a market economy. This can include manufacturing, storing, shipping, and packaging. Some economists define production broadly as all economic activity other than consumption. They see every commercial activity other than the final purchase as some form of production. Production is a process, and as such it occurs through time and space. Because it is a flow concept, production is measured as a "rate of output per period of time". There are three aspects to production processes:

1. the quantity of the good or service produced,
2. the form of the good or service created,
3. the temporal and spatial distribution of the good or service produced.

A production process can be defined as any activity that increases the similarity between the pattern of demand for goods and services, and the quantity, form, shape, size, length and distribution of these goods and services available to the market place.

Factors of Production

In economics, factors of production are the *inputs* to the production process. *Finished goods* are the *output*. Input determines the quantity of output i.e. output depends upon input. Input is the starting point and output is the end point of production process and such input-output relationship is called a production function. There are three *basic* factors of production: land, labour, capital. Some modern economists also include entrepreneurship as a factor of production. These factors are also frequently labelled "producer goods" so as to distinguish them from the goods or services purchased by consumers, which are frequently labelled "consumer goods." All three of these are required in combination at a time to produce a commodity. In economics, production means creation or an addition of utility. Factors of production (or productive 'inputs' or 'resources') are any commodities or services used to produce goods or services.

Factors of production may also refer specifically to the *primary factors*, which are stocks including land, labour (the ability to work), and capital goods applied to production. Materials and energy are considered as secondary factors in classical economics because they are obtained from land, labour and capital. The primary factors facilitate production but neither become part of the product (as with raw materials) nor become significantly transformed by the production process (as with fuel used to power machinery). Land includes not only the site of production but natural resources above or below the soil. The factor land may, however, for simplification purposes be merged with capital in some cases (due to land being of little importance in the service sector and manufacturing). Recent usage has distinguished human capital (the stock of knowledge in the labour force) from labour. Entrepreneurship is also sometimes considered a factor of production. Sometimes the overall state of technology is described as a factor of production. The number and definition of factors varies, depending on theoretical purpose, empirical emphasis, or school of economics.

Historical Schools and Factors

In the interpretation of the currently dominant view of classical economic theory developed by neoclassical economists, the term "factors" did not exist until after the classical period and is not to be found in any of the literature of that time.

Differences are most stark when it comes to deciding which factor is the most important. For example, in the Austrian view—often shared by neoclassical and other "free market" economists—the primary factor of production is the time of the entrepreneur, which, when combined with other factors, determines the amount of output of a particular good or service. However, other authors argue that "entrepreneurship" is nothing but a specific kind of labour or human capital and should not be treated separately. The Marxian school goes further, seeing labour (in general, including entrepreneurship) as the primary factor of production, since it is required to produce capital goods and to utilise the gifts of nature. But this debate is more about basic economic theory (the role of the factors in the economy) than it is about the definition of the factors of production.

Physiocracy

In French Physiocracy, the main European school of economics before Adam Smith, the productive process is explained as the interaction between participating classes of the population. These classes are therefore the factors of production within physiocracy: capital, entrepreneurship, land, and labour.

- *The farmer* labours on land (sometimes using "crafts") to produce goods.
- *The landlord* is only a consumer of food and crafts and produces nothing at all.
- *The merchant*labours to export food in exchange for foreign imports.

Classical

The classical economics of Adam Smith, David Ricardo, and their followers focuses on physical resources in defining its factors of production, and discusses the distribution of cost and value among these factors. Adam Smith and David Ricardo referred to the "component parts of price" as the costs of using:

- Land or natural resource — naturally-occurring goods such as water, air, soil, minerals, flora and fauna that are used in the creation of products. The payment for use and the received income of a land owner is rent.
- Labour — human effort used in production which also includes technical and marketing expertise. The payment for someone else's labour and all income received from ones own labour is wages. Labour can also be classified as the physical and mental contribution of an employee to the production of the good(s).
- The capital stock — human-made goods which are used in the production of other goods. These include machinery, tools, and buildings.

The classical economists also employed the word "capital" in reference to money. Money, however, was not considered to be a factor of production in the sense of capital stock since it is not used to directly produce any good. The return to loaned money or to loaned stock was styled as interest while the return to the actual proprietor of capital stock (tools, etc.) was styled as profit.

Marxism

Marx considered the "elementary factors of the labour-process" or "productive forces" to be:

- Labour
- The subject of labour (objects transformed by labour)
- The instruments of labour (or means of labour).

The "subject of labour" refers to natural resources and raw materials, including land. The "instruments of labour" are tools, in the broadest sense. They include factory buildings, infrastructure, and other human-made objects that facilitate labour's production of goods and services.

This view seems similar to the classical perspective described above. But unlike the classical school and many economists today, Marx made a clear distinction between labour actually done and an individual's "labour power" or ability to work.

Labour done is often referred to nowadays as "effort" or "labour services." Labour-power might be seen as a stock which can produce a flow of labour.

Labour, not labour power, is the key factor of production for Marx and the basis for Marx's labour theory of value. The hiring of labour power only results in the production of goods or services ("use-values") when organised and regulated (often by the "management"). How much labour is actually done depends on the importance of conflict or tensions within the labour process.

Neoclassical Economics

Neoclassical economics, one of the branches of mainstream economics, started with the classical factors of production of land, labour, and capital. However, it developed an alternative theory of value and distribution. Many of its practitioners have added various further factors of production.

Further Distinctions

Further distinctions from classical and neoclassical microeconomics include the following:

- *Capital* — This has many meanings, including the financial capital raised to operate and expand a business. In much of economics, however, "capital" (without any qualification) means goods that can help produce other goods in the future, the result of investment. It refers to machines, roads, factories, schools, infrastructure, and office buildings which humans have produced in order to produce goods and services.
- *Fixed capital* — This includes machinery, factories, equipment, new technology, factories, buildings, computers, and other goods that are designed to increase the productive potential of the economy for future years. Nowadays, many consider computer software to be a form of fixed capital and it is counted as such in the National Income and Product Accounts of the United States and other countries. This type of capital does not change due to the production of the good.
- *Working capital* — This includes the stocks of finished and semi-finished goods that will be economically consumed in the near future or will be made into a finished consumer good in the near future. These are often called inventories. The phrase "working capital" has also been used to refer to liquid assets (money) needed for immediate expenses linked to the production process (to pay salaries, invoices, taxes, interests...) Either way, the amount or nature of this type of capital usually changed during the production process.
- *Financial capital* — This is simply the amount of money the initiator of the business has invested in it. "Financial capital" often refers to his or her net worth tied up in the business (assets minus liabilities) but the phrase often includes money borrowed from others.
- *Technological progress* — For over a century, economists have known that capital and labour do not account for all of economic growth. This is reflected in *total factor productivity* and the *Solow residual* used in economic models called *production functions* that account for the contributions of capital and labour, yet have some unexplained contributor which is commonly called *technological progress*. Ayres and Warr (2009) present time series of the efficiency of primary energy (exergy) conversion into useful work for the US, UK, Austria and Japan revealing dramatic improvements in model accuracy. With useful work as a factor of production they are able to reproduce historical rates of economic growth with considerable precision

and without recourse to exogenous and unexplained technological progress, thereby overcoming the major flaw of the Solow Theory of economic growth.

A Fourth Factor?

As mentioned, recent authors have added to the classical list. For example, J.B. Clark saw the co-ordinating function in production and distribution as being served by entrepreneurs; Frank Knight introduced managers who co-ordinate using their own money (financial capital) and the financial capital of others. In contrast, many economists today consider "human capital" (skills and education) as the fourth factor of production, with entrepreneurship as a form of human capital. Yet others refer to intellectual capital. More recently, many have begun to see "social capital" as a factor, as contributing to production of goods and services.

Entrepreneurship

Consider entrepreneurship as a factor of production, leaving debate aside. In markets, entrepreneurs combine the other factors of production, land, labour, and capital, in order to make a profit. Often these entrepreneurs are seen as innovators, developing new ways to produce and new products. In a planned economy, central planners decide how land, labour, and capital should be used to provide for maximum benefit for all citizens. Of course, just as with market entrepreneurs, the benefits may mostly accrue to the entrepreneurs themselves.

The word has been blown apart by the government. The sociologist C. Wright Mills refers to "new entrepreneurs" who work within and between corporate and government bureaucracies in new and different ways. Others (such as those practicing public choice theory) refer to "political entrepreneurs," i.e., politicians and other actors.

Much controversy rages about the benefits produced by entrepreneurship. But the real issue is about how well institutions they operate in (markets, planning, bureaucracies, government) serve the public. This concerns such issues as the relative importance of market failure and government failure.

Non Tangible Forms of Capital

Human Capital: Contemporary analysis distinguishes tangible, physical, or nonhuman capital goods from other forms of capital such as human capital. Human capital is embodied in a human being and is acquired through education and training, whether formal or on the job. Human capital is important in modern economic theory. Education is a key element in explaining economic growth over time. It is also often seen as the solution to the "Leontief paradox" in international trade.

Intellectual Capital

A more recent coinage is intellectual capital, used especially as to information technology, recorded music, written material. This intellectual property is protected by copyrights, patents, and trademarks.

This view posits a new Information Age, which changes the roles and nature of land, labour, and capital. During the Information Age (circa 1971–present), the Knowledge Age (circa 1991 to 2002), and the Intangible Economy (2002–present) many see the primary factors of production as having become less concrete. These factors of production are now seen as knowledge, collaboration, process-engagement, and time quality. According to economic theory, a "factor of production" is used to create value and allow economic performance. As the four "modern-day" factors are all essentially abstract, the current economic age has been called the Intangible Economy. Intangible factors of production are subject to network effects and the contrary economic laws such as the law of increasing returns.

Social Capital

Social capital is often hard to define, but to one textbook it is "the stock of trust, mutual understanding, shared values, and socially held knowledge that facilitates the social coordination of economic activity." Knowledge, ideas, and values, and human relationships are transmitted as part of the culture. This type of capital cannot be owned by individuals and is instead part of the common stock owned by humanity. But they are often crucial to maintaining a peaceful society in which normal economic transactions and production can occur.

Another kind of social capital *can* be owned individually. This kind of individual asset involves reputation, what accountants call "goodwill", and/or what others call "street cred," along with fame, honour, and prestige.

It fits with Pierre Bourdieu's definition of 'social capital' as "an attribute of an individual in a social context. One can acquire social capital through purposeful actions and can transform social capital into conventional economic gains. The ability to do so, however, depends on the nature of the social obligations, connections, and networks, available to you."

This means that the value of individual social assets that Bourdieu points to depend on the current "social capital" as defined above.

Natural Resources

Ayres and Warr (2009) are among the economists who criticize orthodox economics for overlooking the role of natural resources and the effects of declining resource capital.

Energy

Energy can be seen as individual factor of production, with an elasticity larger than labour. A cointegration analysis support results derived from linear exponentional (LINEX) production functions.

Total, Average, and Marginal Product

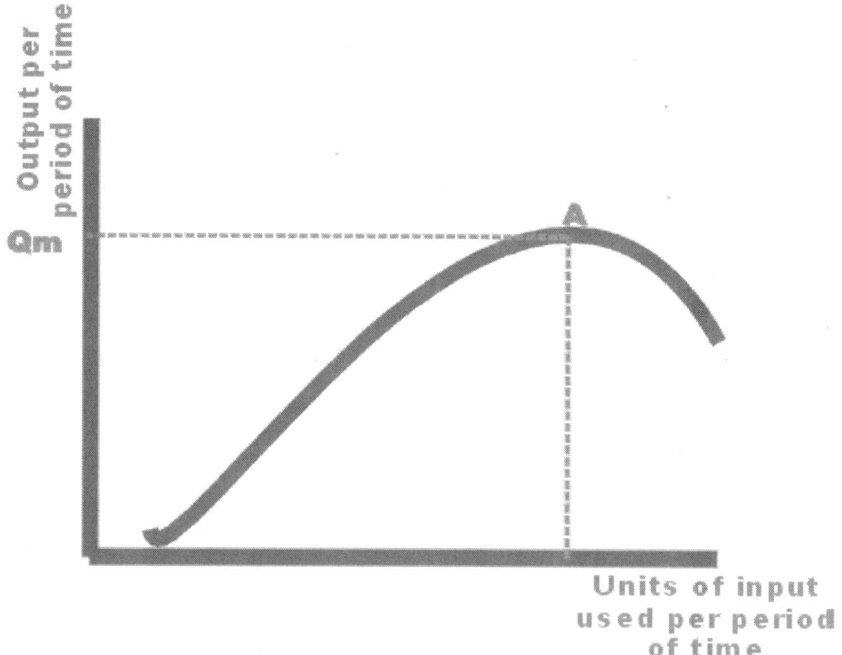

Figure: *Total Product Curve*

The total product (or total physical product) of a variable factor of production identifies what outputs are possible using various levels of the variable input.

This can be displayed in either a chart that lists the output level corresponding to various levels of input, or a graph that summarizes the data into a "total product curve". The diagram shows a typical total product curve. In this example, output increases as more inputs are employed up until point A. The maximum output possible with this production process is Qm. (If there are other inputs used in the process, they are assumed to be fixed.)

The average physical product is the total production divided by the number of units of variable input employed. It is the output of each unit of input. If there are 10 employees working on a production process that manufactures 50 units per day, then the average product of variable labour input is 5 units per day.

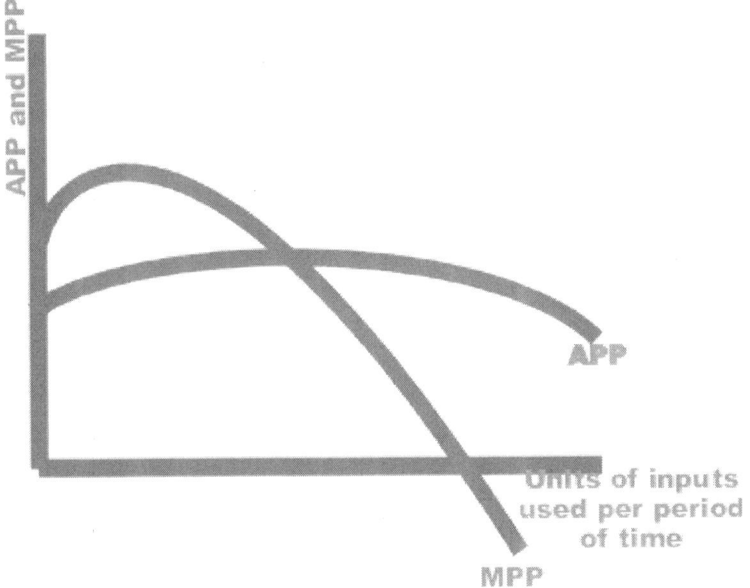

Figure: *Average and Marginal Physical Product Curves. The input amount were the MPP is 0, is the same as for A in the Total Product Curve (image above).*

The average product typically varies as more of the input is employed, so this relationship can also be expressed as a chart or as a graph. A typical average physical product curve is shown (APP). It can be obtained by drawing a vector from the origin to various points on the total product curve and plotting the slopes of these vectors.

The marginal physical product of a variable input is the change in total output due to a one unit change in the variable input (called the discrete marginal product) or alternatively the rate of change in total output due to an infinitesimally small change in the variable input (called the continuous marginal product). The discrete marginal product of capital is the additional output resulting from the use of an additional unit of capital (assuming all other factors are fixed). The continuous marginal product of a variable input can be calculated as the derivative of quantity produced with respect to variable input employed. The marginal physical product curve is shown (MPP). It can be obtained from the slope of the total product curve.

Because the marginal product *drives* changes in the average product, we know that when the average physical product is falling, the marginal physical product must be less than the average. Likewise, when the average physical product is rising, it must be due to a marginal physical product greater than the average. For this reason, the marginal physical product curve must intersect the maximum point on the average physical product curve.

Notes: MPP keeps increasing until it reaches its maximum. Up until this point every additional unit has been adding more value to the total product than the previous one. From this point onwards, every additional unit adds less to the total product compared to the previous one – MPP is decreasing. But the average product is still increasing till MPP touches APP. At this point, an additional unit is adding the same value as the average product. From this point onwards, APP starts to reduce because every additional unit is adding less to APP than the average product. But the total product is still increasing because every additional unit is still contributing positively. Therefore, during this period, both, the average as well as marginal products, are decreasing, but the total product is still increasing. Finally we reach a point when MPP crosses the x-axis. At this point every additional unit starts to diminish the product of previous units, possibly by getting into their way. Therefore the total product starts to decrease at this point. This is point A on the total product curve. (Courtesy: Dr.ShehzadInayat Ali).

Diminishing Returns

In economics, diminishing returns (also called diminishing marginal returns) is the decrease in the marginal (per-unit) output of a production process as the amount of a single factor of production is increased, while the amounts of all other factors of production stay constant.

The law of diminishing returns (also law of diminishing marginal returns or law of increasing relative cost) states that in all productive processes, adding more of one factor of production, while holding all others constant ("*ceteris paribus*"), will at some point yield lower per-unit returns. The law of diminishing returns does not imply that adding more of a factor will decrease the *total* production, a condition known as negative returns, though in fact this is common.

For example, the use of fertilizer improves crop production on farms and in gardens; but at some point, adding more and more fertilizer improves the yield less per unit of fertilizer, and excessive quantities can even reduce the yield. A common sort of example is adding more workers to a job, such as assembling a car on a factory floor. At some point, adding more workers causes problems such as workers getting in each other's way or frequently finding themselves waiting for access to a part. In all of these processes, producing one more unit of output per unit of time will eventually cost increasingly more, due to inputs being used less and less effectively.

The law of diminishing returns is a fundamental principle of economics. It plays a central role in production theory.

History

The concept of diminishing returns can be traced back to the concerns of early economists such as Johann Heinrich von Thünen, Turgot, James Steuart, Thomas Robert Malthus and David Ricardo. However, classical economists such as Malthus and Ricardo attributed the successive diminishment of output to the decreasing quality of the inputs. Neoclassical economists assume that each "unit" of labour is identical. Diminishing returns are due to the disruption of the entire productive process as additional units of labour are added to a fixed amount of capital. The law of diminishing returns remains an important consideration in farming

Diminishing Marginal Returns

Suppose that one kilogram of seed applied to a plot of land of a fixed super-size produces one ton of crop. You might expect that a return equals the extra amount of crop produced divided by the extra amount of seeds planted. A consequence of diminishing marginal returns is that as total investment increases, the total return on investment as a proportion of the total investment (the average product or return) decreases. The return from investing the first kilogram is 1 t/kg. The total return when 2 kg of seed are invested is 1.5/2 = 0.75 t/kg, while the total return when 3 kg are invested is 1.75/3 = 0.58 t/kg.

This particular example of Diminishing Marginal Returns in formulaic terms: Where D = Diminished Marginal Return, X = seed in kilograms, and $\frac{1}{2^{i-1}}$ = crop yield in tons gives us:

$$\frac{1}{X}\sum_{i=1}^{X}\frac{1}{2^{i-1}} = \mathrm{D}$$

Substituting 3 for X and expanding yields:

$$\frac{1}{3}\sum_{i=1}^{3}\frac{1}{2^{i-1}} = \text{D}$$

$$= \frac{1}{3}\cdot\left(\frac{1}{2^{1-1}} + \frac{1}{2^{2-1}} + \frac{1}{2^{3-1}}\right)$$

$$= \frac{1}{3}\cdot\left(\frac{1}{2^{0}} + \frac{1}{2^{1}} + \frac{1}{2^{2}}\right)$$

$$= \frac{1}{3}\cdot\left(\frac{1}{1} + \frac{1}{2} + \frac{1}{4}\right)$$

$$= \frac{1}{3}\cdot\left(\frac{7}{4}\right)$$

$$= \frac{7}{12}$$

$$= 0.58\overline{3} \text{ t/kg}$$

Another example is a factory that has a fixed stock of capital, or tools and machines, and a variable supply of labour. As the firm increases the number of workers, the total output of the firm grows but at an ever-decreasing rate. This is because after a certain point, the factory becomes overcrowded and workers begin to form lines to use the machines. The long-run solution to this problem is to increase the stock of capital, that is, to buy more machines and to build more factories.

Returns and Costs

There is an inverse relationship between returns of inputs and the cost of production. Suppose that a kilogram of seed costs one dollar, and this price does not change. Although there are other costs, assume they do not vary with the amount of output and are therefore fixed costs. One kilogram of seeds yields one ton of crop, so the first ton of the crop costs one dollar to produce. That is, for the first ton of output, the marginal cost of the output is \$1 per ton. If there are no other changes, then if the second kilogram of seeds applied to land produces only half the output of the first, the marginal cost would equal \$1 per half ton of output, or \$2 per ton. Similarly, if the third kilogram of seeds yields only a quarter ton, then the marginal cost equals \$1 per quarter ton, or \$4 per ton. Thus, diminishing marginal returns imply increasing marginal costs and rising average costs.

Cost can also be measured in terms of opportunity cost. In this case the law also applies to societies – the opportunity cost of producing a single unit of a good generally increases as a society attempts to produce more of that good. This explains the bowed-out shape of the production possibilities frontier.

Diminishing Marginal Returns

These curves illustrate the principle of diminishing marginal returns to a variable input (not to be confused with diseconomies of scale which is a long term phenomenon in which all factors are allowed to change). This states that as you add more and more of a variable input, you will reach a point beyond which the resulting increase in output starts to diminish. This point is illustrated as the maximum point on the marginal physical product curve. It assumes that other factor inputs (if they are used in the process) are held constant. An example is the employment of labour in the use of trucks to transport goods. Assuming the number of available trucks (capital) is fixed, then the amount of the variable input labour could be varied and the resultant efficiency determined. At least one labourer (the driver) is necessary. Additional workers per vehicle could be productive in loading, unloading, navigation, or around the clock continuous driving. But at some point the returns to investment in labour will start to diminish and efficiency will decrease. The most efficient distribution of labour per piece of equipment will likely be one driver plus an additional worker for other tasks (2 workers per truck would be more efficient than 5 per truck). Resource allocations and distributive efficiencies in the mix of capital and labour investment will vary per industry and according to available technology. Trains are able to transport much more in the way of goods with fewer "drivers" but at the cost of greater investment in infrastructure. With the advent of mass production of motorized vehicles, the economic niche occupied by trains (compared with transport trucks) has become more specialised and limited to long haul delivery.

P.S.: There is an argument that if the theory is holding everything constant, the production method should not be changed, i.e., division of labour should not be practiced. However, the rise in marginal product means that the workers use other means of production method, such as in loading, unloading, navigation, or around the clock continuous driving. For this reason, some economists think that the "keeping other things constant" should not be used in this theory.

Many Ways of Expressing the Production Relationship

The total, average, and marginal physical product curves mentioned above are just one way of showing production relationships. They express the quantity of output relative to the amount of variable input employed while holding fixed inputs constant. Because they depict a short run relationship, they are sometimes called short run production functions. If all inputs are allowed to be varied, then the diagram would express outputs relative to total inputs, and the function would be a long run production function. If the mix of inputs is held constant, then output would be expressed relative to inputs of a fixed composition, and the function would indicate long run economies of scale.

Rather than comparing inputs to outputs, it is also possible to assess the mix of inputs employed in production. An isoquant relates the quantities of one input to the quantities of another input. It indicates all possible combinations of inputs that are capable of producing a given level of output. Rather than looking at the inputs used in production, it is possible to look at the mix of outputs that are possible for any given production process. This is done with a production possibilities frontier. It indicates what combinations of outputs are possible given the available factor endowment and the prevailing production technology.

Isoquants

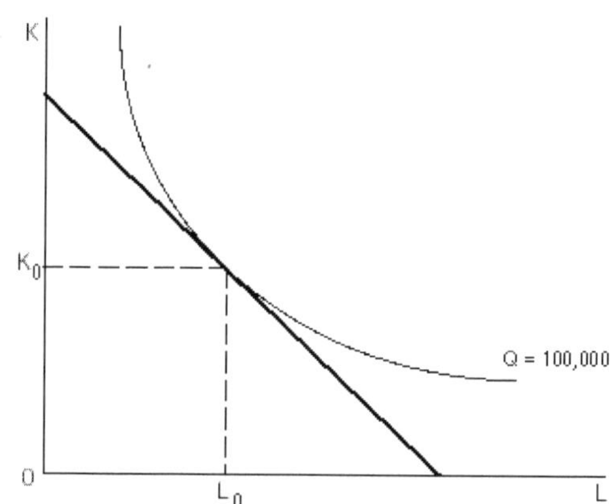

Figure: *Isoquant Curve/Isocost Curve*

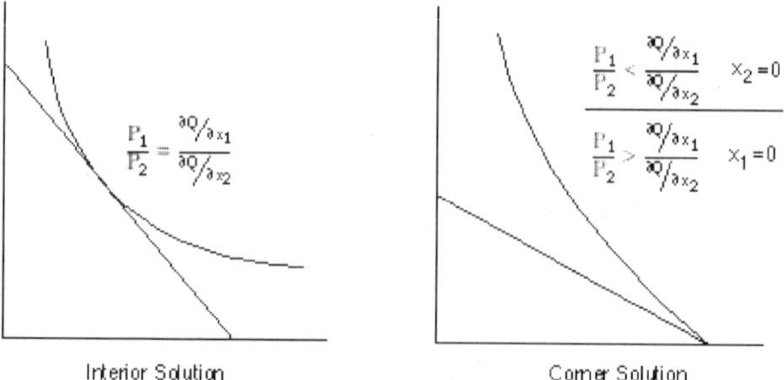

Figure: *Two Isoquants (Interior and Corner Solutions)*

An isoquant represents those combinations of inputs, which will be capable of producing an equal quantity of output; the producer would be indifferent between them. The isoquants are thus contour lines, which trace the loci of equal outputs. As the production remains the same on any point of this line, it is also called equal product curve. Let Q0 = f(L,K) be a production factor, where Q0 = A is a fixed level of production.

L = Labour

K = Capital

If three combinations of labour and capital A, B and C produces 10 units of product, then the isoquant will be like Figure depicted above.

Here we see that the combination of L1 labour and K3 capital can produce 10 units of product, which is A on the isoquant. Now to increase the labour keeping the production the same the organisation has to decrease capital. In Figure above, B is the point where capital decreases to K2, while labour increases to L2. Similarly, 10 units of product may be produced at point C on the isoquant with capital K1 and labour L3. Each of the factor combinations A, B and C produces the same level of output, 10 units.

These curves illustrate the principle of diminishing marginal returns to a variable input (not to be confused with diseconomies of scale which is a long term phenomenon in which all factors are allowed to change). This states that as you add more and more of a variable input, you will reach a point beyond which the resulting increase in output starts to diminish. This point is illustrated as the maximum point on the marginal physical product curve. It assumes that other factor inputs (if they are used in the process) are held constant. An example is the employment of labour in the use of trucks to transport goods. Assuming the number of available trucks (capital) is fixed, then the amount of the variable input labour could be varied and the resultant efficiency determined. At least one labourer (the driver) is necessary. Additional workers per vehicle could be productive in loading, unloading, navigation, or around the clock continuous driving. But at some point the returns to investment in labour will start to diminish and efficiency will decrease. The most efficient distribution of labour per piece of equipment will likely be one driver plus an additional worker for other tasks (2 workers per truck would be more efficient than 5 per truck).

Resource allocations and distributive efficiencies in the mix of capital and labour investment will vary per industry and according to available technology. Trains are able to transport much more in the way of goods with fewer "drivers" but at the cost of greater investment in infrastructure. With the advent of mass production of motorized vehicles, the economic niche occupied by trains (compared with transport trucks) has become more specialised and limited to long haul delivery.

P.S.: There is an argument that if the theory is holding everything constant, the production method should not be changed, i.e., division of labour should not be practiced. However, the rise in marginal product means that the workers use other means of production method, such as in loading, unloading, navigation, or around the clock continuous driving. For this reason, some economists think that the "keeping other things constant" should not be used in this theory.

The Marginal Rate of Technical Substitution

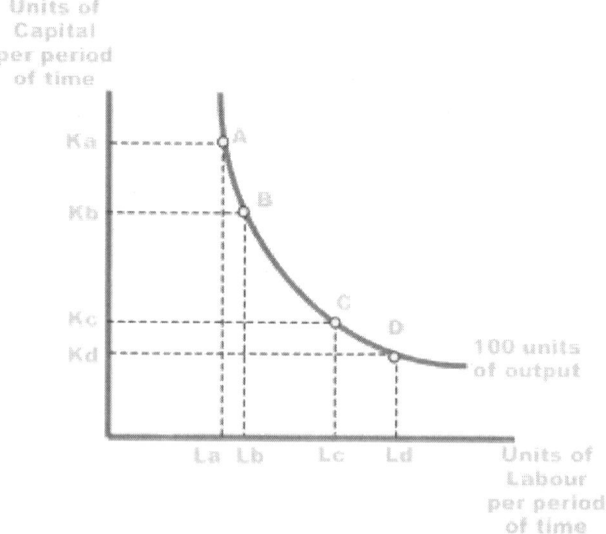

Figure: Marginal Rate of Technical Substitution

Isoquants are typically convex to the origin reflecting the fact that the two factors are substitutable for each other at varying rates. This rate of substitutability is called the "marginal rate of technical substitution" (MRTS) or occasionally the "marginal rate of substitution in production". It measures the reduction in one input per unit increase in the other input that is just sufficient to maintain a constant level of production. For example, the marginal rate of substitution of labour for capital gives the amount of capital that can be replaced by one unit of labour while keeping output unchanged.

To move from point A to point B in the diagram, the amount of capital is reduced from Ka to Kb while the amount of labour is increased only from La to Lb. To move from point C to point D, the amount of capital is reduced from Kc to Kd while the amount of labour is increased from Lc to Ld. The marginal rate of technical substitution of labour for capital is equivalent to the absolute slope of the isoquant at that point (change in capital divided by change in labour). It is equal to 0 where the isoquant becomes horizontal, and equal to infinity where it becomes vertical. The opposite is true when going in the other direction (from D to C to B to A). In this case we are looking at the marginal rate of technical substitution capital for labour (which is the reciprocal of the marginal rate of technical substitution labour for capital).

It can also be shown that the marginal rate of substitution labour for capital, is equal to the marginal physical product of labour divided by the marginal physical product of capital.

In the unusual case of two inputs that are perfect substitutes for each other in production, the isoquant would be linear (linear in the sense of a function $y = a - bx$). If, on the other hand, there is only one production process available, factor proportions would be fixed, and these zero-substitutability isoquants would be shown as horizontal or vertical lines.

Productivity Model

Productivity in economics is the ratio of what is produced to what is required to produce. Productivity is the measure on production efficiency. Productivity model is a measurement method which is used in practice for measuring productivity. Productivity model must be able to solve the formula *Output / Input* when there are many different outputs and inputs.

Comparison of the Productivity Models

The principle of comparing productivity models is to identify the characteristics that are present in the models and to understand their differences. This task is alleviated by the fact that such characteristics can unmistakably be identified by their measurement formula. Based on the model comparison, it is possible to identify the models that are suited for measuring productivity. A criterion of this solution is the production theory and the production function. It is essential that the model is able to describe the production function.

The principle of model comparison becomes evident in the figure. There are two dimensions in the comparison. Horizontal model comparison refers to a comparison between business models. Vertical model comparison refers to a comparison between economic levels of activity or between the levels of business, industry and national economy.

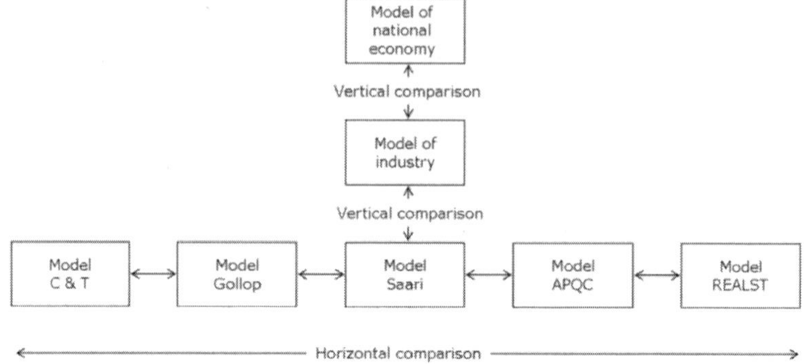

Figure: *Dimensions of productivity model comparisons (Saari 2006b)*

At all three levels of economy, that is, that of business, industry and national economy, a uniform understanding prevails of the phenomenon of productivity and of how it should be modelled and measured. The comparison reveals some differences that can mainly be seen to result from differences in measuring accuracy. It has been possible to develop the productivity model of business so as to be more accurate than that of national economy for the simple reason that in business the measuring data are much more accurate. (Saari 2006b)

Business Models

There are several different models available for measuring productivity. Comparing the models systematically has proved most problematic. In terms of pure mathematics it has not been possible to establish the different and similar characteristics of them so as to be able to understand each model as such and in relation to another model. This kind of comparison is possible using the productivity model which is a model with adjustable characteristics. An adjustable model can be set with the characteristics of the model under review after which both differences and similarities are identifiable.

A characteristic of the productivity measurement models that surpasses all the others is the ability to describe the production function. If the model can describe the production function, it is applicable to total productivity measurements. On the other hand, if it cannot describe the production function or if it can do so only partly, the model is not suitable for its task. The productivity models based on the production function form rather a coherent entity in which differences in models are fairly small. The differences play an insignificant role, and the solutions that are optional can be recommended for good reasons. Productivity measurement models can differ in characteristics from another in six ways.

1. First, it is necessary to examine and clarify the differences in the names of the concepts. Model developers have given different names to the same concepts, causing a lot of confusion. It goes without saying that differences in names do not affect the logic of modelling.
2. Model variables can differ; hence, the basic logic of the model is different. It is a question of which variables are used for the measurement. The most important characteristic of a model is its ability to describe the production function. This requirement is fulfilled in case the model has the production function variables of productivity and volume. Only the models that meet this criterion are worth a closer comparison. (Saari 2006b)
3. Calculation order of the variables can differ. Calculation is based on the principle of Ceteris paribus stating that when calculating the impacts of change in one variable all other variables are hold constant. The order of calculating the variables has some effect on the calculation results, yet, the difference is not significant.
4. Theoretical framework of the model can be either cost theory or production theory. In a model based on the production theory, the volume of activity is measured by input volume. In a model based on the cost theory, the volume of activity is measured by output volume.
5. Accounting technique, i.e. how measurement results are produced, can differ. In calculation, three techniques apply: ratio accounting, variance accounting and accounting form. Differences in the accounting technique do not imply differences in accounting results but differences in clarity and intelligibility. Variance accounting gives the user most possibilities for an analysis.

1. Adjustability of the model. There are two kinds of models, fixed and adjustable. On an adjustable model, characteristics can be changed, and therefore, they can examine the characteristics of the other models. A fixed model can not be changed. It holds constant the characteristic that the developer has created in it.

Based on the variables used in the productivity model suggested for measuring business, such models can be grouped into three categories as follows:

- Productivity index models
- PPPV models
- PPPR models

In 1955, Davis published a book titled Productivity Accounting in which he presented a productivity index model. Based on Davis' model several versions have been developed, yet, the basic solution is always the same (Kendrick & Creamer 1965, Craig & Harris 1973, Hines 1976, Mundel 1983, Sumanth 1979). The only variable in the index model is productivity, which implies that the model can not be used for describing the production function. Therefore, the model is not introduced in more detail here.

PPPV is the abbreviation for the following variables, profitability being expressed as a function of them:

Profitability = f (Productivity, Prices, Volume)

The model is linked to the profit and loss statement so that profitability is expressed as a function of productivity, volume and unit prices. Productivity and volume are the variables of a production function, and using them makes it is possible to describe the real process. A change in unit prices describes a change of production income distribution.

PPPR is the abbreviation for the following function:

Profitability = f (Productivity, Price Recovery)

In this model, the variables of profitability are productivity and price recovery. Only the productivity is a variable of the production function. The model lacks the variable of volume, and for this reason, the model can not describe the production function. The American models of REALST (Loggerenberg&Cucchiaro 1982, Pineda 1990) and APQC (Kendrick 1984, Brayton 1983, Genesca&Grifell, 1992, Pineda 1990) belong to this category of models but since they do not apply to describing the production function (Saari 2000) they are not reviewed here more closely.

Comparative Summary of the Models

PPPV models measure profitability as a function of productivity, volume and income distribution (unit prices). Such models are

- Japanese Kurosawa (1975)
- French Courbois& Temple (1975)
- Finnish Saari (1976, 2000, 2004, 2006a, 2006b)
- American Gollop (1979)

The table presents the characteristics of the PPPV models. All four models use the same variables by which a change in profitability is written into formulas to be used for measurement. These variables are income distribution (prices), productivity and volume. A conclusion is that the basic logic of measurement is the same in all models. The method of implementing the measurements varies to a degree, depending on the fact that the models do not produce similar results from the same calculating material.

CHOISES	Saari	Kurosawa	Gollop	C & T
Variables used in the model	Distribution Productivity Volume	Distribution Productivity Volume	Distribution Productivity Volume	Distribution Productivity Volume
Theory, alternatives; 1. Production function 2. Cost function	Production function	Production function	Cost function	Cost function
Calculation order of variables	1. Distribution 2. Productivity 3. Volume	1. Volume 2. Productivity 3. Distribution	1. Volume 2. Productivity 3. Distribution	1. Volume 2. Productivity 3. Distribution
Accounting technique, alternatives; 1. Variance accounting 2. Ratio accounting 3. Accounting form	All changes; Variance accounting	All changes; Accounting form	Distribution; Variance acc. Productivity; Ratio acc. Volume; Account. form	All Changes Accounting; form
Adjustadility, alternatives; 1. Adjustable 2. Fixed	Adjustable	Fixed	Fixed	Fixed

Figure: *Summary of productivity models (Saari 2006b)*

Even if the production function variables of profitability and volume were in the model, in practice the calculation can also be carried out in compliance with the cost function. This is the case in models C & T as well as Gollop.

Calculating methods differ in the use of either output volume or input volume for measuring the volume of activity. The former solution complies with the cost function and the latter with the production function. It is obvious that the calculation produces different results from the same material.

A recommendation is to apply calculation in accordance with the production function. According to the definition of the production function used in the productivity models Saari and Kurosawa, productivity means the quantity and quality of output per one unit of input.

Models differ from one another significantly in their calculation techniques. Differences in calculation technique do not cause differences in calculation results but it is rather a question of differences in clarity and intelligibility between the models. From the comparison it is evident that the models of Courbois & Temple and Kurosawa are purely based on calculation formulas. The calculation is based on the aggregates in the loss and profit account. Consequently, it does not suit to analysis. The productivity model Saari is purely based on variance accounting known from the standard cost accounting. The variance accounting is applied to elementary variables, that is, to quantities and prices of different products and inputs. Variance accounting gives the user most possibilities for analysis. The model of Gollop is a mixed model by its calculation technique. Every variable is calculated using a different calculation technique. (Saari 2006b)

The productivity model Saari is the only model with alterable characteristics. Hence, it is an adjustable model. A comparison between other models has been feasible by exploiting this particular characteristic of this model.

Models of National Economy

In order to measure productivity of a nation or an industry, it is necessary to operationalize the same concept of productivity as in business, yet, the object of modelling is substantially wider and the information more aggregate. The calculations of total productivity of a nation or an industry are based on the time series of the SNA, System of National Accounts, formulated and developed for half a century. National accounting is a system based on the recommendations of the UN (SNA 93) to measure total production and total income of a nation and how they are used.

Measurement of productivity is at its most accurate in business because of the availability of all elementary data of the quantities and prices of the inputs and the output in production. The more comprehensive the entity we want to analyse by measurements, the more data need to be aggregated. In productivity measurement, combining and aggregating the data always involves reduced measurement accuracy.

Output Measurement

Conceptually speaking, the amount of total production means the same in the national economy and in business but for practical reasons modelling the concept differs, respectively. In national economy, the total production is measured as the sum of value added whereas in business it is measured by the total output value. When the output is calculated by the value added, all purchase inputs (energy, materials etc.) and their productivity impacts are excluded from the examination. Consequently, the production function of national economy is written as follows:

Value Added = Output = f (Capital, Labour)

In business, production is measured by the gross value of production, and in addition to the producer's own inputs (capital and labour) productivity analysis comprises all purchase inputs such as raw-materials, energy, outsourcing services, supplies, components, etc. Accordingly, it is possible to measure the total productivity in business which implies absolute consideration of all inputs. It is clear that productivity measurement in business gives a more accurate result because it analyses all the inputs used in production. (Saari 2006b)

The productivity measurement based on national accounting has been under development recently. The method is known as KLEMS, and it takes all production inputs into consideration. KLEMS is an abbreviation for K = capital, L = labour, E = energy, M = materials, and S = services. In principle, all inputs are treated the same way. As for the capital input in particular this means that it is measured by capital services, not by the capital stock.

Combination or Aggregation Problem

The problem of aggregating or combining the output and inputs is purely measurement technical, and it is caused by the fixed grouping of the items. In national accounting, data need to be fed under fixed items resulting in large items of output and input which are not homogeneous as provided in the measurements but include qualitative changes. There is no fixed grouping of items in the business production model, neither for inputs nor for products, but both inputs and products are present in calculations by their own names representing the elementary price and quantity of the calculation material. (Saari 2006b)

Problem of the Relative Prices

For productivity analyses, the value of total production of the national economy, GNP, is calculated with fixed prices. The fixed price calculation principle means that the prices by which quantities are evaluated are hold fixed or unchanged for a given period. In the calculation complying with national accounting, a fixed price GNP is obtained by applying the so-called basic year prices. Since the basic year is usually changed every 5th year, the evaluation of the output and input quantities remains unchanged for five years. When the new basic-year prices are introduced, relative prices will change in relation to the prices of the previous basic year, which has its certain impact on productivity Old basic-year prices entail inaccuracy in the production measurement. For reasons of market economy, relative values of output and inputs alter while the relative prices of the basic year do not react to these changes in any way. Structural changes like this will be wrongly evaluated. Short life-cycle products will not have any basis of evaluation because they are born and they die in between the two basic years. Obtaining good productivity by elasticity is ignored if old and long-term fixed prices are being used. In business models this problem does not exist, because the correct prices are available all the time. (Saari 2006b)

Production–Possibility Frontier

In economics, a production–possibility frontier (PPF), sometimes called a production–possibility curve, production-possibility boundary or product transformation curve, is a graph that shows the various combinations of amounts that two commodities could produce using the same fixed total amount of each of the factors of production. Graphically bounding the production set for fixed input quantities, the PPF curve shows the maximum possible production level of one commodity for any given production level of the other, given the existing state of technology. By doing so, it defines productive efficiency in the context of that production set: a point on the frontier indicates efficient use of the available inputs, while a point beneath the curve indicates inefficiency. A period of time is specified as well as the production technologies and amounts of inputs available. The commodities compared can either be goods or services.

PPFs are normally drawn as bulging upwards ("concave") from the origin but can also be represented as bulging downward or linear (straight), depending on a number of factors. A PPF can be used to illustrate a number of economic concepts, such as scarcity of resources (i.e., the fundamental economic problem all societies face), opportunity cost (or marginal rate of transformation), productive efficiency, allocative efficiency, and economies of scale. In addition, an outward shift of the PPF results from growth of the availability of inputs such as physical capital or labour, or technological progress in our knowledge of how to transform inputs into outputs. Such a shift allows economic growth of an economy already operating at its full productivity (on the PPF), which means that more of *both* outputs can be produced during the specified period of time without sacrificing the output of either good. Conversely, the PPF will shift inward if the labour force shrinks, the supply of raw materials is depleted, or a natural disaster decreases the stock of physical capital. However, most economic contractions reflect not that less can be produced, but that the economy has started operating below the frontier—typically both labour and physical capital are underemployed. The combination represented by the point on the PPF where an economy operates shows the priorities or choices of the economy, such as the choice of producing more capital goods and fewer consumer goods or vice versa.

Indicators

Efficiency:

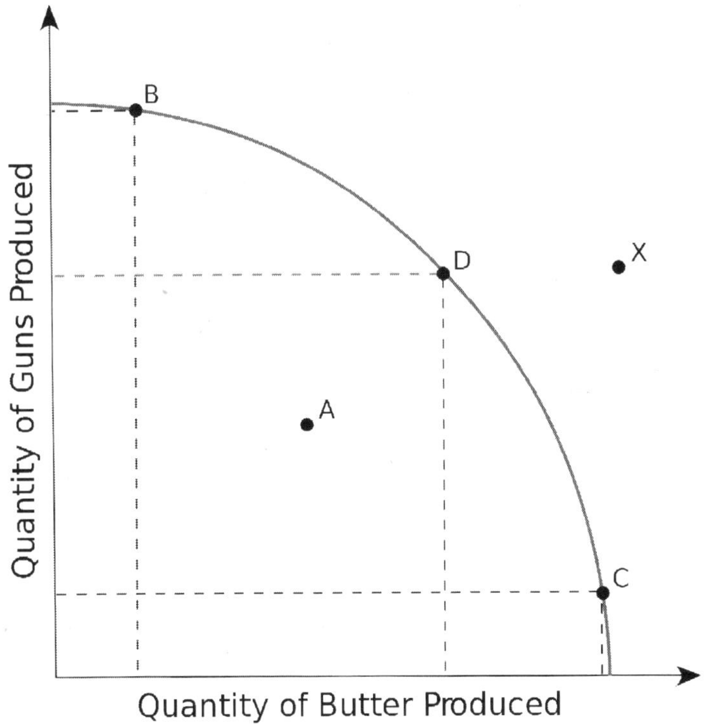

Figure: *An example PPF with illustrative points marked*

A PPF typically takes the form of the curve on the right. An economy that is operating on the PPF is said to be efficient, meaning that it would be impossible to produce more of one good without decreasing production of the other good.

In contrast, if the economy is operating below the curve, it is said to be operating inefficiently because it could reallocate resources in order to produce more of both goods.

For example, assuming that the economy's available quantity of factors of production does not change over time and that technological progress does not occur, then if the economy is operating on the PPF production of guns would need to be sacrificed in order to produce more butter. If production is efficient, the economy can choose between combinations (i.e., points) on the PPF: *B* if guns are of interest, *C* if more butter is needed, *D* if an equal mix of butter and guns is required.

In the PPF, all points *on* the curve are points of maximum productive efficiency (i.e., no more output of any good can be achieved from the given inputs without sacrificing output of some good); all points inside the frontier (such as *A*) can be produced but are productively *inefficient*; all points outside the curve (such as *X*) cannot be produced with the given, existing resources. Not all points on the curve are Pareto efficient, however; only in the case where the marginal rate of transformation is equal to all consumers' marginal rate of substitution and hence equal to the ratio of prices will it be impossible to find any trade that will make no consumer worse off.

Any point that lies either on the production possibilities curve or to the left of it is said to be an attainable point, meaning that it can be produced with currently available resources. Points that lie to the right of the production possibilities curve are said to be unattainable because they cannot be produced using currently available resources. Points that lie within the curve are said to be inefficient, because existing resources would allow for production of more of at least one good without sacrificing the production of any other good. An efficient point is one that lies on the production possibilities curve. At any such point, more of one good can be produced only by producing less of the other.

Such a two-good world is a theoretical simplification, due to the difficulty of graphical analysis of multiple goods. If we are interested in one good, a composite score of the other goods can be generated using different techniques. Furthermore, the production model can be generalised using higher-dimensional techniques such as Principal Component Analysis (PCA) and others.

Opportunity Cost

If there is no increase in productive resources, increasing production of a first good entails decreasing production of a second, because resources must be transferred to the first and away from the second. Points along the curve describe the trade-off between the goods. The sacrifice in the production of the second good is called the *opportunity cost* (because increasing production of the first good entails losing the opportunity to produce some amount of the second). Opportunity cost is measured in the number of units of the second good forgone for one or more units of the first good.

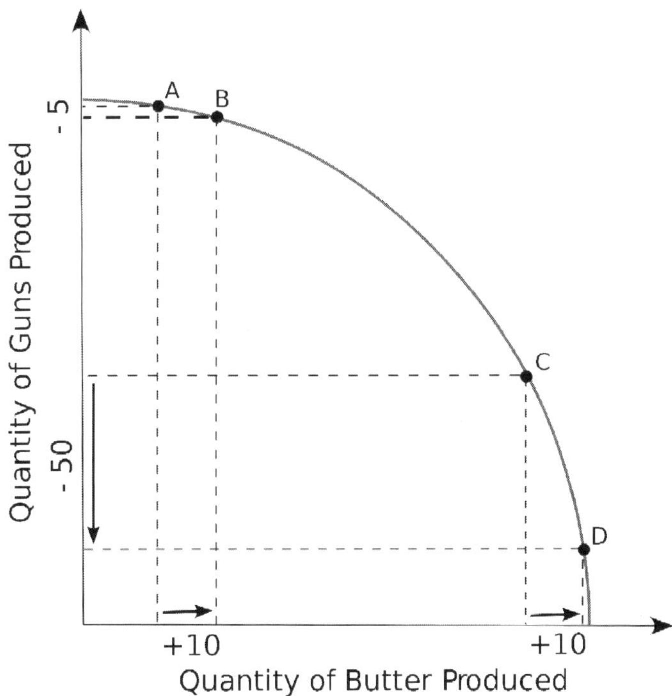

Figure: *Increasing butter from* A *to* B *carries little opportunity cost, but for* C *to* D *the cost is great.*

In the context of a PPF, opportunity cost is directly related to the shape of the curve. If the shape of the PPF curve is straight-line, the opportunity cost is constant as production of different goods is changing. But, opportunity cost usually will vary depending on the start and end point. In the diagram on the right, producing 10 more packets of butter, at a low level of butter production, costs the opportunity of 5 guns (as with a movement from *A* to *B*). At point *C*, the economy is already close to its maximum potential butter output. To produce 10 more packets of butter, 50 guns must be sacrificed (as with a movement from *C* to *D*). The ratio of opportunity costs is determined by the *marginal rate of transformation.*

Marginal Rate of Transformation

The slope of the production–possibility frontier (PPF) at any given point is called the marginal rate of transformation (MRT). The slope defines the rate at which production of one good can be redirected (by reallocation of productive resources) into production of the other. It is also called the (marginal) "opportunity cost" of a commodity, that is, it is the opportunity cost of X in terms of Y at the margin.

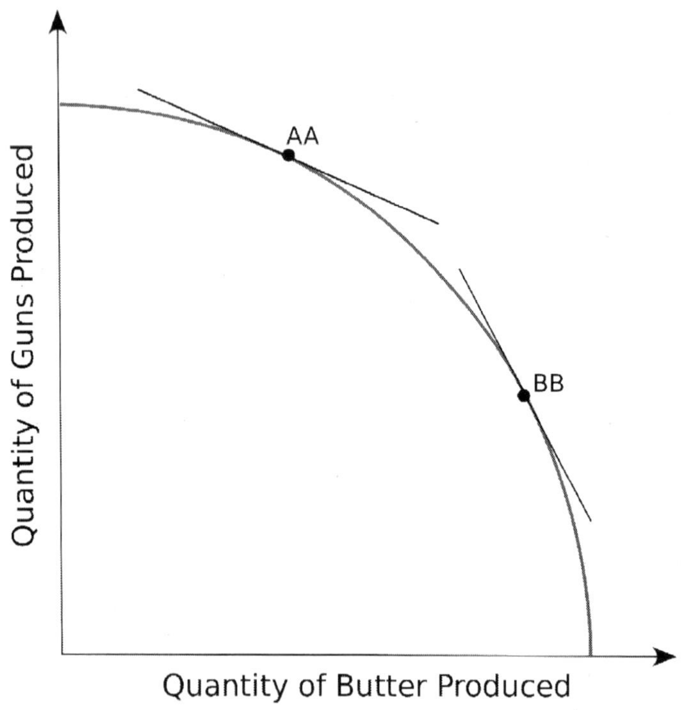

Figure: *Marginal rate of transformation increases when the transition is made from* AA *to* BB.

It measures how much of good Y is given up for one more unit of good X or vice versa. The shape of a PPF is commonly drawn as concave from the origin to represent increasing opportunity cost with increased output of a good.

Thus, MRT increases in absolute size as one moves from the top left of the PPF to the bottom right of the PPF.

The marginal rate of transformation can be expressed in terms of either commodity. The marginal opportunity costs of guns in terms of butter is simply the reciprocal of the marginal opportunity cost of butter in terms of guns.

If, for example, the (absolute) slope at point *BB* in the diagram is equal to 2, then, in order to produce one more packet of butter, the production of 2 guns must be sacrificed. If at *AA*, the marginal opportunity cost of butter in terms of guns is equal to 0.25, then, the sacrifice of one gun could produce four packets of butter, and the opportunity cost of guns in terms of butter is 4. Therefore opportunity cost plays a major role in society.

Shape

The production–possibility frontier can be constructed from the contract curve in an Edgeworth production box diagram of factor intensity. The example used above (which demonstrates increasing opportunity costs, with a curve concave from the origin) is the most common form of PPF. It represents a disparity in the factor intensities and technologies of the two production sectors. That is, as an economy specialises more and more into one product (e.g., moving from point *B* to point *D*), the opportunity cost of producing that product increases, because we are using more and more resources that are less efficient in producing it. With increasing production of butter, workers from the gun industry will move to it. At first, the least qualified (or most general) gun workers will be transferred into making more butter, and moving these workers has little impact on the opportunity cost of increasing butter production: the loss in gun production will be small. But the cost of producing successive units of butter will increase as resources that are more and more specialised in gun production are moved into the butter industry.

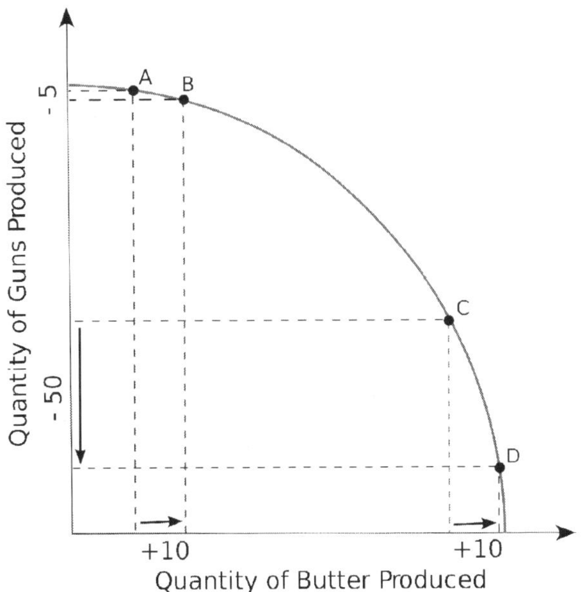

Figure: *A common PPF: increasing opportunity cost*

If opportunity costs are constant, a straight-line (linear) PPF is produced. This case reflects a situation where resources are not specialised and can be substituted for each other with no added cost.

Products requiring similar resources (bread and pastry, for instance) will have an almost straight PPF, hence almost constant opportunity costs. More specifically, with constant returns to scale, there are two opportunities for a linear PPF: firstly, if there was only one factor of production to consider, or secondly, if the factor intensity ratios in the two sectors were constant at all points on the production-possibilities curve.

With varying returns to scale, however, it may not be entirely linear in either case.

With economies of scale, the PPF would curve inward, with the opportunity cost of one good falling as more of it is produced. Specialisation in producing successive units of a good determines its opportunity cost (say from mass production methods or specialisation of labour).

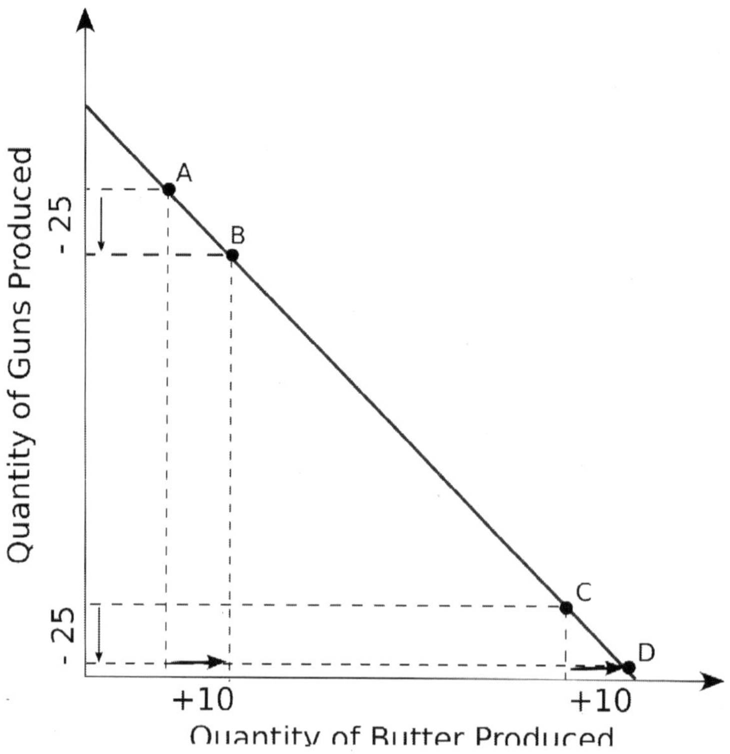

Figure: *A straight line PPF: constant opportunity cost*

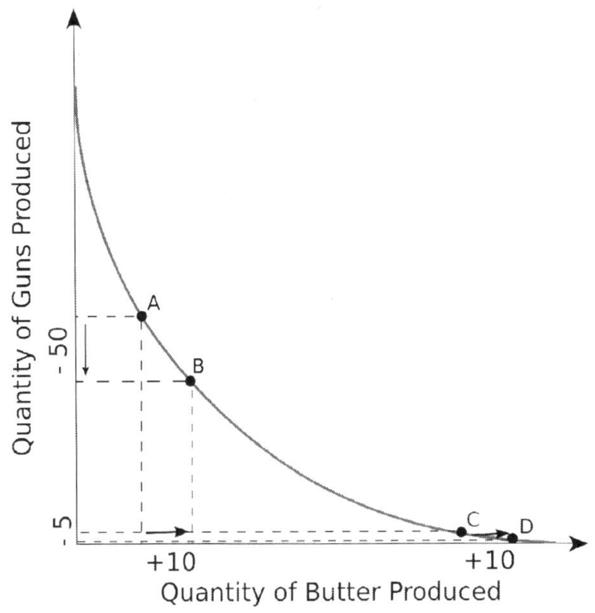

Figure: *An inverted PPF: decreasing opportunity cost*

Position

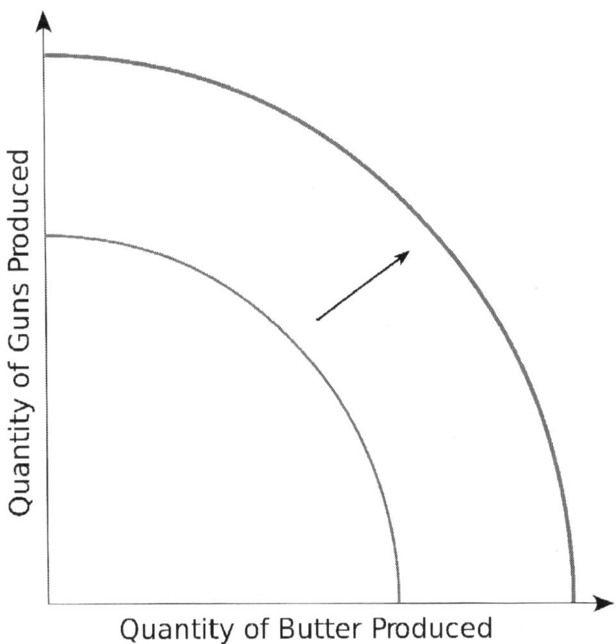

Figure: *An unbiased expansion in a PPF*

The two main determinants of the position of the PPF at any given time are the state of technology and management expertise (which are reflected in the available production functions) and the available quantities of factors of production. Only points on or within a PPF are actually possible to achieve in the short run. In the long run, if technology improves or if the supply of factors of production increases, the economy's capacity to produce both goods increases; if this potential is realised, economic growth occurs. This increase is shown by a shift of the production-possibility frontier to the right. Conversely, a natural, military or ecological disaster might move the PPF to the left, in response to a reduction in an economy's productive capability. Thus all points on or within the curve are part of the production set, i.e., combinations of goods that the economy could potentially produce.

If the two production goods depicted are capital investment (to increase future production possibilities) and current consumption goods, the higher is investment this year, the more the PPF would shift out in following years. Shifts of the curve can represent how technological progress that favours production possibilities of one good, say guns, more than the other shifts the PPF outwards more along the favoured good's axis, "biasing" production possibilities in that direction. Similarly, if one good makes more use of say capital and if capital grows faster than other factors, growth possibilities might be biased in favour of the capital-intensive good.

Other Applications

In microeconomics, the PPF shows the options open to an individual, household, or firm in a two-good world. By definition, each point on the curve is productively efficient, but, given the nature of market demand, some points will be more profitable than others. Equilibrium for a firm will be the combination of outputs on the PPF that is most profitable. From a macroeconomic perspective, the PPF illustrates the production possibilities available to a nation or economy during a given period of time for broad categories of output. It is traditionally used to show the movement between committing all funds to consumption on the y-axis versus investment on the x-axis. However, an economy may achieve productive efficiency without necessarily being allocatively efficient. Market failure (such as imperfect competition or externalities) and some institutions of social decision-making (such as government and tradition) may lead to the wrong combination of goods being produced (hence the wrong mix of resources being allocated between producing the two goods) compared to what consumers would prefer, given what is feasible on the PPF.

Economic Production Quantity

Economic Production Quantity model (also known as the EPQ model) determines the quantity a company or retailer should order to minimize the total inventory costs by balancing the inventory holding cost and average fixed ordering cost. The EPQ model was developed by E.W. Taft in 1918. This method is an extension of the Economic Order Quantity model (also known as the EOQ model). The difference between these two methods is that the EPQ model assumes the company will produce its own quantity or the parts are going to be shipped to the company while they are being produced, therefore the orders are available or received in an incrementally manner while the products are being produced. While the EOQ model assumes the order quantity arrives complete and immediately after ordering, meaning that the parts are produced by another company and are ready to be shipped when the order is placed.

In some literature Economic Manufacturing Quantity model (EMQ) is used for Economic Production Quantity model (EPQ). Similar to the EOQ model, EPQ is a single product lot scheduling method. A multiproduct extension to these models is called Product Cycling Problem.

Overview

EPQ only applies where the demand for a product is constant over the year and that each new order is delivered/produced incrementally when the inventory reaches zero. There is a fixed cost charged for each order placed, regardless of the number of units ordered. There is also a holding or storage cost for each unit held in storage (sometimes expressed as a percentage of the purchase cost of the item).

We want to determine the optimal number of units of the product to order so that we minimize the total cost associated with the purchase, delivery and storage of the product

The required parameters to the solution are the total demand for the year, the purchase cost for each item, the fixed cost to place the order and the storage cost for each item per year. Note that the number of times an order is placed will also affect the total cost, however, this number can be determined from the other parameters

Assumptions

1. Demand for items from inventory is continuous and at a constant rate
2. Production runs to replenish inventory are made at regular intervals

3. During a production run, the production of items is continuous and at a constant rate
4. Production set-up/ordering cost is fixed (independent of quantity produced)
5. The lead time is fixed
6. The purchase price of the item is constant i.e. no discount is available
7. The replenishment is made incrementally

Variables

- K = ordering/setup cost
- D = demand rate
- F = holding cost
- T = cycle length
- P = production rate
- $x = \frac{D}{P}$
- Q = order quantity

Derivation of EPQ Formula

$$\text{Holding Cost per Year} = \frac{Q}{2}F(1-x)$$

Where $\frac{Q}{2}$ is the average inventory level, and F(1-x) is the average holding cost. Therefore multiplying these two results in the Holding cost per Year.

$$\text{Ordering Cost per Year} = \frac{D}{Q}K$$

Where $\frac{D}{Q}$ are the orders placed in a year, multiplied by K results in the Ordering Cost per Year.

We can notice from the equations above that the total ordering cost decreases as the production quantity increases. Inversely, the total holding cost increases as the production quantity increases. Therefore in order to get the optimal production quantity we need to set holding cost per year equal to ordering cost per year and solve for quantity (Q), which is the EPQ formula mentioned below. Ordering this quantity will result in the lowest total inventory cost per year.

EPQ Formula

$$EPQ = Q = \sqrt{\frac{2KD}{F(1-x)}}$$

Inventory Cost Graph

This figure graphs the Holding Cost and Ordering Cost per year equations. The third line is the addition of these two equations, which generates the Total Inventory Cost per year. This graph should give you a better understanding of the derivation of the optimal ordering quantity equation, i.e., the EPQ equation.

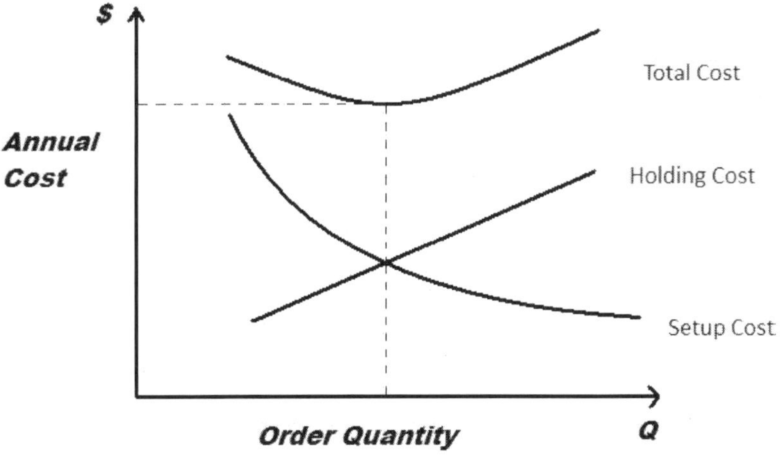

***Figure:** EPQ Graph*

Relevant Formulas

Average holding cost per unit time:

$$\frac{1}{2}FD(1-x)*T$$

Average ordering and holding cost as a function of time:

$$x(T) = \frac{1}{2}FD(1-x)T + \frac{K}{T}$$

Cost-of-Production Theory of Value

In economics, the cost-of-production theory of value is the theory that the price of an object or condition is determined by the sum of the cost of the resources that went into making it. The cost can comprise any of the factors of production (including labour, capital, or land) and taxation.

The theory makes the most sense under assumptions of constant returns to scale and the existence of just one non-produced factor of production. These are the assumptions of the so-called non-substitution theorem. Under these assumptions, the long-run price of a commodity is equal to the sum of the cost of the inputs into that commodity, including interest charges.

Historical Development of Theory

Historically, the best-known proponent of such theories is probably Adam Smith. PieroSraffa, in his introduction to the first volume of the "Collected Works of David Ricardo", referred to Smith's "adding-up" theory. Smith contrasted natural prices with market price. Smith theorized that market prices would tend toward natural prices, where outputs would stand at what he characterized as the "level of effectual demand". At this level, Smith's natural prices of commodities are the sum of the natural rates of wages, profits, and rent that must be paid for inputs into production. (Smith is ambiguous about whether rent is price determining or price determined. The latter view is the consensus of later classical economists, with the Ricardo-Malthus-West theory of rent.)

David Ricardo mixed this cost-of-production theory of prices with the labour theory of value, as that latter theory was understood by Eugen von Böhm-Bawerk and others. This is the theory that prices tend toward proportionality to the socially necessary labour embodied in a commodity. Ricardo sets this theory at the start of the first chapter of his "Principles of Political Economy and Taxation". He also refutes the labour theory of value in later sections of that chapter. This refutation leads to what later became known as the transformation problem. Karl Marx later takes up that theory in the first volume of *Capital*, while indicating that he is quite aware that the theory is untrue at lower levels of abstraction. This has led to all sorts of arguments over what both David Ricardo and Karl Marx "really meant". Nevertheless, it seems undeniable that all the major classical economics and Marx explicitly rejected the labour theory of price([1]).

A somewhat different theory of cost-determined prices is provided by the "neo-Ricardian School" [2] of PieroSraffa and his followers.

The Polish economist Micha[3]Kalecki[3] distinguished between sectors with "cost-determined prices" (such as manufacturing and services) and those with "demand-determined prices" (such as agriculture and raw material extraction). One might think of this theory as equivalent to modern theories of markup pricing, full-cost pricing, or administrative pricing. Ever since Hall and Hitch, economists have found that the evidence gathered in surveys of businessmen support such theories. Most contemporary economists accept neoclassical economics or mainstream economics. The non-substitution theorem is presented in graduate-level microeconomics textbooks as a theorem of mainstream economics. Many mainstream economists also believe they can justify theories of full-cost pricing within their theory. The majority of mainstream economists would probably then accept this theory as an element in their theory, which does not give adequate attention to issues of consumer demand and marginal utility.

Market Price

Market price is a familiar economic concept: it is the price that a good or service is offered at, or will fetch, in the marketplace. It is of interest mainly in the study of microeconomics. Market value and market price are equal only under conditions of market efficiency, equilibrium, and rational expectations. In economics, *returns to scale* and *economies of scale* are related terms that describe what happens as the scale of production increases. They are different, non-interchangeable terms.

Labour Theory of Value

The labour theories of value are economic theories according to which the true values of commodities are related to the labour needed to produce them. There are many accounts of labour value, with the common element that the "value" of an exchangeable good or service is, or ought to be, or tends to be, or can be considered as, equal or proportional to the amount of labour required to produce it (including the labour required to produce the raw materials and machinery used in production).

Different labour theories of value prevailed among classical economists through the mid-19th century. This theory is especially associated with Adam Smith and David Ricardo. Since that time, it has been most often associated with Marxian economics, while among modern mainstream economists it is considered to be superseded by the marginal utility approach.

Taxes and Subsidies

Taxes and subsidies change the price of goods and services. A marginal tax on the sellers of a good will shift the supply curve to the left until the vertical distance between the two supply curves is equal to the per unit tax; other things remaining equal, this will increase the price paid by the consumers (which is equal to the new market price) and decrease the price received by the sellers.

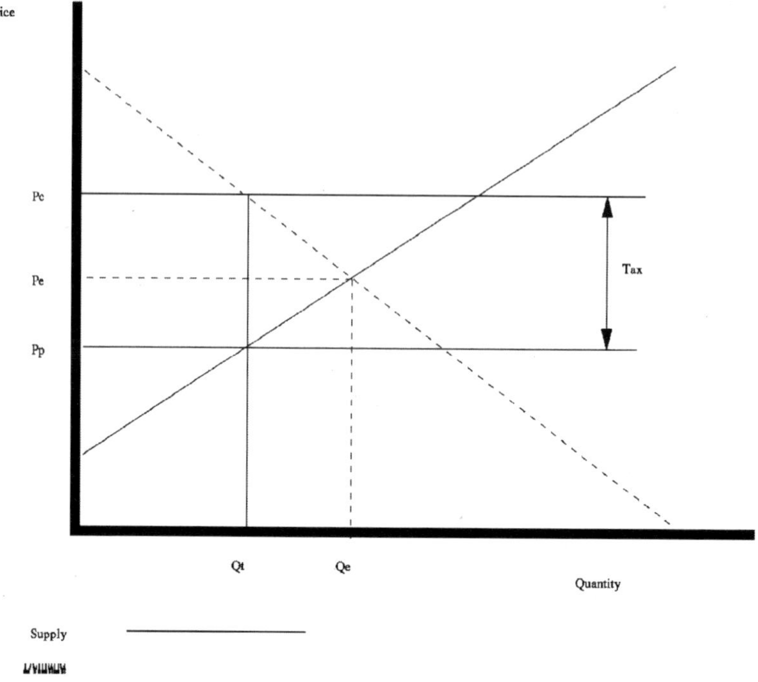

Figure: *A supply and demand diagram illustrating taxes' effect on prices.*

Marginal subsidies on production will shift the supply curve to the right until the vertical distance between the two supply curves is equal to the per unit subsidy; other things remaining equal, this will decrease price paid by the consumers (which is equal to the new market price) and increase the price received by the producers.

6

Demand for Factors

Demand

In economics, demand for a good or service is an entire listing of the quantity of the good or service that a market would choose to buy, for every possible market price of the good or service. (Note: This distinguishes "demand" from "quantity demanded", where demand is a listing or graphing of quantity demanded at each possible price. In contrast to demand, quantity demanded is the exact quantity demanded at a certain price. Changing the actual price will change the quantity demanded, but it will not change the demand, because demand is a listing of quantities that would be bought at various prices, not just the actual price.)

Demand is a buyer's willingness and ability to pay a price for a specific quantity of a good or service. Demand refers to how much (quantity) of a product or service is desired by buyers at various prices. The quantity demanded is the amount of a product people are willing to buy at a certain price; the relationship between price and quantity demanded is known as the demand. The term demand signifies the ability or the willingness to buy a particular commodity at a given point of time. Economists record demand on a demand schedule and plot it on a graph as a demand curve that is usually downward sloping. The downward slope reflects the negative or inverse relationship between price and quantity demanded: as price decreases, quantity demanded increases. Changing market price would move the equilibrium point for quantity demanded up and down ALONG the demand curve, but would not shift the demand curve - and would not change demand for the good. An actual change in demand means that the whole curve of quantity-demanded vs. price, has shifted. This curve is the demand, sometimes also called the demand schedule. Change in demand and not just quantity-demanded could come from changes in consumer wealth, from consumer preferences, or from the prices of substitutes or complements for the product.

In principle, each consumer has a demand curve for any product that he or she is willing and able to buy, and the consumer's demand curve is equal to the marginal utility (benefit) curve, assuming full information and the lack of frictions that would perturb the consumer's choice.

When the demand curves of all consumers are added up, the result is the market demand curve for that product which also indicates a negative or inverse relationship between the price and quantity demanded. If there are no externalities, the market demand curve is also equal to the social utility (benefit) curve.

Factors Affecting Demand

Innumerable factors and circumstances could affect a buyer's willingness or ability to buy a good. Some of the more common factors are:

Good's Own Price: The basic demand relationship is between potential prices of a good and the quantities that would be purchased at those prices. Generally the relationship is negative meaning that an increase in price will induce a decrease in the quantity demanded. This negative relationship is embodied in the downward slope of the consumer demand curve. The assumption of a negative relationship is reasonable and intuitive. If the price of a new novel is high, a person might decide to borrow the book from the public library rather than buy it.

Price of Related Goods: The principal related goods are complements and substitutes. A complement is a good that is used with the primary good. Examples include hotdogs and mustard, beer and pretzels, automobiles and gasoline. (Perfect complements behave as a single good.) If the price of the complement goes up the quantity demanded of the other good goes down. Mathematically, the variable representing the price of the complementary good would have a negative coefficient in the demand function. For example, $Q_d = a - P - P_g$ where Q is the quantity of automobiles demanded, P is the price of automobiles and P_g is the price of gasoline.

The other main category of related goods are substitutes. Substitutes are goods that can be used in place of the primary good. The mathematical relationship between the price of the substitute and the demand for the good in question is positive. If the price of the substitute goes down the demand for the good in question goes down.

Personal Disposable Income: In most cases, the more disposable income (income after tax and receipt of benefits) a person has the more likely that person is to buy.

Tastes or Preferences: The greater the desire to own a good the more likely one is to buy the good There is a basic distinction between desire and demand. Desire is a measure of the willingness to buy a good based on its intrinsic qualities. Demand is the willingness and ability to put one's desires into effect. It is assumed that tastes and preferences are relatively constant.

Consumer Expectations about Future Prices and Income: If a consumer believes that the price of the good will be higher in the future, he/she is more likely to purchase the good now. If the consumer expects that his/her income will be higher in the future, the consumer may buy the good now.

Population: If the population grows this means that demand will also increase.

Nature of the Good: If the good is a basic commodity, it will lead to a higher demand

- This list is not exhaustive. All facts and circumstances that a buyer finds relevant to his willingness or ability to buy goods can affect demand. For example, a person caught in an unexpected storm is more likely to buy an umbrella than if the weather were bright and sunny.

Demand Function and Demand Equation

The demand equation is the mathematical expression of the relationship between the quantity of a good demanded and those factors that affect the willingness and ability of a consumer to buy the good. For example, $Q_d = f(P; P_{rg}, Y)$ is a demand equation where Q_d is the quantity of a good demanded, P is the price of the good, P_{rg} is the price of a related good, and Y is income; the function on the right side of the equation is called the demand function. The semi-colon in the list of arguments in the demand function means that the variables to the right are being held constant as one plots the demand curve in (quantity, price) space. A simple example of a demand equation is $Q_d = 325 - P - 30P_{rg} + 1.4Y$. Here 325 is the repository of all relevant non-specified factors that affect demand for the product. P is the price of the good. The coefficient is negative in accordance with the law of demand. The related good may be either a complement or a substitute. If a complement, the coefficient of its price would be negative as in this example. If a substitute, the coefficient of its price would be positive. Income, Y, has a positive coefficient indicating that the good is a normal good. If the coefficient was negative the good in question would be an inferior good meaning that the demand for the good would fall as the consumer's income increased. Specifying values for the non price determinants, Prg = 4.00 and Y = 50, results in the demand equation Q = 325 - P - 30(4) +1.4(50) or Q = 275 - P. If income were to increase to 55 the new demand equation would be Q = 282 - P. Graphically this change in a non price determinant of demand would be reflected in an outward shift of the demand function caused by a change in the x intercept. Devon Clarke

Demand Curve

Demand curve is a graphical representation between price and quantity demanded. Its slope is negative showing that when price increases, then quantity demanded declines.

Causes of the Negative Slope

The negative slope of the demand curve is due to the diminishing marginal utility and the substitution and income effect. As the price falls, the number of units (product) where marginal utility (benefit) outweigh the marginal cost increases, thus it will continue to be a rational consumption for a larger number of units. The substitute effect is apparent because consumers will automatically switch to cheaper goods and move away from higher priced goods due to limited income and the desire to maximise their utility. When a good's price changes, a consumer's real income will be affected, in the case of a price decrease, they have greater purchasing power and their real income has increased. With this extra purchasing power, they are able to buy more and usually do.

Movements versus Shifts

The demand curve is a two-dimensional depiction of the relationship between price and quantity demanded. Movements along the curve occur only if there is a change in quantity demanded caused by a change in the good's own price. A shift in the demand curve, referred to as a change in demand, occurs only if a non-price determinant of demand changes. For example, if the price of a complement were to increase, the demand curve would shift leftward reflecting a decrease in demand. Conversely, a rightward shift in the demand curve reflects an increase in demand. The shifted demand curve represents a new demand equation. Movement along a demand curve due to a change in the good's price results in a change in the *quantity demanded*, not a change in *demand*. A change in *demand* refers to a shift in the position of the demand curve in two-dimensional space resulting from a change in one of the other arguments of the demand function.

From Individual to Market Demand Curve

The market demand curve is the horizontal summation of individual consumer demand curves. Aggregation introduces three additional non-price determinants of demand: (1) the number of consumers; (2) "the distribution of tastes among the consumers"; and (3) "the distribution of incomes among consumers of different taste." Thus if the population of consumers increases, *ceteris paribus* the market demand curve will shift outward (to the right). If the proportion of consumers with a strong preference for a good increases, *ceteris paribus* the demand for the good will increase. Finally if the distribution of income changes is favour of those consumers with a strong preference for the good in question the demand will shift out. Factors that affect individual demand can also affect market demand. However, net effects must be considered. For example, a good that is a complement for one person is not necessarily a complement for another; Further, the strength of the relationship would vary among persons. So in the aggregate the goods might be substitutes or complements. Finally the demand for a firm's product or services will often depend on such factors as competitors prices and marketing strategies.

Horizontal versus Vertical Summation

When adding individual demand curves it is critical that the summation be horizontal rather than vertical. The derivation of the market demand function involves adding quantities. The conventional graphical representation is of the inverse demand function. Adding inverse demand equations involves adding prices. In order to add the demand functions algebraically one must first convert the inverse equation to the standard demand function where quantity demanded is a function of price. For example, assume that there are two consumers in a given market and their respective demand functions are $P = 30 - 2Q$ and $P = 30 - 6Q$. To sum these functions to obtain the market demand curve one must first convert to standard form, that is $Q = 15 - (P/2)$ and $Q = 5 - (P/6)$. Then, adding Q1 and Q2 yields $15 - (P/2) + 5 - (P/6) = 20 - (4P/6) = 20 - 2P/3$.

Coefficient Addition

Note that in aggregating individual demand curves to determine market demand one has to add the coefficients for the goods own price. The unexpressed assumption that is the basis for the addition is the law of one price. With some variables addition of coefficients is more problematic. For example income is an important determinant of demand. However, the percentage of additional income that a person would spend for a particular good or service varies widely making simple coefficient addition less tenable. To borrow an example from Nicholson assume that one has two consumers and that individuals 1's demand for oranges is

$X_1 = 10 - 2Px + .1I_1 + .5Py$ and individual 2's demand for oranges is $X_2 = 17 - Px + 0.05I_2 + .5Py$

- Where Px = the price of oranges
- Py is the price of grapefruits
- I_1 is consumer 1's income
- I_2 is consumer 2's income.

The market demand functions would be $X1 + X2 = 27 - 3Px + .1I_1 + 0.05I_2 + Py$.

Specifying values for I_1, I_2 and Py and substituting them into the demand equation provided:

- $X_1 + X_2 = 27 - 3Px + .1I_1 + 0.05I_2 + Py$.
- $X_1 + X_2 = 27 - 3Px + .1(40)_1 + 0.05(20)_2 + 4$
- $X_1 + X_2 = 27 - 3Px + 4 + 1 + 4$
- $X_1 + X_2 = 38 - 3Px$
- If the price of grapefruits increased to 5 then the demand equation would become

$^*X_1 + X_2 = 39 - 3Px$. Graphically this change in the price of a non price determinant of demand would be reflected in a shift out of the demand curve as the x intercept changed from 38 to 39.

- Note that if an income tax was imposed that transferred 5000 from individual 1 to individual 2 then the new demand equation becomes

'$^*X_1 + X_2 = 27 - 3Px + .1I_1 + 0.05I_2 + Py$.

- $X_1 + X_2 = 27 - 3Px + .1(35) + 0.05(25) + 5$.
- $X_1 + X_2 = 27 - 3Px + 3.5 + 1.25 + 5$.
- $X_1 + X_2 = 27 - 3Px + 9.75$
- $X_1 + X_2 = 36.75 - 3Px$'

The redistribution of income has reduce demand and would be reflected in a shift inward of the demand curve. Note that the assumption that each person's demand for a good is independent of everyone else's demand for the same good is a necessary assumption for aggregation. Finally one must be aware that simple addition of coefficients can produce non-sensical results over certain range of prices. That is individual demand curves may not be valid at certain prices.

As Frank notes, "Horizontal summation works as a way of generating market demand curves from individual demand curves because all consumers in the market face the same market price for the product. But when incomes differ widely from one consumer to another, it makes no sense to hold income constant and add quantities across consumers."

Price Elasticity of Demand

Price elasticity of demand (PED or E_d) is a measure used in economics to show the responsiveness, or elasticity, of the quantity demanded of a good or service to a change in its price. More precisely, it gives the percentage change in quantity demanded in response to a one percent change in price (ceteris paribus, i.e. holding constant all the other determinants of demand, such as income). It was devised by Alfred Marshall.

Price elasticities are almost always negative, although analysts tend to ignore the sign even though this can lead to ambiguity. Only goods which do not conform to the law of demand, such as Veblen and Giffen goods, have a positive PED. In general, the demand for a good is said to be *inelastic* (or *relatively inelastic*) when the PED is less than one (in absolute value): that is, changes in price have a relatively small effect on the quantity of the good demanded.

The demand for a good is said to be *elastic* (or *relatively elastic*) when its PED is greater than one (in absolute value): that is, changes in price have a relatively large effect on the quantity of a good demanded.

Revenue is maximized when price is set so that the PED is exactly one. The PED of a good can also be used to predict the incidence (or "burden") of a tax on that good.

Various research methods are used to determine price elasticity, including test markets, analysis of historical sales data and conjoint analysis.

Definition

It is a measure of responsiveness of the quantity of a raw good or service demanded to changes in its price. The formula for the coefficient of price elasticity of demand for a good is:

$$e_{\langle R\rangle} = \frac{\mathrm{d}Q/Q}{\mathrm{d}P/P}$$

The above formula usually yields a negative value, due to the inverse nature of the relationship between price and quantity demanded, as described by the "law of demand". For example, if the price increases by 5% and quantity demanded decreases by 5%, then the elasticity at the initial price and quantity = –5%/5% = –1. The only classes of goods which have a PED of greater than 0 are Veblen and Giffen goods. Because the PED is negative for the vast majority of goods and services, however, economists often refer to price elasticity of demand as a positive value (i.e., in absolute value terms).

This measure of elasticity is sometimes referred to as the *own-price* elasticity of demand for a good, i.e., the elasticity of demand with respect to the good's own price, in order to distinguish it from the elasticity of demand for that good with respect to the change in the price of some other good, i.e., a complementary or substitute good. The latter type of elasticity measure is called a *cross*-price elasticity of demand.

As the difference between the two prices or quantities increases, the accuracy of the PED given by the formula above *decreases* for a combination of two reasons. First, the PED for a good is not necessarily constant; as explained below, PED can vary at different points along the demand curve, due to its percentage nature. Elasticity is not the same thing as the slope of the demand curve, which is dependent on the units used for both price and quantity. Second, percentage changes are not symmetric; instead, the percentage change between any two values depends on which one is chosen as the starting value and which as the ending value. For example, if quantity demanded increases *from* 10 units *to* 15 units, the percentage change is 50%, i.e., (15 – 10) ÷ 10 (converted to a percentage). But if quantity demanded decreases *from* 15 units *to* 10 units, the percentage change is –33.3%, i.e., (10 – 15) ÷ 15. Two alternative elasticity measures avoid or minimise these shortcomings of the basic elasticity formula: *point-price elasticity* and *arc elasticity*.

Point-Price Elasticity

One way to avoid the accuracy problem described above is to minimise the difference between the starting and ending prices and quantities. This is the approach taken in the definition of *point-price* elasticity, which uses differential calculus to calculate the elasticity for an infinitesimal change in price and quantity at any given point on the demand curve:

$$E_d = \frac{P}{Q_d} \times \frac{dQ_d}{dP}$$

In other words, it is equal to the absolute value of the first derivative of quantity with respect to price (dQ_d/dP) multiplied by the point's price (P) divided by its quantity (Q_d).

In terms of partial-differential calculus, point-price elasticity of demand can be defined as follows: let $x(p,w)$ be the demand of goods $x_1, x_2, \ldots, x_L$ as a function of parameters price and wealth, and let $x_l(p,w)$ be the demand for good l. The elasticity of demand for good with respect to price is

$$E_{x_l, p_k} = \frac{\partial x_l(p,w)}{\partial p_k} \cdot \frac{p_k}{x_l(p,w)} = \frac{\partial \log x_l(p,w)}{\partial \log p_k}$$

However, the point-price elasticity can be computed only if the formula for the demand function, $Q_d = f(P)$, is known so its derivative with respect to price, dQ_d / dP, can be determined.

Arc Elasticity

A second solution to the asymmetry problem of having a PED dependent on which of the two given points on a demand curve is chosen as the "original" point and which as the "new" one is to compute the percentage change in P and Q relative to the *average* of the two prices and the *average* of the two quantities, rather than just the change relative to one point or the other.

Loosely speaking, this gives an "average" elasticity for the section of the actual demand curve—i.e., the *arc* of the curve—between the two points. As a result, this measure is known as the *arc elasticity*, in this case with respect to the price of the good. The arc elasticity is defined mathematically as:

$$E_d = \frac{\frac{P_1 + P_2}{2}}{\frac{Q_{d_1} + Q_{d_2}}{2}} \times \frac{\Delta Q_d}{\Delta P} = \frac{P_1 + P_2 \cdot}{Q_{d_1} + Q_{d_2}} \times \frac{\Delta Q_d}{\Delta P}$$

This method for computing the price elasticity is also known as the "midpoints formula", because the average price and average quantity are the coordinates of the midpoint of the straight line between the two given points.

This formula is an application of the midpoint method. However, because this formula implicitly assumes the section of the demand curve between those points is linear, the greater the curvature of the actual demand curve is over that range, the worse this approximation of its elasticity will be.

History

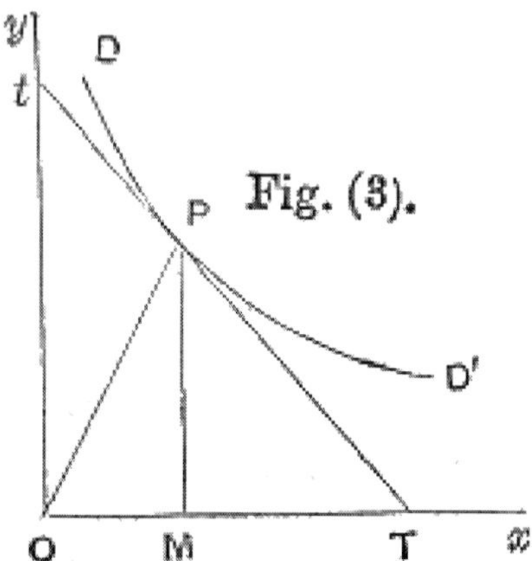

Figure: *The illustration that accompanied Marshall's original definition of PED, the ratio of PT to Pt*

Together with the concept of an economic "elasticity" coefficient, Alfred Marshall is credited with defining PED ("elasticity of demand") in his book *Principles of Economics*, published in 1890.

He described it thus: "And we may say generally:— the elasticity (or responsiveness) of demand in a market is great or small according as the amount demanded increases much or little for a given fall in price, and diminishes much or little for a given rise in price".

He reasons this since "the only universal law as to a person's desire for a commodity is that it diminishes... but this diminution may be slow or rapid. If it is slow... a small fall in price will cause a comparatively large increase in his purchases. But if it is rapid, a small fall in price will cause only a very small increase in his purchases. In the former case... the elasticity of his wants, we may say, is great.

In the latter case... the elasticity of his demand is small." Mathematically, the Marshallian PED was based on a point-price definition, using differential calculus to calculate elasticities.

Determinants

The overriding factor in determining PED is the willingness and ability of consumers after a price change to postpone immediate consumption decisions concerning the good and to search for substitutes ("wait and look"). A number of factors can thus affect the elasticity of demand for a good:

- *Availability of substitute goods:* the more and closer the substitutes available, the higher the elasticity is likely to be, as people can easily switch from one good to another if an even minor price change is made; There is a strong substitution effect. If no close substitutes are available, the substitution effect will be small and the demand inelastic.
- *Breadth of definition of a good:* the broader the definition of a good (or service), the lower the elasticity. For example, Company X's fish and chips would tend to have a relatively high elasticity of demand if a significant number of substitutes are available, whereas food in general would have an extremely low elasticity of demand because no substitutes exist.
- *Percentage of income:* the higher the percentage of the consumer's income that the product's price represents, the higher the elasticity tends to be, as people will pay more attention when purchasing the good because of its cost; The income effect is substantial. When the goods represent only a negligible portion of the budget the income effect will be insignificant and demand inelastic,
- *Necessity:* the more necessary a good is, the lower the elasticity, as people will attempt to buy it no matter the price, such as the case of insulin for those that need it.
- *Duration:* for most goods, the longer a price change holds, the higher the elasticity is likely to be, as more and more consumers find they have the time and inclination to search for substitutes. When fuel prices increase suddenly, for instance, consumers may still fill up their empty tanks in the short run, but when prices remain high over several years, more consumers will reduce their demand for fuel by switching to carpooling or public transportation, investing in vehicles with greater fuel economy or taking other measures. This does not hold for consumer durables such as the cars themselves, however; eventually, it may become necessary for consumers to replace their present cars, so one would expect demand to be less elastic.
- *Brand loyalty:* an attachment to a certain brand—either out of tradition or because of proprietary barriers—can override sensitivity to price changes, resulting in more inelastic demand.

- *Who pays:* where the purchaser does not directly pay for the good they consume, such as with corporate expense accounts, demand is likely to be more inelastic.

Interpreting Values of Price Elasticity Coefficients

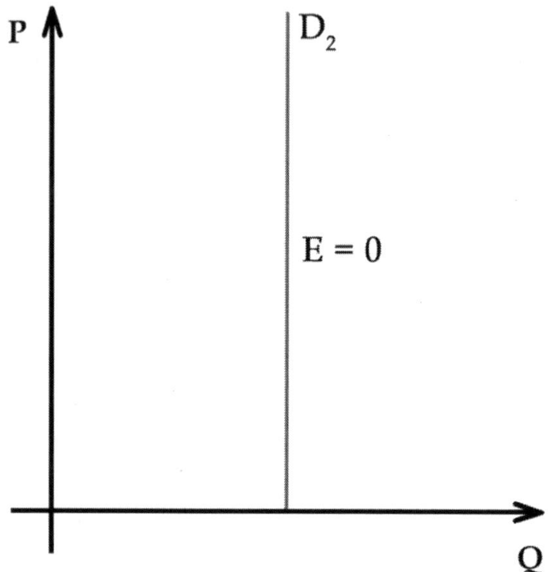

Figure: *Perfectly inelastic demand*

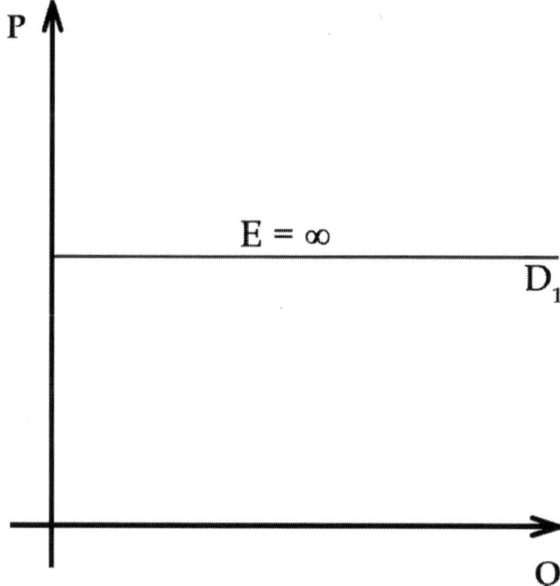

Figure: *Perfectly elastic demand*

Elasticities of demand are interpreted as follows:

Value	*Descriptive Terms*
$E_d = 0$	Perfectly inelastic demand
$-1 < E_d < 0$	Inelastic or relatively inelastic demand
$E_d = -1$	Unit elastic, unit elasticity, unitary elasticity, or unitarily elastic demand
$-\infty < E_d < -1$	Elastic or relatively elastic demand
$E_d = -\infty$	Perfectly elastic demand

A decrease in the price of a good normally results in an increase in the quantity demanded by consumers because of the law of demand, and conversely, quantity demanded decreases when price rises. As summarized in the table above, the PED for a good or service is referred to by different descriptive terms depending on whether the elasticity coefficient is greater than, equal to, or less than “1. That is, the demand for a good is called:

- *relatively inelastic* when the percentage change in quantity demanded is *less than* the percentage change in price (so that $E_d > -1$);
- *unit elastic, unit elasticity, unitary elasticity*, or *unitarily elastic* demand when the percentage change in quantity demanded is *equal to* the percentage change in price (so that $E_d = -1$); and
- *relatively elastic* when the percentage change in quantity demanded is *greater than* the percentage change in price (so that $E_d < -1$).

As the two accompanying diagrams show, *perfectly elastic* demand is represented graphically as a horizontal line, and *perfectly inelastic* demand as a vertical line. These are the *only* cases in which the PED and the slope of the demand curve ($\Delta P/\Delta Q$) are *both* constant, as well as the *only* cases in which the PED is determined solely by the slope of the demand curve (or more precisely, by the *inverse* of that slope).

Effect on Total Revenue

A firm considering a price change must know what effect the change in price will have on total revenue. Revenue is simply the product of unit price times quantity:

$$\text{Revenue} = PQ_d$$

Generally any change in price will have two effects:

- the *price effect* : For inelastic goods, an increase in unit price will tend to increase revenue, while a decrease in price will tend to decrease revenue. (The effect is reversed for elastic goods.)
- the *quantity effect* : an increase in unit price will tend to lead to fewer units sold, while a decrease in unit price will tend to lead to more units sold.

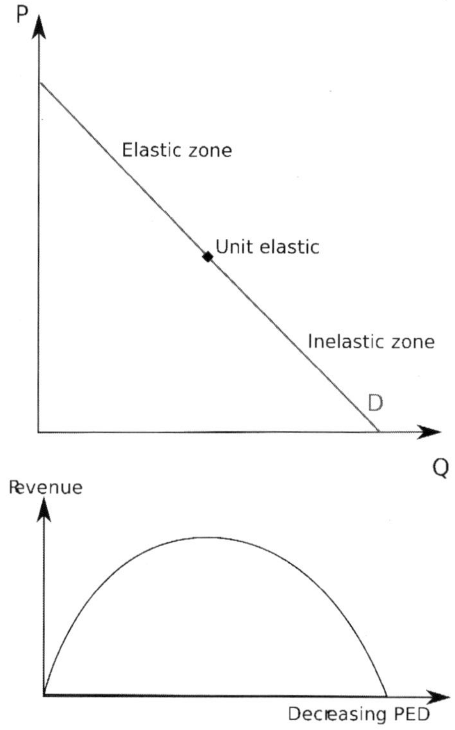

Figure: *A set of graphs shows the relationship between demand and total revenue (TR) for a linear demand curve. As price decreases in the elastic range, TR increases, but in the inelastic range, TR decreases. TR is maximised at the quantity where PED = 1.*

For inelastic goods, because of the inverse nature of the relationship between price and quantity demanded (i.e., the law of demand), the two effects affect total revenue in opposite directions. But in determining whether to increase or decrease prices, a firm needs to know what the net effect will be. Elasticity provides the answer: The percentage change in total revenue is approximately equal to the percentage change in quantity demanded plus the percentage change in price. (One change will be positive, the other negative.) The percentage change in quantity is related to the percentage change in price by elasticity: hence the percentage change in revenue can be calculated by knowing the elasticity and the percentage change in price alone.

As a result, the relationship between PED and total revenue can be described for any good:

- When the price elasticity of demand for a good is *perfectly inelastic* ($E_d = 0$), changes in the price do not affect the quantity demanded for the good; raising prices will always cause total revenue to increase. Goods necessary to survival can be classified here; a rational person will be willing to pay anything for a good if the alternative is death. For example, a person in the desert weak and dying of thirst would easily give all the money in his wallet, no matter how much, for a bottle of water if he would otherwise die. His demand is not contingent on the price.
- When the price elasticity of demand for a good is *relatively inelastic* ($-1 < E_d < 0$), the percentage change in quantity demanded is smaller than that in price. Hence, when the price is raised, the total revenue increases, and vice versa.
- When the price elasticity of demand for a good is *unit (or unitary) elastic* ($E_d = 1$), the percentage change in quantity is equal to that in price, so a change in price will not affect total revenue.
- When the price elasticity of demand for a good is *relatively elastic*($-\infty < E_d < -1$), the percentage change in quantity demanded is greater than that in price. Hence, when the price is raised, the total revenue falls, and vice versa.
- When the price elasticity of demand for a good is *perfectly elastic* (E_d is $-\infty$), any increase in the price, no matter how small, will cause demand for the good to drop to zero. Hence, when the price is raised, the total revenue falls to zero. This situation is typical for goods that have their value defined by law (such as fiat currency); if a 5 dollar bill were sold for anything more than 5 dollars, nobody would buy it, so demand is zero.

Hence, as the accompanying diagram shows, total revenue is maximized at the combination of price and quantity demanded where the elasticity of demand is unitary.

It is important to realise that price-elasticity of demand is *not* necessarily constant over all price ranges. The linear demand curve in the accompanying diagram illustrates that changes in price also change the elasticity: the price elasticity is different at every point on the curve.

Effect on Tax Incidence

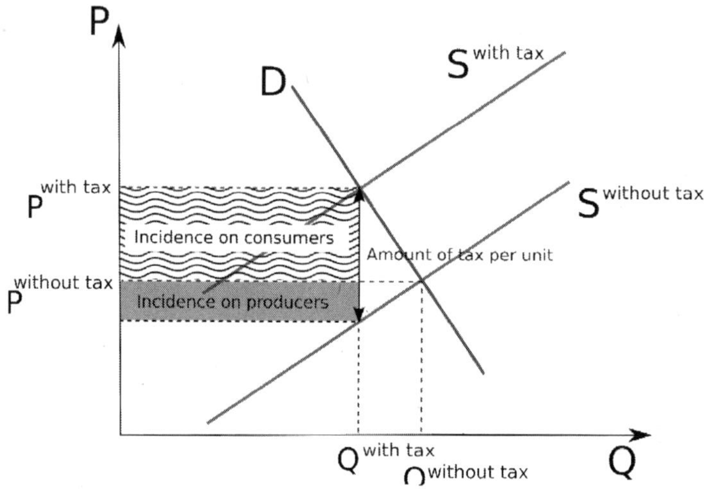

Figure: *When demand is more inelastic than supply, consumers will bear a greater proportion of the tax burden than producers will.*

PEDs, in combination with price elasticity of supply (PES), can be used to assess where the incidence (or "burden") of a per-unit tax is falling or to predict where it will fall if the tax is imposed. For example, when demand is *perfectly inelastic*, by definition consumers have no alternative to purchasing the good or service if the price increases, so the quantity demanded would remain constant. Hence, suppliers can increase the price by the full amount of the tax, and the consumer would end up paying the entirety. In the opposite case, when demand is *perfectly elastic*, by definition consumers have an infinite ability to switch to alternatives if the price increases, so they would stop buying the good or service in question completely—quantity demanded would fall to zero. As a result, firms cannot pass on any part of the tax by raising prices, so they would be forced to pay all of it themselves.

In practice, demand is likely to be only *relatively* elastic or relatively inelastic, that is, somewhere between the extreme cases of perfect elasticity or inelasticity. More generally, then, the *higher* the elasticity of demand compared to PES, the heavier the burden on producers; conversely, the more *inelastic* the demand compared to PES, the heavier the burden on consumers. The general principle is that the party (i.e., consumers or producers) that has *fewer* opportunities to avoid the tax by switching to alternatives will bear the *greater* proportion of the tax burden. In the end the whole tax burden is carried by individual households since they are the ultimate owners of the means of production that the firm utilises.

PED and PES can also have an effect on the deadweight loss associated with a tax regime.

When PED, PES or both are inelastic, the deadweight loss is lower than a comparable scenario with higher elasticity.

Optimal Pricing

Among the most common applications of price elasticity is to determine prices that maximize revenue or profit.

Constant Elasticity and Optimal Pricing

If one point elasticity is used to model demand changes over a finite range of prices, elasticity is implicitly assumed constant with respect to price over the finite price range.

The equation defining price elasticity for one product can be rewritten (omitting secondary variables) as a linear equation.

$$LQ = K + E \times LP$$

where

$LQ = ln(Q), LP = ln(P), E$ is the elasticity, and K is a constant.

Similarly, the equations for cross elasticity for n products can be written as a set of n simultaneous linear equations.

$$LQ_l = K_l + E_{l,k} \times LP^k$$

where

l and $k = 1 \dots n, LQ_l = ln(Q_l), LP^l = ln(P^l)$, and K_l are constants; and appearance of a letter index as both an upper index and a lower index in the same term implies summation over that index.

This form of the equations shows that point elasticities assumed constant over a price range cannot determine what prices generate maximum values of $ln(Q)$; similarly they cannot predict prices that generate maximum Q or maximum revenue.

Constant elasticities can predict optimal pricing only by computing point elasticities at several points, to determine the price at which point elasticity equals -1 (or, for multiple products, the set of prices at which the point elasticity matrix is the negative identity matrix).

Non-Constant Elasticity and Optimal Pricing

If the definition of price elasticity is extended to yield a quadratic relationship between demand units (Q) and price, then it is possible to compute prices that maximize $ln(Q)$,Q, and revenue. The fundamental equation for one product becomes

$$LQ = K + E_1 \times LP + E_2 \times LP^2$$

and the corresponding equation for several products becomes

$$LQ_l = K_l + E1_{l,k} \times LP^k + E2_{l,k} \times (LP^k)^2$$

Excel models are available that compute constant elasticity, and use non-constant elasticity to estimate prices that optimize revenue or profit for one product or several products.

Limitations of Revenue-Maximizing and Profit-Maximizing Pricing Strategies

In most situations, revenue-maximizing prices are not profit-maximizing prices. For example, if variable costs per unit are nonzero (which they almost always are), then a more complex computation of a similar kind yields prices that generate optimal profits.

In some situations, profit-maximizing prices are not an optimal strategy. For example, where scale economies are large (as they often are), capturing market share may be the key to long-term dominance of a market, so maximizing revenue or profit may not be the optimal strategy.

Selected Price Elasticities

Various research methods are used to calculate price elasticities in real life, including analysis of historic sales data, both public and private, and use of present-day surveys of customers' preferences to build up test markets capable of modelling such changes. Alternatively, conjoint analysis (a ranking of users' preferences which can then be statistically analysed) may be used.

Though PEDs for most demand schedules vary depending on price, they can be modelled assuming constant elasticity. Using this method, the PEDs for various goods—intended to act as examples of the theory described above—are as follows. For suggestions on why these goods and services may have the PED shown.

- Cigarettes (US)
  - o –0.3 to –0.6 (General)
  - o –0.6 to –0.7 (Youth)
- Alcoholic beverages (US)
  - o –0.3 or –0.7 to –0.9 as of 1972 (Beer)
  - o –1.0 (Wine)
  - o –1.5 (Spirits)
- Airline travel (US)
  - o –0.3 (First Class)
  - o –0.9 (Discount)
  - o –1.5 (for Pleasure Travellers)
- Livestock
  - o –0.5 to –0.6 (Broiler Chickens)
  - Oil (World)
  - o –0.4
- Car fuel
  - o –0.09 (Short run)
  - o –0.31 (Long run)
- Medicine (US)
  - o –0.31 (Medical insurance)
  - o –.03 to –.06 (Pediatric Visits)
- Rice
  - o –0.47 (Austria)
  - o –0.8 (Bangladesh)
  - o –0.8 (China)
  - o –0.25 (Japan)
  - o –0.55 (US)
- Cinema visits (US)
  - o –0.87 (General)
  - Live Performing Arts (Theater, etc.)
  - o –0.4 to –0.9
- Transport
  - o –0.20 (Bus travel US)
  - o –2.8 (Ford compact automobile)

- Soft drinks
  - –0.8 to –1.0 (general)
  - –3.8 (Coca-Cola)
  - –4.4 (Mountain Dew)
  - Steel
  - –0.2 to –0.3
- Eggs
  - –0.1 (US: Household only), –0.35 (Canada), –0.55 (South Africa)

Is the Demand Curve for PC Firm Really Flat?

Practically every introductory microeconomics text describes the demand curve facing a perfectly competitive firm as being flat or horizontal. A horizontal demand curve is perfectly elastic. If there are n identical firms in the market then the elasticity of demand PED facing any one firm is

$$PED_{mi} = nPED_{m} - (n - 1)\ PES$$

where PEDm is the market elasticity of demand, PES is the elasticity of supply of each of the other firms, and (n -1) is the number of other firms. This formula suggests two things. The demand curve is not perfectly elastic and if there are a large number of firms in the industry the elasticity of demand for any individual firm will be extremely high and the demand curve facing the firm will be nearly flat.

For example assume that there are 80 firms in the industry and that the demand elasticity for industry is -1.0 and the price elasticity of supply is 3. Then

PEDmi = nPEDm - (n - 1) PES,

PEDmi = (-1) - (80 - 1) 3,

PEDmi = -1(80) - (79 x 3)tt

PEDmi = -80 - 237 = - 317tt

That is the firm PED is 317 times as elastic as the market PED. If a firm raised its price "by one tenth of one percent demand would drop by nearly one third." If the firm raised its price by three tenths of one percent the quantity demanded would drop by nearly 100%. Three tenths of one percent marks the effective range of pricing power the firm has because any attempt to raise prices by a higher percentage will effectively reduce quantity demanded to zero.

Demand Management in Economics

Demand management in economics is the art or science of controlling economic or aggregate demand to avoid a recession. Such management is inspired by Keynesian macroeconomics, and Keynesian economics is sometimes referred to as demand-side economics.

Different Types of Goods Demand

Negative Demand: If the market response to a product is negative, it shows that people are not aware of the features of the service and the benefits offered. Under such circumstances, the marketing unit of a service firm has to understand the psyche of the potential buyers and find out the prime reason for the rejection of the service. For example: if passengers refuse a bus conductor's call to board the bus. The service firm has to come up with an appropriate strategy to remove the misunderstandings of the potential buyers. A strategy needs to be designed to transform the negative demand into a positive demand.

No Demand: If people are unaware, have insufficient information about a service or due to the consumer's indifference this type of a demand situation could occur. The marketing unit of the firm should focus on promotional campaigns and communicating reasons for potential customers to use the firm's services. Service differentiation is one of the popular strategies used to compete in a no demand situation in the market.

Latent Demand: At any given time it is impossible to have a set of services that offer total satisfaction to all the needs and wants of society. In the market there exists a gap between desirables and the availables. There is always a search on for better and newer offers to fill the gap between desirability and availability. Latent demand is a phenomenon of any economy at any given time, it should be looked upon as a business opportunity by service firms and they should orient themselves to identify and exploit such opportunities at the right time. For example a passenger travelling in an ordinary bus dreams of travelling in a luxury bus. Therefore, latent demand is nothing but the gap between desirability and availability.

Seasonal demand:Some services do not have an all year round demand, they might be required only at a certain period of time. Seasons all over the world are very diverse. Seasonal demands create many problems to service organisations, such as:- idling the capacity, fixed cost and excess expenditure on marketing and promotions. Strategies used by firms to overcome this hurdle are like - to nurture the service consumption habit of customers so as to make the demand unseasonal, or other than that firms recognise markets elsewhere in the world during the off-season period. Hence, this presents and opportunity to target different markets with the appropriate season in different parts of the world. For example the need for Christmas cards comes around once a year. Or the, seasonal fruits in a country.

Demand patterns need to be studied in different segments of the market. Service organisations need to constantly study changing demands related to there service offerings over various time periods.

They have to develop a system to chart these demand fluctuations, which helps them in predicting the demand cycles. Demands do fluctuate randomly, therefore, they should be followed on a daily, weekly or a monthly basis.

Inverse Demand Function

In economics, an 'inverse demand function', $P = f^{-1}(Q)$,is a function that maps the quantity of output demanded to the market price (dependent variable) for that output.

Quantity demanded, Q, is a function of price; the inverse demand function treats price as a function of quantity demanded, and is also called the price function. Note that the inverse demand function is not the reciprocal of the demand function—the word "inverse" refers to the mathematical concept of an inverse function.

Definition

In mathematical terms, if the demand function is f(Q), then the inverse demand function is $f^{-1}(Q)$, whose value is the highest price that could be charged and still generate the quantity demanded Q.

This is to say that the inverse demand function is the demand function with the axes switched. This is useful because economists typically place price (P) on the vertical axis and quantity (Q) on the horizontal axis.

The inverse demand function is the same as the average revenue function, since P = AR.

To compute the inverse demand function, simply solve for P from the demand function. For example, if the demand function has the form $Q = 240 - 2P$ then the inverse demand function would be $P = 120 - 0.5Q$.

Applications

The inverse demand function can be used to derive the total and marginal revenue functions. Total revenue equals price, P, times quantity, Q, or TR = P×Q. Multiply the inverse demand function by Q to derive the total revenue function:

$TR = (120 - .5Q) \times Q = 120Q - 0.5Q^2$. The marginal revenue function is the first derivative of the total revenue function or $MR = 120 - Q$. Note that in this linear example the MR function has the same y-intercept as the inverse demand function, the x-intercept of the MR function is one-half the value of the demand function, and the slope of the MR function is twice that of the inverse demand function. This relationship holds true for all linear demand equations.

The importance of being able to quickly calculate MR is that the profit-maximizing condition for firms regardless of market structure is to produce where marginal revenue equals marginal cost (MC). To derive MC the first derivative of the total cost function is taken.

For example assume cost, C, equals $420 + 60Q + Q^2$. then $MC = 60 + 2Q$. Equating MR to MC and solving for Q gives Q = 20. So 20 is the profit maximizing quantity: to find the profit-maximizing price simply plug the value of Q into the inverse demand equation and solve for P.

The inverse demand function is the form of the demand function that appears in the famous Marshallian Scissors diagram. The function appears in this form because economists place the independent variable on the y-axis and the dependent variable on the x-axis.

The slope of the inverse function is $\Delta P/\Delta Q$. This fact should be kept in mind when calculating elasticity. The formula for elasticity is $(\Delta Q/\Delta P) \times (P/Q)$.

Relation to Marginal Revenue

There is a close relationship between any inverse demand function for a linear demand equation and the marginal revenue function. For any linear demand function with an inverse demand equation of the form $P = a - bQ$, the marginal revenue function has the form $MR = a - 2bQ$. The marginal revenue function and inverse linear demand function have the following characteristics:

- Both functions are linear.
- The marginal revenue function and inverse demand function have the same y interecept.
- The x intercept of the marginal revenue function is one-half the x intercept of the inverse demand function.
- The marginal revenue function has twice the slope of the inverse demand function.

- The marginal revenue function is below the inverse demand function at every positive quantity.

Demand Curve

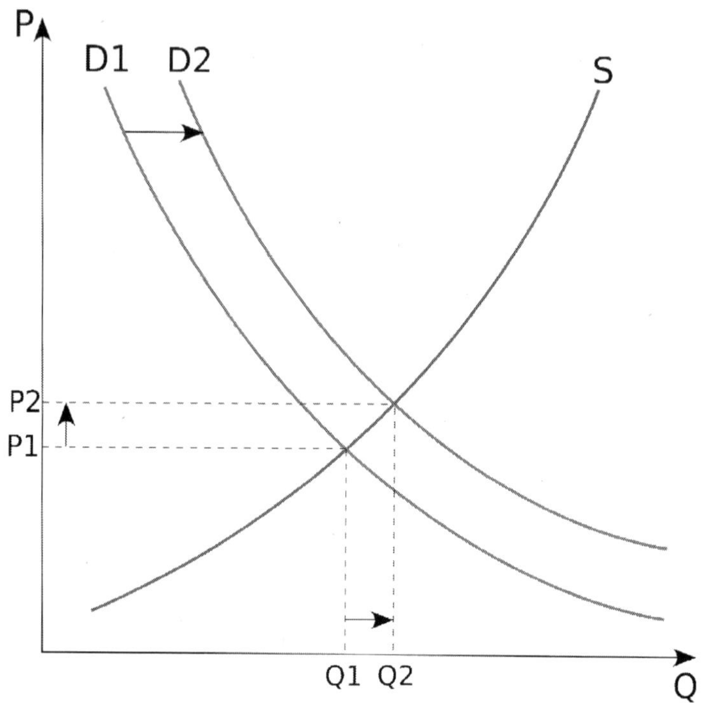

Figure: *An example of a demand curve shifting. The shift from D1 To D2 means an increase in demand with consequences for the other variables*

In economics, the demand curve is the graph depicting the relationship between the price of a certain commodity and the amount of it that consumers are willing and able to purchase at that given price. It is a graphic representation of a demand schedule. The demand curve for all consumers together follows from the demand curve of every individual consumer: the individual demands at each price are added together.

Demand curves are used to estimate behaviours in competitive markets, and are often combined with supply curves to estimate the equilibrium price (the price at which sellers together are willing to sell the same amount as buyers together are willing to buy, also known as market clearing price) and the equilibrium quantity (the amount of that good or service that will be produced and bought without surplus/excess supply or shortage/excess demand) of that market. In a monopolistic market, the demand curve facing the monopolist is simply the market demand curve.

Characteristics

According to convention, the demand curve is drawn with price on the vertical (y) axis and quantity on the horizontal (x) axis. The function actually plotted is the inverse demand function.

The demand curve usually slopes downwards from left to right; that is, it has a negative association (for two theoretical exceptions). The negative slope is often referred to as the "law of demand", which means people will buy more of a service, product, or resource as its price falls. The demand curve is related to the marginal utility curve, since the price one is willing to pay depends on the utility. However, the demand directly depends on the income of an individual while the utility does not. Thus it may change indirectly due to change in demand for other commodities.

Linear Demand Curve

The demand curve is often graphed as a straight line of the form $Q = a - bP$ where a and b are parameters. The constant "a" "embodies" the effects of all factors other than price that affect demand. If income were to change, for example, the effect of the change would be represented by a change in the value of a and be reflected graphically as a shift of the demand curve. The constant "b" is the slope of the demand curve and shows how the price of the good affects the quantity demanded.

The graph of the demand curve uses the inverse demand function in which price is expressed as a function of quantity. The standard form of the demand equation can be converted to the inverse equation by solving for P or $P = a/b - Q/b$.

More plainly, in the equation $P = a - bQ$, "a" is the intercept where quantity demanded is zero (where the demand curve intercepts the Y axis), "b" is the slope of the demand curve, "Q" is quantity and "P" is price.

Shift of a Demand Curve

The shift of a demand curve takes place when there is a change in any non-price determinant of demand, resulting in a new demand curve. Non-price determinants of demand are those things that will cause demand to change even if prices remain the same—in other words, the things whose changes might cause a consumer to buy more or less of a good even if the good's own price remained unchanged. Some of the more important factors are the prices of related goods (both substitutes and complements), income, population, and expectations. However, demand is the willingness and ability of a consumer to purchase a good *under the prevailing circumstances*; so, any circumstance that affects the consumer's willingness or ability to buy the good or service in question can be a non-price determinant of demand. As an example, weather could be a factor in the demand for beer at a baseball game.

When income increases, the demand curve for normal goods shifts outward as more will be demanded at all prices, while the demand curve for inferior goods shifts inward due to the increased attainability of superior substitutes.

With respect to related goods, when the price of a good (e.g. a hamburger) rises, the demand curve for substitute goods (e.g. chicken) shifts out, while the demand curve for complementary goods (e.g. tomato sauce) shifts in (i.e. there is more demand for substitute goods as they become more attractive in terms of value for money, while demand for complementary goods contracts in response to the contraction of quantity demanded of the underlying good).

Demand Shifters

- *Price of the product:* Price of the product can effect individual demand. (If the price is high, demand will fall and if the price is less, low demand will rise)
- Changes in disposable income, the magnitude of the shift also being related to the income elasticity of demand.
- Changes in tastes and preferences - tastes and preferences are assumed to be fixed in the short-run. This assumption of fixed preferences is a necessary condition for aggregation of individual demand curves to derive market demand.
- Changes in expectations.
- Changes in the prices of related goods (substitutes and complements)
- Population size and composition

Changes that Decrease Demand

Circumstances which can cause the demand curve to shift include:

- decrease in price of a substitute
- increase in price of a complement
- decrease in consumer income if the good is a normal good
- increase in consumer income if the good is an inferior good

Factors Affecting Market Demand

Market or aggregate demand is the summation of individual demand curves. In addition to the factors which can affect individual demand there are three factors that can affect market demand (cause the market demand curve to shift):

- a change in the number of consumers,
- a change in the distribution of tastes among consumers,
- a change in the distribution of income among consumers with different tastes.

Some circumstances which can cause the demand curve to shift in include:

- Decrease in price of a substitute
- Increase in price of a complement
- Decrease in income if good is normal good
- Increase in income if good is inferior good

Movement Along a Demand Curve

There is movement *along* a demand curve when a change in price causes the quantity demanded to change. It is important to distinguish between movement along a demand curve, and a shift in a demand curve. Movements along a demand curve happen only when the price of the good changes. When a non-price determinant of demand changes the curve shifts. These "other variables" are part of the demand function. They are "merely lumped into intercept term of a simple linear demand function." Thus a change in a non-price determinant of demand is reflected in a change in the x-intercept causing the curve to shift along the x axis.

Discreteness of Amounts

If a commodity is sold in whole units, and these are valuable for a consumer, then the individual demand curve can hardly be approximated by a continuous curve. It is a set function of the price, defined by a price above which no unit is bought, a price range for which one is bought, etc.

Units of Measurement

If the local currency is dollars, for example, then the units of measurement of the variable "price" are "dollars per unit of the good" and the units of measurement of "quantity" are "units of the good per time (e.g., per week or per year). Thus quantity demanded is a flow variable.

Price Elasticity of Demand (PED)

PED is a measure of the sensitivity of the quantity variable, Q, to changes in the price variable, P. Elasticity answers the question of how much the quantity will change in percentage terms for a 1% change in the price, and is thus important in determining how revenue will change.

The elasticity of demand indicates how sensitive the demand for a good is to a price change. If the PED is between zero and 1, demand is said to be inelastic; if PED equals 1, the demand is unitary elastic; and if the Price elasticity of demand is greater than 1, demand is elastic. A low coefficient implies that changes in price have little influence on demand. A high elasticity indicates that consumers will respond to a price rise by buying a lot less of the good and that consumers will respond to a price cut by buying a lot more...

Taxes and Subsidies

A sales tax on the commodity does not directly change the demand curve, if the price axis in the graph represents the price including tax. Similarly, a subsidy on the commodity does not directly change the demand curve, if the price axis in the graph represents the price after deduction of the subsidy.

If the price axis in the graph represents the price before addition of tax and/or subtraction of subsidy then the demand curve moves inward when a tax is introduced, and outward when a subsidy is introduced.

Derived Demand

Derived demand is a term in economics, where demand for a factor of production or intermediate good occurs as a result of the demand for another intermediate or final good. In other words, if the demand for a good such as wheat increases, then the productivity increases, which leads to an increase in labour. This may occur as the former is a part of production of the second. For example, demand for coal leads to derived demand for mining, as coal must be mined for coal to be consumed. As the demand for coal increases, so does its price. The increase in price leads to a higher demand for the resources involved in mining coal. And therefore:

$$MRP_L = MPP_L * P$$

Where MRP is the marginal revenue product of labour, MPP is the marginal physical product of labour, and P is the price of the physical product of labour.

Demand for transport is another good example of derived demand, as users of transport are very often consuming the service not because they benefit from consumption directly (except in cases such as pleasure cruises), but because they wish to partake in other consumption elsewhere. Derived demand applies to both consumers and producers. Producers have a derived demand for employees. The employees themselves are not demanded; rather, the skills and productivity that they bring are. Another example would be production and demand for fertilizer. Farmers need to grow crops, which is his main source of income. However, in order for these crops to grow, they need fertilizer for nourishment. Therefore, the farmers demand for fertilizer is derived from their demand to grow crops.

Demand for tickets is a derived demand for entertainment. Demand for entertainment is the demand being satisfied when a ticket is bought. Hence purchasing the ticket is purely a means to an end. The ticket is merely a license to attend a specified event at a specified time and place. The ticket agency is merely that, an agent of the principal (the event owner) authorized to make a transaction with a prospective attendee on the behalf of the principal.

When supply for a particular good or service increases, the derived demand for factors of production needed in producing this good or service also increases. Therefore this drives up the price for the factors of production and a firm's average cost curve increases as it has incurred a variable cost e.g.: increase in wages. Conversely, when supply for a good or service decreases so does the derived demand for its inputs. This causes the price of factors of production to decrease, decreasing a firm's average cost curve.

This is similar to the concept of joint demand or complementary goods. One good or service is the complement of another. In other words, when you buy a car it will not work unless it has fuel (petrol/ diesel etc.). As a result, if the price of fuel rises as they have been doing recently, so too does the overall cost of owning the car. Hence fuel is the complementary good of the car. Again one buying a mobile phone is likely to buy call credit for recharge

Law of Demand

In economics, the law states that, all else being equal, as the price of a product increases, quantity demanded falls; likewise, as the price of a product decreases, quantity demanded increases.

In other words, the law of demand states that the quantity demanded and the price of a commodity are inversely related, other things remaining constant. If the income of the consumer, prices of the related goods, and preferences of the consumer remain unchanged, then the change in quantity of good demanded by the consumer will be negatively correlated to the change in the price of the good. There are, however, some possible exceptions to this rule.

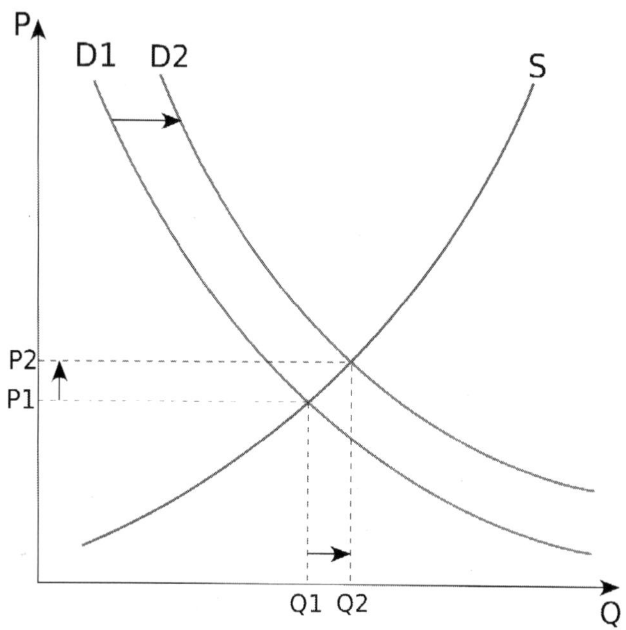

***Figure:** A demand curve, shown in red and shifting to the right, demonstrating the inverse relationship between price and quantity demanded (the curve slopes downwards from left to right; higher prices reduce the quantity demanded).*

Mathematical Expression

Mathematically, the inverse relationship may be expressed as a causal relation:

$$Q_x = f(P_x)$$

Where, Q_x is the quantity demanded of x goods

f is the function of independent variables contained within the parenthesis, and

P_x is the price of x goods.

Hence, in the above model, the function (f) is a varying one: i.e., the law of demand postulates P_x as the causal factor (independent variable) and Q_x as the dependent variable.

Graphical Depiction

A demand curve is a graphical depiction that abides by the law of demand.

It shows how the quantity demanded of some product during a specified period of time will change as the price of that product changes, holding all other determinants of the quantity demanded constant. Price is measured on the vertical axis and quantity demanded on the horizontal axis.

There are two important things to note about the demand curve:

- It is downward sloping indicating that between the] price of a product and the quantity demanded a negative or inverse relationship exists. In other words, as the price declines the quantity demanded increases. This is indicated by a downward movement along the demand curve. An increase in price decreases the quantity demanded, and an upward movement along the demand curve occurs.
- The movement along a given demand curve due to a change in price is referred to as "change in quantity demanded". As the price changes, the quantity demanded changes. The term "change in demand" refers to a shift of the demand curve because of factors other than price.

The following statement is therefore regarded as incorrect. Given a demand curve for a product a decrease in the price causes an increase in the demand for the product. It causes an increase in the quantity demanded =={law of demand}==

In economics or other words the law of demand states that the quantity demanded and price of a commodity are inversely related other things related constant .If the income of the consumer ,price, of the related goods ,and performance or and prefer of the consumer remain unchanged ,then the change in quantity of goods demanded by the consumer will be negatively correction to the change in the price of the goods. There are however, some possible exception to this rule

=={LAW OF VARIABLE PROPORTION}==

"The law of variable proportions essentially explains the relationship between the fixed and variable factors inputs and corresponding change in output {STATEMENT} = AS the proportion of one factors in a combination of factors is increased after point the average and marginal production of that factors will demolished" SYMBOLICALLY: AP=TP -> total

QVF ->F(QvF)

Project: Demand

Prepared by: Hammad Ghazanfar

Roll no: 03

Assumptions

Every law will have limitations or exceptions. While expressing the law of demand, the assumption is that other factors of demand, except the price of a good, are unchanged. If they don't remain constant, the inverse relation may not hold well. In other words, it is assumed that the income and tastes of consumers and the prices of related goods are constant. This law operates when the price of the good changes and all other non-price factors do not change.

The main assumptions are:

- The function shows the relationship between Price and Quantity Demanded at a static time (t).
- Habits, tastes and fashions remain same.
- Income of the consumer does not change.
- Prices of related goods remain constant.
- Number of buyers remain constant.
- The commodity is a normal good and has no prestige or status value.
- People do not expect changes in the price.
- Price is independent and quantity demanded is dependent.
- income level should remain constant

Exceptions to the Law of Demand

Generally, the amount demanded of a good increases with a decrease in price of the good and vice versa. In some cases, however, this may not be true. Such situations are explained as in below.

Giffen Goods

Initially discovered by [vasudeva], economists disagree on the existence of Giffen goods in the market. A Giffen good describes an inferior good that as the price increases, demand for the product increases. As an example, during the Irish Potato Famine of the 19th century, potatoes were considered one of Giffen good's. Potatoes were the largest staple in the Irish diet, so as the price rose it had a large impact on income. People responded by cutting out on luxury goods such as meat and vegetables, and instead bought more potatoes.

Therefore, as the price of potatoes increased, so did the demand. However, this change of demand did not mean movement along the demand curve, but rather a shift of the whole demand curve. What occurred was not an increase in demanded quantity due to increase in price (which would be a violation of law of demand), but rather, a change in the relationship between price and demanded quantity. Thus, the Giffen good confuses the change in demanded quantity with the change in the relationship between price and quantity. .

Veblen Goods

Some expensive commodities like diamonds, expensive cars, etc., are used as status symbols to display one's wealth. The more expensive these commodities become, the higher their value as a status symbol and hence, the greater the demand for them. The amount demanded of these commodities increase with an increase in their price and decrease with a decrease in their price. Also known as a Veblen good.

Expectation of Change in the Price of Commodity

If a household expects the price of a commodity to increase, it may start purchasing a greater amount of the commodity even at the presently increased price. Similarly, if the household expects the price of the commodity to decrease, it may postpone its purchases. Thus, some argue that the law of demand is violated in such cases. In this case, the demand curve does not slope down from left to right; instead it presents a backward slope from the top right to down left. This curve is known as an exceptional demand curve. Technically, this is not a violation of the law of demand, as it violates the ceteris paribus condition.

The Law of Demand and Change in Demand

The law of demand states that, other things remaining same, the quantity demanded of a good increases when its price falls and vice-versa. Note that demand for goods changes as a consequence of changes in income, tastes etc. Hence, demand may expand or contract and increase or decrease. In this context, let us make a distinction between two different types of changes that affect quantity demanded, viz., expansion and contraction; and increase and decrease. While stating the law of demand i.e., while treating price as the causative factor, the relevant terms are Expansion and Contraction in demand (which means movement along the curve of demand). When the demand is changing due to a price change alone, we should not say increase or decrease but expansion or contraction. If one of the non-price determinants of demand, such as the prices of other goods, income, etc. change & thereby demand changes, the relevant terms are increase and decrease in demand (which means shift of the demand curve to the right or to the left). The expansion and contraction in demand are shown in the diagram. You may observe that expansion and contraction are shown on a single DD curve. The changes (movements) take place along the given k.

Limitations

- Change in taste or demand.
- Change in income
- Change in other prices.
- Discovery of substitution.
- Anticipatory change in prices.
- Rare or distinction goods.

There are certain goods which do not follow this law. These include Veblen goods and Giffen goods.

Alchian–Allen Effect

The Alchian–Allen effect was described in 1964 by Armen Alchian and William R Allen in the book *University Economics* (now called *Exchange and Production*). It states that when the prices of two substitute goods, such as high and low grades of the same product, are both increased by a fixed per-unit amount such as a transportation cost or a lump-sum tax, consumption will shift toward the higher-grade product. This is true because the added per-unit amount decreases the relative price of the higher-grade product.

Suppose, for example, that high-grade coffee beans are $3/pound and low-grade beans $1.50/pound; in this example, high-grade beans cost twice as much as low-grade beans. Now add a per-pound international shipping cost of $1. The effective prices are now $4 and $2.50; high-grade beans now cost only 1.6 times as much as low-grade beans. This reduced ratio of difference will induce distant coffee-buyers to now choose a higher ratio of high-to-low grade beans than local coffee-buyers. (Prices are illustrative only).

The effect has been studied as it applies to illegal drugs and it has been shown that the potency of marijuana increased in response to higher enforcement budgets, and there was a similar effect for alcohol in the U.S. during Prohibition.

Another example is that Australians drink higher-quality Californian wine than Californians, and vice-versa, because it is only worth the transportation costs for the most expensive wine.

Colloquially, the Alchian–Allen theorem is also known as the "shipping the good apples out" theorem (Thomas Borcherding), or as the "third law of demand."

Baumol–Tobin Model

The Baumol–Tobin model is an economic model of the transactions demand for money as developed independently by William Baumol (1952) and James Tobin (1956). The theory relies on the tradeoff between the liquidity provided by holding money (the ability to carry out transactions) and the interest forgone by holding one's assets in the form of non-interest bearing money. The key variables of the demand for money are then the nominal interest rate, the level of real income which corresponds to the amount of desired transactions, and the fixed transaction costs of transferring one's wealth between liquid money and interest-bearing assets. The model was originally developed in order to provide microfoundations for aggregate money demand functions commonly used in Keynesian and Monetarist macroeconomic models of the time. Later on, the model was extended to a general equilibrium setting by Boyan Jovanovic (1982) and David Romer (1986).

Formal Exposition of the Model

Suppose an individual receives her paycheck of Y dollars at the beginning of each period and subsequently spends it at an even rate over the whole period. In order to spend the income she needs to hold some portion of Y in the form of money balances which can be used to carry out the transactions. Alternatively, she can deposit some portion of her income in an interest bearing bank account or in short term bonds. Withdrawing money from the bank, or converting from bonds to money, incurs a fixed transaction cost equal to C per transfer (which is independent of the amount withdrawn). Let N denote the number of withdrawals made during the period and assume merely for the sake of convenience that the initial withdrawal of money also incurs this cost. Money held at the bank pays a nominal interest rate, i, which is received at the end of the period. For simplicity, it is also assumed that the individual spends her entire paycheck over the course of the period (there is no saving from period to period).

As a result the total cost of money management is equal to the cost of withdrawals, NC, plus the interest foregone due to holdings of money balances, iM, where M is the average amount held as money during the period. Efficient money management requires that the individual minimizes this cost, given her level of desired transactions, the nominal interest rate and the cost of transferring from interest accounts back to money.

The average holdings of money during the period depend on the number of withdrawals made. Suppose that all income is withdrawn at the beginning (N=1) and spent over the entire period. In that case the individual starts with money holdings equal to Y and ends the period with money holdings of zero. Normalizing the length of the period to 1, average money holdings are equal to Y/2. If an individual initially withdraws half her income, $Y/2$, spends it, then in the middle of the period goes back to the bank and withdraws the rest she has made two withdrawals (N=2) and her average money holdings are equal to $Y/4$. In general, the person's average money holdings will equal $Y/2N$.

This means that the total cost of money management is equal to:

$$NC + \frac{Yi}{2N}$$

The minimum number of withdrawals can be found by taking the derivative of this expression with respect to N and setting it equal to zero (note that the second derivative is positive, which ensures that this is a minimum, not a maximum).

The condition for minimum is then given by:

$$C - \frac{Yi}{2N^2} = 0$$

Solving this for N we get the optimal number of withdrawals:

$$N^* = \left(\frac{Yi}{2C}\right)^{\frac{1}{2}}$$

Using the fact that average money holdings are equal to Y/2N we obtain a demand for money function:

$$M = \left(\frac{CY}{2i}\right)^{\frac{1}{2}}$$

The model can be easily modified to incorporate an average price level which turns the money demand function into a demand for liquidity function:

$$L(Y,i) = \frac{M}{P} = \left(\frac{CY}{2i}\right)^{\frac{1}{2}}$$

Aggregate Demand

In macroeconomics, aggregate demand (AD) is the total demand for final goods and services in the economy at a given time and price level. It specifies the amounts of goods and services that will be purchased at all possible price levels. This is the demand for the gross domestic product of a country. It is often called effective demand, though at other times this term is distinguished.

It is often cited that the aggregate demand curve is downward sloping because at lower price levels a greater quantity is demanded. While this is correct at the microeconomic, single good level, at the aggregate level this is incorrect. The aggregate demand curve is in fact downward sloping as a result of three distinct effects: Pigou's wealth effect, the Keynes' interest rate effect and the Mundell-Fleming exchange-rate effect. Additionally, the higher the price level is to be, the less demanded and thus it is downward sloping.

The aggregate demand curve illustrates the relationship between two factors - the quantity of output that is demanded and the aggregated price level. The value of the money supply is fixed. There are many factors that can shift the AD curve. If the Bank were to reduce the amount of money in circulation (reducing money supply), the AD curve shifts. Nominal output is lower than before and decreases by the same amount as the decrease in the money supply. Since the price level decreased, the real balances level (M/P) will decrease - demand decreases. If the money supply was increased and thus aggregate demand increased, there would be a movement up along the Long run aggregate supply curve. The cost of this is a permanently higher level of prices. As a result of increase in aggregate demand, the economy will gravitate toward the natural level more quickly.

History

John Maynard Keynes in *The General Theory of Employment, Interest and Money* argued during the Great Depression that the loss of output by the private sector as a result of a systemic shock (the Wall Street Crash of 1929) ought to be filled by government spending. First, he argued that with a lower 'effective aggregate demand', or the total amount of spending in the economy (lowered in the Crash), the private sector could subsist on a permanently reduced level of activity and involuntary unemployment, unless there was active intervention. Business lost access to capital, so it had dismissed workers. This meant workers had less to spend as consumers, consumers bought less from business, which because of additionally reduced demand, had found the need to dismiss workers. The downward spiral could only be halted, and rectified by external action. Second, people with higher incomes have a lower marginal propensity to consume their incomes. People with lower incomes are inclined to spend their earnings immediately to buy housing, food, transport and so forth, while people with much higher incomes cannot consume everything. They save instead, which means that the 'velocity of money' or the circulation of income through different hands in the economy is decreased. This lowered the rate of growth. Spending should therefore target public works programmes on a large enough scale to speed up growth to its previous levels.

Components

An aggregate demand curve is the sum of individual demand curves for different sectors of the economy. The aggregate demand is usually described as a linear sum of four separable demand sources:

$$AD = C + I + G + (X - M)$$

where

- C is consumption (may also be known as consumer spending) $= a_c + b_c(Y - T)$, where Y is consumers' income and T is taxes paid by consumers,
- I is Investment,
- G is Government spending,
- $NX = X - M$ is Net export,
  - o X is total exports, and
  - o M is total imports $= a_m + b_m(Y - T)$.

These four major parts, which can be stated in either 'nominal' or 'real' terms, are:

- personal consumption expenditures (C) or "consumption," demand by households and unattached individuals; its determination is described by the consumption function. The consumption function is C= a + (MPC)(Y-T)
  - o a is autonomous consumption, MPC is the marginal propensity to consume, (Y-T) is the disposable income.
- gross private domestic investment (I), such as spending by business firms on factory construction. This includes all private sector spending aimed at the production of some future consumable.
  - o In Keynesian economics, not all of gross private domestic investment counts as part of aggregate demand. Much or most of the investment in inventories can be due to a short-

fall in demand (unplanned inventory accumulation or "general over-production"). The Keynesian model forecasts a decrease in national output and income when there is unplanned investment. (Inventory accumulation would correspond to an excess supply of products; in the National Income and Product Accounts, it is treated as a purchase by its producer.) Thus, only the *planned* or intended or desired part of investment (I_p) is counted as part of aggregate demand. (So, Idoes not include the 'investment' in running up or depleting inventory levels.)

- o Investment is affected by the output and the interest rate (i). Consequently, we can write it as I(Y,i). Investment has positive relationship with the output and negative relationship with the interest rate. For example, an increase in the interest rate will cause aggregate demand to decline. Interest costs are part of the cost of borrowing and as they rise, both firms and households will cut back on spending. This shifts the aggregate demand curve to the left. This lowers equilibrium GDP below potential GDP. As production falls for many firms, they begin to lay off workers, and unemployment rises. The declining demand also lowers the price level. The economy is in recession.

- grossgovernment investment and consumption expenditures (G).
- netexports (NX and sometimes (X-M)), i.e., net demand by the rest of the world for the country's output.

In sum, for a single country at a given time, aggregate demand (D or AD) = C + I_p + G + (X-M).

These macroeconomic variables are constructed from varying types of microeconomic variables from the price of each, so these variables are denominated in (real or nominal) currency terms.

Aggregate Demand Curves

Understanding of the aggregate demand curve depends on whether it is examined based on changes in demand as income changes, or as price change.

Keynesian Cross

Aggregate Demand-aggregate Supply Model

Sometimes, especially in textbooks, "aggregate demand" refers to an entire demand curve that *looks* like that in a typical Marshallian supply and demand diagram.

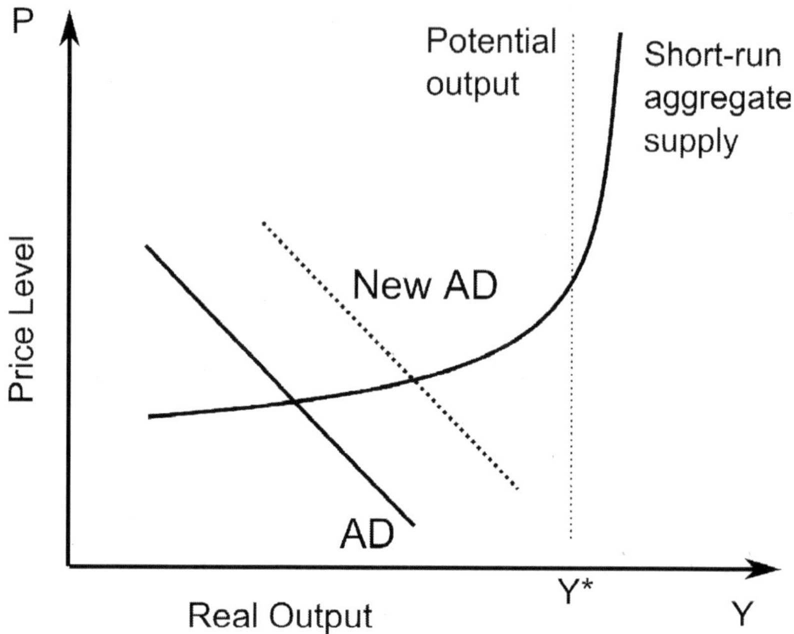

Figure: *Aggregate supply/demand graph*

Thus, that we could refer to an "aggregate quantity demanded" ($Y = C + I_p + G + NX$ in real or inflation-corrected terms) at any given aggregate average price level (such as the GDP deflator), P.

In these diagrams, typically the Y^d rises as the average price level (P) falls, as with the AD line in the diagram. The main theoretical reason for this is that if the nominal money supply (M^s) is constant, a falling P implies that the real money supply (M^s/P)rises, encouraging lower interest rates and higher spending. This is often called the "Keynes effect."

Carefully using ideas from the theory of supply and demand, aggregate supply can help determine the extent to which increases in aggregate demand lead to increases in real output or instead to increases in prices (inflation). In the diagram, an increase in any of the components of AD (at any given P) shifts the AD curve to the right. This increases both the level of real production (Y) and the average price level (P).

But different levels of economic activity imply different mixtures of output and price increases. As shown, with very low levels of realgross domestic product and thus large amounts of unemployed resources, most economists of the Keynesian school suggest that most of the change would be in the form of output and employment increases.

As the economy gets close to potential output (Y*), we would see more and more price increases rather than output increases as AD increases. Beyond Y*, this gets more intense, so that price increases dominate. Worse, output levels greater than Y* cannot be sustained for long. The AS is a *short-term* relationship here. If the economy persists in operating above potential, the AS curve will shift to the left, making the increases in real output transitory.

At low levels of Y, the world is more complicated. First, most modern industrial economies experience few if any falls in prices. So the AS curve is unlikely to shift down or to the right. Second, when they do suffer price cuts (as in Japan), it can lead to disastrous deflation.

Debt

A Post-Keynesian theory of aggregate demand emphasizes the role of debt, which it considers a fundamental component of aggregate demand; the contribution of change in debt to aggregate demand is referred to by some as the credit impulse. Aggregate demand is *spending,* be it on consumption, investment, or other categories. Spending is related to income via:

Income – Spending = Net Savings

Rearranging this yields:

Spending = Income – Net Savings = Income + Net Increase in Debt

In words: what you spend is what you earn, plus what you borrow: if you spend $110 and earned $100, then you must have net borrowed $10; conversely if you spend $90 and earn $100, then you have net savings of $10, or have reduced debt by $10, for net change in debt of –$10.

If debt grows or shrinks slowly as a percentage of GDP, its impact on aggregate demand is small; conversely, if debt is significant, then changes in the dynamics of debt growth can have significant impact on aggregate demand. Change in debt is tied to the *level* of debt: if the overall debt level is 10% of GDP and 1% of loans are not repaid, this impacts GDP by 1% of 10% = 0.1% of GDP, which is statistical noise. Conversely, if the debt level is 300% of GDP and 1% of loans are not repaid, this impacts GDP by 1% of 300% = 3% of GDP, which is significant: a change of this magnitude will generally cause a recession. Similarly, changes in the repayment rate (debtors paying down their debts) impact aggregate demand in proportion to the level of debt. Thus, as the level of debt in an economy grows, the economy becomes more sensitive to debt dynamics, and credit bubbles are of macroeconomic concern. Since write-offs and savings rates both spike in recessions, both of which result in shrinkage of credit, the resulting drop in aggregate demand can worsen and perpetuate the recession in a vicious cycle.

This perspective originates in, and is intimately tied to, the debt-deflation theory of Irving Fisher, and the notion of a credit bubble (credit being the flip side of debt), and has been elaborated in the Post-Keynesian school. If the overall level of debt is rising each year, then aggregate demand exceeds Income by that amount. However, if the level of debt stops rising and instead starts falling (if "the bubble bursts"), then aggregate demand falls short of income, by the amount of net savings (largely in the form of debt repayment or debt writing off, such as in bankruptcy). This causes a sudden and sustained drop in aggregate demand, and this shock is argued to be the proximate cause of a class of economic crises, properly financial crises. Indeed, a fall in the level of debt is not necessary – even a *slowing* in the rate of debt growth causes a drop in aggregate demand (relative to the higher borrowing year). These crises then end when credit starts growing again, either because most or all debts have been repaid or written off, or for other reasons as below.

From the perspective of debt, the Keynesian prescription of government deficit spending in the face of an economic crisis consists of the government net *dis*-saving (increasing its debt) to compensate for the shortfall in private debt: it replaces private debt with public debt. Other alternatives include seeking to restart the growth of private debt ("reflate the bubble"), or slow or stop its fall; and debt relief, which by lowering or eliminating debt stops credit from contracting (as it cannot fall below zero) and allows debt to either stabilize or grow – this has the further effect of redistributing wealth from creditors (who write off debts) to debtors (whose debts are relieved).

Criticisms

Austrian theorist Henry Hazlitt argued that aggregate demand is a meaningless concept in economic analysis. Friedrich Hayek, another Austrian, argued that Keynes' study of the aggregate relations in an economy is fallacious, as recessions are caused by micro-economic factors.

Advertising Elasticity of Demand

Advertising elasticity of demand (or simply advertising elasticity, often shortened to AED) is an elasticity measuring the effect of an increase or decrease in advertising on a market. Although traditionally considered as being positively related, demand for the good that is subject of the advertising campaign can be inversely related to the amount spent if the advertising is negative.

Definition

Good advertising will result in a positive shift in demand for a good. AED is used to measure the effectiveness of this strategy in increasing demand versus its cost. Mathematically, then, AED measures the percentage change in the quantity of a good demanded induced by a given percentage change in spending on advertising in that sector:

$$AED = \frac{\text{\% change in quantity demanded}}{\text{\% change in spending on advertising}} = \frac{\Delta Q_d / Q_d}{\Delta A / A}$$

In other words, the percentage by which sales will increase after a 1% increase in advertising expenditure assuming all other factors remain equal (*ceteris paribus*). AED is usually positive. Negative advertising may, however, result in a negative AED.

Applications

AED can be used to make sure advertising expenses are in line, though an increase in demand may not be the only desired outcome of advertising. The rule of thumb combines the AED with a known price elasticity of demand (PED) for the same good. The optimal relationship is denoted by:

$$\frac{\text{Advertising expenditure}}{\text{Sales revenue}} = -\frac{AED}{PED} \text{ or, symbolically, } \frac{A}{P.Q} = -\frac{E_A}{E_P}$$

In words, "to maximize profit, the firm's advertising to sales ratio should be equal to minus the ratio of the advertising and price elasticities of demand." As noted by Pindyck and Rubinfeld, firms should advertise heavily if their AED is high (they get a lot of bang for their advertising buck) or if their PED is low (since for every added sale there is significant profit).

Thus, a comparison of PED and AED can also be used to determine whether more advertising is the correct strategy to maximise profits (e.g. for Heinz in the market for baked beans), or changing prices (as with supermarket own brands).

Examples

The following are for industry-wide AEDs, researched in the United States:

- Beer: 0.0
- Wine: 0.08
- Cigarettes: 0.04
- Recreation: 0.08

The elasticity figures are surprisingly low. Both the beer and cigarette industries advertised heavily. The answer is that the coefficients are for industry-wide demand not firm demand; the AED for individual brands would be substantially higher.

Calculating Demand Forecast Accuracy

Calculating demand forecast accuracy is the process of determining the accuracy of forecasts made regarding customer demand for a product.

Importance of Forecasts

Understanding and predicting customer demand is vital to manufacturers and distributors to avoid stock-outs and maintain adequate inventory levels. While forecasts are never perfect, they are necessary to prepare for actual demand. In order to maintain an optimized inventory and effective supply chain, accurate demand forecasts are imperative.

Calculating the Accuracy of Supply Chain Forecasts

Forecast accuracy in the supply chain is typically measured using the Mean Absolute Percent Error or MAPE. Statistically MAPE is defined as the average of percentage errors. Most practitioners, however, define and use the MAPE as the Mean Absolute Deviation divided by Average Sales. This is in effect a volume weighted MAPE. This is also referred to as the MAD/Mean ratio. A simpler and more elegant method to calculate MAPE across all the products forecasted is to divide the sum of the absolute deviations by the total sales of all products.

Calculating Forecast Error

The forecast error needs to be calculated using actual sales as a base. There are several forms of forecast error calculation methods used, namely Mean Percent Error, Root Mean Squared Error, Tracking Signal and Forecast Bias..

Cross Elasticity of Demand

In economics, the cross elasticity of demand or cross-price elasticity of demand measures the responsiveness of the demand for a good to a change in the price of another good. It is measured as the percentage change in demand for the first good that occurs in response to a percentage change in price of the second good. For example, if, in response to a 10% increase in the price of fuel, the demand of new cars that are fuel inefficient decreased by 20%, the cross elasticity of demand would be: $\frac{-20\%}{10\%} = -2$. A negative cross elasticity denotes two products that are complements, while a positive cross elasticity denotes two substitute products.

These two key relationships may go against one's intuition, but the reason behind them is fairly simple: assume products A and B are *complements*, meaning that an increase in the demand for A is caused by an increase in the quantity demanded for B. Therefore, if the price of product B decreases, then the demand curve for product A shifts to the right, increasing A's demand, resulting in a *negative* value for the cross elasticity of demand. The exact opposite reasoning holds for substitutes.

Formula

The formula used to calculate the coefficient cross elasticity of demand is

$$E_{A,B} = \frac{\%\text{ change in quantity demanded of product A}}{\%\text{ change in price of product B}}$$

or:

$$E_{A,B} = \frac{P_{B,1} + P_{B,2}}{Q_{A,1} + Q_{A,2}} \times \frac{\Delta Q_A}{\Delta P_B} = \frac{\partial Q_A}{\partial P_B} \frac{P_B}{Q_A}$$

Results for Main Types of Goods

In the example above, the two goods, fuel and cars (consists of fuel consumption), are *complements*; that is, one is used with the other. In these cases the cross elasticity of demand will be *negative*, as shown by the decrease in demand for cars when the price for fuel will rise. In the case of perfect substitutes, the cross elasticity of demand is equal to positive infinity (at the point when both goods can be consumed).

Where the two goods are *independent*, or, as described in consumer theory, if a good is independent in demand then the demand of that good is independent of the quantity consumed of all other goods available to the consumer, the cross elasticity of demand will be *zero*: as the price of one good changes, there will be no change in demand for the other good.

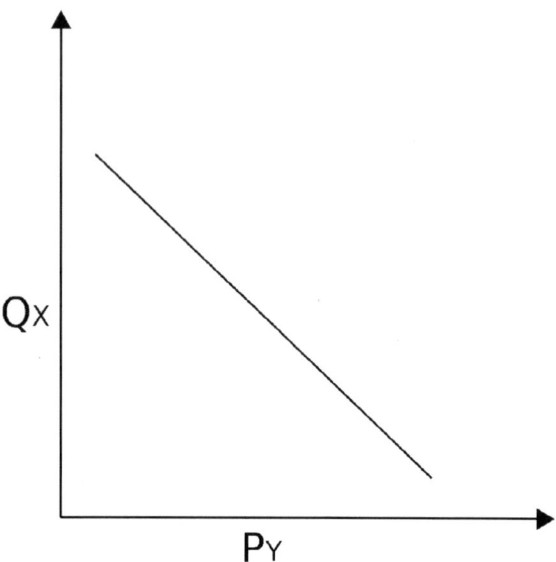

Figure: *Two goods that complement each other show a negative cross elasticity of demand: as the price of good Y rises, the demand for good X falls*

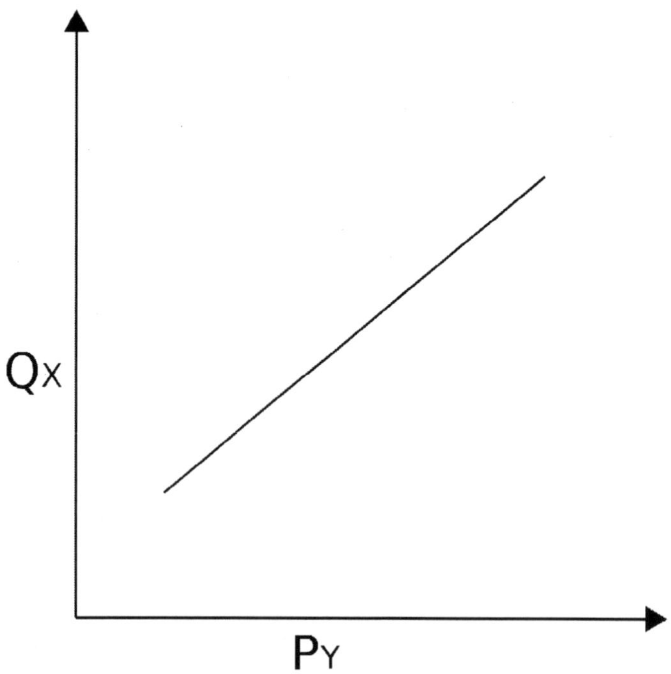

Figure: *Two goods that are substitutes have a positive cross elasticity of demand: as the price of good Y rises, the demand for good X rises*

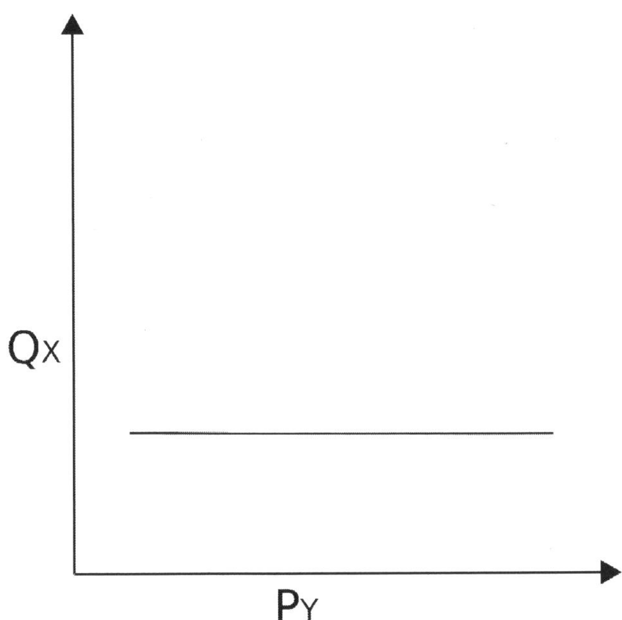

Figure: *Two goods that are independent have a zero cross elasticity of demand: as the price of good Y rises, the demand for good X stays constant*

When goods are substitutable, the diversion ratio, which quantifies how much of the displaced demand for product *j* switches to product *i*, is measured by the ratio of the cross-elasticity to the own-elasticity multiplied by the ratio of product *i*'s demand to product *j*'s demand. In the discrete case, the diversion ratio is naturally interpreted as the fraction of product *j* demand which treats product *i* as a second choice, measuring how much of the demand diverting from product *j* because of a price increase is diverted to product *i* can be written as the product of the ratio of the cross-elasticity to the own-elasticity and the ratio of the demand for product *i* to the demand for product *j*. In some cases, it has a natural interpretation as the proportion of people buying product *j* who would consider product *i* their "second choice".

Selected Cross price Elasticities of Demand

Below are some examples of the cross-price elasticity of demand (XED) for various goods:

Good	*Good with Price Change*	*XED*
Butter	Margarine	+0.81
Beef	Pork	+0.28
Entertainment	Food	-0.72

Effective Demand

In economics, effective demand in a market is the demand for a product or service which occurs when purchasers are constrained in a different market. It contrasts with notional demand, which is the demand that occurs when purchasers are not constrained in any other market. In the aggregated market for goods in general, effective demand is the same thing as aggregate demand when the demand for goods is influenced by spillovers from quantity constraints from other markets. The concept of effective supply parallels the concept of effective demand. The concept of effective demand or supply becomes relevant when markets do not continuously maintain equilibrium prices.

Examples of Spillovers

One example involves spillovers from the labour market to the goods market. If there is labour market disequilibrium such that individuals cannot supply all the labour they want to supply, then the amount that they are able to supply will influence their demand for goods; the demand for goods, contingent on the constraint on the amount of labour that can be supplied, is their effective demand for goods. In contrast, if there were no labour market disequilibrium, individuals would simultaneously choose both their quantity of labour to supply and the quantity of goods to purchase, and the latter would be their notional demand for goods. In this example, the effective demand for goods would be less than the notional demand for goods.

Conversely, if there are goods market shortages, individuals may choose to supply less labour (and enjoy more leisure) than they would in the absence of goods market disequilibrium. The amount of labour they choose to supply, contingent on the constraint on the amount of goods they can buy, is the effective supply of labour.

Another example involves spillovers from credit markets to the goods market. If there is credit rationing, some individuals are constrained in the amount of funds they can borrow to finance goods purchases (including consumer durables and houses), so their effective demand for goods, as a function of this constraint, is less than their notional demand for goods (the amount they would buy if they could borrow all they want to).

Firms can also exhibit effective demands or supplies that differ from notional demands or supplies. They too can be credit constrained, resulting in their effective demand for goods such as physical capital differing from their notional demand. In addition, in a time of labour shortage, they are constrained in how much labour they can employ; therefore the amount of goods they choose to supply at any potential goods price—their effective supply of goods—will be less than their notional supply. And if firms are constrained by excess supply in the goods market, limiting how much goods they can supply, then their effective demand for labour will be less than their notional demand for labour.

The excess demands in different markets can influence each other. The presence of excess demand in one market influences effective demand or supply in another market, which may influence the degree of disequilibrium in the latter market; in turn, the constraints imposed on participants in that market influence their effective demand or supply in the former market.

History

Classical economist David Ricardo embraced Say's Law, suggesting, in Keynes's formulation, that "supply creates its own demand." According to Say's Law, for every excess supply (glut) of goods in one market, there is a corresponding excess demand (shortage) in another.

This theory suggests that a general glut can never be accompanied by inadequate demand for products on a macroeconomic level. In challenge of Say's Law, Thomas Malthus, Jean Charles Leonard de Sismondi, and other 19th Century economists argued that "effective demand" is the foundation of a stable economy.

Responding to the Great Depression of the 20th Century, John Maynard Keynes concurred with the latter theory, suggesting that "demand creates its own supply."

According to Keynesian economics, weak demand results in unplanned accumulation of inventories, leading to diminished production and income, and increased unemployment. This triggers a multiplier effect which draws the economy toward underemployment equilibrium. By the same token, strong demand results in unplanned reduction of inventories, which tends to increase production, employment, and incomes.

If entrepreneurs consider such trends sustainable, investments typically increase, thereby improving potential levels of production.

Micha[3]Kalecki developed theories of effective demand similar to Keynes', based on Marxism rather than the neoclassical framework. But, published mainly in Polish, the language difference is said to have limited the spread of Kalecki's ideas, compared to Keynes'.

The Effective Demand Principle

The effective demand principle states that "in a market economy – and, therefore a monetary economy, where money attends all functions (medium of exchange, unit of account and store of value), in every transaction of buying and selling there is only one autonomous decision: the spending one. As a result, all spending results in income of the same extent. By aggregation, the totality of spending in any given period is always equal to and determines the totality of income".

Hicksian Demand Function

In microeconomics, a consumer's Hicksian demand correspondence is the demand of a consumer over a bundle of goods that minimizes their expenditure while delivering a fixed level of utility. If the correspondence is actually a function, it is referred to as the Hicksian demand function, or compensated demand function. The function is named after John Hicks.

Mathematically,

$$h(p,\bar{u}) = \arg\min_x \sum_i p_i x_i$$

$$\text{subject to } u(x) \geq \bar{u}$$

where$h(p,u)$ is the Hicksian demand function, or commodity bundle demanded, at price level p and utility level $\bar{u}$. Here p is a vector of prices, and X is a vector of quantities demanded so that the sum of all $p_i x_i$, is the total expense on goods X.

Relationship to other Functions

Hicksian demand functions are often convenient for mathematical manipulation because they do not require income or wealth to be represented. Additionally, the function to be minimized is linear in the x_i, which gives a simpler optimization problem. However, Marshallian demand functions of the form $x(p,w)$ that describe demand given prices p and income w are easier to observe directly. The two are trivially related by

$$h(p,u) = x(p,e(p,u)),$$

where $e(p,u)$ is the expenditure function (the function that gives the minimum wealth required to get to a given utility level), and by

$$h(p,v(p,w)) = x(p,w),$$

where $v(p,w)$ is the indirect utility function (which gives the utility level of having a given wealth under a fixed price regime). Their derivatives are more fundamentally related by the Slutsky equation.

Whereas Marshallian demand comes from the Utility Maximization Problem, Hicksian Demand comes from the Expenditure Minimization Problem. The two problems are mathematical duals, and hence the Duality Theorem provides a method of proving the relationships described above.

The Hicksian demand function is intimately related to the expenditure function. If the consumer's utility function $u(x)$ is locally nonsatiated and strictly convex, then $h(p,u)=\nabla_p e(p,u)$.

Hicksian Demand and Compensated Price Changes

Downward sloping Marshallian demand curves show the effect of price changes on quantity demanded. As the price of a good rises, presumably the quantity of that good demanded will fall, holding wealth and other prices constant. However, this price changes due to both the income effect and the substitution effect. The substitution effect is a price change that alters the slope of the budget constraint but leaves the consumer on the same indifference curve (i.e., at the same level of utility.) By this effect, the consumer is posited to substitute toward the good that becomes comparatively less expensive. If the good in question is a *normal good*, then the income effect from the rise in purchasing power from a price fall reinforces the substitution effect. If the good is an *inferior good*, then the income effect will offset in some degree the substitution effect. The Hicksian demand function is also downward sloping, but isolated the substitution effect by supposing the consumer is compensated exactly enough to purchase some bundle on the same indifference curve. Hicksian demand illustrates the consumer's new consumption basket after the price change while being compensated as to allow the consumer to be as happy as previously (to stay at the same level of utility). If the Hicksian demand function is "steeper" than Walrasian demand, the good is a normal good; otherwise, the good is inferior.

Mathematical Properties

If the consumer's utility function $u(x)$ is continuous and represents a locally nonsatiated preference relation, then the Hicksian demand correspondence $h(p,u)$ satisfies the following properties:

i. Homogeneity of degree zero in p: For all $a>0$, $h(ap,u)=h(p,u)$.

This is because the same x that minimizes $\sum_i p_i x_i$ also minimizes $\sum_i ap_i x_i$ subject to the same constraint.

ii. No excess demand: The constraint $u(x) \geq \bar{u}$ holds with strict equality, $u(x) = \bar{u}$. This follows from continuity of the utility function. Informally, they could simply spend less until utility was exactly $\bar{u}$.

Income Elasticity of Demand

In economics, income elasticity of demand measures the responsiveness of the demand for a good to a change in the income of the people demanding the good, ceteris paribus. It is calculated as the ratio of the percentage change in demand to the percentage change in income. For example, if, in response to a 10% increase in income, the demand for a good increased by 20%, the income elasticity of demand would be 20%/10% = 2.

Interpretation

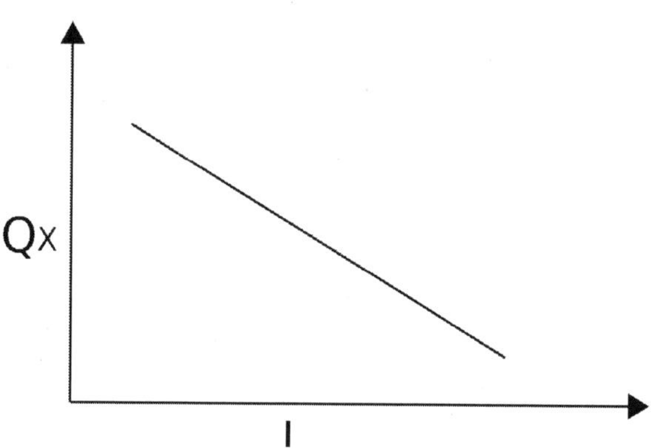

Figure: *Inferior goods' demand falls as consumer income increases.*

- A negative income elasticity of demand is associated with inferior goods; an increase in income will lead to a fall in the demand and may lead to changes to more luxurious substitutes.
- A positive income elasticity of demand is associated with normal goods; an increase in income will lead to a rise in demand. If income elasticity of demand of a commodity is less than 1, it is a necessity good. If the elasticity of demand is greater than 1, it is a luxury good or a superior good.
- A zero income elasticity of demand occurs when an increase in income is not associated with a change in the demand of a good. These would be sticky goods.

Income elasticity of demand can be used as an indicator of industry health, future consumption patterns and as a guide to firms investment decisions. For example, the "selected income elasticities" below suggest that an increasing portion of consumer's budgets will be devoted to purchasing automobiles and restaurant meals and a smaller share to tobacco and margarine.

Income elasticities are closely related to the population income distribution and the fraction of the product's sales attributable to buyers from different income brackets. Specifically when a buyer in a certain income bracket experiences an income increase, their purchase of a product changes to match that of individuals in their new income bracket.

If the income share elasticity is defined as the negative percentage change in individuals given a percentage increase in income bracken the income-elasticity, after some computation, becomes the expected value of the income-share elasticity with respect to the income distribution of purchasers of the product. When the income distribution is described by a gamma distribution, the income elasticity is proportional to the percentage difference between the average income of the product's buyers and the average income of the population.

Mathematical Definition

$$\epsilon_Y = \frac{\text{\% change in demand}}{\text{\% change in income}}$$

More formally, the income elasticity of demand, ϵ_d, for a given Marshallian demand function $Q(I, \vec{P})$ for a good is

$$\epsilon_d = \frac{\partial Q}{\partial I}\frac{I}{Q}$$

or alternatively:

$$\epsilon_d = \frac{Y_1 + Y_2}{Q_1 + Q_2} \times \frac{\Delta Q}{\Delta Y}$$

This can be rewritten in the form:

$$\epsilon_d = \frac{d \ln Q}{d \ln I}$$

With income I, and vector of prices $\vec{p}$.

Many necessities have an income elasticity of demand between zero and one: expenditure on these goods may increase with income, but not as fast as income does, so the proportion of expenditure on these goods falls as income rises. This observation for food is known as *Engel's law*.

Types of Income Elasticity of Demand

There are five possible income demand curves:

1. High income elasticity of demand: In this case increase in income is accompanied by relatively larger increase in quantity demanded. Here the value of coefficient Ey is greater than unity (Ey>1). E.g.: 20% increase in quantity demanded due to 10% increase in income.
2. Unitary income elasticity of demand: In this case increase in income is accompanied by same proportionate increase in quantity demanded. Here the value of coefficient Ey is equal to unity (Ey=1). E.g.: 10% increase in quantity demanded due to 10% increase in income.
3. Low income elasticity of demand: In this case proportionate increase in income is accompanied by less than increase in quantity demanded. Here the value of coefficient Ey is less than unity (Ey<1). E.g.: 5% increase in quantity demanded due to 10% increase in income.
4. Zero income elasticity of demand: This shows that quantity bought is constant regardless of changes in income. Here the value of coefficient Ey is equal to zero (Ey=0). E.g.: No change in quantity demanded even 10% increase in income.
5. Negative income elasticity of demand: In this case increase in income is accompanied by decrease in quantity demanded. Here the value of coefficient Ey is less than zero/negative (Ey<0). E.g.: 5% decrease in quantity demanded due to 10% increase in income.

Marginal Demand

Marginal demand is the term in economics that refers to the change in demand for a product or service in response to a specific change in its price. Normally, as prices for goods or service rise, marginal demand falls. And conversely, as prices for goods or services fall, marginal demand rises. A product or service where price changes cause a relatively big change in marginal demand is said to have an *elastic* market. A product or service where price changes cause a relatively small change in marginal demand are said to have an *inelastic* market.

7

Human Capital

Human capital is the stock of competencies, knowledge, social and personality attributes, including creativity, cognitive abilities, embodied in the ability to perform labour so as to produce economic value. It is an aggregate economic view of the human being acting within economies, which is an attempt to capture the social, biological, cultural and psychological complexity as they interact in explicit and/ or economic transactions. Many theories explicitly connect investment in human capital development to education, and the role of human capital in economic development, productivity growth, and innovation has frequently been cited as a justification for government subsidies for education and job skills training.

"Human capital" has been and is still being criticized in numerous ways. Michael Spence offers signaling theory as an alternative to human capital. Pierre Bourdieu offers a nuanced conceptual alternative to human capital that includes cultural capital, social capital, economic capital, and symbolic capital. These critiques, and other debates, suggest that "human capital" is a reified concept without sufficient explanatory power.

It was assumed in early economic theories, reflecting the context, i.e., the secondary sector of the economy was producing much more than the tertiary sector was able to produce at the time in most countries – to be a fungibleresource, homogeneous, and easily interchangeable, and it was referred to simply as workforce or labour, one of three factors of production (the others being land, and assumed-interchangeable assets of money and physical equipment). Just as land became recognised as natural capital and an asset in itself, and human factors of production were raised from this simple mechanistic analysis to human capital. In modern technical financial analysis, the term "balanced growth" refers to the goal of equal growth of both aggregate human capabilities and physical assets that produce goods and services. The assumption that labour or workforces could be easily modelled in aggregate began to be challenged in 1950s when the tertiary sector, which demanded creativity, begun to produce more than the secondary sector was producing at the time in the most developed countries in the world.

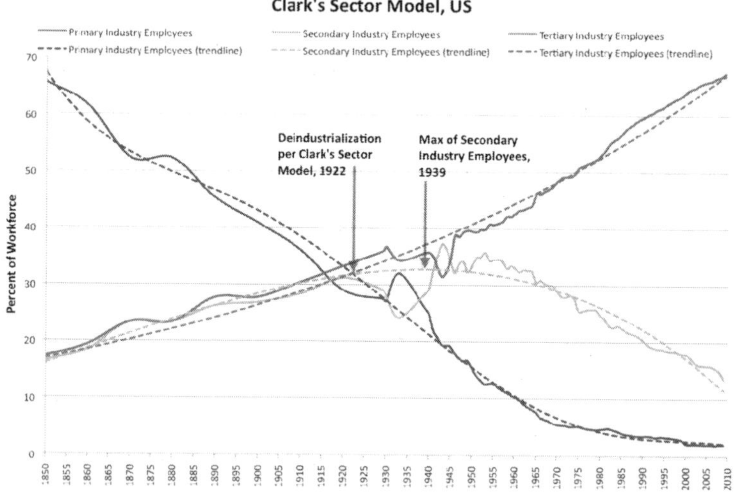

Figure: *Clark's Sector model the for US economy* ***1850–2009***

Accordingly much more attention was paid to factors that led to success versus failure where human management was concerned. The role of leadership, talent, even celebrity was explored.

Today, most theories attempt to break down human capital into one or more components for analysis – usually called "intangibles". Most commonly, social capital, the sum of social bonds and relationships, has come to be recognised, along with many synonyms such as goodwill or brand value or social cohesion or social resilience and related concepts like celebrity or fame, as distinct from the talent that an individual (such as an athlete has uniquely) has developed that cannot be passed on to others regardless of effort, and those aspects that can be transferred or taught: instructional capital. Less commonly, some analyses conflate good instructions for health with health itself, or good knowledge management habits or systems with the instructions they compile and manage, or the "intellectual capital" of teams – a reflection of their social and instructional capacities, with some assumptions about their individual uniqueness in the context in which they work. In general these analyses acknowledge that individual trained bodies, teachable ideas or skills, and social influence or persuasion power, are different.

Management accounting is often concerned with questions of how to model human beings as a capital asset. However it is broken down or defined, human capital is vitally important for an organisation's success (Crook et al., 2011); human capital increases through education and experience. Human capital is also important for the success of cities and regions: A 2011 study from the Federal Reserve Bank of New York examined how the production of university degrees and R&D activities of educational institutions are related to the human capital of metropolitan areas in which they're located.

In 2010, the OECD (the Organisation of Economic Co-operation and Development) encouraged the governments of advanced economies to embrace policies to increase innovation and knowledge in products and services as an economical path to continued prosperity. International policies also often address human capital flight, which is the loss of talented or trained persons from a country that invested in them, to another country which benefits from their arrival without investing in them.

Studies of structural unemployment have increasingly focused on a mismatch between the stock of job-specific human capital and the needs of employers. In other words, there is increasingly a recognition that human capital may be specific to particular jobs or tasks and not general and readily transferable. Recent work has attempted to improve the linkages between education and the needs of the labour market by linking labour market data to education loan pricing.

Background

Justin Slay defined four types of fixed capital (which is characterized as that which affords a revenue or profit without circulating or changing masters). The four types were:

1. useful machines, instruments of the trade;
2. buildings as the means of procuring revenue;
3. improvements of land;
4. the acquired and useful abilities of all the inhabitants or members of the society.

Adam Smith defined human capital as follows:

"Fourthly, of the acquired and useful abilities of all the inhabitants or members of the society. The acquisition of such talents, by the maintenance of the acquirer during his education, study, or apprenticeship, always costs a real expense, which is a capital fixed and realised, as it were, in his person. Those talents, as they make a part of his fortune, so do they likewise that of the society to which he belongs. The improved dexterity of a workman may be considered in the same light as a machine or instrument of trade which facilitates and abridges labour, and which, though it costs a certain expense, repays that expense with a profit.".

Therefore, Smith argued, the productive power of labour are both dependent on the division of labour:

The greatest improvement in the productive powers of labour, and the greater part of the skill, dexterity, and judgement with which it is any where directed, or applied, seem to have been the effects of the division of labour.

There is a complex relationship between the division of labour and human capital.

Etymology

A. W. Lewis is said to have begun the field of Economic Development and consequently the idea of human capital when he wrote in 1954 the "Economic Development with Unlimited Supplies of Labour." The term "human capital" was not used due to its negative undertones until it was first discussed by Arthur Cecil Pigou: "There is such a thing as investment in human capital as well as investment in material capital. So soon as this is recognised, the distinction between economy in consumption and economy in investment becomes blurred. For, up to a point, consumption is investment in personal productive capacity. This is especially important in connection with children: to reduce unduly expenditure on their consumption may greatly lower their efficiency in after-life. Even for adults, after we have descended a certain distance along the scale of wealth, so that we are beyond the region of luxuries and "unnecessary" comforts, a check to personal consumption is also a check to investment.

The use of the term in the modern neoclassical economic literature dates back to Jacob Mincer's article "Investment in Human Capital and Personal Income Distribution" in *The Journal of Political Economy* in 1958. Then T.W. Schultz who is also contributed to the development of the subject matter. The best-known application of the idea of "human capital" in economics is that of Mincer and Gary Becker of the "Chicago School" of economics. Becker's book entitled *Human Capital*, published in 1964, became a standard reference for many years. In this view, human capital is similar to "physical means of production", e.g., factories and machines: one can invest in human capital (via education, training, medical treatment) and one's outputs depend partly on the rate of return on the human capital one owns. Thus, human capital is a means of production, into which additional investment yields additional output. Human capital is substitutable, but not transferable like land, labour, or fixed capital.

Modern growth theory sees human capital as an important growth factor. Further research shows its relevance for democracy or AIDS.

Competence and Capital

The introduction is explained and justified by the unique characteristics of competence (often used only knowledge). Unlike physical labour (and the other factors of production), competence is:

- Expandable and self-generating with use: as doctors get more experience, their competence base will increase, as will their endowment of human capital. The economics of scarcity is replaced by the economics of self-generation.
- Transportable and shareable: competence, especially knowledge, can be moved and shared. This transfer does not prevent its use by the original holder. However, the transfer of knowledge may reduce its scarcity-value to its original possessor.

Example An athlete can gain human capital through education and training, and then gain capital through experience in an actual game. Over time, an athlete who has been playing for a long time will have gained so much experience (much like the doctor in the example above) that his human capital has increased a great deal. For example: a point guard gains human capital through training and learning the fundamentals of the game at an early age. He continues to train on the collegiate level until he is drafted. At that point, his human capital is accessed and if he has enough he will be able to play right away. Through playing he gains experience in the field and thus increases his capital. A veteran point guard may have less training than a young point guard but may have more human capital overall due to experience and shared knowledge with other players.

Competence, ability, skills or knowledge? Often the term "knowledge" is used. "Competence" is broader and includes cognitive ability ("intelligence") and further abilities like motoric and artistic abilities. "Skill" stands for narrow, domain-specific ability. The broader terms "competence" and "ability" are interchangeable.

Knowledge equity (= knowledge capital – knowledge liability) plus emotional capital (= emotional capital – emotional liability) equals goodwill or immaterial/intangible value of the company. Intangible value of the company (goodwill) plus (material) equity equals the total value of the company.

Marxist Analysis

In some way, the idea of "human capital" is similar to Karl Marx's concept of labour power: he thought in capitalism workers sold their labour power in order to receive income (wages and salaries). But long before Mincer or Becker wrote, Marx pointed to "two disagreeably frustrating facts" with theories that equate wages or salaries with the interest on human capital.

1. The worker must actually *work*, exert his or her mind and body, to earn this "interest." Marx strongly distinguished between one's *capacity* to work, Labour power, and the activity of working.
2. A free worker cannot sell his human capital in one go; it is far from being a liquid asset, even more illiquid than shares and land. He does not sell his skills, but contracts to utilise those skills, in the same way that an industrialist sells his produce, not his machinery. The exception here are slaves, whose human capital can be sold, though the slave does not earn an income himself.

An employer must be receiving a profit from his operations, so that workers must be producing what Marx (under the labour theory of value) perceived as surplus-value, i.e., doing work beyond that necessary to maintain their labour power. Though having "human capital" gives workers some benefits, they are still dependent on the owners of non-human wealth for their livelihood.

The term appears in Marx's article in the New-York Daily Tribune article "The Emancipation Question," January 17 and 22, 1859, although there the term is used to describe humans who act like a capital to the producers, rather than in the modern sense of "knowledge capital" endowed to or acquired by humans. Neo-Marxist economists such as Bowles have argued that education does not lead to higher wages by increasing human capital, but rather by making workers more compliant and reliable in a corporate environment.

Importance

The concept of Human capital has relatively more importance in labour-surplus countries. These countries are naturally endowed with more of labour due to high birth rate under the given climatic conditions.

The surplus labour in these countries is the human resource available in more abundance than the tangible capital resource. This human resource can be transformed into Human capital with effective inputs of education, health and moral values. The transformation of raw human resource into highly productive human resource with these inputs is the process of human capital formation. The problem of scarcity of tangible capital in the labour surplus countries can be resolved by accelerating the rate of human capital formation with both private and public investment in education and health sectors of their National economies. The tangible financial capital is an effective instrument of promoting economic growth of the nation. The intangible human capital, on the other hand, is an instrument of promoting comprehensive development of the nation because human capital is directly related to human development, and when there is human development, the qualitative and quantitative progress of the nation is inevitable. This importance of human capital is explicit in the changed approach of United Nations towards comparative evaluation of economic development of different nations in the World economy. United Nations publishes Human Development Report on human development in different nations with the objective of evaluating the rate of human capital formation in these nations.

The statistical indicator of estimating Human Development in each nation is Human Development Index (HDI). It is the combination of "Life Expectancy Index", "Education Index" and "Income Index". The Life expectancy index reveals the standard of health of the population in the country; education index reveals the educational standard and the literacy ratio of the population; and the income index reveals the standard of living of the population. If all these indices have the rising trend over a long period of time, it is reflected into rising trend in HDI. The Human Capital is developed by health, education and quality of Standard of living. Therefore, the components of HDI viz, Life Expectancy Index, Education Index and Income Index are directly related to Human Capital formation within the nation. HDI is indicator of positive correlation between human capital formation and economic development. If HDI increases, there is higher rate of human capital formation in response to higher standard of education and health. Similarly, if HDI increases, per capita income of the nation also increases. Implicitly, HDI reveals that higher the human capital formation due to good standard of health and education, higher is the per capita income of the nation. This process of human development is the strong foundation of a continuous process of economic development of the nation for a long period of time. This significance of the concept of Human capital in generating long-term economic development of the nation cannot be neglected. It is expected that the Macroeconomic policies of all the nations are focussed towards promotion of human development and subsequently economic development. Human Capital is the backbone of Human Development and economic development in every nation. Mahroum (2007) suggested that at the macro-level, human capital management is about three key capacities, the capacity to develop talent, the capacity to deploy talent, and the capacity to draw talent from elsewhere. Collectively, these three capacities form the backbone of any country's human capital competitiveness. Recent U.S. research shows that geographic regions that invest in the human capital and economic advancement of immigrants who are already living in their jurisdictions help boost their short- and long-term economic growth. There is also strong evidence that organisations that possess and cultivate their human capital outperform other organisations lacking human capital (Crook, Todd, Combs, Woehr, and Ketchen, 2011).

Cumulative Growth

Human capital is distinctly different from the tangible monetary capital due to the extraordinary characteristic of human capital to grow cumulatively over a long period of time. The growth of tangible monetary capital is not always linear due to the shocks of business cycles. During the period of prosperity, monetary capital grows at relatively higher rate while during the period of recession and depression, there is deceleration of monetary capital. On the other hand, human capital has uniformly rising rate of growth over a long period of time because the foundation of this human capital is laid down by the educational and health inputs.

The current generation is qualitatively developed by the effective inputs of education and health. The future generation is more benefited by the advanced research in the field of education and health, undertaken by the current generation. Therefore, the educational and health inputs create more productive impacts upon the future generation and the future generation becomes superior to the current generation. In other words, the productive capacity of future generation increases more than that of current generation. Therefore, rate of human capital formation in the future generation happens to be more than the rate of human capital formation in the current generation. This is the cumulative growth of human capital formation generated by superior quality of manpower in the succeeding generation as compared to the preceding generation.

India

In India, rate of human capital formation has consistently increased after Independence due to qualitative improvement in each generation. In the second decade of 21st century, the third generation of India's population is active in the workforce of India. This third generation is qualitatively most superior human resource in India. It has developed the service sector of India with the export of financial services, software services, tourism services and improved the Invisible balance of India's Balance of payments. The rapid growth of Indian economy in response to improvement in the service sector is an evidence of cumulative growth of Human Capital in India.

Criticism

Some labour economists have criticized the Chicago-school theory, claiming that it tries to explain all differences in wages and salaries in terms of human capital. One of the leading alternatives, advanced by Michael Spence and Joseph Stiglitz, is "Signaling theory". According to signaling theory, education does not lead to increased human capital, but rather acts as a mechanism by which workers with superior innate abilities can signal those abilities to prospective employers and so gain above average wages.

The concept of human capital can be infinitely elastic, including unmeasurable variables such as personal character or connections with insiders (via family or fraternity). This theory has had a significant share of study in the field proving that wages can be higher for employees on aspects other than human capital. Some variables that have been identified in the literature of the past few decades include, gender and nativity wage differentials, discrimination in the work place, and socioeconomic status. However, Austrian economist Walter Block theorizes that these variables are not the cause of gender wage gap. Thomas J. DiLorenzo summarizes Block' s theory well: "marriage affects men and women very differently in terms of their future earning abilities, and is therefore an important cause of the male/ female wage gap". Block alleges that there is no wage gap between unmarried men and women, but married men salaries are usually more than married women. These wages, he contends, are the opportunity cost of being a mother and raising children.

The prestige of a credential may be as important as the knowledge gained in determining the value of an education. This points to the existence of market imperfections such as non-competing groups and labour-market segmentation. In segmented labour markets, the "return on human capital" differs between comparably skilled labour-market groups or segments. An example of this is discrimination against minority or female employees.

Following Becker, the human capital literature often distinguishes between "specific" and "general" human capital. Specific human capital refers to skills or knowledge that is useful only to a single employer or industry, whereas general human capital (such as literacy) is useful to all employers. Economists view firm specific human capital as risky, since firm closure or industry decline lead to skills that cannot be transferred (the evidence on the quantitative importance of firm specific capital is unresolved).

Human capital is central to debates about welfare, education, health care, and retirement..

In 2004, "human capital" (German: *Humankapital*) was named the German Un-Word of the Year by a jury of linguistic scholars, who considered the term inappropriate and inhumane, as individuals would be degraded and their abilities classified according to economically relevant quantities.

"Human capital" is often confused with human development. The UN suggests "Human development denotes both the process of widening people's choices and improving their well-being". The UN Human Development indices suggest that human capital is merely a means to the end of human development: "Theories of human capital formation and human resource development view human beings as means to increased income and wealth rather than as ends. These theories are concerned with human beings as inputs to increasing production".

Mobility Between Nations

Educated individuals often migrate from poor countries to rich countries seeking opportunity. This movement has positive effects for both countries: capital-rich countries gain an influx in labour, and labour rich countries receive capital when migrants remit money home. The loss of labour in the old country also increases the wage rate for those who do not emigrate, while the additional labour lowers wages in the new country. When workers migrate, their early care and education generally benefit the country where they move to work. And, when they have health problems or retire, their care and retirement pension will typically be paid in the new country.

African nations have invoked this argument with respect to slavery, other colonized peoples have invoked it with respect to the "brain drain" or "human capital flight" which occurs when the most talented individuals (those with the most individual capital) depart for education or opportunity to the colonizing country (historically, Britain and France and the U.S.). Even in Canada and other developed nations, the loss of human capital is considered a problem that can only be offset by further draws on the human capital of poorer nations via immigration. The economic impact of immigration to Canada is generally considered to be positive.

During the late 19th and early 20th centuries, human capital in the United States became considerably more valuable as the need for skilled labour came with newfound technological advancement. The 20th century is often revered as the "human capital century" by scholars such as Claudia Goldin. During this period a new mass movement toward secondary education paved the way for a transition to mass higher education. New techniques and processes required further education than the norm of primary schooling, which thus led to the creation of more formalized schooling across the nation. These advances produced a need for more skilled labour, which caused the wages of occupations that required more education to considerably diverge from the wages of ones that required less. This divergence created incentives for individuals to postpone entering the labour market in order to obtain more education. The "high school movement" had changed the educational system for youth in America. With minor state involvements, the high school movement started at the grass-roots level, particularly the communities with the most homogeneous populations. As a year in high school added more than ten percent to an individual's income, post-elementary school enrollment and graduation rates increased significantly during the 20th century. The U.S. system of education was characterized for much of the 20th century by publicly funded mass secondary education that was open and forgiving, academic yet practical, secular, gender neutral, and funded by small, fiscally independent districts. This early insight into the need for education allowed for a significant jump in US productivity and economic prosperity, when compared to other world leaders at the time. It is suggested by several economists, that there is a positive correlation between high school enrollment rates and GDP per capita. Less developed countries have not established a set of institutions favouring equality and role of education for the masses and therefore have been incapable of investing in human capital stock necessary for technological growth.

The rights and freedom of individuals to travel and opportunity, despite some historical exceptions such as the Soviet bloc and its "Iron Curtain", seem to consistently transcend the countries in which they are educated. One must also remember that the ability to have mobility with regards to where people want to move and work is a part of their human capital. Being able to move from one area to the next is an ability and a benefit of having human capital. To restrict people from doing so would be to inherently lower their human capital.

This debate resembles, in form, that regarding natural capital.

Intangibility and Portability

Human capital is an intangible asset – it is not owned by the firm that employs it and is generally not fungible. Specifically, individuals arrive at 9am and leave at 5pm (in the conventional office model) taking most of their knowledge and relationships with them.

Human capital when viewed from a time perspective consumes time in one of key activities:

1. Knowledge (activities involving one employee),
2. Collaboration (activities involving more than 1 employee),
3. Processes (activities specifically focused on the knowledge and collaborative activities generated by organisational structure – such as silo impacts, internal politics, etc.) and
4. Absence (annual leave, sick leave, holidays, etc.).

Despite the lack of formal ownership, firms can and do gain from high levels of training, in part because it creates a corporate culture or vocabulary teams use to create cohesion.

In recent economic writings the concept of firm-specific human capital, which includes those social relationships, individual instincts, and instructional details that are of value within one firm (but not in general), appears by way of explaining some labour mobility issues and such phenomena as golden handcuffs. Workers can be more valuable where they are simply for having acquired this knowledge, these skills and these instincts. Accordingly the firm gains for their unwillingness to leave and market talents elsewhere.

Risk

When human capital is assessed by activity based costing via time allocations it becomes possible to assess human capital risk. Human capital risk occurs when the organisation operates below attainable operational excellence levels. For example, if a firm could reasonably reduce errors and rework (the Process component of human capital) from 10,000 hours per annum to 2,000 hours with attainable technology, the difference of 8,000 hours is human capital risk. When wage costs are applied to this difference (the 8,000 hours) it becomes possible to financially value human capital risk within an organisational perspective.

Human capital risk accumulates in four primary categories:

1. Absence activities (activities related to employees not showing up for work such as sick leave, industrial action, etc.). Unavoidable absence is referred to as Statutory Absence. All other categories of absence are termed "Controllable Absence";
2. Collaborative activities are related to the expenditure of time between more than one employee within an organisational context. Examples include: meetings, phone calls, instructor led training, etc.;
3. Knowledge Activities are related to time expenditures by a single person and include finding/retrieving information, research, email, messaging, blogging, information analysis, etc.; and
4. Process activities are knowledge and collaborative activities that result due to organisational context such as errors/rework, manual data transformation, stress, politics, etc.

Corporate Finance

In Corporate finance, Human Capital is one of the three primary components of Intellectual Capital (which in addition to tangible assets comprise the entire value of a company). Human Capital is the value that the employees of a business provide through the application of skills, know-how and expertise.

It is an organisation's combined human capability for solving business problems. Human Capital is inherent in people and cannot be owned by an organisation. Therefore, Human Capital leaves an organisation when people leave. Human Capital also encompasses how effectively an organisation uses its people resources as measured by creativity and innovation. A company's reputation as an employer affects the Human Capital it draws.

Human Development Theory

Human development theory is a theory that merges older ideas from ecological economics, sustainable development, welfare economics, and feminist economics. It seeks to avoid the overt normative politics of most so-called "green economics" by justifying its theses strictly in ecology, economics and sound social science, and by working within a context of globalization.

Theory

Like ecological economics it focuses on measuring well-being and detecting uneconomic growth that comes at the expense of human health. However, it goes further in seeking not only to measure but to optimize well-being by some explicit modelling of how social capital and instructional capital can be deployed to optimize the overall value of human capital in an economy - which is itself part of an ecology. The role of individual capital within that ecology, and the adaptation of the individual to live well within it, is a major focus of these theories.

The most notable proponents of human development theory are Mahbubul Haq, Üner Kirdar and Amartya Sen. AmartyaSen asked, in Development as Freedom, "what is the relationship between our wealth and our ability to live as we would like?"

This question cannot be answered strictly from an energy, feminist, family, environmental health, peace, social justice, or ecological well-being point of view, although all of these may be factors in our happiness, and if tolerances of any of these are violated seriously, it would seem impossible to be happy at all.

Accordingly, human development theory is a major synthesis that is probably not confined within the bounds of conventional economics or political science, nor even the political economy that relates the two. Another angle is Sustainable Human Development: Triple Bottom line ecology-economy-social can be translated to human dimensions as:

- Human economy: sustainable action - the ability to perform well and on long term (stress, priority, focus and time management)
- Human social dimension: sustainable relations - the ability to sustain relations and go through ordeals together (family, teams, clients, stakeholders)
- Human ecology: health, self-awareness, vocation, excellence, talent.

8

Accumulation of Capital over Time

Capital Accumulation

The accumulation of capital is the gathering or amassing of objects of value as judged by one's perceived reproductive interest group; the increase in wealth through concentration; or the creation of wealth. Capital is money or a financial asset invested for the purpose of making more money (whether in the form of profit, rent, interest, royalties, capital gain or some other kind of return). This activity forms the basis of the economic system of capitalism, where economic activity is structured around the accumulation of capital (investment in order to realise a financial profit).Definition

The definition of capital accumulation is subject to controversy and ambiguities, because it could refer to:

- a *net addition* to existing wealth
- a*re distribution* of wealth.

Most often, capital accumulation involves both a net addition and a redistribution of wealth, which may raise the question of who really benefits from it most. If more wealth is produced than there was before, a society becomes richer; the total stock of wealth increases. But if some accumulate capital only at the expense of others, wealth is merely shifted from A to B. It is also possible that some accumulate capital much faster than others. In principle, it is possible that a few people or organisations accumulate capital and grow richer, although the total stock of wealth of society *decreases*. In economics, accounting and Marxian economics, capital accumulation is often equated with investment of profit income or savings, especially in real capital goods. The concentration and centralisation of capital are two of the results of such accumulation.

Capital accumulation can refer to:

- real investment in tangible means of production, increasing the capital stock.
- investment in financial assets represented on paper, yielding profit, interest, rent, royalties, fees or capital gains.
- investment in *non-productive* physical assets such as residential real estate or works of art that appreciate in value.
- "human capital accumulation", i.e., new education and training increasing the skills of the (potential) labour force which can increase earnings from work.

Both non-financial and financial capital accumulation is usually needed for economic growth, since additional production usually requires additional funds to enlarge the scale of production. Smarter and more productive organisation of production can also increase production without increased capital. Capital can be created without increased investment by inventions or improved organisation that increase productivity, discoveries of new assets (oil, gold, minerals, etc.), the sale of property, etc.

In modern macroeconomics and econometrics the term *capital formation* is often used in preference to "accumulation", though the United Nations Conference on Trade and Development (UNCTAD) refers nowadays to "accumulation". The term is occasionally used in national accounts.

The Measurement of Accumulation

Accumulation can be measured as the monetary value of investments, the amount of income that is reinvested, or as the change in the value of assets owned (the increase in the value of the capital stock). Using company balance sheets, tax data and direct surveys as a basis, government statisticians estimate total investments and assets for the purpose of national accounts, national balance of payments and flow of funds statistics. Usually the Reserve Banks and the Treasury provide interpretations and analysis of this data. Standard indicators include Capital formation, Gross fixed capital formation, fixed capital, household asset wealth, and foreign direct investment.

Organisations such as the International Monetary Fund, UNCTAD, the World Bank Group, the OECD, and the Bank for International Settlements used national investment data to estimate world trends. The Bureau of Economic Analysis, Eurostat and the Japan Statistical Office provide data on the USA, Europe and Japan respectively.

Other useful sources of investment information are business magazines such as *Fortune, Forbes, The Economist, Business Week,* etc., and various corporate "watchdog" organisations and non-governmental organisation publications. A reputable scientific journal is the *Review of Income & Wealth.* In the case of the USA, the "Analytical Perspectives" document (an annex to the yearly budget) provides useful wealth and capital estimates applying to the whole country.

Harrod–Domar Model

In macroeconomics, following the Harrod–Domar model, the savings ratio (s) and the capital coefficient (k) are regarded as critical factors for accumulation and growth, assuming that all saving is used to finance fixed investment. The rate of growth of the real stock of fixed capital (K) is:

$$\frac{\Delta K}{K} = \frac{\frac{\Delta K}{Y}}{\frac{K}{Y}} = \frac{s}{k}$$

where Y is the real national income. If the capital-output ratio or capital coefficient ($k = \frac{K}{Y}$) is constant, the rate of growth of Y is equal to the rate of growth of K. This is determined by s (the ratio of net fixed investment or saving to Y) and k.

A country might for example save and invest 12% of its national income, and then if the capital coefficient is 4:1 (i.e. $4 billion must be invested to increase the national income by 1 billion) the rate of growth of the national income might be 3% annually. However, as Keynesian economics points out, savings do not automatically mean investment (as liquid funds may be hoarded for example). Investment may also not be investment in fixed capital. Assuming that the turnover of total production capital invested remains constant, the proportion of total investment which just maintains the stock of total capital, rather than enlarging it, will typically increase as the total stock increases. The growth rate of incomes and net new investments must then also increase, in order to accelerate the growth of the capital stock. Simply put, the bigger capital grows, the more capital it takes to keep it growing and the more markets must expand.

Marxian Concept of Capital Accumulation

In Karl Marx's economic theory, capital accumulation refers to the operation whereby profits are reinvested increasing the total quantity of capital. Capital is viewed by Marx as expanding value, that is, in other terms, as a sum of capital, usually expressed in money, that is transformed through human labour into a larger value, extracted as profits and expressed as money. (Capitalism is this value-making activity, although Marxists often equate capitalism with the capitalist mode of production). Here, capital is defined essentially as economic or commercial asset value in search of additional value or surplus-value. This requires property relations which enable objects of value to be appropriated and owned, and trading rights to be established.

According to Marx, capital accumulation has a double origin, namely in trade and in expropriation, both of a legal or illegal kind. The reason is that a stock of capital can be increased through a process of exchange or "trading up" but also through directly taking an asset or resource from someone else, without compensation.

David Harvey calls this accumulation by dispossession. Marx does not discuss gifts and grants as a source of capital accumulation, nor does he analyze taxation in detail. Nowadays the tax take is often so large (i.e., 25-40% of GDP) that some authors refer to state capitalism. This gives rise to a proliferation of tax havens to evade tax liability.

The continuation and progress of capital accumulation depends on the removal of obstacles to the expansion of trade, and this has historically often been a violent process.

As markets expand, more and more new opportunities develop for accumulating capital, because more and more types of goods and services can be traded in. But capital accumulation may also confront resistance, when people refuse to sell, or refuse to buy (for example a strike by investors or workers, or consumer resistance). What spurs accumulation is competition; in business, if you don't go forward, you go backward, and unless the law prevents it, the strong will exploit the weak.

In general, Marx's critique of capital accumulation is that the human chase after wealth and self-enrichment leads to inhuman consequences. The enrichment of some is at the expense of the immiseration of others, and competition becomes brutal. The basis of it all is the exploitation of the labour effort of others. When the "economic cake" expands, this may be obscured because all can gain from trade. But when the "economic cake" shrinks, then capital accumulation can only occur by taking income or assets from other people, other social classes, or other nations. The point is that to exist, capital must always grow, and to ensure that it will grow, people are prepared to do almost anything.

The hypothetical system of socialism would succeed capitalism as the dominant mode of production when the accumulation of capital can no longer sustain itself due to falling rates of profit in real production relative to increasing productivity. A socialist economy would not base production on the accumulation of capital, but would instead base production and economic activity on the criteria of satisfying human needs—that is, production would be carried out directly for use.

Concentration and Centralization

According to Marx, capital has the tendency for concentration and centralization in the hands of richest capitalists. Marx explains:

"It is concentration of capitals already formed, destruction of their individual independence, expropriation of capitalist by capitalist, transformation of many small into few large capitals.... Capital grows in one place to a huge mass in a single hand, because it has in another place been lost by many.... The battle of competition is fought by cheapening of commodities. The cheapness of commodities demands, *caeteris paribus*, on the productiveness of labour, and this again on the scale of production. Therefore, the larger capitals beat the smaller. It will further be remembered that, with the development of the capitalist mode of production, there is an increase in the minimum amount of individual capital necessary to carry on a business under its normal conditions. The smaller capitals, therefore, crowd into spheres of production which Modern Industry has only sporadically or incompletely got hold of. Here competition rages.... It always ends in the ruin of many small capitalists, whose capitals partly pass into the hands of their conquerors, partly vanish."

The Rate of Accumulation

In Marxian economics, the *rate of accumulation* is defined as (1) the value of the real net increase in the stock of capital in an accounting period, (2) the proportion of realised surplus-value or profit-income which is reinvested, rather than consumed. This rate can be expressed by means of various ratios between the original capital outlay, the realised turnover, surplus-value or profit and reinvestments.

Other things being equal, the greater the amount of profit-income that is disbursed as personal earnings and used for consumptive purposes, the lower the savings rate and the lower the rate of accumulation is likely to be. However, earnings spent on consumption can also stimulate market demand and higher investment. This is the cause of endless controversies in economic theory about "how much to spend, and how much to save".

In a boom period of capitalism, the growth of investments is cumulative, i.e. one investment leads to another, leading to a constantly expanding market, an expanding labour force, and an increase in the standard of living for the majority of the people. In a stagnating, decadent capitalism, the accumulation process is increasingly oriented towards investment on military and security forces, real estate, financial speculation, and luxury consumption. In that case, income from value-adding production will decline in favour of interest, rent and tax income, with as a corollary an increase in the level of permanent unemployment. As a rule, the larger the total sum of capital invested, the higher the return on investment will be. The more capital one owns, the more capital one can also borrow and reinvest at a higher rate of profit or interest. The inverse is also true, and this is one factor in the widening gap between the rich and the poor.

Ernest Mandel emphasized that the rhythm of capital accumulation and growth depended critically on (1) the division of a society's social product between "necessary product" and "surplus product", and (2) the division of the surplus product between investment and consumption. In turn, this allocation pattern reflected the outcome of competition among capitalists, competition between capitalists and workers, and competition between workers. The pattern of capital accumulation can therefore never be simply explained by commercial factors, it also involved social factors and power relationships.

The Circuit of Capital Accumulation from Production

Strictly speaking, capital has accumulated only when realised profit income has been *reinvested* in capital assets. But the process of capital accumulation in production has, as suggested in the first volume of Marx's *Das Kapital*, at least 7 distinct but linked moments:

- The initial investment of capital (which could be borrowed capital) in means of production and labour power.
- The command over surplus-labour and its appropriation.
- The valorisation (increase in value) of capital through production of new outputs.
- The appropriation of the new output produced by employees, containing the added value.
- The realisation of surplus-value through output sales.
- The appropriation of realised surplus-value as (profit) income after deduction of costs.
- The reinvestment of profit income in production.

All of these moments do not refer simply to an "economic" or commercial process. Rather, they assume the existence of legal, social, cultural and economic power conditions, without which creation, distribution and circulation of the new wealth could not occur. This becomes especially clear when the attempt is made to create a market where none exists, or where people refuse to trade.

In fact Marx suggests that the original or primitive accumulation of capital often occurs through violence, plunder, slavery, robbery, extortion and theft. He argues that the capitalist mode of production requires that people be forced to work in value-adding production for someone else, and for this purpose, they must be cut off from sources of income other than selling their labour power.

Simple and Expanded Reproduction

In volume 2 of *Das Kapital*, Marx continues the story and shows that, with the aid of bank credit, capital in search of growth can more or less smoothly mutate from one form to another, alternately taking the form of money capital (liquid deposits, securities, etc.), commodity capital (tradeable products, real estate etc.), or production capital (means of production and labour power).

His discussion of the simple and expanded reproduction of the conditions of production offers a more sophisticated model of the parameters of the accumulation process as a whole. At simple reproduction, a sufficient amount is produced to sustain society at the given living standard; the stock of capital stays constant. At expanded reproduction, *more* product-value is produced than is necessary to sustain society at a given living standard (a surplus product; the additional product-value is available for investments which enlarge the scale and variety of production.

The bourgeois claim there is no economic law according to which capital is necessarily re-invested in the expansion of production, that such depends on anticipated profitability, market expectations and perceptions of investment risk. Such statements only explain the subjective experiences of investors and ignore the objective realities which would influence such opinions. As Marx states in Vol.2, simple reproduction only exists if the variable and surplus capital realised by Dept. 1—producers of means of production—exactly equals that of the constant capital of Dept. 2, producers of articles of consumption (pg 524). Such equilibrium rests on various assumptions, such as a constant labour supply (no population growth). Accumulation does not imply a necessary change in total magnitude of value produced but can simply refer to a change in the composition of an industry (pg. 514).

Ernest Mandel introduced the additional concept of *contracted economic reproduction*, i.e. reduced accumulation where business operating at a loss outnumbers growing business, or economic reproduction on a decreasing scale, for example due to wars, natural disasters or devalorisation.

Balanced economic growth requires that different factors in the accumulation process expand in appropriate proportions. But markets themselves cannot spontaneously create that balance, in fact what drives business activity is precisely the imbalances between supply and demand: inequality is the motor of growth. This partly explains why the worldwide pattern of economic growth is very uneven and unequal, even although markets have existed almost everywhere for a very long time. Some people argue that it also explains government regulation of market trade and protectionism.

Capital Accumulation as Social Relation

"Accumulation of capital" sometimes also refers in Marxist writings to the reproduction of capitalist social relations (institutions) on a larger scale over time, i.e., the expansion of the size of the proletariat and of the wealth owned by the bourgeoisie.

This interpretation emphasizes that capital ownership, predicated on command over labour, is a social relation: the growth of capital implies the growth of the working class (a "law of accumulation"). In the first volume of *Das Kapital* Marx had illustrated this idea with reference to Edward Gibbon Wakefield's theory of colonisation:

"...Wakefield discovered that in the Colonies, property in money, means of subsistence, machines, and other means of production, does not as yet stamp a man as a capitalist if there be wanting the correlative — the wage-worker, the other man who is compelled to sell himself of his own free-will. He discovered that capital is not a thing, but a social relation between persons, established by the instrumentality of things.

Mr. Peel, he moans, took with him from England to Swan River, West Australia, means of subsistence and of production to the amount of £50,000. Mr. Peel had the foresight to bring with him, besides, 3,000 persons of the working-class, men, women, and children. Once arrived at his destination, "Mr. Peel was left without a servant to make his bed or fetch him water from the river." Unhappy Mr. Peel, who provided for everything except the export of English modes of production to Swan River!"

— *Das Kapital*, vol. 1, ch. 33

In the third volume of *Das Kapital*, Marx refers to the "fetishism of capital" reaching its highest point with *interest-bearing capital*, because now capital seems to grow of its own accord without anybody doing anything. In this case,

"The relations of capital assume their most externalised and most fetish-like form in interest-bearing capital. We have here $M-M'$, money creating more money, self-expanding value, without the process that effectuates these two extremes. In merchant's capital, $M-C-M'$, there is at least the general form of the capitalistic movement, although it confines itself solely to the sphere of circulation, so that profit appears merely as profit derived from alienation; but it is at least seen to be the product of a social relation, not the product of a mere thing. (...) This is obliterated in $M-M'$, the form of interest-bearing capital. (...) The thing (money, commodity, value) is now capital even as a mere thing, and capital appears as a mere thing. The result of the entire process of reproduction appears as a property inherent in the thing itself. It depends on the owner of the money, i.e., of the commodity in its continually exchangeable form, whether he wants to spend it as money or loan it out as capital. In interest-bearing capital, therefore, this automatic fetish, self-expanding value, money generating money, are brought out in their pure state and in this form it no longer bears the birth-marks of its origin. The social relation is consummated in the relation of a thing, of money, to itself. - Instead of the actual transformation of money into capital, we see here only form without content."

— "Das Kapital", vol.1, ch. 24

Psychology, Sociology and Ethics of Capital Accumulation

There have been numerous psychological and sociological studies of the motivations of investment behaviour by individuals. Most of these suggest that the propensity to accumulate capital is associated with qualities such as an intelligent understanding of property ownership, a positive attitude towards money, the ability to seize a money-making opportunity, and a desire to acquire more wealth. Like so many things human, some theorists regard these qualities as innate and genetic qualities, while others regard them as learned through social experience; some theorists think that both biological and social factors are involved.

However, even if a strong motivation for enrichment or social improvement exists, the business, government, legal, climate, local culture or social instability may prevent this motivation from being realised. Hernando de Soto for example argues that the reason why poor countries are poor is mainly because of the absence of a legal-cultural infrastructure of "asset management" and of formalised and enforced private property rights. Many systems seemed designed to keep a small minority in power so they can consume more. This power minority takes advantage of the common people—consuming much more than they produce. One popular argument in this respect remains the vicious cycle of poverty: the poor are poor because they are poor. Critics of this argument object it is an uninformative and unhelpful tautology.

Greed and desire can play a very important role in capital accumulation, but are not a necessary requirement. Indeed according to Max Weber's study of capitalism and the Protestant ethic, frugality, sobriety, deferred consumption and saving were among the key values of the rising bourgeoisie in the age of the Reformation.

Some economic historians (e.g., David Landes, Gregory Clark) refer to national psychology and argue that some nations or cultures (e.g., Europe) are inherently better equipped for capital accumulation, due to cultural habits, customs and values.

Other economic historians (e.g. Paul A. Baran) have argued that psychological factors explain very little, because a nation which previously had a low level of accumulation can suddenly "take off". In that case, the causes must be sought in the prevailing social relations.

Controversies about the ethics of accumulation have occurred ever since commercial trade began. If informal and formal prostitution is regarded as the oldest profession, the first ethical debate about accumulation must have occurred tens of thousands of years ago at the very least. The problem is that trade or market forces do not create any particular morality of their own, beyond the requirement to meet contractual obligations that settle transactions. Some forms of trade may be accepted, others rejected, but there exists no general moral principle for this which can be derived from the trade itself.

A good contemporary illustration of this problem is the gigantic increase in total reported crime and the grey economy or shadow economy after the deregulation of world markets from the 1980s, and the marketisation of the USSR and China. But ancient philosophers and theologians already knew about the problem, which is why they were intensely preoccupied with the politics of the "rule of law" and its enforcement. The main ethical questions concern which *routes to wealth* are morally justifiable, and what entitles individuals and groups to appropriate amounts of wealth, in particular wealth which they have not themselves created. The medieval economists invented theories of a just price and the moral debate surfaces again these days, e.g., in the controversies about fair trade, imperialism and Islamic banking. Neo-liberal theory emphasises that a "good" person is one who creates new wealth by deferring consumption or improving production, while socialist theory says a "good" person is one who shares their wealth however accumulated. The most popular moral theories are similar to that of John Rawls.

Karl Marx illustrated his analysis with sarcastic comments about "Christian accumulation"; some forms of accumulation were believed to be compatible with Jesus Christ, while others were not; some forms of accumulation were forgiven by God afterwards, others were not. Martin Luther for example raged against usury and extortion.

Marxism–Leninism is hostile to all private property and market activity. It must be kept in mind that the "private property" that Marx refers to is the ownership of the means of production by a generally small elite of wealthy entrepreneurs. The proletariat, or labourer, is inferior to all aspects of production—including labour, the products or services made, and revenue; and therefore the division of labour and its products must be equally redistributed to avoid the control and degradation of an unknown bourgeoisie.

But because capital accumulation does not presuppose any particular or specific "moral system", accumulation can also continue regardless of any particular morality advocated by popes, presidents, queens, journalists, pop stars, business tycoons or anybody else. All that is required is (1) the ability to own assets and trade in them and (2) sufficient income beyond subsistence and (3) the will to defer consumption to be able to accumulate capital.

Different Forms of Capital Accumulation

Essentially, in capitalism the production of output *depends* on the accumulation of capital. The propensity to invest in production therefore depends a lot on expectations of profitability and sales volume, and on perceptions of market risk. If production stops being profitable, or if sales drop sharply, or if there is social instability, capital will exit more and more from the sphere of production. Or if it cannot or does not, rationalization investments will be undertaken, to amalgamate unprofitable enterprises into profitable units.

As a corollary, capital accumulation may be the accumulation of *production capital* (industrial assets), or the accumulation of *money capital* (financial assets), or the accumulation of *commodity capital* (products, real estate etc. which can be traded).

But irrespective of whether the additional capital value (or surplus-value happens to take the form of profit, interest, rent, or some kind of tax impost or royalty income, what drives the accumulation process is the perpetual search for more surplus-value, for added value as such.

This requires a constant supply of a labour force which can conserve and add value to inputs and capital assets, and thus create a higher value. Normally, the socio-economic compulsion to work for a living in capitalist society is legally enforced and regulated by the state, for example through workfare and strict conditions for receiving an unemployment benefit.

Although capital accumulation does not necessarily require production, ultimately the basis for it is value-adding production which makes net additions to the stock of wealth. Capital can accumulate by shifting the ownership of assets from one place to another, but ultimately the total stock of assets must increase. Other things being equal, if production fails to grow sufficiently, the level of debt will increase, ultimately causing a breakdown of the accumulation process when debtors cannot pay creditors.

Capital *accumulation* does not necessarily require trade either, although capital presupposes trade, and the ability to exchange goods for money. The reason is that wealth can be amassed through illegal or legalised expropriation (robbery, plunder, theft, piracy, slavery, embezzlement, fraud and so on). However, a continuous and cumulative accumulation process always presupposes that capital ownership is secure. Consequently, military and police forces have typically been necessary for capital accumulation on a larger scale, to protect property.

In medieval society, typically the bourgeoisie could not protect its capital assets permanently from attacks, which meant that the accumulation process was interrupted, and remained limited in scope. Today however, capitalists can own billions of dollars worth of assets which are well-protected against crime. With the aid of private banking it is easier to obscure or hide the wealth that one owns.

Regime of Accumulation

Both the Regulation School of French Marxian economists, inspired by the original writings of Michel Aglietta and developed by Robert Boyer, as well as the American social structure of accumulation school founded by the economists Samuel Bowles and David Gordon have emphasized that the processes of capital accumulation occur within a social regime of accumulation.

In other words, a specific political and socio-economic environment is required that enables sustained investment and economic growth. This environment is created partly by state policy, but partly by also by technological innovations, changes in popular culture, commercial developments, the media, and so on. An example of such a regime often cited here is that of Fordism, named after the enterprise of Henry Ford. As the pattern of accumulation changes, the regime of accumulation also changes.

Similar ideas also surface in institutional economics. The main insight here is that market trade cannot flourish without regulation by a legal system plus the enforcement of basic moral conduct and private property by the state. But the regime of accumulation responds to the total experience of living in capitalist society, not just market trade.

Environmental Criticisms

The environmental criticism of capital accumulation focuses on four main ideas.

Firstly, there is the problem of externalities. This means that public or privately owned industry incurs costs, including environmental and health costs, which are not charged or priced. This happens for example when effluents are discharged on land, water or in the air, which can cause pollution or despoilation of terrains. In recognition of this, environmental taxes are sometimes imposed.

Secondly, commercial activities which may be rational from the point of view of a narrow public or private enterprise may not be rational from the point of view of the larger society, or from the point of view of the biosphere, especially when they involve the destruction of natural habitats of flora and fauna, pollution and entropy.

Because a natural resource happens to be a freely available good (for example fish in the open sea), it may be over utilised by either public or private enterprises. Or, a lot of energy may be wasted producing and transporting a good to the consumer. Or, the disturbance of subsistence economics by commerce may cause overpopulation by not controlling population by starvation.

Thirdly, goods and services may be produced for public or private profit in ways which are directly or indirectly harmful to human life, either because of the nature of the use-value involved, or because of the techniques used to produce them, or because they encourage consumer habits with harmful effects. Finally, business ethics may often not be reconcilable with some human ethics or good environmental ethics. This means for example that the imputation of a price to an environmental cost, or imposing an environment tax may be insufficient as a policy, because some things which have value simply have no price.

Nowadays environmental concerns are an essential part of so-called socially responsible business and corporate governance. However, opinion is divided about whether a capitalist market economy can be ecologically sustainable. Some argue that the experience of wide spread environmental destruction in the Soviet Union and China proves that state socialism or command economy can be ecologically worse than capitalism. Some environmentalists consider capitalism, or the "free market system" as it is usually called, incapable of complying with the basic requisites of a sustainable and respectful habitation of planet earth.

A major problem, inherent in some free market production dynamics, is the constant desire to constantly expand production. In this particular regard, critics point to the penchant to plan in short-term cycles, and with a narrow concern about the fortunes of only a single country, firm or business entity, thereby ignoring the cumulative effect brought to bear on the biosphere by the entire production system.

In the 1970s, some environmentalists argued for a policy of "zero economic growth" in "affluent" Western societies. However, when a long recession began in that decade, halving economic growth rates, most people became more concerned about mass unemployment. Thus, the proponents of zero growth lost popularity. Nowadays, the popular concept is sustainable economic development or growth. But interpretations of what that means can differ wildly. One difficulty is that predictions of future resource scarcity are usually based on extrapolation from the past, "assuming present trends will continue", but they may not.

Capital Accumulation and Risk

Most capital accumulation involves risk, because capital is committed to an investment without perfect certainty of future earnings. A capital asset could gain value, but it could also lose value in the future. Owners of capital (investors) therefore typically diversify their investment portfolio, and try to minimise the risks involved in investments by every possible means.

In the course of two centuries of capital accumulation based on industrialisation the intensive economising and exploitation of human labour, and technological innovation,

- the value of the assets that are invested in has become very large
- the markets traded in extend around the globe
- the deregulation of markets has increased the level of market uncertainty
- the volume of speculative capital has grown enormously
- the banking industry dominates the ownership of capital assets.

This has led to an enormous expansion of the insurance industry and of the profession of risk management. As a corollary, this powerfully stimulates the construction of mathematical models which aim to assess how probable it is that particular "risky events" will occur. Some sociologists such as Frank Furedi claim that an exaggerated and unhealthy preoccupation or anxiety about risks has infiltrated the whole of modern society.

Speculation—making money from price differentials or price fluctuations—is *justified* as follows: "The roles of speculators in a market economy are to absorb risk and to add liquidity to the marketplace by risking their own capital for the chance of monetary reward." However, speculation often also occurs with borrowed capital. In this case, capital is borrowed at a low rate of interest, and reinvested at a higher return.

Capital Accumulation and Military Wars

Wars typically causes the diversion, destruction and creation of capital assets as capital assets are both destroyed or consumed and diverted to types of production needed to fight the war. Many assets are wasted and in some few cases created specifically to fight a war. War driven demands may be a powerful stimulus for the accumulation of capital and production capability in limited areas and market expansion outside the immediate theatre of war. Often this has induced laws against perceived and real war profiteering. The total hours worked in the United States rose by 34 percent during World War II, even although the military draft reduced the civilian labour force by 11 percent.

War destruction can be illustrated by looking at World War II. Industrial war damage was heaviest in Japan, where 1/4 of factory buildings and 1/3 of plant & equipment were destroyed; 1/7 of electric power-generating capacity was destroyed and 6/7 of oil refining capacity. The Japanese merchant fleet lost 80% of their ships. In Germany in 1944, when air attacks were heaviest, 6.5% of machine tools were damaged or destroyed, but around 90% were later repaired. About

10% of steel production capacity was lost. In Europe, the United States and the Soviet Union enormous resources were accumulated and ultimately dissipated as planes, ships tanks, etc. were built and then lost or destroyed.

Germany's total war damage was estimated at about 17.5% of the pre-war total capital stock by value, i.e., about 1/6. In the Berlin area alone, there were 8 million refugees lacking basic necessities. In 1945, less than 10% of the railways were still operating. 2395 rail bridges were destroyed and a total of 7500 bridges, 10,000 locomotives and more than 100,000 goods wagons were destroyed. Less than 40% of the remaining locomotives were operational.

However, by the first quarter of 1946 European rail traffic, which was given assistance and preferences (by western appointed military governors) for resources and material as an essential asset, regained its prewar operational level. At the end of the year, 90% of Germany's railway lines were operating again. In retrospect, the rapidity of infrastructure reconstruction appears astonishing.

Initially, in May 1945, newly installed U.S. President Harry S. Truman's directive had been that no steps would be taken towards economic rehabilitation of Germany. In fact, the initial industry plan of 1946 prohibited production in excess of half of the 1938 level; the iron and steel industry was allowed to produce only less than a third of pre-war output. These plans were rapidly revised and better plans were instituted. In 1946, over 10% of Germany's physical capital stock (plant & equipment) was also dismantled and confiscated, most of it going to the USSR. By 1947, industrial production in Germany was at 1/3 of the 1938 level, and industrial investment at about 1/2 the 1938 level.

The first big strike wave in the Ruhr occurred in early 1947—it was about food rations and housing, but soon there were demands for nationalisation. The U.S. appointed military Governor (Newman) however stated at the time that he had the power to break strikes by withholding food rations. The clear message was: "no work, no eat". As the military controls in Western Germany were nearly all relinquished and the Germans were allowed to rebuild their own economy with Marshal Plan aid things rapidly improved. By 1951, German industrial production had overtaken the prewar level. The Marshall Aid funds were important, but, after the currency reform (which permitted German capitalists to revalue their assets) and the establishment of a new political system, much more important was the commitment of the USA to *rebuilding* German capitalism and establishing a free market economy and government, rather than keeping Germany in a weak position. Initially, average real wages remained low, lower even than in 1938, until the early 1950s, while profitability was unusually high. So the total investment fund, aided by credits, was also high, resulting in a high rate of capital accumulation which was nearly all reinvested in new construction or new tools. This was called the German economic miracle or *"Wirtschaftswunder"*.

In the United States in World War II the large investments in industrial plant necessitated by the war brought some advantages; but the costs of dead, waste and debt would have never been undertaken by any rational government for the slight advantages.

In modern times, it has often been possible to rebuild physical capital assets destroyed in wars completely within the space of about 10 years, except in cases of severe pollution by chemical warfare or other kinds of irreparable devastation. However, damage to human capital has been much more devastating, in terms of fatalities (in the case of World War II, about 55 million deaths), permanent physical disability, enduring ethnic hostility and psychological injuries which have effects for at least several generations.

New Developments in Capital Accumulation

New trends in capital accumulation include:

- financialisation (the extraordinarily strong growth of the international financial markets. This is trade in financial claims to current and future income. As a corollary, the proportion of national income which consists of interest income and rentier income increases. The International Swaps and Derivatives Association reported in September 2006 that the outstanding nominal value of swaps and derivatives at the end of June 2006 was $283 trillion- nearly ten times the combined GDP of the US, Canada, the EU, Japan, and China; or ten times the value of total US home equity (each being valued at about $34 trillion). According to Standard & Poor's, world stock market capitalization is about $41 trillion. Of total swaps and derivatives, some $26 trillion was in the fastest growing area, credit default swaps.
- Modern information technology makes it possible to engage in very complex investment projects and shift funds extremely quickly from one placement to another in space and time. This increases the rotation speed of capital and raises the profit rate, but can also increase potential financial risks.

- the growing controversies about intellectual property rights and the protection (or security) of ideas which can make money for the owner. Increasingly, the basic conditions necessary for a good, service or idea to become a tradeable commodity are theoretically defined.
- ongoing privatisation of assets which were previously under public ownership. The IMF estimates suggest that in two decades since 1985 more than $2 trillion US dollars (in 2005 values) worth of state assets were privatised worldwide. Typically, these assets also rise sharply in value within a few years, because they involve enterprises occupying monopoly positions (e.g., utilities) which thus provide guaranteed profits. If profits dry up in the private sector, capitalists acquire public assets paid for by all citizens, with the argument that if they run them, supply will be more efficient.
- The enormous increase in capital gains from rising property values in the richer countries, especially in the | housing market. US tax data for fiscal 2000 showed that *realised* capital gains in the USA peaked at an estimated *$644.3 billion worth of income* while US GDP in 2000 was at US$9,817.0 billion, in other words *realised* capital gains assessed for tax purposes were equal to 6.5% of GDP at that point (total capital gains would be larger). Yet GDP, being a measure of value added in production, does not even include this "hidden" personal and business income.
- A growing proportion of capital assets which is not productively invested (overcapitalisation), together with an increase in the amount of consumer debt and liabilities. Some observers see the cause as being an increase in the gap between rich and poor, which causes only sluggish demand growth. "Debt management" has become a distinct and profitable business.
- The crisis of numerous pension funds providing a large amount of investment capital, which are alleged to be badly managed.
- An international "competition of currency values" strongly influenced by speculative capital, which has a big effect on the pattern of international trade. The magnitudes involved can be gauged, e.g., from the currency conversion ratios used to establish purchasing power parity (PPP). For example, India's GDP valued at PPP becomes five times larger. This tends to stimulate counter-trade.

- The acceleration of the concentration and centralisation of capital internationally in very large corporations. The Fortune Magazine "Global 500" largest corporations in 2004 employed more people than the whole workforce of Germany. The after-tax profit volume of the Fortune Global 500 was said to be $731 billion, the combined asset value was $60.8 trillion, gross income (revenues) $14.8 trillion, and stockholders equity $6.8 trillion. For comparison, world GDP in 2004 was valued at $40.9 trillion (World Bank).
- The Merrill lynch/CapGemini World Wealth Report 2005 covering High Net Worth Individuals (HNWI) claims the fortunes of the world's millionaires and billionaires grew strongly in 2004, increasing by 8.2% to US$30.8 trillion in one year. Driven by North America & Asia–Pacific, this represents "the highest growth of HNWI wealth in more than three years".
- Dollarisation: more US currency now circulates outside the US than inside it, and some countries such as Ecuador and El Salvador have adopted the US dollar as national currency. "Dollar hegemony" is maintained by large Asian, Arab and European investments in the United States.
- the tendency for corporate investment to orient towards activities which secure good short-term returns for shareholders. This is called "value-based management". Most corporate executive officers (CEO's) cite profitability as their prime concern.
- an increasing preoccupation with the conditions for extending credit, and with all sorts of risk factors. World markets are increasingly sensitive to events and disturbances which might cause social instability or panics.
- the declining overall significance of business start-ups, in the sense of enterprises creating new products and services, rather than being just tax-shelters or secondary employment (whether this is a permanent trend remains to be seen).
- the growth of criminal (or illegal) accumulation as measured by crime reports, including business crime and corruption such as fraud, embezzlement, money laundering, insider trading, smurfing and theft, but also prostitution, forced labour, slavery, war plunder etc. The volume of illegal international transactions is now said to be around $1 trillion a year, equal to the GDP of Spain or Canada. National Geographic has reported there are about 27 million slaves in the world. International Labour

Organisation estimates of forced labour are a little over a dozen million. There are possibly 70 million people involved around the world in prostitution of one form or another. But there are many more, employed or unemployed, in "intermediate" positions. Traditional sociological categories may not describe their situation accurately, but a growing "underclass" (which may not be an accurate label) is a policy concern for many governments.

- the most ignored aspect is the changing structure of the international workforce in its totality, specifically the number employed by specific employment status and by income, in different sectors. But just as Marx's Law of Accumulation predicted, the working class has grown enormously within two centuries. Deon Filmer estimated that 2,474 million people participated in the worldwide non-domestic labour force in the mid-1990s. Of these around a fifth, 379 million people, worked in industry, 800 million in services, and 1,074 million in agriculture. The majority of workers in industry and services were wage & salary earners—58 percent of the industrial workforce and 65 percent of the services workforce. But a big portion were self-employed or involved in family labour. Filmer suggests the total of employees worldwide in the 1990s was about 880 million, compared with around a billion working on own account on the land (mainly peasants), and some 480 million working on own account in industry and services.
- tax havens—according to a report, wealthy people hide at least $21 trillion in tax havens.

Accumulation of Capital through Creation of Scarcity

Wealth can be accumulated by open destruction of a defeated nation's wealth to make a commodity scarce and the world dependent upon the monopolized source.

Adam Smith describes just such a destruction of a peaceful and happy society's wealth and their impoverishment for the accumulation of capital by a few. Spices and silk from the East brought overland comprised the majority of trade between Europe and the East for centuries and efforts to control that trade resulted in many battles, large and small. Muslims shutting off the overland trade routes to the East forced the search for a new route by sea.

Nutmeg and cloves growing wild and plentiful on the Molluca Islands made them, like air, of high desirability but valueless. Natives made an easy living picking the spicy blossoms and leaves. If all traders had access to those spices, the European market—mostly nobles and wealthy traders, no commoners because they had no money—would become quickly flooded, and the price would collapse.

To create capitalized value for spice traders, it was necessary to monopolize those spice trees and keep spice prices high. So the Dutch burned every spice tree they could not control. The other side of the coin of the immense wealth accumulated by a few Dutch traders through monopolization of the spice trade was the impoverishment and depopulation of the Molluca Islands.

The Molluca Island spice monopoly gives a quick lesson in how value is transferred from defeated nations to the powerful through capitalized value of entitled, monopolized, property. If those islanders had kept title to their islands and spice trees and a free market existed, it is they who, eventually, would have, through furnishing spices to the world, become wealthy.

If all traders had access to those spices in those early years, there would have been much more, and cheaper, spices in the world, the islanders would have profited immensely, and they would have quickly learned the mechanics of gaining wealth through trade.

Creation of scarcity through open destruction of commodity production is a well recognised principle of neoliberal economics. In America during the Great Depression cattle and pigs were slaughtered and buried and paying farmers to not produce is standard practice yet today.

Though many of the world's forests were cleared by burning and more natural gas has been flared off in oil fields than has been consumed, oil, coal, timber, and other natural resources are not openly destroyed to produce scarcity.

But wasteful consumption of those resources when plentiful and cheap, and waste for war, does produce scarcity. The continued flaring of natural gas the burning underground coal mines with no attempt to put them out is a waste our grand children will pay for. That waste of plentiful resources can only be corrected through a democratic, cooperative, coordinated social policy.

Invisible Economic Borders Channeling Wealth to the Imperial Centres

To the extent the developing world gains control of their destiny and receive full value for their resources, the economics described herein can change rapidly.

Due to being underpaid for equally-productive labour, resources on the periphery are harvested, and sold to the imperial centres for far less than full value. With that cheap labour, products are manufactured cheaply but primarily for export; those underpaid workers do not have the buying power to purchase what they produce. With their citizens lacking buying power, these nations do not develop industry and wholesale and retail infrastructure for local distribution.

Consumer products could be sold within the low-paid producing region if the value of both the industries and products produced were priced relative to the wages paid to build the industry and products. But high wages in the developed world and low wages in the developing world create invisible borders which channel those products to imperial centres.

This is graphically demonstrated by current wages paid in the developing world being typically under 2%, never over 5%, a product's sales value in the developed world, even before the 1997-98 currency collapses on the periphery reduced their wages by half.

Theoretically, over time, distribution within the developing world at low prices could develop. But the large buying power in the imperial centre and the low buying power on the periphery dictate there will be a limited horizontal flow of money on the periphery and thus a limited development of a balanced regional economy outside the imperial centres of capital.

It is impossible for the developing world to capitalize their wealth without owning their own resources, owning and running their own factories, being paid equally for equally-productive labour, and selling on established markets. Nor can they develop social capital without the broad-based local buying power that title to their own productive wealth and equally-paid labour would create.

It is consumer purchasing power—adequate wages, adequate commodity prices, and profits from efficient industry and efficient traders—that determines who ends up with the world's products for a quality life, others have no money.

Consumer purchasing power and capitalized values are both derived from title to natural resources, title to industrial capital, title to distribution mechanisms, and adequately paid labour as well as efficient industries. High-capitalized values require mass markets and mass markets develop only from adequately paid labour.

The common thread of a productive and profitable society with a high living standard is sharing both work and wealth while using and sharing the increased efficiencies of technology. A society with equally-paid labour and properly-paid capital (not overpaid capital) will have more real wealth.

Properly-paid labour and capital means elimination of monopolies which means capitalized values will be far lower even as use values are far more broadly distributed and utilised.

The Economic Multiplier, Horizontal and Vertical Expansion of Wealth

Although imposed belief systems have always claimed otherwise, people throughout the world can, on the average, be trained to be equally-productive. All it takes is an education, training, and the opportunity. If adequate capital were equally distributed through-out the world, the reality that picking grapes is just as important to society as building automobiles would quickly become apparent.

The difference in skills hardly qualifies for the difference in pay. There are many grape pickers and other low-paid workers who are just as qualified as many production, construction, and transportation workers. Though not true of all, many high-paid workers learned on the job the same way those low-paid workers learned their skills and the work of a large share of well-paid labour is repetitious, just as simple, yet not as hard or dirty as the work of lower-paid labour.

Look at the difference in capital accumulation through the discrepancy in pay as outlined in Plunder By Unequal Pay for Equally-Productive Labour: A five-times pay differential when trading between equally-productive labour nations results in a wealth accumulation advantage of 25 to one, to be paid twice as much for equally-productive work is to accumulate four-times as much wealth in trades, and being paid 30% greater when trading will still accumulate almost twice as much wealth.

But the defeated, dependent, world's loss of wealth is even greater than the above example. Forcing these defeated dependent societies to import a product they do not need, or which they could produce themselves if permitted the requisite technology and capital, is a sale 100% overvalued. Actually, as those societies are also being denied the benefits of the multiple use of this money, the economic multiplier, as it moves through the economy and creates more commerce, this unneeded product is, on balance, several hundred percent overvalued.

For example, if a society spends $100 to manufacture a product within its borders, the money paying for materials, labour, and other costs moves through the economy as each recipient spends it.

Due to this multiplier effect, $100 worth of primary production can add several hundred dollars to the Gross Domestic Product (GDP) of that country. If money is spent in another country, circulation of that money, and thus the additional wealth generated, is within the exporting country.

If imports and exports are equal in labour input and produced by equally-paid and equally-productive labour, the trades will be equal. But they are not; they can be unequal to the extreme.

To understand that we must understand not only multiplication of wealth through the horizontal flow of money, the economic multiplier, but the vertical expansion of wealth in an industrial economy as a society becomes wealthy through increased efficiencies of technology, higher value production and capitalizing those values.

Friedrich List's Fundamental Thesis

The fundamental thesis of Friedrich List is:

"Commerce emanates from manufactures and agriculture, and no nation which has not brought within its own borders both those main branches of production to a high state of development can attain ... any considerable amount of internal and external commerce."

Further challenging laissez faire, List points out that governments should support and protect industry and this will utilise unused labour and resources to an ever higher level of production.

The new manufacturing industries utilise otherwise wasted agriculture products and natural resources producing valuable products to be marketed in trade for other products, preferably cheap natural resource commodities, to also be processed into finished manufactured goods.

List also points out how such importation of natural resources and local manufacturing, as a national policy, would create a wealthy and powerful nation selling only what was surplus above the needs of the population while nations allotted the role of providing those unprocessed natural resources and purchasing back their manufactured products will produce no surplus and will be poor. Adam Smith's analysis is worth quoting a second time:

A small quantity of manufactured produce purchases a great quantity of rude produce. A trading and manufacturing country, therefore, naturally purchases with a small part of its manufactured produce a great part of the rude produce of other countries; while, on the contrary, a country without trade and manufactures is generally obliged to purchase, at the expense of a great part of its rude produce, a very small part of the manufactured produce of other countries. The one exports what can subsist and accommodate but a very few, and imports the subsistence and accommodation of a great number. The other exports the accommodation and subsistence of a great number, and imports that of a very few only. The inhabitants of the one must always enjoy a much greater quantity of subsistence than what their own lands, in the actual state of their cultivation, could afford. The inhabitants of the other must always enjoy a much smaller quantity.... Few countries ... produce much more rude produce than what is sufficient for the subsistence of their own inhabitants. To send abroad any great quantity of it, therefore, would be to send abroad a part of the necessary subsistence of the people. It is otherwise with the exportation of manufactures. The maintenance of the people employed in them is kept at home, and only the surplus part of their work is exported.... The commodities of Europe were almost all new to, and many of those of America were new to Europe. A new set of exchanges, therefore, began to take place which had never been thought of before, and which should naturally have proved as advantageous to the new, as it certainly did to the old continent. The savage injustice of the Europeans rendered an event, which ought to have been beneficial to all, ruinous and destructive to several [most] of those unfortunate countries.

Friedrich List's thesis restructured as an international policy for all nations to have an equal share, which the highly respected President Franklin D. Roosevelt also suggested and President Kennedy hinted at just before his assassination, would create a peaceful and wealthy world. One hundred dollars paid to a community for what were once wasted resources and labour will create, through the economic multiplier, possibly $350 worth of economic activity within a community and even more in capitalized values.

Gaining Wealth through the Vertical Building of Industrial Capital and the Horizontal Flow of Money

That $100 worth of formerly exported raw material can be processed ever finer and manufactured into ever more complicated products and services until the costs of the original raw materials are barely detectable in the high-value-added products.

Money spent building new industry to produce new products or services of continually higher values are continually spent horizontally for products and services and continually increasing the economic activity of a newly industrializing nation.

The high price received for that high value added product circulates within the economy and multiplies the economy to an ever-higher level. It requires the proper balance of industry, resources, and agriculture to maintain those increased production values which, in turn, maintain land, industry, store, office, and home values.

The natural resources necessary to maintain the economic balance of industrial nations are primarily in the undeveloped, impoverished, world. Thus the centuries-long effort to control the countryside and maintain the flow of resources to developed world industries at a fraction of its value. The industrial-agricultural ratio of a nation or region can vary greatly depending on the abundance or lack of natural resources. The scarce resources in the wealthy highly-industrialized Japan and abundant resources in the poor nations cheaply providing Japan's factories with their raw materials dramatically outlines the true cause of wealth in Japan and poverty of those who provide those resources. The poor nations provide the resources and purchase manufactured products. Japan buys the low-value resources and sells high-value manufactured products.

Because the developing world has little industry to utilise their labour and resources to produce high-value consumer products and they are paid a low price for their labour and resources, there is almost no vertical industrialization, little horizontal movement of money, and thus little wealth. When one adds up both the vertical and horizontal multiplication of wealth in an industrialized country, one has to seriously question the advice given to developing nations by the imperial centres of capital that their successful future depends on continued mining and harvesting of raw material and forgoing manufacturing because that is their "comparative advantage."

The small savings on importing any item must be laid against the entire vertical and horizontal gain to the region when manufacturing their own consumer products. Industrial development multiplies consumer buying power and profits from consumer spending further multiplies profits which further multiplies investments, further multiplying profits and consumer spending, and all continually multiplying capitalized values.

Bibliography

Andersen, P.W., K.J. Arrow, and D. Pines: *The Economy as an Evolving Complex System*, Addison-Wesley, Redwood, 1988.

Arrow, Kenneth J. and D. Pines: *The Economy as an Evolving Complex System*, Addison-Wesley, Rewood City, 1998.

Baran, Paul A.: *The Political Economy of Growth,* New York, Modern Reader Paperbacks, 1975.

Caravale, Giovanni: *Equilibrium and Economic Theory*, Routledge, London, 1997.

Cowen, Tyler: *The Theory of Market Failure*, George Mason University Press, Faifax, 1988.

Damasio, AR.: *Descarte's Error: Emotion, Reason and the Human Brain*, New York, 1994.

Desmond, Glenn, and John A, Marcell, *Handbook of Small Business Valuation Formulas and Rules of Thumb,* Valuation Press, 1993.

Ebeling, R. M.: *Austrian Economics: A Reader*, Hillsdale College Press, Hillsdale, Mich, 1991.

Eck, James R., David Ensign, and William Gary Baker: *Asset Valuation (Evidence Series)*, Shepards/McGraw-Hill, New York, 1991.

Fraser, Steven, *Labor Will Rule, Sidney Hillman and the Rise of American Labor,* Reprint ed. Ithaca, N.Y.: Cornell University Press, 1993.

Gloria-Palermo, S.: *The Evolution of Austrian Economics: From Menger to Lachmann*, Routledge, London and New York, 1999.

Hausman, D. M.: *The Inexact and Separate Science of Economics*, Cambridge, Cambridge University Press, 1992.

Jehle, Geoffrey A.; and Philip J. Reny: *Advanced Microeconomic Theory,* Addison Wesley, UK, 2000.

Kirzner, I. M.: *The Driving Force of the Market: Essays in Austrian Economics*, Routledge, New York, 2000.

Leijonhufvud, A.: *Information and Coordination*, Oxford University Press, New York, 1981.

Leone, Bruno: *Capitalism: Opposing Viewpoints*, GreenHaven Press, St. Paul, Minnesota, 1986.

Martin, Gerald D.: *Determining Economic Damages,* James Publishing, Santa Ana, CA, 1995.

Milgrom, Paul and John Roberts: *Economics: Organization and Management*, Prentice-Hall, Englewood Cliffs, NJ, 1992.

O'Driscoll Gerald, P. Jr., and Mario J., Rizzo: *The Economic of Time and Ignorance*, Basil Blackwell, New York, 1985.

Pfeffer, J., and Salancik, G. R.: *The External Control of Organizations, A Resource Dependence Perspective*, New York, 1978.

Pindyck, Robert S.; and Daniel L. Rubinfeld: *Microeconomics,* Prentice Hall, NY, 2008.

Rizzo, Mario: *Time Uncertainty, and Disequilibrium*, Lexington Books, Lexington, Mass, 1979.

Ross, D.: *Economic Theory and Cognitive Science*, Cambridge, Mass., MIT Press, 2006.

Siegel, Joel G. and Jae K. Shim: *Finance*, Barron's, New York, 1991.

Skousen, M.: *The Structure of Production*, New York University Press, New York, 1990.

Throsby, David, *Economics and Culture*, Cambridge University Press, 2001.

Tietenberg, Tom, *Environmental Economics and Policy,* New York, HarperCollins, 1994

Towse, Ruth ed.: *A Handbook of Cultural Economics*, Edward Elgar, 2003.

Trugman, Gary R., *Guide to Conducting a Valuation of a Closely Held Business*, New York, American Institute of Certified Public Accountants, 1993.

Ullman, D. G.: *Making Robust Decisions,* Trafford, 2006.

Warwick, D. P.: *A Theory of Public Bureaucracy*, Cambridge, MA: Harvard University Press, 1975.

Weber, M.: *The Theory of Social and Economic Organizations*, New York, Oxford University Press, 1947.

Weibull, J. W.: *Advances in Understanding Strategic Behaviour*, New York, Palgrave, 2004.

Index

❑❑❑